Constant Fouard

The Christ

the Son of God, a life of Our Lord and Saviour Jesus Christ - Vol. 1

Constant Fouard

The Christ
the Son of God, a life of Our Lord and Saviour Jesus Christ - Vol. 1

ISBN/EAN: 9783337314767

Printed in Europe, USA, Canada, Australia, Japan

Cover: Foto ©Lupo / pixelio.de

More available books at **www.hansebooks.com**

THE SON OF GOD

A LIFE OF OUR LORD AND SAVIOUR JESUS CHRIST

By THE ABBÉ CONSTANT FOUARD

Translated from the Fifth Edition with the Author's sanction

By GEORGE F. X. GRIFFITH

With an Introduction

By CARDINAL MANNING

Volume I.

NEW YORK AND LONDON
LONGMANS, GREEN, AND CO.
1891

INTRODUCTION.

THE knowledge of French is so widely diffused in English society that publishers wisely refuse to undertake to print translations from the French, excepting only works of science or of special value. Nevertheless Messrs. Longman have very wisely undertaken to publish an English translation of "*La Vie de N. S. Jesus Christ*" by Abbé Fouard, Professor of Theology in Rouen. Such a work will be read by multitudes who do not command a knowledge of the French language.

This singularly able and excellent work can need no commendation. It is already in its fifth edition. When it first appeared it had the commendation of the late Cardinal de Bonnechose, Archbishop of Rouen, who well described it as uniting "the consolations of piety with the explanations of true science on the text of Scripture." In 1881 Leo XIII. sent his benediction to the author, and many cardinals and a large number of the bishops of France gave it their approbation.

Abbé Fouard describes his book in these words: "This Life of Jesus is an act of faith." By a deliberate judgment he refused to admit both controversy and criticism. He would not prefix even an introduction establishing the authenticity of the Gospels. Nevertheless he has given in the notes to his preface a brief summary of those who have attacked the books of the New Testament, and those who have defended them, together with a long list of authors, French, English, and German, on which his history is founded.

Throughout the whole course of his work abundant notes are found at the foot of the page to interpret the text, and to illustrate the events recorded, by extensive researches made by himself in his pilgrimage to the Holy Land.

Abbé Fouard calls attention to a fact which appears seldom to be borne in mind. He says it was only in the Middle Ages that men began to write the life of our Lord. From the beginning until then the living and Divine tradition of faith, in which the name, the person, the character, the words, and the works of our Divine Saviour pervaded the Christian world, was enough to draw the hearts of men to Himself. The uninspired writers, founding themselves upon the living consciousness of the faith, wrote of their Divine Master as of a Person to whom they bore a personal relation. They interpreted the Scriptures of the New Testament as it were in His presence and by the memory of His own teaching. Their baptismal creed, which came to them "by hearing," filled them with "the word of Christ" and the knowledge of His mind,—for instance, the Homilies of Saint John Chrysostom in the East, and of Saint Augustin in the West. Their teaching was not historical, but didactic and devotional, of which the *Catena Aurea* of Saint Thomas is a full proof.

The intellectual state of the following ages took an historical form. Then began the compilation of the life of our Lord. Jansenius of Ghent, Salmeron, Tillemont, Calmet, and De Ligny began to reduce the sacred history to chronological order. From that day to this the life of our Lord has been elaborated more and more in the way of history; until at last some men, ceasing to realize their personal relation to a Living Person, have come to regard Him as an historical person, to whom they owe no duty, or as a mythical person who never existed.

Not so among those who inherit the living and Divine consciousness which animated the early ages of the faith. The name, the person, the character, the words, and the works of our Divine Master have ever been perpetuated in the daily life of those who adore Him in the unity of the faith. The history of Abbé Fouard unites the sacred narrative of the three-and-thirty years of our Saviour's earthly life with the living consciousness of faith, in which the mutual personal relation and the mutual personal love of the Divine Master and His Disciples are as living and sustaining at this day as they were when He ascended into Heaven. To all such this Life of Our Lord will be a golden book.

HENRY EDWARD CARDINAL MANNING.

PREFACE.

THIS Life of Jesus is an Act of Faith. We have had no intention of pursuing through these pages a controversy in which so many minds have been matched since the opening of our century; we only desire to make the Saviour better known and loved. Surely the times are propitious; for the Gospels, combated at a thousand points, have triumphed over their critics. The attacking party and the defenders alike appear exhausted. What is left for this our generation, unless it be to avail ourselves of the inspired Witnesses and by drawing from them an account of the actions of Jesus, demonstrate that He, Whose death some have published to the world, lives still, is indeed the very Life itself?

Yet since such a throng of writers have already essayed the same plan, any attempt to rewrite the life of the Saviour after them may seem superfluous. Our excuse is in the sublimity of its Subject, which no study can encompass wholly: for the Divinity of the Christ is the object of eternal contemplation, and as in every age His Humanity appears under new features, so it will always demand a different portraiture. This is why we have so many Narratives, which, one after another, have sketched that Figure, Whose proper lineaments we need but recall to mind, in order to perceive all that these great writers leave still to be attempted.

The Gospels, explained by their pastors, sufficed the faithful in the first ages of Christianity. The Saviour's daily life on earth, the places and the dates of his wondrous deeds, were still too memorable, too vividly impressed upon their minds, for need of any reminder to refresh their memory. It was by dying for Him that these heroic generations confessed the Lord Jesus. Yet, even then, error had endeavored to deface the figure of the Divine Master, and the apocryphal gospels show to what a state it would have degraded Him. To dispel these visionary mists it was only necessary to confront them with the Witnesses of the doings of the Christ. This task was imposed upon Tatian of Syria in the second century, upon Ammonius in the third, upon Eusebius of Cæsarea in the fourth. By arranging the Evangelists' Record of the facts, in their order of occurrence, they composed therefrom a *Harmony of the Gospels*.[1]

Some of the Fathers followed this example, but the majority among them were busied rather in interpreting the Doctrine of the Saviour, and it was only in the Middle Ages that lives of Jesus began to be written. Even at that period the historians meditate more than they describe. Only read the "Chain of Gold" by Saint Thomas, the "Holy Eminences" attributed to the Seraphic Doctor, the austere pages of Ludolphe le Chartreux; everywhere you feel the flame of love which feeds at their heart; it seems as though these men, for whom the body exists no longer, could not study the Saviour by any light save that of Tabor. Giotto has painted this transfigured Christ on the walls of Assisi, and we see him there, even as the Middle Ages adored Him, permitting the streaming rays of His Divinity to escape and irradiate His body, His head crowned with a glory as magnificent when suffering the scourges of the executioners as in the triumph of the Resurrection. It was indeed a figure which was typical of those ages of faith and charity, more absorbed in imitating that Model, than anxious to set forth its details in the cold light of day.

In the centuries that followed the life of Jesus assumed a more

---

[1] A Harmony or Concordance is the name given to the various works in which expositors endeavor to reconcile the Evangelists' Narratives, and dispose the events in chronological order. Those cited above are the first efforts of this description of which there is any record extant; others in great number have succeeded them. The most noteworthy will be found elsewhere, in the list of works of which we have availed ourselves.

doctrinal shape. Jansenius of Ghent, Salmeron, Tillemont, and Calmet enriched their commentaries with treasures of erudition; unhappily they did not base their researches upon a Narrative, which would make the life of the Saviour natural and effective. Père de Ligny profited by the labors of his predecessors; but like them he neglected the rules of art, and contented himself with arranging the Gospel texts in their chronological order, merely inserting the glosses requisite to preserve the connection. Even after his work the History of Jesus Christ remained still unwritten.

But while these expositors crowded into their pages the traditions of eighteen centuries, the Reformation, after having overturned the faith of our fathers in Germany, began to undermine its very foundations. The Holy Books, though for a long time revered, were in their turn assaulted by Error; authenticity, inspiration, veracity, all were called in question.[1] Strauss came to consider Jesus as a fabulous personage; Baur treats the Gospel as a legend, resting upon an historical foundation, but fanciful and imaginary so far as its wonders are concerned. Such venturesome essays among ancient beliefs could not fail to attract the genius of Frenchmen, lovers of clearness and light, and it only needed the artistic and imaginative skill of M. Renan to lend a certain glitter to their inventions.

Their success was not, however, lasting. England, always severely serious in the domain of Science, treated this work, which had so astonished us, as a Romance. Germany smiled to see that we were taking theories already refuted by them, for the final verdict of exegetical criticism.[2] To-day what remains of the scandal to which it gave rise? No doctrine, no new

[1] See *La Bible et les découvertes modernes*, par M. Vigouroux, prêtre de Saint-Sulpice, t. I.: *Esquisse de l'histoire du rationalisme biblique en Allemagne*.

[2] "The Work as it is composed," writes Ewald, "reflects little credit upon the Country which produced it, and could scarcely have had its origin among other surroundings than those in which it was conceived." "M. Renan's book," adds Keim, "is more than anything else a Parisian production, — a superficial compound; it is of no moment to the scholar, who will find nothing in it adapted to his use." (See *M. Renan, Réfuté par les rationalistes allemands*, por Mgr. Meignan.)

school ; only one more name to write under that of Celsus, Marcion, and all the rest, who for eighteen centuries have attacked the Godhead in Jesus Christ. Like so many others, this last assault has been fruitless, the figment has faded away, — yet only to give place to theories more formidable, as they are more specious and sophistical.

Scorning Tradition, which might have enlightened them, these hardy expositors would have us accept the Gospels as Apostolic teaching augmented and disfigured by the addition of a new body of texts in the course of years. To their apprehension the sacred Writings are not therefore a History, made from the original, but a compilation from a succession of narratives ; and nothing could be more ingenious, yet at the same time more arbitrary, than their innumerable speculations, which are always at variance with each other, as they vainly strive to point out what were, after all, the original features of the Books we possess to-day. We can see toward what end these innovators are working. By rejecting any settled dates for the Gospels, they in fact destroy all their authority ; for what credence could be accorded to a confused collection of reminiscences, jotted down by a thousand various hands and in epochs most at variance in spirit. Concede this point and there would be an end of all certitude as regards the Life of Jesus. Indeed all powers that lie deepest down in the Christian heart have risen in defence of the Heavenly Message. Marvels of erudition have been accomplished, and the Protestant churches, whence sprung the evil, have not been the last in exorcising it. Even in the judgment of liberal investigation, truth rests on the side of Tradition ; our Gospels are still regarded as the work of those who either saw the Master Himself, or heard His Apostles. Written by the Spirit of God, independently of each other, they shine forth in the white light of truth with a radiance which nothing can obscure.

We shall be forgiven for not restating here the proofs which have put the authenticity and veracity of this Record beyond cavil or suspicion ; one volume would not be enough to contain them. Our wisest course was to refer the reader to the apologists who have triumphantly defended them,[1] and pursue the plan which we have indicated above : to gather from the Gospels a History of Jesus, — comparing the four holy Witnesses in order to show how their Narratives, varying as they do in form, intention, and origin, nevertheless explain and confirm each other. To attain this object, let us see what guides we shall follow.

The first and most trustworthy of all is the Gospel itself. We possess it in the very language which the sacred Historians employed,[2] and one must read it in the original tongue to appreciate all its charms ; but it is quite as necessary not to neglect the Versions which were composed from the first ages ; for,

[1] See the *Introductions* written by Hug, Adalbert Maïer, and Reithmayr : Tholuck, *The Credibility of the Evangelical History* ; the English works of Norton and Westcott ; in France, *De la Croyance due à l'Évangile*, by M. Wallon, and *Les Évangiles*, by Mgr. Meignan. Bossuet was content to dismiss the question with a few lines, -- "that great concourse of different nations who received and translated the Holy Books agree both as to their date and as to their Authors. The Pagans never contradicted Tradition on this point. Neither Celsus, who attacked the sacred Books almost at the outset of Christianity, nor Julian the Apostate, although he neither ignored nor neglected anything whereby he might discredit them, nor has any other Pagan ever suggested the idea that they were of supposititious origin. On the contrary, one and all have credited them with the same authorship as the Christians. The heretics of olden times, although the authority of these same Books was oppressive to them, dared not assert that they were not the words of the Disciples of our Lord. Some of these heretics, moreover, had witnessed the beginnings of the Church, and had seen the Books of the Gospel written beneath their own eyes ; thus any deception which could possibly have insinuated itself would have been brought to light too promptly to succeed. It is true that after the Apostles' death, and when the Church had already penetrated into all lands, Marcion and Manes, always the most daring as they were the most ignorant among the heretics, . . . dared to say that three of the Gospels were forgeries. . . . But what proofs did they advance ? Only visions ; not one positive fact. . . . To invalidate the good faith of the Church, it was considered requisite for them to have possession of some original documents differing from hers, or some other ascertainable proof. Summoned to produce such proof, they and their disciples were silent, and by their silence have left an indubitable evidence that in the second century of Christianity, in which they wrote, there was not even an indication of unreliability, nor the least supposition which could be brought forward against the Tradition of the Church." (*Discours sur l'Histoire universelle*, ii[e] partie, c. xxvii.).

[2] We do not even except the First Gospel, for it appears most likely to us that the Greek Version from S. Matthew's original Aramean was made by the Apostle himself.

while they enlighten us as to the original meaning of the text, they enable us at the same time to decide between different readings. Every one knows, indeed, that there are no longer any Greek Manuscripts of the first three centuries, and that the oldest copies are only duplicates, made three hundred years after the epoch in which the Evangelists lived.[1] During that long period of transmission, different readings were multiplied, yet viewed as a guarantee of the genuineness of the original, no evidence equals the translations written by disciples of the Apostles, because they give us a faithful reflection of the Greek Gospels, as they were known at the birth of the Church.[2]

[1] Not to overload these notes with details, we shall not mention any readings besides those given by the five most ancient and most important Manuscripts: The Codex Sinaïticus (א), found by Tischendorf in the Monastery of Sinai in 1859: this Manuscript dates back to the fourth century. The Codex Vaticanus (B), belonging to the same period as the preceding, is preserved in the library of the Vatican. The Codex Alexandrinus (A), sent by the Patriarch of Constantinople, Cyril Lucar, to Charles I., in 1628, and kept ever since in the British Museum. The Codex Ephræmi (C). The parchment of this manuscript had been washed sufficiently to receive the text of S. Ephrem's Works; hence the name. The ancient text has been restored, and it forms one of the treasures of the National Library. The Codex Bezæ, or Cantabrigiensis (D), given by Beza to the University of Cambridge. These last three manuscripts date back to the fifth century. As regards these Codices, consult Reithmayr's *Introduction*, and Scrivener's *Introduction to the Criticism of the New Testament*, pp. 76-103.

[2] We mean by this the most ancient Versions, which are the following: The Italic, a Latin translation of the first century; two of the Syriac Versions, the Peshito (The Simple), composed at the beginning of the second century, and the Cureton, so named from the Canon of Westminster, who discovered it among the Syriac manuscripts of the British Museum. The latter Version, in which some believe we possess the original Aramean of S. Matthew, is older than the Peshito, and consequently goes back to the very days of the Apostles. Important as these first translations are, no one among them equals the Vulgate. We know what careful zeal S. Jerome brought to its composition, taking every advantage of his predecessors' labors, and referring to the most ancient manuscripts in the Greek text, in order to revise and correct the Italic; so that it is with perfect justice that the Church, having declared it authentic in every respect, accords it the same authority as to an original in everything which concerns faith and morals. In addition, we shall quote from the Coptic, Ethiopian, and Gothic Versions, done in the fourth century, with the Armenian, which dates from the fifth. (See, as to these Versions, the *Manuel Biblique*, par l'abbé F. Vigouroux, t. I. pp. 137-193; Reithmayr's *Introduction*, and *Les Études Publiques*, par l'abbé Le Hir, t. 1. p. 251.)

Upon this question it is equally incumbent upon us to consult the first Fathers; their preaching, as it is little more than a commentary upon the Good Tidings, reproduces the Gospel for us, almost in its entirety, and, consequently we can reconstruct from their Homilies so many Versions antedating any which we know to-day. But it is principally because they explain holy Writ that they must ever remain our teachers. No research, no science, however profound it may be, can supply us with what they then possessed, — the actual world as Jesus found it, the self-same aspect of localities and affairs, and further still, their opportunities for daily intercourse with those of the faithful, who, having lived in the society of the Apostles, could relate their instructions. All these circumstances once taken into consideration, lend such tremendous weight to the teaching of the Fathers that even Protestant theologians have been struck by it. They declare that "To evade or contravene that common belief which existed among them would be foolish and unavailing, it would be to struggle against the resistless rush of a torrent."[1] We have purposely employed the phraseology of Waterland and Bull; although the evidence of liberal investigation, it is no less uncompromising than the rulings of the Council of Trent.[2]

Accordingly we shall endeavor to follow Tradition closely in interpreting those words of the Saviour which are the immovable foundation of Christian Dogma. Here there is no room for novelties, for Truth is unchangeable. Yet it is not enough, in a Life of the Christ, to set forth the Evangelical Doctrine; it is necessary to describe the places where the years of the Saviour's life were spent; to learn from contemporary history what thoughts then occupied men's minds, what manner of people they were among whom Jesus lived. Upon these points the Gospels are

---

[1] "It is absurd to imagine that all the Churches should combine in the same error, and conspire together to corrupt the doctrine of Christ." (Dr. Waterland, *On the Use and Value of Ecclesiastical Antiquity.* Works, vol. v., pp. 253-383.) "But I have and always shall have a religious scruple in interpreting the Holy Scriptures against the stream of all the fathers and ancient doctors" (Bull, *Defensio fidei Nicænæ*, I. 1, 9. Oxford Translation).

[2] *Concilium Tridentinum*, sessio quarta.

sparing of detail; written for readers of their own era who had under their very eyes the life of the Orient, they are constantly making allusions to customs differing widely from ours, and suppose that their readers are familiar with manners to which we indeed are more or less strangers. This is the vanished world it behoves us to re-habilitate here, in order that the Gospel may be understood as it was in the day of its appearance.

Just now it would seem that everything is ripe for such a restoration of the past. Never has the East been better known; the Aramaic Paraphrases, the traditions contained in the Talmud and the Jewish writers have been tediously conned over; Egypt and Assyria, which traced such deep marks upon the monuments of Judea, have at last revealed the secrets of their institutions; in a word, the knowledge of Hebrew antiquities has become as entire and intelligible to our generation as the archæology of Greece and Rome. At the same time learned achievements in Chronology, based upon astronomical calculations, have established the dates for us, even to the month and the day. Who does not see the advantages offered by such vast stores of knowledge? We cannot even set down here the long array of authors whose works we have examined, and to whom we have been indebted. A list of those by whose labors we have profited most is placed in the front of this Volume, and it will show that we have borrowed much from Germany and England. Nevertheless, however highly we may have esteemed our predecessors, we have been studious to refer to original sources and to accept nothing except upon trustworthy testimony.

An inestimable advantage has been accorded us, above and beyond all these others, — one which has enabled us to make the places in which the Saviour lived better known and realized. Surrounded by friends who lent us a coöperation which was as intelligent and sympathetic as it was kindly, we traversed the Holy Land, "from Dan to Beer-Sheba," from Gaza to Libanus, following the Master step by step, over those hilltops which were the witnesses of His birth, into the valley of the shadow of death, wherein He faced temptation; and along the borders of the lake which He loved. On every hand we have seen the same world which met the eyes of Jesus, — the cities, whose gates still close so soon as ever the first torchlight flares up in the deepening twilight to dispel the darkness from their dwellings; the troops of dogs overrunning the deserted streets, still venturing to lick the beggar's body as he lies yonder by the rich man's threshold; the pomp and ceremony of the marriage-feasts, the banqueting-hall, with the wedding-guests reclining on purple and fine linen; the wail of the mourners, the clamor of their lamentations mingling with the shrill notes of the flutes; and as we enter each town we still hear the plaintive monotone of the blind man's appeal, while the leper still attracts attention to his malady by piercing moans; thence to the Desert of Jericho, — the lonely track winding over wild and gloomy heights, where the Bedouin, gaunt and hollow-eyed with hunger, now as then lies in wait for the traveller who may fall within his reach. In the Gospels all these pictures are indicated in a line, by a single stroke; it is only when viewed under the Eastern sky that they regain their fresh colors, in their clear native atmosphere.

It will be asked what rules we have observed in settling the relationship of the Narratives. Saint Luke has given us the order of events connected with the Childhood of Jesus; Saint John, those which bear upon the beginnings of His Ministry. Indeed, the latter often goes so far as to mention the day and hour. Unfortunately, his testimony leaves much untold concerning the whole public life, or at least he only furnishes us with striking incidents, evidently selected with the design of setting forth the Divinity of the Saviour in higher relief. We must recur to the Synoptical Writers[1] to discover the sequence of events. Certainly, no research could require more careful handling; for the Evangelists, as their name implies, are bearers of Good News, — Glad Tidings,[2] — and in telling it to the world the Apostles have endeavored, not so much to give us a complete chronicle, accompanied with precise dates, as simply to show forth in Jesus the

---

[1] This name has been applied to the first three Evangelists, because their narratives agree in general arrangement, and may be taken in at a glance. S. John has adopted an entirely different method.

[2] Εὐαγγέλιον, from εὖ, "well," and ἀγγέλλειν, "to announce."

Christ Whom they adored. Saint Matthew thinks of Him only as the Royal Messiah; to Saint Mark, He lives, the Son of God; as Saint Luke sees Him, He is the Saviour of the world. Each, absorbed in his own one view of the Fact Divine, recounts only what bears particularly upon his controlling thought.

In fact, Saint Matthew resolutely sacrifices chronology by attempting to associate marvellous occurrences more effectively, which actually took place under very different circumstances, and to this end connects parables which, without doubt, the Christ did not utter in the same discourse. The object of the Evangelist in grouping the doctrines, miracles, and parables of the Saviour is to mass the streaming rays of light in which the Life of Jesus gleamed upon his sight, and by thus concentrating events render them of a more radiant glory.

Saint Mark and Saint Luke have not neglected the succession of occurrences to such a marked degree. In fact the latter, in so many words, announces that it is his intention to conform his Narrative to their order. "Since so many," he says in his Prologue, "have undertaken to compose a narrative of the things believed among us[1] in the manner in which those transmitted them to us who from the beginning did themselves witness them, and have been ministers of the Word, so I likewise, after having followed the course of all these things from their earliest outset,[2] have conceived the plan of recounting these matters to you in their order,[3] most excellent Theophilus,[4] that thus you may be better able to recognize the truth of that which has been taught

---

[1] The Vulgate translates πεπληροφορημένων by "quæ in nobis completæ sunt rerum;" but the Greek text, the Syriac Version, and the interpretation of many Fathers, allow us to give this word the more exact sense of, "matters firmly accepted and believed by us."

[2] Ἄνωθεν: "Alte petito principio." Jansenius Yprentius, Tetrateuchus.

[3] Καθεξῆς signifies in this passage, as commonly elsewhere in the Greek language, "observing the order of events" (Thucydides, ii. 1, 5, 26). It is the sense usually given to the word by S. Luke (vii. 11; Acts xxi. 1; xxv. 17; xxvii. 18), as well as that demanded by the connection of ideas. (See Tischendorf, Synopsis Evangelica, xiv.)

[4] The title Κράτιστε would indicate that Theophilus was of high rank (Acts xxiii. 26; xxiv. 3; xxvi. 2); but neither Scripture nor Tradition makes us any better acquainted with this noble personage.

you." These words clearly denote Saint Luke's intention to leave Theophilus, not simply an authentic record of the preaching of the Apostles, but furthermore, to construct a work in accordance with the rules of history. Wherefore, to insure perfect confidence in his work, he reminds him that he has been a careful student of the facts, that he has set them forth from their inception, with great exactness and in the order in which they took place. Hence he is fittest to be our guide in the disposition of events chronicled by the three synoptical writers, and we shall follow him with all the more confidence from the fact that his Narrative is generally in harmony with that of Saint Mark.

We know too well what difficulties this question of chronology presents to think of insisting on the arrangement which we have adopted for this Life of the Lord. The main duty was to set some certain date for the principal events; for even if it could be proved that such and such miracles, or certain words of the Master, occurred a few weeks earlier or later, variances of this nature would affect the arrangement of His History very little. As to the minor events, whose order still remains subject to difference of opinion, we have thought it best to adopt what seemed the most reasonable construction, referring, in the Notes and Appendices, to the arguments which supported our preference.

In spite of all the care taken by our untiring friends in correcting this effort, more than one error has undoubtedly escaped our notice, and the work must still remain unworthy of its Subject. We have no other ground for hoping well of it beyond the knowledge of its fidelity to Tradition, whose voice, growing more eloquent as it comes down the ages, is now without a rival in its office as Interpreter of the Saviour's words and deeds. God grant that it may have lost nothing of its force by coming from our lips. May its mighty truth touch men's hearts and revive therein their faith in Jesus. More than ever is the aid of that Divine Master now needed, for the latter years of the century grow daily more threatening. A secret disquiet alarms the most steadfast natures; an increasing license is disturbing men's minds, as the divisions of society become every day more apparent. The Christ is no longer among them, to console the poor and wretched ones, who, bent beneath their burdens, still angrily spurn his loving-kindness, while the rich and powerful call sadly for a Deliverer. For salvation, for help, they can turn nowhere but unto Jesus. Upon Him depends all that this world, all that our country has still to hope for or expect. Shattered and broken, menaced on every side, she shall surely rise again upon that day, when, with her children all re-united in the Christ, she shall have but one heart, one mind, one soul, in the sight of God. May our humble efforts be not altogether ineffectual in speeding that regeneration for which all hearts are longing. It is the single purpose of this Book, and the sole glory we could desire for it.

Boisguillaume (Institution Join-Lambert),
    25 Decembre, 1879.

BIBLIOGRAPHICAL LIST.

ALFORD. The Greek Testament, sixth edition. London, 1868.
AMBROSE (S.). Patrologie Latine de Migne, t. xv.-xvii.
ANDREWS. The Life of Our Lord upon the Earth. London, 1863.
ANGER. Synopsis Evangeliorum, cum locis qui supersunt parallelis litterarum et traditionum Irenæo antiquiorum. Lipsiæ, 1851.
AUGUSTINE (S.). Opera, édition Gaume, t. iii. v.

BACUEZ et VIGOUROUX. Manuel Biblique. Paris, 1880.
BARONIUS. Annales Ecclesiastici, t. i. Parisiis.
BEDE. Patrologie latine, t. xcii.
BENGEL. Gnomon Novi Testamenti. Stuttgartiæ, 1860.
BINGHAM. Origines Ecclesiasticæ. Halæ, 1724.
BISPING. Erklärung des Evangeliums nach Matthæus. Munster, 1867.
BONAVENTURE (S.). Meditationes Vitæ Christi, editio Lugdun., 1668, t. vi.
BOSSUET. Méditations sur l'Évangile. — Élévations sur les Mystères, édit. Vivès, t. vi. et vii.
BOUGAUD. Le Christianisme et les temps présents. Paris, 1875.
BUXTORF. Synagoga Judaïca. Basileæ, 1661.
—— Lexicon Chaldaicum, Talmudicum et Rabbinicum. Basileæ, 1639.

CALMET. Dictionnaire de la Bible. Paris, 1730.
—— Commentaire littéral sur tous les livres de l'Ancien et du Nouveau Testament. Paris, 1714.
CASPARI. Chronologische geographische Einleitung in das Leben Jesu Christi. Hamburg, 1869.
CHRYSOSTOM (S. JOHN). Opera, édit. Gaume, t. vi.-viii.
CLEMENT OF ALEXANDRIA. Patrologie grecque, t. viii., ix.
COLERIDGE. The Public Life of Our Lord. London, 1874, 1875.
CORLUY. Commentarius in Evangelium S. Joannis. Gandavi, 1880.
CORNELIUS A LAPIDE. Commentaria, édit. Vivès. Paris, 1858.

CYPRIAN (S.). Patrologie latine, t. iv.
CYRIL OF ALEXANDRIA (S.). Patrologie grecque, t. lxxii.-lxxiv.
CYRIL OF JERUSALEM (S.). Patrologie grecque, t. xxxiii.

DANKO. Historia Revelationis Divinæ Novi Testamenti. Vindobonæ, 1867.
DAVIDSON. Introduction to the New Testament. London, 1868.
DEHAUT. L'Évangile médité, défendu et expliqué. Paris, 1875.
DELITZSCH Jesus und Hillel. Erlangen, 1867.
—— Ein Tag in Capernaum. Leipzig, 1873.
—— Jüdisches Handwerkerleben zur Zeit Jesu. Erlangen, 1869.
DERENBOURG Essai sur l'histoire et la géographie de la Palestine, d'après les Thalmuds. Paris, 1867.
DIDYMUS. Patrologie grecque, t xxxix.
DILLMANN. Das Buch Henoch. Leipzig. 1853.
DÖLLINGER. Paganisme et Judaïsme. Bruxelles, 1858.
DUPANLOUP (Mgr). Histoire de N.-S. Jésus-Christ. Paris, 1872.

EBRARD. The Gospel History. Edinburgh, 1863.
—— Ecce Homo. London, 1866
ELLICOTT. Historical Lectures on the Life of Our Lord Jesus Christ. London, 1868.
EPIPHANIUS. Patrologie grecque, t. xli-xliii.
ERASMUS. Annotationes in Novum Testamentum. Bâle, 1516.
EUSEBIUS. Patrologie grecque, t. xx., xxiv.
EUTHYMIUS ZIGABENUS. Patrologie grecque, t. cxxix.
EWALD. Geschichte. Gottingen, 1866.
—— Die drei ersten Evangelien. Gottingen, 1870.

FABER. Bethlehem. London, 1865.
FARRAR. Life of Christ. London, 1874.
FILLION. Évangile selon S. Matthieu et S. Marc, 1878, 1879; dans la Bible de Lethielleux. Paris.
FOISSET. Histoire de Jésus-Christ. Paris, 1863.
FRIEDLIEB. Archäologie der Leidensgeschichte unsers Herrn Jesu Christi. Bonn, 1843.

GEIKIE. The Life and Words of Christ. London, 1877.
GREGORY THE GREAT (S.). Patrologie latine, t. lxxvi., lxxix.
GRESWELL. Harmonia Evangelica. Oxford, 1840.
GRINFIELD. Novum Testamentum Græcum; editio Hellenistica. London. 1843.

GRINFIELD. Scholia Hellenistica in Novum Testamentum. London, 1848.
GROTIUS. Annotationes in Novum Testamentum. Paris, 1644.
GUÉRIN. Description géographique, historique et archéologique de la Palestine. — JUDÉE. — SAMARIE. Paris, 1868-1875.

HASE. Das Leben Jesu. Leipzig, 1835.
HENGSTENBERG. Commentary on the Gospel of S. John. Edinburgh, 1871.
—— Christology of the Old Testament. Edinburgh, 1871.
—— Vorlesungen über die Leidensgeschichte. Leipzig, 1875.
HERVEY. On the Genealogies of Our Lord. Cambridge, 1853.
HILARY (S.). Patrologie latine, t. ix.
HUG. Einleitung in die Schriften des Neuen Testaments. Stuttgart, 1847.

IRENÆUS (S.). Patrologie grecque, t. vii.

JAHN. Archæologia Biblica. Oxford, 1836.
JANSENIUS GANDENTIUS. Concordia Evangelica. Lugduni, 1684.
JANSENIUS YPRENTIUS. Tetrateuchus. Avenione, 1853.
JEROME (S.). Patrologie latine, t. xxvi., xxix., xxx.
JOSEPHUS. Opera, édit. Didot. Paris, 1845-1847.
JOST. Geschichte des Judenthums. Leipzig, 1857.
JUSTIN (S.). Patrologie grecque, t. vi.

KITTO. Cyclopædia of Biblical Literature. Edinburgh, 1869.

LANGE. Life of Christ. Edinburgh, 1864.
—— Commentar über Matthäus, Markus, Johannes. Bielefeld, 1860.
LANGEN. Die letzten Lebenstage Jesu.
LEO (S.). Patrologie latine, t. liv.
LIÉVIN DE HAMME. Guide indicateur des sanctuaires et lieux historiques de la terre sainte. Louvain, 1876.
LIGHTFOOT. Horæ Hebraïcæ. Oxford, 1859.
LIGNY (DE). Histoire de la vie de Jésus-Christ. Paris, 1830.
LUCAS BRUGENTIUS. Commentarius in Evangelia. Anvers, 1606.
LUCKE. Commentar über das Evangelium des Johannes. Bonn, 1840.
LUDOLPHE LE CHARTREUX. Vita Christi e sacris Evangeliis sanctorumque Patrum fontibus derivata. Strasbourg, 1474.
LUTHARDT. Das Johanneische Evangelium. Nürnberg, 1853.

MALDONATUS. Commentarii in IV Evangelistas. Lutetiæ Parisiorum, 1629.
MAUDUIT. L'Évangile analysé. Paris, 1843.
MEIGNAN (M**gr**). Les Évangiles. Bar-le-Duc, 1864.
MÉMAIN Études chronologiques pour l'histoire de N.-S Jésus-Christ. Paris, 1867.
MESSMER. Erklärung des Johannes Evangeliums. Innsbruck, 1860.
MEYER. Kritish exegetischer Commentar über das Neue Testament. Gottingen, 1858.
MILL Observations on the attempted application of pantheistic principles to the theory and historic criticism of the Gospel. Cambridge, 1861.
MILMAN. History of Christianity. London, 1867
—— History of the Jews. London, 1866
MURRAY Handbook for Syria and Palestine.

NEANDER Das Leben Jesu Christi. Hamburg, 1845.

OLSHAUSEN. Biblischer Commentar. Kœnigsberg, 1830.
OOSTERZEE. Das Evangelium nach Lukas. Bielefeld, 1867
ORIGEN. Patrologie grecque, t. xiii., xiv.

PATRIZI De Evangeliis libri tres. Friburgi Brisgoviæ, 1853.
—— In Marcum Commentarium. Romæ, 1862.
—— In Joannem Commentarium. Romæ, 1857.
PHILO. Opera omnia. Lipsiæ, 1828.
PRESSENSÉ (DE). Jésus-Christ, son temps, sa vie, son œuvre. Paris.

REITHMAYR. Introduction aux livres du Nouveau Testament, traduction du P. de Valroger. Paris, 1861.
RELAND. Antiquitates Sacræ. Utrecht, 1712.
RENAN. Les Origines du christianisme. Paris.
ROBINSON. Biblical Researches in Palestine. London, 1867.
—— Harmony of the Four Gospels. Boston, 1845.
—— Lexicon of the New Testament. Edinburgh, 1876.
ROUTH. Reliquiæ Sacræ. Oxford, 1846.

SACY (DE). La sainte Bible en latin et en français, avec des explications du sens littéral et du sens spirituel. Paris, 1804.
SALMERON. Commentarius in Evangelia et Acta. Coloniæ, 1602.
SCHEGG. Sechs Bücher des Lebens Jesu. Freiburg in Breisgau, 1875.
SCHOETTGEN. Horæ Hebraïcæ et Talmudicæ. Dresden und Leipzig. 1733.

SCRIVENER. Introduction to the Criticism of the New Testament. Cambridge, 1861.
SEPP. Das Leben Jesu. Regensburg, 1865.
SMITH. Dictionary of the Bible. London, 1863.
STANLEY Sinaï and Palestine. London, 1866.
STAPPFER. Idées religieuses des Juifs au temps de Notre-Seigneur. Paris, 1878.

TERTULLIAN. Patrologie latine, t. i., ii.
THILO. Codex Apocryphus Novi Testamenti. Leipzig, 1832.
THOLUCK. Philologisch-theologische Auslegung der Bergpredigt. Hamburg, 1835.
—— Commentar zum Evangelium Joannis. Hamburg, 1844.
THOMAS AQUINAS (S.). Catena Aurea in IV Evangelia. Paris, 1636.
THOMSON. The Land and The Book. London, 1863.
TILLEMONT. Mémoires pour servir à l'Histoire ecclésiastique. Paris, 1693.
TISCHENDORF. Evangelia Apocrypha. Leipzig, 1876.
—— Synopsis Evangelica. Leipzig. 1871.
TOBLER. Topographie von Jerusalem. Berlin, 1854.
TRENCH. Notes on the Parables. London, 1841.
—— Notes on the Miracles. London, 1847.
—— Studies on the Gospel. London, 1867.
—— Synonyms of the New Testament. London, 1871.

VARIOT. Les Évangiles Apocryphes. Paris, 1878.
VEUILLOT (L). Vie de Notre-Seigneur Jésus-Christ. Paris, 1864.

WAHL. Clavis Novi Testamenti. Lipsiæ, 1843.
WALLON. De la Croyance due à l'Évangile. Paris, 1866.
—— Vie de N.-S. Jésus-Christ. Paris, 1865.
—— Les saints Évangiles, traduction tirée de Bossuet. Paris, 1863.
WESTCOTT. Introduction to the Study of the Gospels. London, 1867.
—— A General Survey of the History of the Canon of the New Testament. London, 1870.
WIESELER. Chronologische Synopse der Vier Evangelien. Hamburg, 1843.
WINER. Biblisches Realwörterbuch. Leipzig, 1847.
—— Grammatik der Neutestamentlichen Sprachidioms. Leipzig, 1867.
WORDSWORTH. The New Testament of Our Lord. London. 1870.

THE TRANSLATOR'S ADVERTISEMENT.

THE only words contained in Monsieur Fouard's Fifth Edition which we have omitted here come under the heading, *Avant-Propos de la Seconde Edition*, — a short page and a half in length, in recognition of the popular and critical welcome the work had received, and as an acknowledgment of indebtedness to the prelates and professors whose counsels and corrections had helped largely toward perfecting later editions, but most of all for an expression of gratitude to that princely Scholar, Leo XIII., whose Brief of April 2, 1881, conferred upon our Author the Apostolic benediction, with the Theologian's congratulations. Besides the Holy Father, many Cardinals and ecclesiastics have testified to their delight at the learning and faith, which indeed have made their impression upon every reader of this Life, from the humblest Christian to the great servant of God and God's people, under whose patronage we are happy in being able to place this translation.

A word of explanation on some technical points may be of service to the student. Bossuet's translation of the Gospels was preferred by the Abbé Fouard, because, as he says, "though oftentimes full of archaisms and curious felicities of speech, yet, since it is always luminous, and the work of a genius, it conveys the Master's meaning better than any other." Here the method to be followed by the interpreter was fixed beyond cavil by his original. The Author is well known on the Continent as a Hellenist, and his helpful re-settings of the hallowed sentences are not the least valuable feature of his periods, which bear their burthen of erudition so happily. A cursory comparison will demonstrate the impossibility of making any received English Version take the place of our Author's illuminations of ancient Codices.

But Professor Fouard is eminent also as a Hebraist; hence, in some instances, he has not hesitated to revise the spelling of proper names, in consonance with our fuller understanding of their derivation and significance: for the more familiar names, however, he retains the usual Vulgate form. Doubtless he lays as little stress upon such technical divergences as do all who set the matter higher than the manner. But here, as everywhere else, needless to say, our sole aim has been to find the fairest equivalent of the original form. Perhaps we may be pardoned for adding that we have been far from desiring to introduce strange forms into the present orthographical chaos, which to-day offers us such differences as Nabuchodonosor and Nebuchadnezzar, to dismay the Catholic or non-Catholic layman.

Finally, it would betoken something like ingratitude to let this edition go out without a word of recognition for its many well-wishers: for, after the Abbé Fouard himself, whose unvarying courtesy has contributed toward making our toil altogether a pleasure, this Book stands to the Very Reverend Thomas S. Campbell, S. J., and to other dear friends of his Company, in relations much like that of a son to his home and kinsfolk; while, continuing the figure, our translation has the honor of claiming as its Godfather and Mentor that ripe scholar and theologian, the Reverend Professor Fivez, of the New York Provincial Seminary. To his self-sacrificing interest and generosity we owe it that no greater blunders have been committed than now, perchance, and despite all such affectionate pains, must meet the eyes of our indulgent reader.

G. F. X. G.

Day of St. Anthony of Padua,
    St. Joseph's Seminary, TROY, N. Y.

TABLE OF CONTENTS.

VOLUME I.

	PAGE
INTRODUCTION BY CARDINAL MANNING	v
AUTHOR'S PREFACE	ix
BIBLIOGRAPHICAL LIST	xxi
THE TRANSLATOR'S ADVERTISEMENT	xxvii

Book First.

THE CHILDHOOD OF JESUS.

CHAPTER I.

JUDEA IN THE TIME OF JESUS.

Decline of the Machabees. — Reign of Herod the Great. — The Sanhedrin: its constitution; its authority in the time of Herod. — Jewish sects: Pharisees, Sadducees, Essenes. — Erroneous ideas among the Jews concerning the Messiah. — The true Messiah foretold in the Scriptures 3

CHAPTER II.

THE BIRTH OF THE PRECURSOR.

I. THE VISION OF ZACHARY.

Youttah, Zachary's abode. — The Sacrifice of Perfumes. — Appearance of the Angel Gabriel. — Elizabeth conceives a son . . . 17

II. THE CIRCUMCISION OF JOHN THE BAPTIST.

Ceremonies of Circumcision. — The name John given him by Zachary. — The *Benedictus* 23

CHAPTER III.

THE INCARNATION.

I. THE ANNUNCIATION.

Mary betrothed to Joseph. — Appearance of the Angel Gabriel in the home at Nazareth. — The Angelical Salutation. — The Word made flesh 28

II. THE VISITATION.

Journey from Nazareth to Youttah. — Mary in the dwelling of Elizabeth. — The *Magnificat* 35

CHAPTER IV.

THE NATIVITY.

I. THE APPEARANCE OF THE ANGEL TO JOSEPH. — THE CENSUS OF QUIRINIUS.

Joseph's misgivings. — An Angel of the Lord appears to him. — Joseph marries Mary. — The numbering of the Roman Empire ordered by Augustus, completed in Judea by Quirinius. — The Genealogical Tables of Bethlehem. — Genealogy of the parents of Jesus 39

II. THE NATIVITY.

The Inn at Bethlehem. — The Cave. — Birth of Jesus 46

III. THE ADORATION OF THE SHEPHERDS.

Appearance of the Angelic hosts. — *Gloria in excelsis.* — The Shepherds worship Jesus in His crib 51

IV. THE CIRCUMCISION AND THE PRESENTATION IN THE TEMPLE.

Jesus circumcised on the eighth day. — The Name of Jesus. — Mary's Purification. — The old man Simeon. — *Nunc Dimittis.* — Anna the Prophetess 54

CHAPTER V

THE EPIPHANY.

I. THE MAGI.

The Magi of Persian origin; their beliefs. — Appearance of the Star. — The Magi in Jerusalem; Herod's perturbation. — The Adoration of the Magi 61

II. THE FLIGHT INTO EGYPT AND THE HOLY INNOCENTS.

Secret departure of the Magi. — The Holy Family in Egypt. — Massacre of the Holy Innocents. — Testimony of Macrobius. — Herod's death. — Return of the Holy Family to Nazareth . . . 68

CHAPTER VI.

JESUS AT NAZARETH.

I. THE CHILDHOOD OF JESUS

Interior development of Jesus. — Jesus in the arms of Mary. — Galilee of the Gentiles. — Nazareth 77

II. JESUS AMONG THE DOCTORS.

Route from Nazareth to Jerusalem. — The Galileans' caravans. — The Child Jesus among the Doctors 81

III. HIDDEN LIFE OF JESUS AT NAZARETH.

Jesus in the Carpenter's shop at Nazareth. — Home life of the Holy Family. — The Lord's brethren 86

Book Second.

THE BEGINNINGS OF THE MINISTRY OF JESUS.

CHAPTER I.

THE EPOCH AND THE LOCALITIES IN WHICH JESUS EXERCISED HIS MINISTRY.

Period in which John Baptist appeared. — Principal epochs in the life of Jesus. — The territory wherein Jesus preached. — Government of Judea in the time of Jesus 93

CHAPTER II.

THE MISSION OF JOHN BAPTIST.

"John's Desert." — The two Precursors. — John Baptist's preaching. — Baptism of Jesus 106

CHAPTER III.

THE TEMPTATION.

Jesus impelled into the wilderness by the Holy Ghost. — Mystery involved in a God's being tempted. — The threefold Temptation . 120

CHAPTER IV.

JOHN BAPTIST'S TESTIMONY, AND THE FIRST DISCIPLES OF JESUS.

The Sanhedrin's Embassy. — John's testimony. — The Voice crying in the wilderness. — The Lamb of God. — Calling of the first disciples 129

CHAPTER V.

THE WEDDING FESTIVITIES AT CANA.

Ceremonies of Jewish weddings. — Mary at the wedding in Cana. — The water changed into wine. — The first Sign given by Jesus . 140

CHAPTER VI.

GENESARETH.

The Lake and Plain of Genesareth. — Cities of the Lake: Tiberias, Capharnaum, Bethsaïda, Chorozaïn 148

Book Third.

FIRST YEAR OF THE MINISTRY OF JESUS.

CHAPTER I.

THE FIRST PASCH IN THE MINISTRY OF JESUS.

I. THE HUCKSTERS DRIVEN FROM THE TEMPLE.   PAGE

Jesus' first sojourn at Capharnaum. — Merchants and money-changers expelled from the porches. — A Temple destroyed and rebuilt in three days 163

II. NICODEMUS.

The second birth. — The breath of the Spirit. — The things of Heaven. — The Light and the darkness 169

CHAPTER II.

JOHN BAPTIST'S LAST TESTIMONY.

Ministry of Jesus in Judea. — Baptism performed by the disciples of Jesus. — Discussion between John's disciples and the Jews concerning the purifications. — Renewed testimony from the Forerunner. — Sinful union of Herod Antipas with Herodias. — John Baptist imprisoned in the fortress of Macheronte 175

CHAPTER III.

THE SAMARITAN.

Sichem. — The woman of Samaria. — The Spring of living water. — The true worshippers. — Jesus and the Samaritans 186

CHAPTER IV.

JESUS DRIVEN OUT OF NAZARETH.

Jesus in Galilee. — Outward appearance of Jesus. — The Jewish synagogues. — Jesus driven from the synagogue at Nazareth. — The child of the officer of Capharnaum 197

VOL. I. — *c*

CHAPTER V.

THE FIRST ACTS DURING THE MINISTRY OF JESUS IN GALILEE.

I. THE CALLING OF THE FIRST DISCIPLES.   PAGE

Jesus makes His home at Capharnaum. — Calling of the sons of Jonas
 and of Zebedee 208

II. A SABBATH DAY AT CAPHARNAUM.

A possessed person healed in the synagogue. — Simon's mother-in-
 law. — Numberless cures on the Sabbath evening 211

III. THE MIRACULOUS DRAUGHT OF FISHES. — HEALING OF
 A LEPER.

Jesus at Bethsaïda. — The miraculous draught of fishes, symbol of
 the Apostles' ministry. — First mission trip into Galilee. — Healing of a leper 217

IV. HEALING OF A PARALYTIC.

The Sanhedrin's spies. — Paralytic healed by Jesus 222

V. THE CALLING OF LEVI.

The publicans. — Their business hateful to the Jews. — Levi joins
 the company of Jesus 225

Book Fourth.

SECOND YEAR OF THE MINISTRY OF JESUS.

CHAPTER I.

THE SECOND PASCHAL SEASON IN THE MINISTRY OF JESUS.

I. THE POOL OF BETHESDA.

The paralytic at the pool of Bethesda. — Jesus and the Sanhedrin-
 Councillors. — Jesus accused of violating the Sabbatic prescriptions   231

II. A Sabbath Walk through the Fields.

The disciples pluck ears of corn on the Sabbath. — David and the Loaves of Proposition. — The Sabbath made for man, not man for the Sabbath 237

III. The Man with the Withered Hand.

Jesus in the synagogue cures a man with a withered hand. — The Sanhedrin's spies make common cause with the Herodians. — Jesus withdraws to escape their attacks 242

CHAPTER II.

THE TWELVE APOSTLES.

Jesus upon the heights of Kourn Hattin. — He chooses the Twelve Apostles. — Character of each 246

CHAPTER III.

THE SERMON ON THE MOUNT.

Scope and character of the Sermon. — The Beatitudes. — The Ancient Law and the New. — The Lord's Prayer. — Trust in God. — Conclusion of the Master's discourse 259

CHAPTER IV.

CAPHARNAUM AND NAIM.

I. The Centurion of Capharnaum.

Rare qualities of the Centurion of Capharnaum. — Jesus heals his servant 274

II. The Son of the Widow of Naim.

Naim. — Funeral rites in Jewry. — Jesus heals the widow's son . . 278

III. The Message sent by John the Baptist.

John's disciples as deputies before Jesus. — The miracles as Signs of the Christ. — John more than a Prophet. — The least in God's Kingdom greater than John 280

IV. THE SINFUL WOMAN AT THE BANQUET GIVEN BY SIMON.

Jesus among the Pharisees. — The sinner at the Master's feet. — The two debtors. — The Magdalene in Jewish and Christian Tradition 285

CHAPTER V.

THE PARABLES.

Second mission into Galilee. — The holy women. — The Mother and brothers of Jesus. — Beelzebub. — The sin against the Holy Spirit. — Change in the Master's teaching. — Parables of the kingdom of God 293

CHAPTER VI.

MIRACLES DONE IN GERGESA AND CAPHARNAUM.

I. THE POSSESSED CREATURES OF GERGESA.

The tempest stilled. — The possessed men. — The herd of swine . . 308

II. THE BANQUET GIVEN BY LEVI — THE WOMAN WITH THE ISSUE OF BLOOD. — THE DAUGHTER OF JAÏRUS.

Publicans and sinners. — John's disciples. — Healing of a woman with an issue of blood. — The daughter of Jaïru 313

CHAPTER VII.

THE MISSION OF THE APOSTLES. — DEATH OF THE PRECURSOR.

I. THE MISSION OF THE APOSTLES.

Third mission-journey into Galilee. — Jesus at Nazareth. — Duties of the Apostles. — Their Mission 323

II. DEATH OF JOHN THE BAPTIST.

John in prison at Macheronte. — Celebration of Herod's birthday. — Herodias and Salome. — The Baptist put to death. — Herod's remorseful terrors. — Jesus withdraws to the domain of Philip . 330

CHAPTER VIII.

THE BREAD OF LIFE.

I. THE MULTIPLICATION OF THE LOAVES.   PAGE

Bethsaïda-Julias. — Multiplication of the five loaves and the two fishes. — Jesus alone on the mountain-top. — The Apostles overtaken by storm. — Jesus walking on the waves of the Lake. — Manifold cures in the land of Genesareth 336

II. THE PROMISE OF THE EUCHARIST.

Jesus in the synagogue at Capharnaum. — Manna and the Bread of Heaven. — Murmurings among the people of Capharnaum. — Jesus the Bread of Life. — To eat the Flesh and to drink the Blood of the Christ. — The disciples scandalized. — Peter's protestation of the Faith of the Twelve 344

Appendix.

I.	JERUSALEM AND THE TEMPLE	357
II.	THE "WORD" OF SAINT JOHN .	362
III.	THE GENEALOGIES OF THE GOSPEL	373
IV.	THE STAR OF THE MAGI	382
V.	THE BRETHREN OF THE LORD . .	383
VI.	THE SAMARITANS	386
VII.	THE FESTIVAL IN THE FIFTH CHAPTER OF SAINT JOHN .	389
VIII.	THE POOL OF BETHESDA	391

MAP OF JUDEA IN THE TIME OF OUR LORD JESUS CHRIST   *Frontispiece*

MAP OF THE LAKE OF GENESARETH 148

ERRATA.

Vol. I. p.	xiv, n. 2,	for "in every respect,"	read "in all its parts."
	14, n. 2,	"Alexandria,"	"Alexandre."
	73, n. 3,	"*Phthiarisis*,"	"*Phthiriasis.*"
	211, l. 28,	"Peter and Simon,"	"Peter and Andrew."
	269, n. 4,	"two feet and a half,"	"one foot and a half."
	356,	"ΘΟΕΥ,"	"ΘΕΟΥ."
	390, l. 14,	"on Mount Sion,"	"of Jerusalem."
Vol. II. p.	310, l. 15,	"linen,"	"cloth."
	315, l. 20,	"Vienna,"	"Vienne."
	317, l. 23,	"eastward,"	"westward."

ADDENDA.

Vol. I. p. 144, line 30, for "pay any heed to her," etc., read "pay heed directly to her.[2]

Vol. I. p. 144, add note, [2] S. Gregory of Nyssa (*Patrologie grecque* † xliv. p. 1308); S. Bernard (*Patrologie latine*, † clxxxiii. p. 160). Cf. Maldonatus: *Comment. in Joan.*, Cap. ii. 13.

Vol. II. p. 354, n. 4, add, [4] John xx. 11, 18. Mark xvi. 9. — "Quamquam Dominus primo dicatur apparuisse Magdalenae, pietas tamen non parum suadet ut credamus Dominum prius apparuisse dilectissimae suae matri, licet eam praetermiserint Evangelistae, quod ad confirmandam filii resurrectionem inefficax esset matris testimonium. . . . Quamquam etiam videri possit Dominum ideo non apparuisse subito matri quod illam in fide resurrectionis sciret non vacillare, propter quod non ita cum reliquis sepulcrum adiit, sicut cum reliquis astitit cruci." Jansenius Gaudentius (*Comment. in Concord. Evang.* Cap. cxlv. p. 1045).

BOOK FIRST.

THE CHILDHOOD OF JESUS.

ΚΑΤΑ ΛΟΥΚΑΝ.

ά. λδ΄, λέ.

Εἶπεν δὲ Μαριὰμ πρὸς τὸν ἄγγελον· Πῶς ἔσται τοῦτο, ἐπεὶ ἄνδρα οὐ γινώσκω;

Καὶ ἀποκριθεὶς ὁ ἄγγελος εἶπεν αὐτῇ· Πνεῦμα ἅγιον ἐπελεύσεται ἐπὶ σέ καὶ δύναμις Ὑψίστου ἐπισκιάσει σοι· διὸ καὶ τὸ γεννώμενον Ἅγιον κληθήσεται ΥΙΟΣ ΘΕΟΥ.

The Angel's Testimony.

And Mary said to the Angel: How shall this be done, because I know not man?

Then answering the Angel said: "The Holy Spirit shall come upon thee, and the power of the Most High shall overshadow thee; and therefore also The Holy which shall be born of Thee shall be called THE SON OF GOD.

SAINT LUKE.

i. 34, 36.

THE CHRIST, THE SON OF GOD.

Book First.

THE CHILDHOOD OF JESUS.

CHAPTER I.

JUDEA IN THE TIME OF JESUS.

JUDEA in the time of the Christ was despoiled of all her splendor. The Machabees, pontiffs and kings of Israel during one century, had in that time seen their glories vanish, together with their virtues. The power, so nobly exercised by Judas and his brothers, degenerated into despotism under their successors; their religious zeal became ambition; and the concord which had existed among the sons of Mathathias gave place to such profound divisions that, sixty-six years before the Christian era, Hyrcanus and Aristobulus, two brothers sprung from this illustrious stock, were compelled to invoke the arbitration of Pompey to adjust their feuds and dissensions. The Roman general, already master of Syria, solemnly adjudged their differences at Damascus, and pronounced in favor of Hyrcanus. Resorting to arms, Aristobulus hazarded a desperate defence from the Mountain of the Temple; but in vain, — defeat was inevitable. Hyrcanus remained sovereign of Judea, but under the authority of the governors of Syria and with the simple title of Ethnarch. Jerusalem for the first time saw the eagles within her walls. Pompey crossed the threshold of the Holy of Holies, and gazed in astonishment upon that Sanctuary, devoid of idol or image. The sovereignty of Juda had run its course; the servitude of Israel was begun.

Very soon Hyrcanus lost even the shadow of command which had been spared him. Cæsar, the conqueror of Pompey, united Palestine to the kingdom of Edom, and gave the government of these countries to an Idumean of noble race, Antipater. Phasaël and Herod, two sons of this prince, lent him their aid in the administration of affairs, — one assuming the government of Galilee, the other that of Judea; but their united efforts were ineffectual for the maintaining of a peace of any long duration. A descendant of the Machabees, Aristobulus, the brother of Hyrcanus, made his escape from Rome, where he was held as a captive, and essayed to regain the throne of his fathers, aided by his sons, Alexander and Antigonus. The arms of the last-named prince alone achieved any success; he made Phasaël prisoner, and constrained him to take his own life. Herod, more fortunate than his brother, eluded their conqueror, hurried to Rome, and was declared by the senate King of Judea. After three years of conflict, the victorious Latin legions reëstablished his rule in Jerusalem. This was in the year 37 before Jesus Christ.

The patronage of Rome, which never belied its promises, Herod's own native genius for ruling, his union with Mariamne, the daughter of Hyrcanus, their former ethnarch, — all seemed to insure him a tranquil reign. Yet the Idumean found in his nationality, his unhoped-for successes, his own restless and suspicious nature, too many sources of disquiet to permit of any peaceable enjoyment of his power. He could take no repose while a remnant of the Machabean line remained alive. Two princes of that family, as well as his father-in-law, — Hyrcanus himself, broken down by years and misfortunes, — were the first victims of Herod's distrust; then came the turn of Mariamne, the only one of his wives whom he had really loved; and finally, neither the two children he had had by her, nor Antipater (son of Doris, and his first-born) were spared the penalty of such suspicions. Only the death of the tyrant could set a limit to these cruelties.

In vain did Herod beautify Judea with splendid monuments, in order to divert attention from the bloody tragedies which encrimsoned his marble palaces. To the Jews, his vast amphitheatres were the scenes of spectacles as detestable as they were abhorrent. The Baths and the Porticos introduced novel customs; and the Roman eagle which spread its wings within the Temple profaned its sanctity. During thirty-four years the prince wearied himself in fruitless endeavors to make the people forget his origin and their servitude. Everything did but remind this nation, shuddering under his yoke, that the sceptre had indeed passed from the sons of Jacob to those of Esau.

Amid this universal demolition of Judaic institutions, one body alone withstood the tempests and retained its authority; this was the Sanhedrin, — the National Council, established by Moses according to some, while according to others it was first convened after the Captivity. The ascendency which the prophets and doctors possessed over the people in those days of exile, the absence of the priests and of all external surroundings of their worship, the debasement into which the royal family had fallen after the return from Babylon, the difficulties surrounding any political and religious restoration, — all these considerations had led the Jews to regard this sovereign assembly as a substitute for the Monarchy.

The functions of the Sanhedrin were to interpret the Law, to adjudge more important cases, and to exercise an exact surveillance over the administration of affairs. Hence it became at one and the same time Parliament, High Court of Justice, and the supreme resort of instruction in Judea.[1] Its seventy-one[2] members represented the three

---

[1] Josephus, *Antiquitates*, xiv. 9, 3; *Sanhedrin*, 19.

[2] Jewish writers do not agree as to the number composing the body of the Sanhedrin. The majority suppose that there were seventy-one members for a lasting memorial of that first Council of Israel, in which seventy elders took part, together with Moses, who presided over their delibera-

classes of the nation: the Priests (that is to say, the chiefs of the twenty-four sacerdotal classes), with whom were associated, under Herod and the Romans, the Pontiffs (who were in this manner deprived of any temporal authority by their foreign masters); and the Scribes, as doctors and interpreters of the Law; together with the Ancients, chosen from among the elders of each tribe and family.

During four hundred years the authority of this Council had remained absolute. Herod was the first to sap its strength; but shrewd as he showed himself in usurping all other powers, he could not entirely cripple the Sanhedrin. That mighty assembly continued its sittings in the very face of the tyrant, and survived his dynasty; for we see it, under the Romans, asserting its right to settle all questions of doctrine, to administer justice, and to direct in secret the movements of the people.

This, then, is the poor ghost of authority to which the power of Israel was finally reduced; yet what must be said of the deterioration of religion and manners? The last of the Machabees had allowed the Pontificate to be dishonored by permitting the Scribes to assume a predominant influence. Relinquished to these doctors, so zealous to discuss in their elaborate commentaries the most trivial minutiae, the laws became mere matter for futile argument; and the numerous Sects, each one arrogating to itself the right of interpreting the Law, furnish a most striking proof of the decline of Israel. The fame of three of these great parties has lived up to this day, — the Pharisees, Sadducees, and Essenes, and (according to the testimony of Josephus [1]) to be acquainted with this trio is to understand the ethics and the morals of all their contemporaries.

Whatever uncertainty we may feel as to the origin of Pharisaism, we believe its sources should be sought in

---

tions. Others, however, would raise the number to seventy-two; these do not include Moses with the seventy Councillors, but hold that the other two representatives were Eldad and Medad, upon whom the Spirit of the Lord descended, when in company with the Seventy (Num. xi. 16–30). Selden, *De Synedriis*, lib. ii. cap. iv.

[1] Josephus, *Bellum Judaïcum*, ii. 8, 2.

that isolation which the Law of Jehovah imposed upon the Jews as a nation. To shun contact with idolatrous peoples, in order to preserve the worship of God in its purity, was one of the precepts constantly reiterated by Moses and the Prophets. On the return from Babylon, Esdras and Nehemiah insisted upon this point with all the more earnestness because the defences which they could erect about the Holy Land were so feeble and so frequently infringed upon. This exclusiveness became a duty still more rigorous when the Syrian kings made apostasy obligatory, and when the High Priests Menelaus and Alcimus betrayed the faith by becoming the allies of their persecutors. All the generous hearts that Israel could count upon henceforth entrenched themselves in their despair, forming a band of picked souls whose zeal procured them the name of the Pietists,—the Assideäns.[1]

Under the leadership of Mathathias and his sons these children of Abraham had proved themselves invincible. Nothing was wanting of all that goes to make true heroism,—austere, indomitable courage, a noble scorn of death, a living faith in the God who was their Protector, and in the Angels, who were their ministers and His. But peace once reëstablished, this impetuous virtue knew not how to restrain itself; zeal developed into fanaticism; the love of fatherland gradually narrowed into a hatred of strangers; to fly from their impure contact became a law for these Assideäns,—a law which they desired to impose upon all Israel. From this, in fact, came the Aramaïc name of Parousch,[2] Pharisee (that is to say, a Separatist), which was given them by those Jews who opposed their teachings.

Neither the Machabees nor the priests who surrounded them followed the Pharisees in these views. Obliged to maintain political relations with other countries, yielding moreover to the attractions of power and wealth, the new princes of Judea rejected the maxims prescribed by these zealots; they confined their observance to the letter of the

---

[1] חֲסִידִים, 1 Mach. ii. 42.
[2] פְּרוּשִׁים, From the root פָּרַשׁ, to separate.

law, to the *sedacha*,¹ so highly praised in the holy Books, and it was from this trait that they got the name of Sadducees (or The Just), to whom they were fond of likening themselves. Such, in the days of the Machabees, were the diverse tendencies of the Pharisees and Sadducees; let us see how far they had developed their theories at the time of the birth of Jesus.

Each proceeded along the downward path it had marked out for itself. The Pontiff kings and the chiefs of the sacerdotal body fortified themselves in their holdings, endeavoring, in the administration of public business, to conserve their tottering forces by intrigue and shrewdly-planned alliances; while, with the neighboring nations, they maintained their reciprocal relations with more rigor in proportion as the independence of Judea began to be more generally menaced. From this habitual intercourse with the Pagan world the faith of the Sadducees grew weaker, and the Epicurean doctrines, which so largely obtained at Rome, attained an influence over them also. If they really retained their belief in the Creator, God, they did not concede to Him any active participation in the government of the world. "The Law once given to the people," they said, "Jehovah withdrew into the repose of Eternity, and abandoned man to his own free-will, unchecked and unheeded."² Very soon they came to deny the Immortality of the Soul, the Resurrection of the body, and the existence of the Angels.³ Priests of Jehovah, for the most part, they still continued to observe the laws, and acquitted themselves of their sacred functions; but, even so, they railed against the scrupulosity of the zealots.

"The Pharisees," they would say ironically, "torment themselves to no purpose in this life of ours, since they will gain nothing for their pains in this world or any other."⁴

The laxity of this aristocracy, full of disdain for the people and of friendly toleration for the Gentiles, had

---

¹ צְדָקָה, righteousness.
² Josephus, *Bellum Judaicum*, ii. 8, 14; *Antiquitates*, xiii. 5, 9.
³ Josephus, *Antiquitates*, xviii. 1, 4.
⁴ *Aboth of Rabbi Nathan*, v.

been at all times a scandal to the Pharisees, who therefore showed themselves the more ardent to protect the orthodoxy which was thus threatened. According to the Rabbinical expression, they multiplied "hedge after hedge" about the Law, and would have had their prescriptions as strictly obligatory upon all as were the Precepts of the Lord. To lend some show of reason to their pretensions, they asserted that there was no Commandment of which Moses had not given an oral interpretation. To collect these traditions and from them to construct a complement to the entire Mosaical ordinance, became their aim. Colleges of learned doctors were formed to enter into the minutiae of these Rules, and the people who, since the Captivity, had ceased to understand the original Hebrew [1] of the holy Books, received these decisions as the words of God himself. The instruction which they received from the Pharisee-Scribes is, therefore, at this epoch, all the religion that Israel retained; to discover what that Doctrine was, it suffices simply to open the Talmud.[2]

No speculative theology, no considerations concerning the Divine Being, or the Soul, or the end of man, or the things of Eternity; only ardent discussions as to puerile observances; scrupulosity as to what was lawful pushed to the last extreme of absurdity, while but faintly and infrequently does some inspired sentence recall the God of Horeb and Sinai. Past all doubt the Pharisees guarded the Law of their God most faithfully; yet, in that Law, the exact payment of Tithes, interminable Ablutions, and especially the observance of the Sabbath, absorbed all their attention. It would be useless to enumerate the one thousand two hundred and seventy-nine Rules which a Jew must have always before his eyes, if he would not violate

---

[1] 2 Esdras, viii.
[2] It was not until the sixth century that, through the efforts of Rabbi Rabina and Rabbi Jose, who were at the head of the Schools of Sora and Pumpadita, the Talmud was given to the world in an available form; but in the year 166 we find Rabbi Simon, the son of Gamaliel, already beginning to collect the materials for that vast compilation. The traditions and the precepts then put in writing, had up to that time been transmitted by word of mouth in the Jewish schools.

the "Quiescence of Sanctity," — the Precepts ordained for the conduct of guests at public banquets, the innumerable Contaminations to which all were declared to be exposed.

Such a yoke as this was intolerable; the Sadducees threw it off openly, the Scribes resigned themselves to enduring it, merely for the sake of appearances; but, for the most part, under their religious exterior, they concealed nothing but bigotry and hypocrisy. The Talmudic writers have torn the mask from the true features of the Pharisaism of their times; nothing could be imagined more mind-deadening and wretched in its effects than the Rules observed by these zealots, in order to regulate their comportment and to overawe the masses. And so we see them, presently, in order to give an added gravity to their carriage, shortening their steps so that their feet might always meet in their mincing gait. Again, that they might never look upon a woman, some kept their eyes so obstinately fixed upon the ground as often to result in sudden collisions with the walls, while others, preserving a still more exact modesty, enveloped their heads in sacks and walked the streets like blind men.[1]

If disposed to believe that these are but satirical exaggerations, that this picture overdoes the reality, you need only turn over a few pages of the Talmud to discover how far hypocrisy was elaborated into a practical science. Read the ten chapters devoted to the "Eroubin," that is, the expedients to which it was permissible to resort in evading the Law, in the event of its becoming too inconvenient. For example, the "Sabbatic Rest" forbade the transporting of any load or burden further than two thousand cubits. In order to double this measure, it was enough to have deposited some food, the night before, at the furthest point in the legal distance. By this act a presumptive domicile was conferred, from which it was allowed to proceed again for another two thousand cubits in any direction.[2] Should the Pharisee perceive that one of his animals

---

[1] Talmud of Babylon, *Sotah*, 22 *b*; Talmud of Jerusalem, *Berachot*, ix.
[2] *Essai sur l'histoire et la géographie de la Palestine, d'après les Thalmuds*, par J. Derenbourg, p. 143.

was about to die, he was permitted to kill the creature, without violating the holy Sabbath Rest, provided he swallowed a morsel, of the size of an olive, taken from the beast's carcass, thus indicating that he had been obliged to butcher it for nourishment. It was allowable for him to buy and sell also; the only precaution he must observe was not to pay until the morrow.[1] We would not venture to add to this list the licentious excesses tolerated by the Rabbis, merely on condition that they were concealed under an impenetrable mask of secrecy.[2]

Is it necessary to mention the fact that, however widespread among the masses was this decadence, there were many noble exceptions still to be found in Israel, many Scribes who were worthy descendants of the Assideäns, true heirs of their faith and virtues. The Gospels speak the praises of more than one,[3] the Talmud names still others, and, among the first of all, stands Hillel. His poverty, borne with such dignified serenity, his steadfast, unswerving constancy, his zeal, his charity have rendered him justly celebrated. It was he, indeed, who instructed the contemporaries of Jesus in maxims almost Christian in spirit:—

"Love and strive after peace."

"Love mankind and reconcile it to the Law."

"He who magnifies his own worth debases it."

"What am I, if I neglect my soul? If I have no care for it, who will take care of it for me? If I do not think of these things now, when shall I do so?"[4]

Dazzled by his epigrammatical brilliancy, many have unreasonably exalted this Rabbi by attempting to make him an historical peer of the Christ. They forget that Hillel never accomplished anything which can be compared to the works of the Saviour.[5] Like the other Doc-

---

[1] *Essai sur l'histoire et la géographie de la Palestine, d'après les Thalmuds*, par J. Derenbourg, p. 144.

[2] Talmud of Babylon, *Kiddouschin*, 40 a ; *Chagigah*, 16 a.

[3] John iii. 1 ; xiii. 42 ; xix. 38 ; Mark xv. 43 ; Luke xxiii. 51.

[4] *Aboth*, i. 11, 14.

[5] "Hillel will never pass for the true founder of Christianity. In Ethics, as in Art, words count for nothing, deeds are everything." (Renan, *Vie de Jésus*, v.)

tors of his day, while commentating upon the Pharisaic laws, he confined his efforts to making that yoke bearable, and spoke only in the schools of Jerusalem to a small group of chosen disciples. Indeed he even shared in the disdain of the Scribes for the poor and humble; this haughty saying comes from him: "No man without education can escape evil-doing; no man of the common people has ever attained unto piety."[1] In a word, Hillel was an illustrious Scribe, Jesus is God. Between such there is no comparison possible.

And finally, we have still to speak of the strangest of all the Jewish sects, — the Essenes. On the western borders of the Dead Sea, where the streams of Engedi empty into the lake, a verdant oasis gladdens the eye, wearied with those desert stretches of land, devastated by the fire of divine retribution. In its green recesses there lived (quoting the words of Pliny) "an eternal people, where there was never any one born."[2] No woman, no child, was ever found among them; youths only were admitted, and only after long probation. The Essene, on the day of his reception, received the white garment in which he was robed at all the repasts of the community, the towel-cloth needed for his numerous ablutions, and an instrument which served as axe or spade, and designed for cutting and digging trenches and sewers, in which all ref-

---

[1] McCaul, *Old Paths*, p. 6, 158, etc. What a difference between the Saviour's teaching and the puerile trifles which Hillel discusses! One of his celebrated discourses deals with this weighty question: "Is it lawful to eat an egg which a hen has laid during a feast day, when this feast falls upon a Sabbath?" Actually this inquiry seemed so serious to the Rabbis of the period that a whole Treatise in the Talmud has taken its name from it (*The Egg Book*, Betsa). Even when Hillel's teaching is most admirable, it is too often incomplete and unsatisfactory. The most gracious of all his maxims (borrowed from Leviticus xix. 18), "Whatsoever thou wouldst not desire for thyself, do it not unto thy neighbor," omits all duties which man owes to his God, for the great Rabbi immediately adds: "In this lieth all the Law, the rest is naught but a commentary upon it." (*Sabbath*, 31 *a*). We have purposely kept the Rabbi's weak points in the background, — such strange decisions, for instance, as the one in which he declares that a husband may disown his wife on the most frivolous pretexts, as that of serving him with a badly cooked meal. (*Gittin*, 90.)

[2] Pliny, *Historia Naturalis*, v. 15.

use was buried with the greatest care, lest by any uncleanness they should sully the purity of the sun's rays. A rigorous discipline was imposed upon all; absolute obedience, perpetual abstinence and mortification were obligatory; their only punishment was excommunication, by which the condemned man was constrained to live upon herbs, and thus die slowly of hunger.

What were the hopes, what were the fanatic dreams which could sustain the Essene in his rude life? It is hard indeed to tell, for a terrible law sealed their lips and on the rack of torture they refused to expose their mysteries. All that any one knows to-day is that they worshipped the Sun; that they believed, like the Pythagoreans, in an ethereal soul, which is, for a time, confined within the body. Their aversion to the sacrifices of the Temple, and for the flesh of animals, their linen vestments, their prohibition of speech, all remind one of the Orphics[1] whom Plato knew. Yet what was, in reality, the teaching of this Sect? No one can say with any certainty, for it was not long-lived, and it kept its secret to the end inviolate. However, it matters little or nothing so far as it affects the history of Jewish religions, since the doctrine of these ascetics was never popular; being confined to the initiated, it had but a feeble influence upon the general populace of Israel.

If we wish to understand the feelings and thoughts of these average Jews, we must look to the writings of that period. So, listen to this paragraph, found in the Book of Enoch: "In those days there shall be a wondrous change for the elect. The light of day shall shine for them without shadow and without night; all majesty, all honor shall attend upon them. In those days the earth shall render up every treasure which she possesses; the Kingdom of Death also, Hell itself, and all that has been intrusted unto them . . . The elect shall build their dwelling within a land of delights; a new Temple shall be erected for the Great King, more spacious, more resplendent than the

---

[1] Pauly, *Real Encyclopædie:* ORPHEUS.

first, and all the flocks of the earth shall be led thither unto sacrifice." "In that place," pursues the author of these Messianic dreams, "I see a never-failing fountain of justice, whence flow innumerable streams of wisdom on every side, and all those who have thirst shall come hither and drink.... From over that new Earth the ancient heavens shall fade away, to give place unto another heaven, wherein the stars shall give forth sevenfold more light than before; and thenceforth the innumerable days shall succeed each other in an happiness that shall know no end."[1]

Their Sybilline Oracles have added to this description, so flattering to the senses, further promises of a felicity more terrestrial still. "The people of the Mighty God shall bathe in seas of gold and of silver, their garments shall be of purple; all lands and oceans shall pour their treasures at their feet, and the Saints shall reign amid unceasing delights. The tiger shall graze side by side with the kid; the olive tree shall be crowned with imperishable fruits; milk, whiter than the snow, shall spring up from the fountains, and the young child shall play with the asp and the serpent without fear."[2] It would be easy to multiply quotations. The Fourth Book of Esdras, the Psalms of Solomon, the Jewish writers of Alexandria, bear witness everywhere to the same longings; everywhere we find these dreams of a people aspiring to a higher destiny, to a fuller fruition, yet looking for it only amid the things of earth and from temporal pleasures.

All, indeed, as we have pointed out, did not partake of these material sentiments. In this degenerate people, in the midst of this carnal Israel, the spiritual Israel was still alive, a chosen band, predestined to be of the Kingdom of the Christ, holy souls who, by piously pondering the inspired truths, had therein discovered the proper lineaments

---

[1] *Das Buch Henoch*, übersetzt von Dillmann, xc., xci.

[2] These quotations are taken from the Third Book of the *Oracles*, which, with the exception of a few fragments (v. 1-96, 818-828, etc.), go as far back as the times of the Machabees (*Oracula Sibyllina*, edition of Alexandria, ii. p. 318).

of the picture which Prophecy had painted of the true Messiah.

In the very hour of man's fall God had declared to Adam that One should be born of the seed of the woman; and thereafter He set apart, from the race of Sem, one people, of the stock of Abraham, and from that people one tribe, — the tribe of Juda,[1] — from which was to be born the Messiah.

That mysterious Figure stands forth still more clearly, more perspicuously, as the years hasten on toward the realizing of all expectation of Him. As Moses sees Him, He is a Prophet, his equal in power; in David's eyes He is a King, His Son, heir to his glories, as well as his misfortunes.[2] His very Name is discovered to the Psalmist; this King of all times to come and of the timeless Eternity is to be called the Anointed of God, the Christ, the Messiah.[3] One after another the Prophets added each a line to the limning of this portraiture which foreshadowed the advent of Divinity. Bethlehem is to be His birthplace, Galilee His native land, a Virgin His Mother.[4] He will preach the Good News to the pure and humble of heart. He will enter Sion mounted upon the foal of an ass.[5] He shall be despised and rejected, led to the slaughter as a Lamb; His vestments shall be parted, lots shall be cast for His tunic, His hands and His feet pierced; vinegar shall moisten His lips.[6] Yet shall He become subject to the malefactor's death only that He may show forth the glory of His Resurrection; His soul snatched from the deep pit, and His body from corruption, that He may seat Himself upon the right hand of Jehovah, henceforth to reign forever in the world of human hearts.[7]

Prophecy had been advanced to this point of certainty when Malachy appeared, the last of the Seers. It was he

---

[1] Gen. iii. 15; ix. 26; xii. 3; xlix. 8.
[2] Deut. xviii. 18; 2 Kings vii. 13; 3 Kings xi. 34; Psal., passim.
[3] Ps. xliv. 8.
[4] Mich. v. 2; Is. ix. 1-7; vii. 14; lxi. 1.
[5] Zach. ix. 9; Is. liii. 3, 7.
[6] Ps. xxi. 19; xxi. 17; lxviii. 22.
[7] Is. xi. 10; Ps. xv. 10; cix. 1.

who finished the painting, by his foretelling of the precursor of Jesus. This Herald of the Messiah would arise from among the children of Levi; so then the Prophet fixes his gaze upon that tribe. If he scourges the vices of the priesthood, their scandalous alliances with the daughters of Gentiles; if he proclaims a New Sacrifice, offered from the rising unto the setting of the sun,[1] and casts aside as worthless the defiled oblations of Israel, it is to prefigure the Forerunner, as he was to separate himself from the Levites, going forth before the face of the Messiah, preparing the way for Him: "Presently shall He come to His Temple, the Saviour whom you seek, and the Angel of the Testament whom you desire. Behold, He cometh, sayeth the Lord of Hosts."[2]

Such was the Messiah for Whom all true Israelites waited in expectation; such the Precursor, to be sent before Him, and of whose birth Saint Luke will give us the account.

[1] Mal. ii. 1–11; i. 10–12.   [2] Id. iii. 1.

CHAPTER II.

THE BIRTH OF THE PRECURSOR.

I. THE VISION OF ZACHARY.

Luke i. 5-25.

FOR four centuries the world had waited for the fulfilment of these Prophecies. The reign of Herod had almost reached its end; and the old king, beginning at last to realize that he was descending slowly, surely to the tomb, stands out a lonely figure in the palace which his bloodstained hands had made so bare and empty. Uneasy forebodings disturbed the souls of men. Suddenly from Jerusalem, and from the Temple,[1] a voice broke the silence of suspense in words that spoke deliverance and salvation.

Among the many Levites of that time, there was a priest named Zachary, of the family of Abia, the eighth of the divisions[2] which, by turns, took part in the divine

---

[1] We speak of the holy City and the Temple in this Life of Jesus so very often, that some description of them seems necessary. It will be found in Appendix I.

[2] Ἐξ ἐφημερίας: Luke xv. Ἐφημερία (properly, the ministry of each day) in this connection refers to the religious services performed during the week by the priesthood, divided into twenty-four classes, together with the company of Levites who were employed in their allotted functions. This arrangement was instituted by David, who left the rank of each class to be decided by lot (1 Par. xxiv. 5; 2 Par. xxiii. 5: Josephus, *Antiquitates*, vii. 11). The Captivity had, it is true, disturbed this order, since only four of the sacerdotal Families returned from Babylon; but their members were distributed once more into twenty-four classes, and each group kept its primitive title as if it were composed of the actual descendants of that Levite whose name it bore. Thus the sacred ministry was restored in the same form which it had at the foundation of the Temple (1 Esdras, ii. 36-62; Lightfoot, *Horæ Hebraicæ*, in Luc. 1, 5).

service. Reduced as they were upon the return from captivity, the sons of Levi were not slow to increase in number; and thus they were soon forced to seek residences outside of Jerusalem, in the ancient sacerdotal cities.[1] Hebron and Youttah[2] had seen their levitical population returning to the old homes, and it was probably the latter of these towns[3] which was the dwelling-place of Zachary. Situated to the south of Hebron, and at some considerable distance from it, Youttah stretches along the slope of a hill, in the heart of the mountains of Juda. In this retreat Zachary lived with his wife Elizabeth, who was also of the sacerdotal tribe. The sequestered pair "were just in the sight of God, and walked without reproach in the commandments and laws of the Lord."[4] Yet they found

---

[1] Following their ancient customs, the Levites intrusted with the performance of the sacred music resided in villages near the city (2 Esdr. xii. 28; 1 Paral. ix. 16); but the priests, whose ministry only called them to the Temple twice a year, lived at a distance, in the sacerdotal cities of Juda.

[2] Josue, xv. 55; xxi. 16.

[3] Luke i. 39. The tradition which gives Hebron as the home of Zachary only goes back to the ninth century (*Acta Sanctorum*, xxiv. junii); and, further, there is little likelihood that S. Luke, if he were speaking of such a well-known town, would have employed so vague a term as "the city of Juda." Whenever he uses this expression he adds the name of the place as well: πόλις Ναζαρέτ (Luke ii. 4); πόλις Ἰόππη (Acts xi. 5, etc.). Ἰούδα is in all probability only a softened pronunciation of the Hebrew Ἰούτα Youttah (יוטה), for the Greek δ is frequently used where the Hebrew has ט. This hypothesis, first proposed by Reland, has been adopted by the majority of modern critics, among others by P. Patrizi (*De Evangeliis*, lib. iii. diss. x. cap. i.), and Robinson (*Biblical Researches*, i. 494, note; 206, note). On the other hand, M. Guérin (*Judée*, tome i. chap. 5) and Frère Liévin (*Guide Indicateur*), following certain local traditions, have preferred to locate the birthplace of the Baptist near to Jerusalem, and so have fixed upon Aïn Karim, which has the Desert of John and the Monastery of Mar Zacharia in the vicinity. But to our mind these vague indications are not enough to outweigh the authority of the ancient traditions, which give the region about Hebron as his native country.

[4] Luke i. 6. Ἐντολαί, the precepts of the natural law, confirmed by the decalogue (Rom. vii. 8, 13); δικαιώματα, the positive precepts added to the law of nature (Rom. ii. 26; viii. 4). Ἀβραάμ ἐφύλαξε τὰς ἐντολάς μου καὶ τὰ δικαιώματά μου (Gen. xxvi. 5). This distinction, though it is the only one which can be drawn between these two terms, is nevertheless neither very certain nor always reliable; it is enough to read over Psalm cxviii. in order to be convinced that they were often to be regarded as synonymous expressions.

their piety put to a severe test; for, childless while they were both far advanced in age, they had finally lost all hope of God's ever blessing them by raising up offspring to the barren daughter of Levi.

The time drew round for Zachary to join his associates of the Class of Abia, and to fulfil his functions in the Temple; he therefore took his way to Jerusalem. Each Class was accustomed to decide the division of the various offices by lot; that of Incense-Burner fell to the husband of Elizabeth.[1] It was the highest of all the sacerdotal duties, and was performed with a solemnity of ritual which it behoves us to describe more in detail.

The altar of gold, whereon was offered the sacrifice of perfumes, stood in the midst of the Holy Place, between the Seven-branched Candlestick and the Table of the Bread of Proposition; only a single veil separated it from the Holy of Holies, despoiled in Zachary's time of its Ark of the Covenant. Everything about the Sanctuary must be made ready beforehand,—the flames of the lamps trimmed and brightened, the ashes removed from the altar, and a fresh fire enkindled upon it before the entrance of the priest. Upon his appearance all stood aside, and the people, crowding back beneath the porches, prayed there in silence.[2] The officiating Minister alone advanced within the Holy Place, and, at a signal given by a prince of the priesthood, must cast the precious perfumes upon the flame; then, having bowed down before the Holy of Holies, he receded slowly, stepping backwards, that he might not turn his face away from the altar. A bell gave warning of his withdrawal and the Benediction which he bestowed upon the people.[3] Immediately Levites intoned the sacred hymns, and the music of the Temple, combining with their voices, formed a symphony so powerful (the Rabbinical writers say) that it could be heard in Jericho.[4]

Although this ceremonial was observed twice every day,

---

[1] Luke i. 9.
[2] Luke i. 10. *Tamid*, 3, 6, 9 ; 6, 1 ; *Ioma*, 5, 1, etc.
[3] Num. vi. 24-26.
[4] Lightfoot, *Horæ Hebraicæ*, in Luc. i.

—in the morning and at evening,—the Jews never assisted thereat without a secret tremor of anxiety; for the priest, who entered within the Sanctuary, was their Representative, and the incense burned beneath his hands was for a figure of the prayers of all. Should Jehovah reject his offering, if He should strike him to the earth for some legal impurity, then indeed would Israel be overwhelmed by the same blow. It was from this cause the impatience of the crowd arose, and the promptitude with which the Minister acquitted himself of his functions, that he might not prolong the general emotion.

But on this day these fears were quickened to terror; for Zachary tarried much longer than the wonted time in the Holy Place.[1] He appeared at last, trembling, dumb; his lips so suddenly sealed, his gesticulations, his agitation, all declared that some portentous spectacle had burst upon his sight. Did he write down his marvellous vision at once? The sacred text would not seem to imply as much. "He remained dumb,"[2] it says; as if it would signify that his heart, as well as his tongue, refused to reveal immediately the celestial apparition, or that he would await that hour for disclosing it in which God Himself would open his lips. This, then, is what Zachary at last made known.

He was about to enter within when, to the right of the altar from which arose white clouds of incense, of a sudden an Angel appeared. Seeing this, terror overwhelmed the priest; but the Angel spoke to him:[3]—

"Fear not at all, Zachary! Your prayer is heard; your wife Elizabeth shall conceive a son, and you shall give him the name of John. This child shall be your joy and your delight, and the multitude shall rejoice at his nativity. For he shall be great before the Lord; he shall not drink of wine nor of aught that doth inebriate, and he shall be filled with the Holy Spirit even from his mother's womb. He shall convert many of the children of Israel to the Lord their God; and he himself shall walk before Him[4] in the

---

[1] Luke i. 21.   [2] Luke i. 22.   [3] Luke i. 11-17.
[4] 'Ενώπιον αὐτοῦ, that is to say, κυρίου τοῦ Θεοῦ αὐτῶν: before the Lord God.

spirit and might[1] of Elias; that he may turn the hearts of the fathers unto the children,[2] the unbelieving unto the wisdom of the righteous,[3] and prepare for the Lord a perfect people."

Malachy, whose prediction the Angel here recalls, had foretold that two Forerunners should herald the Messiah's appearance: one, John the Baptist, was to announce His first Advent;[4] Elias, the other Envoy of Heaven, in the latter days of the world, shall descend from his chariot of fire to prepare men for the return of the Christ.[5] Yet in spite of the diversity of their missions, John was to be

---

[1] Δυνάμει, the power, not of working miracles, for this S. John seems not to have possessed (John x. 41), but the mighty force of his example and the commanding efficacy of his speech.

[2] Malach. iv. 6. That power of drawing together the hearts of men, which prophecy reserves to Elias, does not mean merely reconciliation and peace between families, as Meyer would have it (*Handbuch über das Evangelium des Lukas,* in loco) and Alford with him (Greek Testament, *in loco*); it signifies such faith as that of Abraham, and the mighty power of those first fathers of Israel living again in their children. By reminding us of the law given upon Horeb, Malachy shows clearly that he has these holy Patriarchs in mind: more than this, the Angel, after having quoted the first words of the Prophet, "He shall turn the hearts of the fathers unto the children," proceeds to explain what was to be the nature of this reconciliation: "He shall bring back the unbelieving to wisdom, and thus he shall prepare for the Lord a people made ready for His coming." Hence it was to be the duty of Elias, as it was the Mission of his prototype John, to arouse the fervor of olden days in the hearts of Israel. "Est sensus, ut etiam filii sic intelligant legem, id est Judæi, quemadmodum patres eam intellexerunt, id est prophetæ, in quibus erat et ipse Moyses" (S. Augustine, *De Civitate Dei,* xx. 29).

[3] Φρόνησις, the practical innate sense of justice, which makes us do what seems right and good to us.

[4] "Behold I send My Angel before Me, and he shall prepare the way. Presently shall He come unto His Temple, the Saviour whom you seek, and the Angel of the Testament whom you desire. Behold He cometh, saith the Lord of Hosts" (Malach. iii. 1).

[5] "Remember the law of Moses, My servant, which I have given you upon Horeb. Behold, I send you Elias the Prophet, before the day of the Lord, the great and dreadful Day; and he shall turn the hearts of the fathers to their children, and the heart of the children to their parents, lest I come and strike the earth with anathema" (Malach. iv. 4, 6). Evidently the Prophet is speaking here of the last days of the world and the coming of Elias, and by using the words of this second prophecy in speaking of John Baptist the Angel Gabriel would foretell how closely the latter, by the holiness of his life, was to bear before the eyes of the world the perfect likeness of the Thesbite.

another Elias, because in him would be enkindled the very soul of the Thesbite,—the same strong spirit, the same glowing genius,—a fiery nature which should lead captive the sons of Israel by word and example, and bring them back to the virtues of their fathers. Engrossed in the contemplation of so perfect a resemblance, the Jews had never, in their thoughts of them, separated these two forerunners of the Messiah.

God did not demand of Zachary a more illuminated intuition, nor that he should foresee clearly everything that the Angel's announcement implied; all that was required of him was that he should believe implicitly in the Message, however mysterious it might seem. Too haughty for such simple faith, the Levite still demurred; he dared to demand a sign before he would yield any credence to the divine communication.

"How shall I know the truth of these words?" he answered. "I am old, and my wife is advanced in age."

To overcome and dissipate this incredulity, the Angel deigned to disclose his own dignity.

"I am Gabriel,"[1] he said, "one of the ministering Spirits, standing ever in the presence of God, whom the Lord has sent to speak to you and to announce to you these good tidings. Look you, therefore, you shall be dumb and shall not be able to speak until the day wherein these things shall take place, because you have not believed my words, which shall be accomplished in their time."

Zachary must needs have humbled himself under the hand which chastised him. He retreated from the sanctuary dumb; only by his signs of awe and terror could he respond to the breathless throng, now quite disquieted by his long delay, and at once all the people knew that he had seen a vision in the Temple.

---

[1] Gabriel, גַּבְרִי אֵל, the man of God. It would seem as if the Almighty had made this Prince of the Angels the special Minister of that which we call the greatest work of the Godhead,—the Incarnation. It was he who was sent to Daniel to announce the near Advent of the Saint of saints (Dan. ix. 21-24); and it was he who was soon to be sent to Mary.

The days of his ministry being fulfilled,¹ he betook himself to his home. A little later Elizabeth, his wife, conceived, and for five months secluded herself, " because," as she said, " the Lord hath dealt thus with me, since he has willed to take away my reproach among men." Nothing could be more natural than this desire to retreat from the world. It was but seemly, indeed, to prevent the curiosity and malice of rumor from busying itself with such a marvel as was this unhoped-for conception.

II. The Circumcision of John the Baptist.

Luke i. 57–80.

" The time being come for Elizabeth to be delivered,² she brought forth a son ; and her neighbors and kinsfolk being made aware that God had manifested His mercy towards her, shared in her joy, and on the eighth day they all gathered unto the circumcision of the infant."

This consecration to the God of Abraham was celebrated in every family with solemn festivity. Ten witnesses surrounded the child ; while the father, or some other of the relatives present, made with an instrument of stone the bloody incision.³ Zachary did not perform the sacred rite in person, for his moveless lips could not pronounce the benedictions incidental to it. So also, when at the close of the ceremony they desired, according to ancient custom, to confer a name upon the child,⁴ and would have called him Zachary after the father, the latter neither heard nor comprehended.⁵

---

[1] Luke i. 23–25.   [2] Luke i. 57–59.
[3] Buxtorf, *Synagoga Judaica*, cap. iii. ; Otho, *Lexicon Rabbinicum*, p. 133.
[4] Luke i. 59–63. Children receive their names after circumcision, in memory of the events which took place at the institution of this rite. At that time Abram and Sarai changed their names to Abraham and Sara (Gen. xvii.).
[5] Zachary was deaf as well as dumb ; $\Delta\iota\acute{\epsilon}\mu\epsilon\nu\epsilon\nu\ \kappa\omega\phi\acute{o}s$ (Luke i. 22). $K\omega\phi\acute{o}s$ means a deaf-mute.

Elizabeth, however, withstood them. "No," she said; "he shall be called John."

"But," it was objected, "none of your kindred bear that name."

She persisted none the less in her design. Turning toward the father, who stood before them a mute and wistful spectator of this scene, she asked him by signs what name he wished to give the child.

Zachary, taking up his tablets, wrote thereon, "John is his name." [1]

Then, while they were still filled with astonishment, suddenly the lips of the old man were opened, his tongue was loosed, and he spoke aloud in thanksgiving to the Lord.[2] At this prodigy their wondering delight gave place to fear and awe. From that dwelling, endeared to God, the thrill of emotion spread swiftly throughout the surrounding country; so that shortly, among the mountains of Juda, nothing else was spoken of beside these marvels; and those who heard the tale treasured it up in thoughtful silence, musing in their breasts, "What an one, think ye, shall this child be?" For the hand of God was upon him.

With his hearing and speech Zachary recovered the divine favor, and, filled with the Spirit, he prophesied. As sung every night in our churches, the Hymn of the holy old man is like an echo of the ancient prophecies of Israel. Jehovah visits His people to save them from their enemies, — from the hand of those who hate them; the Redemption is revealed unto the eyes of this Levite, even as the dying Moses beheld it,[3] and as Ezechiel[4] and countless others had represented it, — mighty and resistless as

---

[1] The name John is an expression which signifies Grace, or Mercy of Jehovah, יְהוֹחָנָן ; in the Septuagint Ἰωανάν (1 Par. vi. 9; xii. 4, etc.), from יָּה, Jah, an abbreviated form of Jehovah, and חָנָה, grace. The names of Zachary and Elizabeth have a like mystical meaning. Zachary reminds us that Jehovah is mindful of His people זָכַר, to remember ; יָּה, Jehovah. Elizabeth alludes to the covenant of God ; אֵל, God ; and שָׁבַע, to swear.

[2] Luke i. 63–67.
[3] Deut. xxxiii. 17.
[4] Ezech. xxix. 21.

the horned frontal of the savage beast which spreads terror round about its path. Yet, beneath this rude imagery — the last vestiges of an almost vanished era — there is a tenderer tone which predominates withal. The salvation of Israel is no longer that which the carnal-minded Jews had fancied, — the triumph of their race, the joys and riches of this world. It is Salvation in righteousness and holiness, won by penitence and the remission of sins. The God of Zachary is no longer a Jehovah who, as He moves among men, sows horror and death about Him, but a God with bowels of merciful compassion, shining upon the world like a holy, beneficent Light. It is as if, very different from the mornings of earth, this marvellous Orient, this great New Dawn, would be made visible, not on the horizon, but on high, within the heavens,[1] thus to make it manifest to the world that He came, not to consume it with the scorching heats of noontide, but to spread about His pathway the pure light of a clear, cloudless daybreak. Hence, though Jewish in its form, this chant is essentially Christian. Struck with its beauty in the original Arameän, Saint Luke sought to reproduce, not only the thoughts, but the figures as well, foreign as they are to the genius of the Greek tongue. To this fact is due the obscurity and, at the same time, the peculiar charm of this Hymn : —

> Blessed be the Lord, the God of Israel,
>   because He hath looked down upon His people,
>   and hath wrought their Redemption ;[2]
> He hath raised up, in the house of David His son,
>   an invincible power (as it were an Horn[3]),
>   to be our Salvation :

---

[1] Ἀνατολὴ ἐξ ὕψους (Luke i. 78).

[2] Luke i. 68-79. Λύτρωσιν, a moral deliverance rather than the political enfranchisement of the new Israel.

[3] Κέρας ; it is a metaphor suggested by the nature of certain wild animals, which are weak and defenceless if robbed of their horns and antlers, but, armed with those weapons, are so terrible when they stand at bay. "This majestic and awe-inspiring phrase, as it is used in Scripture, expresses a splendor, and at the same time an incomparable strength, whereby the enemy is to be scattered and dismayed" (Bossuet, *Élévations sur les mystères*, xv⁰ semaine, iii⁰ élévation). Κέρας σωτηρίας, the genitive form,

(according to that which He hath promised us,
   by the mouth of the holy Prophets,
   from the beginning of Time ;)
a Salvation¹ whereby He will preserve us
   from our enemies,
   out of the hands of them that hate us :
for the accomplishment of His Loving-Kindness
   unto our fathers ;
and as a remembrance² of His holy Covenant,
   the Oath³ which He swore to Abraham our father ;
so that, delivered from the hands of our enemies,
   and freed from fear, we may worship Him,
in righteousness and holiness⁴ in His sight,
   even all the days of our life.
And thou, child, shalt be called
   the Prophet of the Most High.
Thou shalt walk before the Lord,
   to prepare His ways,
to declare⁵ unto His people Salvation,
   in the pardon of their sins,
pardon through the bowels⁶ of mercy
   of our God :

which has the force of a word in apposition : a Horn, a Power, which is to be our Salvation (Winer, *Grammatik des Neutestamentlichen Spruchidioms*, 1867, par. 59, 8).

¹ Σωτηρίαν may be made to depend on ἐλάλησε ; however, it would seem to be more natural to consider καθὼς κτλ . . . as a parenthesis, and σωτηρίαν as the development of this thought : "A Horn, a Salvation, . . . whose peculiar property it is to deliver us from our enemies."

² Ποιῆσαι . . . καὶ μνησθῆναι : these two infinitives depend upon σωτηρίαν, and thus declare the design of God in working out our salvation.

³ Ὅρκον, in apposition to διαθήκης, is put in the accusative because of the position of ὄν in the sentence : "The Testament of God to our fathers, that is, the Covenant He once made with them."

⁴ The entire moral and religious restoration of God's people is embodied in those two words ; ὁσιότης bestows a divine consecration upon δικαιοσύνη.

⁵ Τοῦ δοῦναι . . . indicates the end to which John was to look while he was thus preparing the ways of the Lord, — spreading the knowledge of salvation, and proclaiming that this salvation was to consist in a washing away of all sins.

⁶ Διὰ σπλάγχνα must not be separated from the preceding phrase, ἐν ἀφέσει ἁμαρτιῶν, the remission of sins accorded us by His tender mercies, any more than from the following phrase : ἐν οἷς ἐπεσκέψατο, . . . that is, the bowels of compassion begotten in the Orient.

whereby a Star, rising[1] to the heights of heaven,
    hath visited us;
illumining them that sit in the shadow
    and in the darkness of death,
leading our steps within the paths of peace.

The halo which overhung the cradle of John might not last in all its early splendor; for the design of God was, in silence and in solitude, to form of him the greatest of the children of men. The glorified dwelling-place of Zachary disappears immediately from our range of vision. All that we know is that God's Spirit came upon the Baptist even in his childhood and impelled him to retire to the Desert. "The child grew," says Saint Luke,[2] "and his soul was strengthened, and he was in the Desert until the day of his manifestation in Israel."

---

[1] Ἀνατολή is the word by which the Septuagint generally translates צֶמַח, "a branch," "an offshoot," whatever springs up, darts out, or gushes forth, and hence the streaming rays of light; here, in all probability, it refers to the Star of Jacob (Num. xxiv. 17), or, better still, to the Sun of Truth appearing unexpectedly, not upon the horizon, but beaming from the summit of the great arch of heaven: ἐξ ὕψους. "The true Daybreak will come upon us from the high celestial places, inasmuch as it cometh from the Bosom of the Father to enlighten our souls" (Bossuet, *Élévations sur les mystères*, xve semaine, iiie élévation).

[2] Luke i. 80.

CHAPTER III.

THE INCARNATION.

I. THE ANNUNCIATION.

Luke i. 26-38 ; John i. 1-18.

Six months after the conception of John,[1] Gabriel received of God a new Mission. This time it was neither to the Temple nor to the holy city that he must needs betake himself, but to Nazareth,—an obscure village of Galilee. He was sent thither to a young kinswoman of Elizabeth, named Mary,[2] who was betrothed to a descendant of the House of David called Joseph. Sprung likewise from the seed of the Great King,[3] she was, according to the testi-

---

[1] Luke i. 26.

[2] Mary was of the Tribe of Juda (Luke i. 32), and Elizabeth was a daughter of Aaron (Luke i. 5). To understand how they could be cousins (Luke i. 36), although belonging to different tribes, we need only suppose that their mothers were sisters and of the tribe of Juda ; and hence one might have married one of the Levites, whereas the other found a husband in her own Family. There was no law forbidding the Levites to take wives from other tribes ; the High Priest was the only one who could wed none but the daughter of a levite (Philo, *De Monarchia*, ii. 11 ; Exod. vi. 23).

[3] Nowhere in the Gospel is it distinctly asserted that Mary was a descendant of David ; nevertheless it leaves us to understand as much. For Jesus, indeed, was born of her, not by any human commerce, but by the operation of a Divine Mystery (Matt. i. 18 ; Luke i. 34); therefore He is, properly speaking, her Son, and hers alone. Now, this her Son is called by S. Matthew the Son of David (Matt. i. 1 ; compare S. Paul, Rom. i. 3) ; very evidently this can only be understood to mean that Mary was likewise a daughter of the Great King. The most ancient Fathers are unanimous upon this point, and the apocryphal gospels took the same view (S. Justin, *Adversus Tryphonem*, 23, 45, 100 ; S. Irenæus,

mony of Tradition, the daughter of Joachim and Anna,[1] and had but one sister, named, like herself, Mary. Her parents, being deprived of male offspring, had been forced, in order to insure the legal transmission of their property, to affiance the two sisters to two young men of the same lineage.[2]

We do not know what combination of circumstances had banished these descendants of the kings of Israel from Bethlehem, the home of their family; yet we must believe that, sharing in the destinies of their race, they had all fallen into poverty and obscurity; for neither their ancestry nor the prophecies which promised the throne to a Son of David awoke the morbid suspicions of Herod. The lives of the betrothed pair in the retired village of Nazareth were passed in complete separation from each other, and in a state bordering upon destitution. Joseph was a carpenter; Mary worked, as he did, with her hands.[3] Thus, then, it was an humble dwelling-place, this cottage of Joachim and Anna, which the Angel from Heaven visited; for, in accordance with the custom of the daughters of Juda, Mary was expected to seclude herself in the privacy of her home from the day on which her troth was plighted.

But it was not merely for these few days that Mary had hoped to shelter her virginity within that lowly retirement. A light, which never before shone upon the mothers of Israel, had discovered to her the value of per-

---

Adversus Hæreses, 3, 21, 5; Julius Africanus, *Epistola ad Aristidem*, etc.; *Protevangelium Jacobi*, 10). The *Testament of the Twelve Fathers* is the only one which differs from the others; this last makes the Messiah born of Juda and Levi. It is hard to understand how Ewald, with only this solitary and untrustworthy authority, can hold that Jesus belonged to the Tribe of Levi.

[1] See Dom Calmet, *Dictionnaire de la Bible*: JOACHIM.

[2] This hypothesis, founded upon the well-known law contained in Numbers (xxxvi. 6), is the only one by which we can explain why Mary, despite her intention to preserve her Virginity, came to be betrothed to S. Joseph.

[3] Matt. xiii. 55. "An ancient tradition tells us that she too earned her own daily bread by daily toils; this is why Jesus is called by the most ancient of the Fathers 'fabri et quæstuariæ Filius.'" (Bossuet, *Élévations sur les mystères*, xiie semaine, 1re élévation.)

petual continence, and she was resolved never to know man.[1] How was she to reconcile this inspiration from Heaven with the promise made for her by her parents? It was a period of perplexity and an agonizing ordeal, this to which Mary was subjected from the time of her betrothal, and it was destined to cause her an even more profound trouble on the day of the Angelical Message.[2]

A little to the westward of Nazareth there is a fountain which bears the name of Mary. The Greeks have erected close at hand their Church of the Annunciation. They hold that the Angel uttered his salutation to the Virgin on that spot, when at evening she had set out from the village on her way thither to draw water. This legend, taken from the Proto-gospel of Saint James, is not based upon any reliable foundation, and Christian art is more truly inspired when it represents the Virgin as kneeling in the privacy of her chamber at the hour in which the Angel appeared to her.[3]

Doubtless by those same vows of chastity she had hastened the day of the coming of the Messiah, when the celestial messenger appeared before her eyes[4] and said:

---

[1] The question asked by Mary, "How may this happen, since I know not man?" has no meaning at all unless we suppose that she had formed a steadfast resolution to remain a virgin; for certainly she had only to look forward to the near fulfilment of her plighted troth, and thus her natural motherhood would be the accomplishment of the Angel's Message. It was only a reasonable conclusion which the Fathers drew from Mary's own words, that she had consecrated her Virginity to Heaven. (S. Augustine, *De Virginitate*, 4, etc.)

[2] Here we follow the opinion of P. Patrizi (*De Evangeliis*, lib. i. diss. xv. cap. ii.), and with him we think that by these words S. Matthew means to have us understand that Mary was only affianced at the time of the Annunciation: $M\nu\eta\sigma\tau\epsilon\upsilon\theta\epsilon\iota\sigma\eta s$ ... $\pi\rho\iota\nu\ \dot{\eta}\ \sigma\upsilon\nu\epsilon\lambda\theta\epsilon\hat{\iota}\nu\ a\upsilon\tau o\upsilon s$ ... (i. 18) ... $\Delta\iota\epsilon\gamma\epsilon\rho\theta\epsilon\iota s\ \delta\dot{\epsilon}\ \dot{o}\ '\text{I}\omega\sigma\dot{\eta}\phi$ ... $\pi\alpha\rho\dot{\epsilon}\lambda\alpha\beta\epsilon\ \tau\dot{\eta}\nu\ \gamma\upsilon\nu\alpha\hat{\iota}\kappa\alpha\ a\upsilon\tau o\hat{\upsilon}$ ... (i. 24). In fact, the reason given by Christian antiquity for the marriage of the Virgin was the necessity by which she would be bound to preserve her honor as Mother of the King; but in olden times would it not be thought enough to know that she was betrothed when Jesus was conceived? S. Hilary (*in Matt.* i.), S. Epiphanius (*Hær.* lxxviii. par. 8), S. Jerome (*in Matt.* i.), and S. John Chrysostom (*Hom.* iv. 2, *in Matt.*) have all held the latter view, and their opinion seems to be the most plausible one.

[3] Εἰσελθών. (Luke i. 28.)

[4] Luke i. 28-33.

"Hail, full of grace,[1] the Lord is with you; you are blessed among all women."[2]

Yet, having heard this, she was troubled at his saying, and she thought within herself what could be the meaning of such a salutation. But the Angel resumed:—

"Fear not at all, Mary; you have found grace in God's sight. And behold you shall conceive in your womb and shall bear a Son, and you shall give Him the name of Jesus. He shall be great, and He shall be called the Son of the Most-High, and the Lord God shall give to Him the throne of David His father: He shall reign eternally in the house of Jacob, and of His Kingdom there shall be no end."

Mary had meditated much upon the Prophecies; she could not therefore mistake the purport of the Angel's announcement. This child, Son of the Most-High, King and Saviour of men for all eternity, — this could only be the Messiah; and to her was to accrue the honor of bringing forth the Desired of Days. But the daughter of David had resolved to remain a Virgin for God's sake, and despite this promise that she should be the Mother of a God she continued steadfast in her inspired design.

Unable to make the Angel's words harmonize with this

[1] Exegetical critics of the Protestant persuasion, in their anxiety to prevent any cultus of Mary, generally render the word κεχαριτωμένη by "thou who hast found favor with God;" but the translation in the Vulgate, "gratiâ plena," is that given by a majority of the versions and by the Latin Fathers. The Church has never feared that this interpretation would give any occasion for superstitious worship; she has always known how to mark with perfect clearness the difference between the plenitude of grace which is in Jesus, and that which the Holy Bible attributes to Mary and to the Saints (Acts vi. 8). "Very different is the fulness of power which is in the waters at the fountain-head from the plenitude possessed by the streams and channels which draw their life from it." (Maldonatus, *in Luc.* i. 29.)

[2] Εὐλογημένη may signify, "blessed beyond all women," or "proclaimed blessed by all women." The first sense, which is the one adopted by the Vulgate, seems more natural. Tischendorf suppresses this member of the sentence, and in fact it is not to be found in his Manuscript of Sinaï, nor in that of the Vatican; but since it is in the text of the Latin and Syriac versions, and in the manuscripts of Alexandria, Ephraim, and Beza, we surely have grave reasons for retaining it.

vow, "How may this be," she replied,[1] "since I know not man?"

Gabriel immediately enlightened her. "The Holy Ghost shall come upon you," he said, "and the Power of the Most-High shall enfold you within His Shadow; therefore it is that the Holy One which shall be born of you shall be called the Son of God. And behold your cousin Elizabeth also has conceived a son in her old age; and it is now the sixth month for her who is called barren, because nothing is impossible unto God."

This was sufficient to insure Mary's entire abandonment to the Will of the Almighty. She bowed down before the Seraphic Messenger: "I am the handmaid of the Lord," she said; "let it be done unto me according to Thy word." And forthwith the Angel withdrew from her sight.

What happened then in the little house of Nazareth?

In one line John has expressed the unspeakable thought: "The Word was made flesh, and took up its habitation with us."[2] The Word, — that is to say, the Eternal and substantial Utterance of God, His own, and only Son: "A Son who was not born at the commandment of His Father, but Who, by puissance and by plenitude, flashed forth from His Bosom, God of God, Light of Light."[3]

Of the Word we can learn little enough from the first three Evangelists; so intent are they upon tracing the footsteps upon earth of the God made Man that they speak of His Divine nature but rarely;[4] yet this is not at all the case with John.[5] The beloved Disciple of Jesus had drawn from the heart of His Master a relish and a perception of the

---

[1] Luke i. 34–38.
[2] John i. 14.
[3] S. Basil, *Oratio de Fide*, Hom. xxv.
[4] "The other three Evangelists, albeit they had walked the earth with the man-God, have said but little of His Divinity; but this man [John], as though it irked him to walk the earth, as if even at this, the very outset of his speaking, the heavens had thundered, hath raised himself not only above our world, . . . but above all the hosts of Angels . . . and, finding his way to Him by Whom all things are made, sayeth: In the beginning was the Word." (S. Augustine, *in Joannem*, tract. xxxvi. 1.)
[5] The doctrine of the Word of S. John and the origin of this term is considered in Appendix II.

highest Mysteries. So when, following Matthew, Mark, and Luke, he took up his pen to write "that which his eyes had seen, his ears heard, that which his hands had touched of the Word of life,"[1] stifled in the thick atmosphere of the lower world of thought, he spurns the air with strong eagle-pinions, and rising far aloft above the earth and the heavens, he penetrates to the Throne of Him Whose life he would recount. From those fearful heights his first word rang forth like a peal of thunder upon the ears of the Christians of Ephesus, who knelt in prayer and fasting round about him.[2]

"In the beginning was the Word,
"And the Word was with God,
"And the Word was God;
"He it is Who was with God in the beginning.
"All things have been made by Him, and without Him is nothing made that has been made.
"In Him was the life, and the life was the Light of men.[3]
"And the Word was made flesh," adds Saint John; that is to say, has formed unto Himself a body out of the most pure blood of Mary, — the Eternal Father has produced,

[1] 1 John i. 1.
[2] "Ecclesiastica narrat historia, cum a patribus Joannes cogeretur ut scriberet, ita facturum se respondisse, si, indicto jejunio, in commune omnes Deum deprecarentur; quo expleto, revelatione saturatus, in illud proœmium cœlo veniens eructavit: 'In principio erat Verbum.'" (S. Jerome, *in Matthæum, Proœmium;* Eusebius, *Historia Ecclesiastica,* vi. 14; *Fragment de Muratori.*)
[3] John i. 1-4. In the Bosom of God the Light is Life because the divine Attributes are only the different aspects of one only and infinite Action of the Godhead. Far away in those unfathomable depths the Life hath robed Itself in splendor, wherefore it is the Light and the Truth. Several of the Fathers, among the rest S. Justin (*in Joan.*, Tractatus i. 16-18), punctuate this passage differently: "All things that have been made are the Life which is in Him, and that Life is the Light of men;" that is to say, all creatures, before they were called into existence, were contemplated and foreseen by the Word. Therefore, in their conception (when they were the perfect models of imperfect things) they formed the subject of His high Counsels, and thus by partaking of His thoughts, they also had part in Him, even as He is; they were like Him, the Life Itself. The masterpiece of the artist only exists in the intelligence which has conceived it; for canvas and marble cannot convey the contemplated ideal. So it is with created things: they can find their completion only in that Eternal Thought, wherein everything is Life and the Light of Life.

in the bosom of the Virgin, that same Son whom He has, from all eternity, begotten within His own Bosom. In that all-happy moment, this blood, this virginal body found itself pervaded and absorbed by God: "The Word was made flesh, that the flesh might become God."[1]

And this union was not to be transitory; for the purpose of the Word is to consummate His union with man, "to dwell amongst us," "to pitch His tent[2] in our midst," which is the force of the words used in the original text. This last word of the Evangelist carries an allusion to the luminous cloud which had enveloped the Tabernacle long ago to show that Jehovah sojourned in the midst of His people.[3] In the time of Jesus, the sanctuary of Herod was empty of its Ark of the Covenant, nor did its curtain of glory any more screen the Holy Receptacle. John shows how the Word did take up its abode in the midst of Israel, of a truth. "He has pitched His Tent in our midst," he says, "and we have seen His glory," not blazing by brilliant intervals, as did that of the ancient Cloud, but streaming upon the world in rays of splendor, which are the effulgence of grace and truth, — Grace, by which we mean the Life divine that animates our souls; Truth, by which we mean the Light of God that illuminates them.

"We have all received of this fulness," he pursues;[4] "a

---

[1] John i. 14, "Verbum caro factum est, ut caro fieret Deus." (S. Ambrose.)

[2] Ἐσκήνωσεν. (John i. 14.)

[3] The pavilion for the Ark was hardly finished when this Cloud disappeared (Exod. xl. 32; Num. ix. 15). On the day when the Temple was dedicated, we again see the same Cloud streaming with rays of glory, and awful to behold: "Neither could the priests enter there any longer, nor acquit themselves of their functions, by reason of the Cloud, because the Glory of Jehovah had filled the holy House, and Solomon cried out: Jehovah hath said that He would pitch His tent in a Cloud." (3 Kings viii. 10-12.) And then, when this ceremony was concluded, the Divine Vapor was no more visible from without its Tabernacle, and yet all Israel knew that it still abode within the Holy of Holies, between the Cherubim which overshadow the propitiatory with their wings, and that so Jehovah continued to make His habitation in that mysterious Cloud until the day when Nabuchodonosor destroyed the Temple.

[4] John i. 16-18. "Interposito breviter Joannis testimonio, pergit declarare illam quam dixerat plenitudinem gratiæ et veritatis." (Jansenius Yprentius, *in Joan.* i. 15.)

grace more abounding has succeeded the ancient gifts[1] of Jehovah to the Jews." "Moses did but give us the Law, we have gained grace and truth by Jesus Christ. Moses had never beheld Jehovah save through the splendrous mists of Sinai, — for never has any one seen God ; He, the one and only Son (the only-begotten God,[2] according to another reading), — He who, in the Bosom of God,[3] exists in His very Presence, — He alone can declare to us, of Himself, what He is."

Such, in the eyes of Saint John, was the Salvation which the Son of Mary came to accomplish. The Truth must, then, at Its Incarnation, illumine the eyes long blinded to the light;[4] grace must flow in cleansing streams there where sin had soiled the very springs of our natural life ;[5] and the Word, embodied in our flesh, must repair the ruined handiwork of the Creative Word, of the Word Which was in the beginning.

II. The Visitation.

Luke i. 39-56.

In those days Mary, rising up, went in haste toward the mountainous country, to the city of Youttah.[6] What

---

[1] "Gratiam pro gratia." "The New Covenant in place of the ancient alliance." This interpretation, which is also that of the Greek Fathers, seems to us the most natural one. The different meanings given to this passage may be seen in Father Corluy's work. (*Commentarius in Evangelium Joannis*, p. 36.)

[2] The reading μονογενὴς Υἱός is to be found in the Latin versions, in the Syriac of Cureton, and in the majority of manuscripts, as well as in the Latin Fathers. But the other form, μονογενὴς Θεός, has also an imposing array of authorities, — the manuscripts of the Vatican and Sinaï, the Codex Ephræmi, the Peshito, S. Theodotus, S. Epiphanus, and Didymus.

[3] Ὁ ὤν εἰς τὸν κόλπον does not mean : "He Who reposes in the Bosom of the Father," ἐν τῷ κόλπῳ. On the contrary, the preposition εἰς with the accusative signifies that the Word is living, operating within the Bosom of the Father, begotten by Him, and ceaselessly turning back upon this Its Well-spring of Life.

[4] Ἀλήθεια (John i. 17), as opposed to τὸ φῶς (i. 4).

[5] Χάρις (John i. 17), as opposed to ζωή (i. 4).

[6] Luke i. 39. See above, p. 22.

prompted her to undertake so long a journey?—one so unusual, too, when we recall how strict was the seclusion which custom had imposed upon a young Jewess after her betrothal?[1] Are we to believe that Joseph, having had knowledge of Mary's state, rejected her, and that she sought consolation in the society of Elizabeth, as well as escape from the hard-heartedness of men;[2] or, better still, was she not led by a longing to unburden her heart, which was now overbrimming with its new gladness, and so sought the company of a soul capable of understanding her? Elizabeth shared with her in these bountiful blessings of the Lord; thus she had been designated by the Angel as Mary's natural confidant. Was there not in all this an adequate motive for the Virgin's disregard of those rigorous Jewish customs?

It took only a few days for Mary to go from Nazareth to Youttah.[3] She traversed Judea, screening herself beneath the veil of a humility already perfect,—indeed, so forgetful was she of the eminence to which she had been elevated over all Creation, that she gladly humbled herself thus, in order to discourse with her kinswoman of the divine honors vouchsafed to them. Wherefore, so soon as Elizabeth heard Mary's salutation within her dwelling, the child leaped within her, and revealed to her the Presence of the Incarnate God.[4]

"You are blessed from among all women," she cried out, "and the Fruit of your womb is blessed. And whence is this to me, that the Mother of my Lord should come unto me?"

This knowledge of the secrets of Heaven Elizabeth owed to the Precursor, who was aroused within the maternal

---

[1] Philo, *De Specialibus Legibus*, iii. 31; *Ketoubot*, vii. 6.

[2] This hypothesis has been adopted by Lange, who has made a poetical use of it in his *Vie de Jésus*; but it is hardly probable that Mary would have departed so far from her usual maidenly reserve as to confide the secret of her motherhood to Joseph, and certainly there was no occasion for her to do so just at this time, and before her journey southward.

[3] From Nazareth to Hebron is generally called a five days' journey.

[4] Luke i. 40-45.

bosom, that so he might salute Jesus; this is what she declared, adding, —

"So soon as the voice of your salutation came to my ears, the child that I bear leaped in my breast." Then, reflecting upon the incredulity and chastisement of her husband, which set the serene faith of Mary in so much higher relief, —

"Blessed," she cried, "is she who hath believed that the word which the Lord hath spoken to her shall be accomplished."[1]

Amid these transports of surprise and joy Mary remained calm and recollected; her lips opened at last, but it was to praise God for this new largess of His bounty toward her, for His providence toward the world, for His merciful goodness to all Israel; these three ideas sustain the burden of the whole Magnificat.[2]

> "My soul doth glorify the Lord,
>   and my spirit[3] is made exceeding glad
>   in God my Saviour.
> Because He hath regarded the lowliness
>   of His handmaid :
> and behold all generations
>   shall proclaim me Blessed.
> For the All-Powerful hath done great things to me :
>   and Holy is His Name ;
> and His mercy reacheth from age to age,
>   unto those who fear Him."

Turning from the marvellous effects of the Eternal Holiness, the Love Eternal, in her regard, Mary's glance sweeps over the world; it seems to her flashing vision as

---

[1] Elsewhere S. Luke gives this same sense to ὅτι (Acts xxvii. 25). The Vulgate translates it differently: "Beata, quæ credidisti, quoniam perficientur ea quæ dicta sunt tibi a Domino." "Blessed art thou who hast believed, because those things shall be accomplished that were spoken to thee by the Lord."

[2] Luke i. 40-55.

[3] Ψυχή is the soul considered in its relations to the body whereby it gives it life. Πνεῦμα, on the other hand, is used to designate its immaterial and more elevated attributes.

lying prostrate at the feet of that Almighty One, Whom she knew she was soon to bring forth unto it.

> "He hath showed forth the Might of His arm,
> He hath scattered those who were proudly elated
>   in the thoughts of their hearts.
> He casteth the powerful headlong from their thrones,
>   and hath lifted up the humble.
> He hath filled the hungry with food,
>   and sent away the rich with empty hands."

This great upheaval in human destinies must result in the triumph of the veritable Israel, and in this thought the sacred Canticle finds its final note of joy.

> "He hath taken under His protection
> Israel, His servant,
> Being mindful of His mercies to Abraham
>   and to His people, from generation to generation."

Nor need we marvel at the sight of Mary pouring forth her feeling under this poetic form. In the East, where song is the natural expression of every emotion, only a few thoughts are requisite to the development of a poem. Inspired simply by the remembrance of the hymns of Israel,[1] and by the grace of which she was the spotless Vessel, the Virgin, uplifted upon the wings of the Divine Spirit, drew from her enraptured soul the measure of this Canticle, as simple as it is sublime.[2]

---

[1] P. Patrizi (*De Evangeliis*, lib. iii. dissert. xi.) has collected the passages in the Old Testament which Mary may have had in mind when she broke forth into her Canticle of joy. Nothing could show better how she had grown up with the knowledge of the holy books; for almost every phrase which she uses had been already consecrated by association with the revealed word.

[2] It is the opinion of some modern critics that the Magnificat is but a poetical abridgment of such conversations as took place during those months which Mary passed with her kinsfolk. Thus their simple words were finally transformed into a Song, which of course would be religiously preserved in a family like that of Zachary, and so would come to the knowledge of S. Luke. This supposition seems to us as uncalled for as it certainly is unnecessary.

CHAPTER IV.

THE NATIVITY.

I. THE APPEARANCE OF THE ANGEL TO JOSEPH. — THE CENSUS OF QUIRINIUS.

Matt. i. 18–25 ; Luke ii. 1–15.

AFTER nearly three months passed in her cousin's home, Mary returned to Nazareth.[1] That she was soon to be a mother was, of course, at once made known, and Joseph was made acquainted with the bitterest of all human sorrows.[2] He could not hesitate as to the duty of repudiating this affianced maiden, whom honor would not permit him to retain; yet, as "he was just," and knew the severity of the Law towards the sinning woman, he resolved to spare Mary.[3] The betrothment, considered among Jews as sacred as the marriage tie, like it could be broken by divorce;[4] but although the Act of Separation was public in its nature, yet, in certain cases, usage allowed of its being drawn up in secret.[5] Joseph chose this plan, which was

---

[1] Luke i. 36.
[2] Matt. i. 18, 19.
[3] Did the laws which ordered that the sinful wife be put away and publicly denounced also apply to the faithless betrothed? There are good reasons for doubting it; however, public opinion appears to have obliged a lover to renounce an unfaithful maiden. (Selden, *Uxor Ebraica*, lib. iii. cap. xviii.)
[4] Selden, *Uxor Ebr.*, lib. ii. cap. i.; lib. iii. cap. xviii.
[5] There cannot be any question here of a public divorce, for Joseph's intention was not to defame the character of Mary (Matt. i. 19). So too there is little likelihood that Joseph could have contemplated a separation by common consent and without letters of divorce, since the Law formally

at the same time in accordance with his duty and his grief.

But while he was sadly pondering this step the Angel of the Lord appeared to him in a dream, and said to him,[1] "Joseph, son of David, be not afraid to take unto you Mary, your espoused; for That which is born in her is of the Holy Spirit. She shall bring forth a Son, and you shall give to Him the name of Jesus[2] (which means a Saviour); He it is Who shall save His people from their sins." "This," adds Saint Matthew,[3] "was done to accomplish what the Lord had said by the mouth of the Prophet:"[4] "Behold a Virgin shall conceive in her womb, and shall bring forth a Son, and He shall be called[5] Emmanuel, that is, God with us."[6]

When Joseph had arisen from his sleep, he had no other thought beyond the desire to fulfil the command of the Angel. He was eager to repair the unmerited outrage Mary had suffered in his thoughts. Nuptial ceremonies at

---

forbade any such course (Deut. xxiv. 1). All he wished was to acquit himself of the legal formalities, and as secretly as possible. Now, although the deed of divorce was ostensibly a public act (Ewald, *Alterthümer*, p. 224), there is nothing to show that it could not be effected privately, and Abarbanel supposes that under certain circumstances the cause for breaking off the covenanted union was not disclosed. (Buxtorf, *De Divortio*.)

[1] Matt. i. 20, 21.

[2] Ἰησοῦς is the same name as Jehoshua, יְהוֹשֻׁעַ, in the Law and the prophecies; Jeshoua, יֵשׁוּעַ, in the hagiographies. The name signifies "the Salvation of the Lord." (See Philo, *De Mutatione nominum*, par. 21.)

[3] Matt. i. 22, 23.

[4] Isaias vii. 14. In regard to this prophecy, and particularly as to the real meaning of the word עַלְמָה, consult *Les trois grands prophètes*, par M. Le Hir, pp. 58-80, and the same writer's *Études bibliques*, t. i. pp. 64-67.

[5] Καλέσουσιν. The Hebrew has קָרָאת. "Verbum *Careth*, quod omnes interpretati sunt Vocabis, potest intelligi et Vocabit; quod ipsa scilicet virgo quæ concipiet et pariet, hoc Christum appellatura sit nomine." (S. Jerome, *in loco*.)

[6] Ἐμμανουήλ, "God with us," עִמָּנוּ אֵל. Nowhere do we read that Jesus was ever called by this name; hence we can only look upon it "as one of those mystical titles which the Prophets give in a spiritual sense, in order to express certain effects of the divine power, without any consequent necessity that the person thus described use it as his surname." (Bossuet, *Élévations sur les mystères*, xvi⁰ semaine, iv⁰ élévation.)

once ushered the young spouse into his house, but "he knew her not," pursues the sacred text, "until the day wherein she brought forth a Son[1] and gave to Him the name of Jesus." Not that after His birth Joseph ceased to respect the virginal temple in which Jesus was incarnate. Christian tradition has always shrunk with horror from the thought that Mary, whose taintless blood had mingled with the blood of a God, could ever have forfeited the purity of God's Tabernacle, the habitation of His overshadowing cloud, and the Ark of the Lord. Saint Matthew's only thought here was to emphasize the miraculous nature of her maiden Motherhood, and to declare the fulfilment of Isaiah's prediction that "a Virgin shall conceive and bring forth a Son."[2]

Nazareth, which was to be the abode of Jesus for many long years, did not witness His birth. The prophecies had reserved that glory for Bethlehem; and the whole world, at the destined hour of His birth, was disturbed, that these predictions might be accomplished. "In those days," says the sacred text,[3] "an enrollment of the empire brought Joseph and Mary to Bethlehem, the edict which prescribed it emanating from Augustus." This prince, at that time, held the whole world in his sovereign grasp. The adopted son of Cæsar, he had inherited his projects, and of these the most considerable and wide-reaching in its consequences consisted in a registration of the Roman world.[4] This general taking of statistics was to include a valuation of all the resources of the provinces, and a reapportionment of the tax-list. Interrupted for a while, the work of Cæsar was pushed forward again by Augustus,

---

[1] The majority of the versions (Vulgate, Peshito, Ethiopian, Armenian) give the text: τὸν Υἱὸν αὐτῆς τὸν πρωτότοκον, which we find in the Codex Ephræmi and that of Beza. The Syriac of Cureton and the manuscripts of the Vatican and of Sinaï have simply ἔτεκεν Υἱόν. Theophylactus and Euthymius, who have the reading πρωτότοκον, also add that invaluable commentary πρῶτος καὶ μόνος, "first and only."

[2] Matt. i. 22, 25.

[3] Luke ii. 1, 2.

[4] According to Æthicus Ister (*Cosmographia*), the decree of the Senate which ordered this work dated as far back as the consulate of Julius Cæsar and Anthony, 44 B. C. Compare Orosus, lib. i. 2.

who, besides a description of the various lands, added a recapitulation of their subjects. Twenty Commissioners, whose probity had recommended them to the favor of the prince, were despatched into the countries which bore the yoke of obedience to him,[1] and there they devoted twenty-five years to this work.[2] The result was inscribed by the hand of Augustus himself, in a Book called by Suetonius, "Statistics of the Empire."[3] "It was," says Tacitus, "a pictorial reflection of the imperial acquisitions; herein one might see how many of the citizens and of the allies were under arms, the number of fleets, kingdoms, provinces, the revenues from tribute and toll gatherers, an estimate of necessary expenditures as well as of perquisites."[4]

In what year did the decretal for this universal census become operative? It is difficult to decide. The three censuses attributed to Augustus upon the bas-relief at Ancyrus[5] seem to refer simply to the regular numbering of the people of Rome, made by the Censors once every five years. Apparently Augustus promulgated this edict when, feeling himself to be at last absolute master of the Empire, he forthwith devoted all his energies to its consolidation.[6]

[1] Suidas, *Lexicon*, Ἀπογραφή. Cassiodorus, *Variarum*, lib. iii. 52.
[2] Æthicus tells us that it lasted twenty-four or twenty-five years. See Ritschl, *Vermessung der Romischen Reichs*, and Egger, *Examen des Historiens d'Auguste*, p. 50.
[3] Suetonius, *Augustus*, 101 : " Breviarium imperii."
[4] Tacitus, *Annales*, i. 11. Dion Cassius, lvi. 33.
[5] Augustus had commanded that a representation of his mighty deeds, as written out by himself, should be graven upon brass about the base of his mausoleum in the Field of Mars (Suetonius, *Augustus*, 101). The town of Ancyrus had this inscription copied upon marble, and placed it in the temple which it raised to the god Augustus. These last tables, very much mutilated, have come down to us. The matter is clearly explained in the *Exploration archéologique* of MM. Perrot and Guillaume, and in Mommsen's *Res gestæ divi Augusti*.
[6] M. Wallon (*De la Croyance due à l'Évangile*, partie ii. c. ii) has proved that the silence of Tacitus, Suetonius, and Dionysius Cassius, does not invalidate the existence of this edict, and that the testimony of the land-surveyors of Cassiodorus and Suidas implies some such Act. We will only cite this passage from Frontinus · " Huic addendæ sunt mensuræ limitum et terminorum ex libris Augusti et Neronis Cæsarum : sed et Balbi mensoris, qui, temporibus Augusti, omnium provinciarum et civitatum formas et mensuras compertas in commentarios retulit, et legem agrariam per universitatem provinciarum distinxit et declaravit."

Even the allied kingdoms must needs make this act of submission, and Saint Luke informs us that its performance was brought about in Judea at the time in which Jesus was born.[1] "This first enrolling," he adds, "was made by Quirinius, Governor of Syria;"[2] in other words it was made authoritative by Saturninus, as Tertullian tells us;[3] was continued under his successor Varus; and hence it could not have been consummated until the time when Quirinius first took in hand the government of Syria.[4]

Ten years later this same distinguished ex-consul, having been despatched to Judea to reduce it to the condition of a Roman province, found himself obliged to rectify his earlier efforts, and to make a new census in order definitely to regulate the tribute. From this fact comes the care with which Saint Luke would distinguish between the two enrolments.[5] If the first has left fewer traces among Jew-

---

[1] It has been asked how this census, ordered by Augustus, could be made to apply to a kingdom which had kept its autonomy and its king. To understand this we must remember that the States so allied to Rome were considered as part of the Empire (Suetonius, *Augustus*, 48; Strabo, xvii.; Tacitus, *Annales*, i. 11; vi. 41), and that Judea in particular was kept under Augustus's personal direction. After being subjugated and made liable to tribute by Pompey, it owed the shadow of liberty which it still possessed to Herod's shrewd political address. This prince was at first protected by Octavius, as he had been by Cæsar; but his excesses, and the war which he declared on his own responsibility against the king of Arabia, drew from the Emperor that severe admonition: "Hitherto I have treated you as a friend; henceforth I shall treat you as a subject" (Josephus, *Antiquitates*, xvi. 9, 3). In this way he was informed that Judea would be reduced to a Roman province; after that announcement, what else was to be expected but that Augustus would extend the schedule to include this country, if only as a preliminary step to a more complete subjugation?

[2] Luke ii. 2.

[3] Tertullian, *Adversus Marcionem*, iv. 19.

[4] The researches of Zumpt and of Mommsen have finally established the fact that Quirinius was twice Governor of Syria at the time of Herod's death (750), and. ten years later, as is expressly told us by Josephus (*Antiquitates*, xvii. 13, 5; xviii. 1, 1 et 2, 1. See Mommsen, *Res gestæ divi Augusti*, and Zumpt, *De Syria Romana provincia*, pp. 97, 98).

[5] Josephus, without mentioning this first muster in so many words, seems to allude to it, however: "Six thousand Pharisees," says he, "refused to swear, when all Judea took the oath of fidelity to Cæsar Augustus and to the interests of the king." And he adds that the names of the nonjurors were brought to Herod, who fined them (Josephus, *Antiquitates*,

ish annals, and caused no such bloody revolts[1] as did the second, it is because it was merely a description of the peoples and their goods, involving neither any levy of taxes nor military service;[2] but most of all is it due to the fact that Herod was still alive, and, by shrewd political address, was able to manipulate the workings of this enforced enrolment. In fact we can see how this Roman Census, taken under the eyes of the Imperial Commissioners was, notwithstanding, administered according to Jewish forms.

Now the Israelites were in the habit of taking an account of their population, not in their place of residence or birth, but by assembling themselves according to the Family and the Tribe, whence each one had sprung.[3] A muster of Judea, therefore, was nothing less than a revision of the Genealogical Tables. These precious Archives were carefully kept and highly treasured by the particular city which was by way of being regarded as the first fatherland of each Family. David was born at Bethlehem: it was to this town therefore that Joseph must betake himself, "for he was of the Tribe and Family" of the Great King.[4]

Two of the Evangelists had held in their hands the

---

xvii. 2, 4). Hence the oath was accompanied by a registering of names, and as the time in which it was enforced (about 748) tallies with the date of Judea's subjection to the Roman Census, there is good reason to suppose that they were one and the same event. (See Sanclemente, *De vulgaris ærœ emandatione*, lib. iii. 3; Patrizi, *De Evangeliis*, lib. iii. dissert. xviii. 33.)

[1] Acts v. 37; Josephus, *Antiquitates*, xviii. 1, 1; *Bellum Judaïcum*, ii. 9, 2.

[2] M. Wallon has set forth the very valid reasons for holding this theory in his learned dissertation upon the Census taken by Quirinius (*De la Croyance due à l'Évangile*, part. ii. chap. iii).

[3] When in the desert of Sinaï God commanded Moses to number the people, He told him to take the names of the Israelites according to each man's Tribe and Family (Num. i. 2). The terms made use of by S. Luke, οἶκος and πατριά, correspond to those which we find in the Hebrew text: מִשְׁפָּחוֹת, which designates the Tribe, πατριά (Luke ii. 4), and בֵּית אָבוֹת, the household of the fathers; that is, the various Families which composed each Tribe, οἶκος (Luke ii. 4).

[4] Luke ii. 4, 5.

Genealogical Tables of Bethlehem; naturally each searched therein after what would most clearly support his individual point of view. Saint Matthew, occupied in the collection of evidence which would reveal in Jesus, the King and the Messiah promised to Israel, for his part only demanded of these Archives an endorsement of Joseph's royal ancestry. Saint Luke, writing for the Gentiles, interests himself solely in the natural filiation, and he shows us in what order of generation the second Adam traces His lineage up to the first man, and thus to God Himself.[1]

One might very well marvel that the sacred historians, who have given us these genealogies of Joseph, should have passed over in silence that of Mary, if it were not so well known that, according to the teaching of Tradition, the Virgin was a near relative, probably the niece, of Joseph,[2] and that, in consequence, her paternity corresponded with that of her husband. The family trees of the parents of

[1] As to the genealogies of S. Matthew and S. Luke, see Appendix III.

[2] In what degree of kinship did Mary stand to Joseph? As Scripture is silent on this point, we must consult Tradition; and a careful examination of all the testimony has led our soberest critics to arrive at these conclusions: (1) that Joseph (of the house of Panther) had two brothers, named Cleophas (Alpheus) and Joachim; (2) that Mary, daughter of the last named, was consequently the niece of Joseph. This opinion, although not certain, seems at least very well supported by the facts (see the Bollandists, *Acta Sanctorum*, 19 Martii; Zacharia, *Raccolta di Dissertaz.* t. i. diss. v. 3; and especially Father Patrizi, *De Evangeliis*, lib. iii. dissert. ix. cap. xx.). Everything indicates that Joseph was still young when he married Mary. "Without one exception," says M. de Rossi, "every sarcophagus and monument of the first four centuries gives a type of manhood for S. Joseph which is very different from the figure we encounter nowadays; he is always represented as a young man and beardless (*Bulletino di Archeologia cristiana*, 1865, pp. 26-32, and 66-72. Compare with this *Rome souterraine*, par Paul Allard, p. 332). It is only in the fourth century that certain Fathers, after consulting the apocryphal gospels, made S. Joseph an old man. S. Epiphanius even goes so far as to give his age as about forty-four years. Our more conservative theologians have not hesitated to discard these recent traditions. "Juvenis, vel vir, triginta, quadragintave annorum," says Suarez, *in* 3ᵃᵐ *divi Thomæ*, disputatio vii. sectio iii. And forasmuch as it was God's design to cover the maiden motherhood of Mary beneath the veil of marriage, thus to shield the honor of Jesus from idle rumor, so, likewise, no such unusual and shocking difference in the ages of the pair would have been allowed, lest it should cast a shade of ridicule upon their union.

Jesus being the same, nothing could be more natural for the Evangelists than to set down these pedigrees just as they found them in the records at Bethlehem; for the Jews were prone to overlook the descent of their women-folk, by giving only that of the men.

II. The Nativity.

Luke ii. 4–7.

So then, to inscribe himself in the Public Registers, the carpenter of Nazareth quitted his native hills of Zabulon. His young wife too, made the journey with him. Everything drew her to Bethlehem; a secret inspiration from Heaven as well as her affection for Joseph. Perhaps, too, there was some obligation for her appearance in person at the enrolling, as being the heiress of her family.

Four days of foot-travel separate Nazareth from the city of David. Mary, as her time was so near, made the distance very slowly, for winter makes the roads rough, and the holy Family journeyed on foot, doubtless, like other poor pilgrims. Leaving behind them the plain of Esdrelon, En-Gannim, Sichem, and Sion, about two hours from the last-named town they perceived at length the dwellings of Bethlehem.

This village is located upon a long and whitish hill, whose slope, covered with vines, olive, and fig trees, forms a circle of terraces, rising one above another in regular curves, like steps in a stairway of verdure. On the summit rests to-day a heavy pile of sombre buildings; it is the Church of the Nativity, which screens the holy Grotto, and round about it are the three convents built by the Latins, the Greeks, and the Armenians. From these heights, at a glance of the eye, we can descry, far below us, the fertile valleys, the ancient domain of Boaz and of Jesse, the far-away pastures, where, protecting their herds from the mountain lions, there had grown up that intrepid race of Shepherds, which once supplied Israel with the noblest of her captains.

As they entered Bethlehem they would first encounter the hostlery, of which the Khan of modern Oriental villages is still a fair copy, a huge square enclosed by porticos; here, under the shelter of some rude galleries, the ground being raised a foot or two above the level, travellers are spreading out their mats upon the narrow platform, while all about them beasts of burden block up the courtyard; such was the aspect of the place before which Joseph and Mary presented themselves.

The concourse of strangers in those busy days of the registration, the poverty of these late comers, the very condition of Mary, all promised the humble pair a cold welcome. So it happened that they received the reply, "that there was no room for them;"[1] and despite their fatigue they must needs seek elsewhere for some resting-place. The chalk-hills of Judea are honey-combed with innumerable caves. One of these excavations, close by the inn, was used as a shelter for such beasts as the public stables were unable to accommodate. Mary, according to the testimony of Tradition,[2] could find no other refuge but this. And there, amid the straw which served as bedding for the beasts,[3] far from all assistance, on a cold winter's

[1] Luke ii. 7.
[2] From the earliest times Christians have always regarded the stable in which Jesus was born as one of those hill-caves. S. Justin (born at Sichem about 103) says in so many words: "Joseph, not knowing where to find lodgings in Bethlehem, withdrew to a grotto near the village" (*Adversus Tryphonem*, 78). Origen assures us that they still showed this cavern with the manger in his day; and beside this, we know how frequently these numerous excavations served in Judea as a shelter for animals. It was in one of these retreats that S. Jerome passed the thirty years which he consecrated to prayer and study; and it was close to the Crib that he wrote the Vulgate and his famous Commentaries; and it was there too that he wished to die. To-day the manger is no longer in the cave; but a star of gold, lighted by sixteen lamps, stands out against the white marble slabs with which the walls are covered, and an inscription recalls that upon this spot Mary brought the Saviour into the world: HIC DE VIRGINE MARIA JESUS CHRISTUS NATUS EST.
[3] The tradition which declares that an ass and an ox stood over the crib is to be referred to the first centuries; for in the year 343, we find Christian sculptors making use of it (Rossi, *Inscriptiones christianæ*, t. i. p. 51).

night,[1] the hour came for her to be delivered, and she brought forth unto the world, Jesus.

The object of assault for nineteen centuries, this humble Birth, the adoration of some, to others has seemed but a folly and a libel.

"Preserve me from it all!" cried the impious Marcion, in the very first centuries. "Away with these pitiful swaddling-bands and this manger, unworthy of the God whom I adore."

In vain did Tertullian reply, "Nothing is more worthy of God than that, in order to save man, He should trample under foot our perishable grandeur, and so adjudge these joys unworthy of Himself and His."[2] In vain have all our

---

Probably it has no other origin than those words of Isaias: "The ox knoweth his master, and the ass the stable of his lord," which was afterwards supported by a mistaken interpretation of Habacuc iii. 2. Instead of the reading, "Lord, Thou shalt make known Thy work in the midst of the years," the Septuagint and the Italic Version have, "Thou shalt manifest Thyself between two animals " (Ἐν μέσῳ δύο ζώων γνωσθήσῃ: "In medio duorum animalium innotesceris"). Hence, without doubt, arose the pious legend which has been perpetuated even to our day (see Tillemont, *Mémoires*, i. 447).

[1] There is no reason to reject the tradition which fixes the twenty-fifth of December as the date of the Saviour's Nativity. It has been generally accepted since the fourth century, and the modern Chronologists have rarely disputed it. Wieseler (*Chronologische Synopse der Evangelien*, p. 140) prefers to put it in the beginning of January, and certainly it could not have been later than the first days of February, since Jesus Christ was presented in the Temple forty days after His Birth; and the Presentation must have preceded the month of April, which is the date of Herod's death. S. Luke, it is true, shows us the shepherds passing the night out in the pasture-lands at the moment of Jesus' birth, and, according to the Talmudists, this was not their custom except in the period from March to November. But the writers, whose testimony we now quote, were only speaking of the general practices of the country, and it might well be that at such a juncture, when strangers were pouring into Bethlehem, the people thereabouts would put their flocks out to pasture in the more sheltered valleys, in order to make room in their stables for the beasts of burden which otherwise would block up the village streets. The temperature is not the same over all Palestine; thus, although the valley of the Jordan escapes the sharpest spells of winter, still, almost every year snow is visible along the mountains. Even on the fifth of April, M. Gu rin has recorded a heavy fall of snow covering the streets of Jerusalem (*S aa ri*, t. i. p. 47). During five years, the highest temperature observed by Barclay in that city was 33°; the lowest, 3°.3; medium, 17°.

[2] Quæcumque adhuc ut pusilla et infirma et indigna colligitis ad destructionem Creatoris, simplici et certa ratione proponam: Deum non

Doctors who have followed him made manifest to us the High Counsel, so full of wisdom and merciful compassion, which moved the Word Incarnate to this Self-abasement; the God that was born of a woman and laid in a manger[1] has offended the haughty spirit of man, and Marcion's cry is repeated still from century to century.

Without going as far as this in their impatient scorn, the Christians of this same era sought to dignify the humility of their God by fanciful prodigies. They would have us believe that the glory, which Jesus rejected, enveloped His cradle; that Mary, upon her entrance into the sombre grotto, filled it with a noon-tide radiance; that the Angels, in robes of splendor, hung over them in trailing legions; that the stars retarded their heavenly motions to contemplate the Birth of God, to shed upon Him their gentle rays; that the manger itself was resplendent with a great lustre, and that all eyes were veiled, unable to sustain the gorgeous glare.[2]

Very different from this is the simple story of the Gospel; here there is no outward pomp; all the glory of the crib lies in its inherent loveliness. It is only the soul that is illumined by it; 'tis to the heart alone it speaks. Furthermore, we must not forget that here, by anything we add to the Majesty of the Christ, we detract just so much from His Love. The Word, in order to save us, has not disdained the womb of a Virgin; why, then, should we blush at the lowliness of our God? The

---

potuisse humanos congressus inire, nisi humanos et sensus et affectus suscepisset, per quos vim majestatis suæ, intolerabilem utique humanæ mediocritati, humilitate temperaret, sibi quidem indigna, homini autem necessaria, et ita jam Deo digna, quia nihil tam dignum Deo, quam salus hominis" (Tertullian, *Adversus Marcionem*, lib. ii. cap. xxvii.). "Quales et quanti eum fasces producerent! Qualis purpura de humeris ejus floreret! Quale aurum de capite radiaret, nisi gloriam sæculi alienam et sibi et suis judicasset! Igitur quæ noluit, rejecit; quæ rejecit, damnavit" (Tertullian, *De Idololatria*, cap. xviii.).

[1] This crib, made of clay, was the manger of the animals which were stabled in the cavern (Tillemont, *Mémoires pour servir à l' histoire ecclésiastique*, t. i. p. 448).

[2] *Arabian Gospel of the Childhood*, iii.; *Apocryphal Gospel of S. Matthew*, xiii.

more profound it appears the more it forces us to love Him.[1]

Nevertheless, though Mary knew all the natural cares of motherhood, she was yet unacquainted with all those evils which are the penalty of sin,—the sorrows and the heavy-heartedness into which all daughters of Adam must fall.[2] We should not even say that her Motherhood was like that of Eve, in the age of innocence; for as she was a greater than Eve so hers was the unparalleled happiness of preserving her Virgin purity in bearing the Divine Child.[3] When Jesus was born, it was as when the ripe fruit is parted from the branch that bore it, so cheerful, so comfortable, and attended with all joys was the coming of the Christ-Child into the world.[4]

So Saint Luke shows us this Virgin Mother, immediately upon her deliverance, lavishing upon her Holy Infant the cares ordinarily left to strangers; she envelopes Him in swaddling bands and lays Him to rest amid the straw of the manger.[5] "She must cloak the New Adam from the cold winter air; reverence, too, bade her clothe the Babe, as well as did necessity. Cover Him, Mary; cover that tender Baby body; shield Him in thy maiden bosom! Dost understand thy Motherhood? Hast thou not any perturbation at beholding this thine infant One? Hast thou no fear to bare unto Him thy maternal breasts? For what Child is this, Who reaches up to thee His divine hands? Adore Him even whilst thou dost nourish Him, what time the Angels summon new hosts of invisible worshippers."[6]

---

[1] S. Jerome, *Adversus Helvidium*, 18.
[2] Suarez, Disp. xiii. *in* 3ᵃᵐ *divi Thomæ;* Cajetan, *in* 3ᵃᵐ *divi Thomæ*, quæstio xxxv. art vi.
[3] "Virgo ante partum, in partu, post partum" (S. Augustine, *Sermo* cxxiii.).
[4] S. Jerome, *Adversus Helvidium*, 8.
[5] Luke ii. 7.
[6] Bossuet, *Élévations sur les mystères*, xviᵉ semaine, iiiᵉ élévation.

III. THE ADORATION OF THE SHEPHERDS.

Luke ii. 8-20.

To the east of Bethlehem there extend toward the Dead Sea one of the greenest of valleys. In olden times there stood in that place "the Tower of the Herds,"[1] near which Jacob had pitched his tent, there to mourn his dearly loved Rachel. Ruth had gleaned in those happy fields, and the boy David tended there his father's flocks. To-day, in that same valley, the olive trees overshadow a lonely crypt. Consecrated to the Holy Angels, this sanctuary marks the spot over which the heavens were opened to reveal to Earth the coming of its Saviour.[2]

"Certain of the shepherds," says Saint Luke, "were guarding their flocks and keeping their watches through the night. Then suddenly the Angel of the Lord appeared unto them, the glory of the Lord[3] enveloped them in light, and they were seized with a great terror." For to the sons of Israel no splendor could emanate from the skies, without recalling the flaming heights of Sinai and the dread Jehovah, Whom no man might look upon and live.[4]

Straightway the Angel reassured them. "Be not afraid," he said; "I am come to announce good tidings of great joy unto you and unto all your people. To-day, in the city of David, is born to you a Saviour, the Christ, the Lord;[5] and behold the sign by which you shall know him:

---

[1] Migdal Eder. Gen. xxxv. 21; S. Jerome, *Liber de situ et nominibus:* BETHLEHEM.

[2] We are confirmed in our fidelity to the traditions which place the apparition of the Angels at Deir Er-Ralouat. The objections which M. Guarmani has made against this time-honored belief do not appear unanswerable; they are clearly set forth and learnedly discussed by M. Guérin in his *Description de la Judée*, chap. vii.

[3] Luke ii. 8-12. Doubtless by those words: δόξα Κυρίου, S. Luke alludes also to that luminous Cloud which overhung the Tabernacle; for in the Old Testament it is often called "the Glory of the Lord" (Exod. xl. 32; 3 Kings viii. 10, 11, etc.).

[4] Exod. xx. 18, 19.

[5] Χριστὸς Κύριος. This is the only instance where the holy Records make use of these two titles associated in this manner (Κύριον καὶ Χριστόν

you shall find an Infant, wrapt in swaddling clothes and lying in a manger."

A manger, an infant, to work out their salvation! What strange tidings are these! The Wonderful, the Mighty God, the Father of Eternity, the Messiah, for whose glorious coming Israel was in expectation, has revealed Himself at last in nakedness, in abandonment, in the midst of the straw of a stable! What a sudden reversal of the most dearly cherished dreams of the Jews! They must needs be simple and docile hearts who could receive this Message. And so the Angel bore the glad tidings, neither to the Doctors of the Law nor to the great ones of earth, but to these shepherds; and in them he found that which he was seeking, — the Faith of Abraham, of Isaac and of Jacob.

Their gentle souls were all aglow upon his words, and suddenly, while their eyes were still drinking in the celestial radiance, all at once they saw that the Angel was not alone; a multitude of spirits, all hosts of Heaven, surrounded them,[1] and the Angelic choir entoned the chant whose echoes resound each day in the holy mystery of the Mass, —

" Glory to God in the highest of the heavens, and peace upon Earth unto all men beloved of God!"[2]

The shepherds heard with rapture this concert of the Angels; and when it had faded away into the far depths of the skies, and the Messengers of God had gone from their sight, " Let us go to Bethlehem," they cried to one another immediately, " and see this which has happened, — see this which the Lord has made known to us."

of the Acts ii. 36, and τῷ Κυρίῳ Χριστῷ δουλεύετε in the Epistle to the Colossians, iii. 24, receive each a particular meaning from the context). Κύριος is made to refer here peculiarly to the Lord, Jehovah; the Christ is the Messiah, Who is none other than God Himself.

[1] Luke ii. 13-15.

[2] The reading ἐν ἀνθρώποις εὐδοκίας should be adhered to, for it is that of the Vulgate and the most ancient manuscripts, — that of Sinaï, the Vatican, Cambridge, and the Alexandrine. " The word in the original which we render as 'good-will' is used to signify the good-will which God has for us, and thus declares that peace is given unto men so loved by God " (Bossuet, *Élévations*, xvie semaine, ixe élévation).

And making haste to depart, they ascended the hill.[1] Upon its heights they found the cave; in the dumb beast's crib lay an Infant, wrapt in swaddling bands and laid amidst the straw; over Him knelt a young Mother, a thoughtful and silent man.

It was the sign given from on High; they recognized it; and their faith bursting forth into joyous transports, they recounted to those who surrounded them all that had been said to them concerning this Child. The sudden arrival of the shepherds, their search throughout the village had attracted attention. Soon the throng of listeners grew in numbers, and "all were in admiration at this tale which the shepherds related." [2]

Having rendered their testimony to the heavenly origin of the Babe, "the shepherds returned, glorifying and praising God for all the things which they had heard and seen, even as He had made known unto them." Midmost of all this concert of delighted homage the Mother of Jesus was silent. "Treasuring up all these things, she pondered over them in her heart," [3] until the day when Saint Luke wrote them down at her inspiration; for it would seem certain that in this portion of his Gospel, which is so entirely different from all the other accounts, we are reading the very words of Mary. This story, at once so simple and so tender, betrays the Virgin's hand and the Mother's heart.[4]

---

[1] Luke ii. 16, 17.
[2] Luke ii. 18-20.
[3] Luke ii. 19.
[4] All the critics concede that the two first chapters of S. Luke have an Hebraïc coloring, a touch of artlessness and innocence which does not accord with the ordinary manner of the Evangelist, fond as he is of his scholarly phrases. Evidently, in this part he has borrowed now and again from the actual words of some eye-witness of the Saviour's earlier years; the simplicity of the tale and the perfect recollection of all the hymns make us naturally think at once of the Mother of Jesus. "Ea quæ (Lucas) narrat de Christo puero, ab ipsa hujus matre audisse credendum omnino est. Qua de re consentientes habemus nonnullos etiam de schola Rationalistarum" (Patrizi, *De Evangeliis*, lib. 1, cap. iii. quæst. 4).

IV. The Circumcision and the Presentation in the Temple.

Luke vi. 21-38.

What happened after the departure of the shepherds? Were the emotions which their tale had excited lasting? Did the citizens of Bethlehem make all haste to offer Mary that dwelling[1] where the Magi were soon to find her?

The Gospel, while it notes this change of abode, does not tell either at what time or in what manner it was effected; certainly, to worldly eyes, there was nothing of distinction about this poor Family of the Saviour; and therefore it is most probable that the attention, so suddenly attracted to them by the shepherds, was as promptly drawn away by the more exciting incidents of the Census-taking. For, eight days later, when the Babe was to be circumcised, the same Evangelist, who tells us how great was the gathering on the same event happening in the life of John Baptist, now simply remarks of Jesus: "On the eighth day He was circumcised."[2]

Apparently it was Joseph who performed the sacred rite,[3] and so shed the first drops of the Blood Divine. The Christ, in order to fulfil all justice, was required to endure this humiliation, and bear in His body the stigma of the sins which He had taken upon Himself. Yet He only underwent circumcision that He might set us free from its bondage, by substituting for it a purification more elevated, one wholly spiritual,—that of the heart and of the heart's evil desires.

It was the time for giving the Child His Name. The

---

[1] Matt. ii. 11.
[2] Luke ii. 21.
[3] Although the circumcision of Jesus seems to have taken place without any ceremony of note, it did however require the presence of certain witnesses for the Religious Act, that being the invariable custom among the Jews (Buxtorf, *Synagoga Judaica*, cap. ii.; Otho, *Lexicon Rabbinicum*, etc.).

Angel had apprised them by a heavenly mandate that He should be called Jesus,[1] — a name that spoke of Salvation to the Jews, and recalled thoughts of their entrance into the promised land and of the return from Captivity.[2] The sublimest of the titles of the Christ — the Messiah[3] — only compasses in its meaning the Majesty of the Son of God, — that Anointment by which he was consecrated King and Pontiff; the name Jesus signifies One who has loved us even to the dying for us; it bears in upon the heart with a profounder impress of love, a celestial sweetness, a secret relish of salvation, and a foretaste of our deliverance.

The Law commanded that this first-born should be presented in the Temple; as it is written: "Every male child that cometh from the mother's womb shall be consecrated to the Lord;"[4] and it was necessary for Mary to be purified, since the Levitical canons declared every woman unclean after the birth of her offspring. During forty days, if it were a son, eighty if a daughter, she was forbidden to approach the Sanctuary.[5] The custom among the mothers of Israel was to pass this time secluded in their homes until the day on which the expiatory sacrifice was to purify

---

[1] Luke ii. 21.

[2] Jehoshua, Jeshua, Jeshu, were the three forms under which the name of Israël's Deliverer was spoken or written. As a shadow of the true Saviour it was borne by Joshua, son of Nonn, who brought the people into the Holy Land, and by Joshua, son of Josedec, who, with Zorobabel, led them back from the Captivity in Babylon (1 Esdr. ii. 2 : iii. 2).

[3] Christ, Χριστός, is simply the Greek translation of the Hebrew word קָשִׁיחַ, "The Anointed."

[4] Luke ii. 22-24. God gave this command to Moses after the flight from Egypt (Exod. xiii. 2). Thus, as Sovereign Master of all things, He reserved the first-fruits of each family, in order that by this means the others might be consecrated to Him in the person of these their choicest offerings. Indeed they had, in a special manner, belonged to Him ever since the night when He had exterminated the first-born of the Egyptians, and spared the eldest of the children of Israel; the lives then saved by Him were owed to Him by every claim of gratitude. Later on, in place of the eldest sons of each family, He chose to call the sons of Levi to be His servants; and only the first-born, who exceeded the number of two hundred and seventy-three Levites fixed by the Law, were to be redeemed by the payment of five shekels (Num. iii. 12, 44, 45). A last disposition extended this duty (of paying purchase-money for every first-born) to include the whole nation (Num. xviii. 15, 16).

[5] Lev. xii.

them. They offered, then, a year-old lamb for a holocaust, and a turtle dove or a young pigeon for a Sin-offering. In kind consideration for the poor, the Law permitted them in place of a lamb, which would have been too costly, to make presentation simply of two turtle doves or two young pigeons. Such was the obligation to which the Virgin submitted herself, although she knew nothing of the common misfortunes of women in her stainless generation.

On the fortieth day following the Nativity "the time of their purification was accomplished."[1] The sacred text extends the expiation entailed upon the mother so as to include Jesus also; for since the Law considered everything impure that had been touched by the woman during this period, the child she bore in her arms was excommunicated as much as the mother. So Joseph and Mary went up to Jerusalem to consecrate Jesus to the Lord; the five shekels[2] of the Sanctuary relieved Him of the obligation to remain as a Server at the altars, and the "Sacrifice of the Poor" was offered for the purification of them both.

"Now there was at this time in Jerusalem a just man, and one who feared God, named Simeon, who lived in expectation of the consolation of Israel. The Holy Ghost was with him, and it had been revealed to him by this Spirit of God that he should not surely die, before he had seen the Christ of the Lord."[3]

The terms of which Saint Luke makes use in speaking of this aged man indicate that he had in mind a distinguished personage, perhaps even the famous Scribe[4]

---

[1] Luke ii. 22. The Vulgate and the Latin versions have the reading contained in the Cambridge manuscript, καθαρισμοῦ αὐτοῦ; however, the other form, αὐτῶν, which gives it a meaning much more easy to understand, should be preferred, for we find it in the most ancient manuscripts, — the Alexandrine, those of the Vatican and of Sinaï, — and in a majority of the Versions (Syriac, Coptic, Gothic, etc.). "Quod cur rejiciamus non sane est ; quum Moyses lege sanciverit ut is quoque pollui censeretur et purgatione indigere, qui pollutum tangeret, pueri nascentes polluerentur necesse erat contactu matris, ipso partu pollutæ" (Patrizi, De Evangeliis, liv. iii. dissert. xxv. 6).

[2] About four dollars in our money.
[3] Luke ii. 25, 26.
[4] Μέγας διδάσκαλος (*Gospel of Nicodemus*).

Rabban [1] Simeon, son of Hillel. Indeed there is a perfect resemblance in this sketch of his to the historical Simeon, — a similarity in age and residence, an equally high-souled zeal, with the same saintliness of life. The Talmud, which expatiates complacently upon the grand-parents and sons of Hillel, preserves an expressive silence as to Simeon;[2] and this doubtless because it would gladly bury in oblivion a President of the Sanhedrin who celebrated the birth of Jesus, and who had thoughts anent the Messiah[3] which differed very widely from those of his contemporaries, so widely in fact that the latter finally deposed him from the presidency of the Supreme Council.[4]

At the moment when Mary and Joseph were approaching the Sanctuary that indwelling Spirit, moving within the old man's heart, was conducting him to the Temple.[5] There was nothing in their exterior to draw his gaze upon them, — a poor family making their Sin-offering, while in the arms of the mother there lay a little Child; and yet it was enough for him. To the eyes of the Seer this Infant

---

[1] Rabban, that is, the Master above all others. Simeon is the first Scribe whose name was honored with this superlative title (see Lightfoot, *Harmonia iv. Evangel.*, pars. i. sect. iv.).

[2] Lightfoot, *Horæ Hebraicæ*, in Luc. ii. 34.

[3] Poli, *Synopsis Critic.*, ad Luc.

[4] On this question see Patrizi (*De Evangeliis*, lib. iii. dissert. 26) and Witsius (*Miscellanea sacra*, i. 21, 14). The objections which have been made to Father Patrizi's conclusions are: (1) That Simeon, son of Hillel, was still alive some time after the Nativity; (2) that his son Gamaliel is known not as a Christian, but as a Pharisee; (3) that S. Luke would not have spoken of so famous a Doctor in such vague terms as "Now there was then at Jerusalem a man named Simeon." These difficulties can all be disposed of, for (1) the sacred text (Luke ii. 26) does not say that Simeon died after having seen the Lord, but that his eyes were not to be closed in death before he had beheld Him; (2) as for Gamaliel, it may easily be believed that, holding as high rank as he did among the Pharisees, he would not at once follow his father's example; but though outwardly he remained attached to this sect, he had nevertheless an openly professed sympathy for the doctrine and the disciples of Jesus; he undertook their defence before the Sanhedrin (Acts v. 34), and the primitive traditions assert that he died a Christian (*Recognitiones*, i. 65; Photius, *Cod.*, 171); (3) to dispose of the last objection, it is enough to remark that S. Luke was writing for Gentiles, to whom the doctors of Israel were known hardly at all.

[5] Luke ii. 27, 28.

appeared, what indeed He was, the long-expected Salvation, the Consolation which he had waited for so long, the one and only Object of his vows. Simeon took Him into his arms, and in an ecstasy of the Divine Spirit he intoned this Canticle: —

> "Now hath it come to pass, O Lord,
>   that Thou dost deliver[1] Thy servant:
> "according to Thy word,
>   he will go in peace.
> "For mine eyes have seen Thy Salvation:
>   that Salvation which Thou hast prepared
>   in the face of all the nations:
> "even as a Light, which shall reveal Itself
>   unto the Gentiles
> "and the Glory of Israel, Thy people."

Meanwhile "the father and the mother of the Child were filled with wonder at the things which he had spoken of Him, and Simeon blessed Him;"[2] but as his eyes fell upon Mary, he perceived in prophetic vision all that this Mother was to suffer. Then, holding up the Babe before her, —

"He Whom you now look upon," he said, "is for the ruin[3] and the resurrection of many in Israel. He shall be a Man rejected and denied.[4] As for you, a sword of sorrow shall pierce your soul."[5]

Then, reverting to the Son of Mary and to the trials that awaited Him, he revealed what would ensue: "And thus,"

---

[1] Luke ii. 29–33. Ἀπολύεις, "Thou deliverest me, Thou makest my chains to fall from me."

[2] Luke ii. 34, 35.

[3] Πτῶσιν, the Stumbling Block and Rock of Offence, on which unbelief shall fall and be dashed to pieces (Is. viii. 14).

[4] Σημεῖον ἀντιλεγόμενον, that is to say, the perfect Ensample of a man who is disowned and despised, whose life shows what it is to be rejected by all men. The Hebraïc turn of expression, translated by the Greek words εἶναι εἰς σημεῖον, has no other meaning (Rosenmüller, *in loco*)

[5] Καὶ σοῦ δὲ αὐτῆς τὴν ψυχήν, κτλ . . . should be considered as a parenthetical thought. The connective, ὅπως ἄν, in this way refers to the preceding phrase, "The Christ shall be an Ensample of all adversities," and hence it means not "in order that . . .," but "in such wise that the thoughts of many shall be revealed."

he added, "the thoughts which many hide in their hearts shall be revealed;" that is to say, in the Presence of the Christ, — He who was to be for the scandal and the scorn of this world, — before Him all secret thoughts should be unveiled. He would distinguish in this way between those who dreamed of riches, glory, and temporal happiness as part of the coming of the Messiah, and those who, seeking Him for Himself, are prepared to welcome Him under whatever form he may appear.

Mary listened in silence to this menacing prediction. Such as she appears to us now in the Temple, such she ever remains throughout the whole Gospel, — enveloped in her modesty, her heart at times flooded with joys which no language can express, but oftener resigned under the sword which even now tore this Mother's heart in expectation of the end.

"There was present also a Prophetess named Anna, daughter of Phanuel, of the tribe of Aser,[1] of a very advanced age. She had lived seven years with her husband since her virginity, and she had remained a widow up to her eighty-fourth year,[2] never leaving the Temple, and serving God night and day in fasting and prayer." It was this zeal for the House of God which merited for her that she should find therein, and therein adore, her Saviour. As she was coming into the Temple at that same moment, she recognized the Child, Whom Simeon had blessed, rendered thanks to Heaven for unveiling to her eyes this Mystery,

---

[1] Luke ii. 36. "Perhaps it was to show that Jesus Christ finds His worshippers among many tribes, and hence in this number was also found the Tribe of Aser, to which Jacob and Moses had promised only "good bread, oil in abundance," and in a word, "the riches of the mines of iron and of copper" (Gen. xlix. 20; Deuter. xxxiii. 24, 25). But now, in the person of this widow, note how "the soft finery of the kings and nations of earth, the good things of the land, are all changed to fasting and mortification" (Bossuet, *Élévations sur les mystères*, xviiie semaine, xxie élévation).

[2] The reading χήρα ἕως ἐτῶν ὀγδοήκοντα τεσσάρων, which declares how, during her long widowhood, the holy Anna was steadfast in her fidelity to her first husband, has been preferred by Lachmann and Tischendorf; and with good reason, since we find it in the Vulgate, in most of the Versions, in the Alexandrine Manuscript, and in that of the Vatican. The received text gives ὡς in place of ἕως.

and praising the Lord her God,[1] she spoke of Him to all those who awaited the redemption of Israel.

The Lord, the God praised by the Prophetess, is manifestly Jesus; to Anna, daughter of Phanuel, belongs, then, the signal honor of having first announced to Jerusalem the Divinity of the Christ, which other most illustrious witnesses were soon to publish to the world.

[1] The reading Κυρίῳ is based on the authority of the Alexandrine Manuscript and a majority of the Versions (Vulgate, Syriac, Gothic, etc.). We find Θεῷ in the manuscripts of the Vatican and of Sinaï, and in the Codex Bezæ. Tischendorf has adopted the latter form in his Eighth Edition.

CHAPTER V.

THE EPIPHANY.

I. THE MAGI.

Matt. ii. 1–11.

WHILE Joseph and Mary were leaving Jerusalem,[1] a rich caravan was entering it. "These were certain Magi[2] of the Orient," says Saint Matthew. This word, borrowed from the religious terminology of the Persians, is used here to designate the Sacerdotal Class; and it would seem to indicate, therefore, that the Magi were priests of that nation. This feeling is confirmed by the paintings in the catacombs, where we see the Magi always robed in the costume of the Persians,—the high head-dress, the tunic girded at the loins, over which floats a mantle thrown back over the

---

[1] After having related the facts which we have been considering, S. Luke adds: "And when they had fulfilled all things according to the Law of the Lord, they went back to Galilee, to their town of Nazareth" (Luke ii. 39). From this some have concluded that Joseph returned to that town before the adoration of the Magi, not to remain, but to set in order what he possessed there, so as to establish himself at Bethlehem. Thus it would be after his return that the adoration of the Magi and the flight into Egypt took place. Father Patrizi has adopted this hypothesis, but it only seems to us to complicate the sequence of events needlessly; for the text of S. Luke does not necessarily imply that the return of the Holy Family to Galilee followed immediately after the Purification.

[2] In the Pehlvi (the vulgar tongue of Persia in the time of Sassanides), Mogh is the word for Priest (Hyde, *De Religione veterum Persarum*, p. 372). Fürst (*Hebräisches Handwörterbuch:* מַג) thinks that the proper meaning of the word is "a sage," as the Hebrew and the Aramean translated it by חַכָּם. Other philologists give it the sense of "a grandee;" these connected it with the root, מַג (Magh), the Sanscrit Mahat: Magnate = Μέγας = Magnus.

shoulders, the legs either bare or covered with boots, closely bound with thongs after the fashion of this people.[1]

Ministers of a religion far superior to any of the numerous forms of Paganism, the Magi appear to have worshipped at all times One Supreme Divinity,[2] toward whom they observed an austere cult. There were neither altars nor statues in their temples; their choirs never marched with other than reverent gravity, sending up to God their solemn chants and prayers.

These noble beliefs had survived intact among the Persians up to the time when, under the guidance of Cyrus, they ascended into the plains of Mesopotamia. There mingling with the Chaldean Magi,[3] if they did not preserve the purity of their faith, they however came under the potent influence which the Israelite captives exercised upon their conquerors at that period, and in particular

---

[1] Martigny, *Dictionnaire des Antiquités chrétiennes*, article MAGES. The traditions of the Syrian Church and the Greek Fathers give Persia as the native country of the Magi. Tertullian and S. Justin do not agree with these witnesses. The nature of the presents offered to Jesus have made them think at once of Arabia, the land of gold, of frankincense, and myrrh. See Patrizi (*De Evangeliis*, lib. iii. dissertat. xxvii. cap. ii. pars i.).

[2] His name was Aouramazda (Ormuzd), "the luminous, the resplendent, the mightiest and the best, most perfect and most active, very intelligent and very beautiful" (Yacna, i. 1). This supreme and uncreated God has created all things; as the Principle of Good He only distributes blessings, but while drawing into life the forces which were to rule matter, He could not prevent the appearance (resulting from the action and reaction of those same properties) of a destructive genius, Angromaïnyous (Ahriman), "The Worker of Death." This latest-born spirit sows naught but sin and darkness through the world, and indeed seems to be all-powerful for evil; nevertheless, at the end of time he shall see his forces completely destroyed, and he shall be constrained to acknowledge the sovereignty of Aouramazda (Spiegel, *Erânische Alterthumskunde*, t. ii. pp. 121-158).

[3] Although the title Magi is of Persian origin, it was known among the Babylonians before Cyrus; in fact, we find the Chief Magi mentioned in the number of those officials sent to Jerusalem by Nabuchodonosor (Jer. xxxix. 3). Among the Chaldeans this name was evidently used to designate an ancient and powerful race, to whom the sacerdotal office was reserved. Though not so near the revealed Truths as were the Magi of Persia and Media, given also to the worship of fire and other superstitious practices, they however had not neglected more lofty studies; astronomy especially had an honorable place among them, for we know that their observations, which were forwarded to Aristotle by Callisthenes, covered a period of nineteen hundred and three years (Aristotle, *De Cœlo*, ii.).

under the teachings of Daniel. It is a fact, which we know from Scripture, that this Prophet, after his introduction into the palace of Nabuchodonosor, showed himself ten times as wise as the priests and soothsayers of Chaldea,[1] and hence he was placed at their head through the favor of the prince. His ascendency only increased under the four succeeding princes and the three dynasties, and was afterwards confirmed by the triumph of the Persians; for these new victors sympathized with the hatred which Israel had ever felt for idolatry.[2]

Being made subject in this manner to the authority of Daniel, the Magi—Chaldean as well as Persian—could not possibly have been ignorant of his predictions concerning a Messiah, in which he had gone so far as to mark the year, the month, and the hour of His Birth. They had learned from him that the Saint of Saints, who should receive the divine Anointment, was that very One whom Balaam had beheld rising from Jacob like a Star.[3] From the Magi these prophecies were disseminated among the people; and in the time of Jesus there was a settled conviction, cherished likewise throughout all the East, that a King was to arise from Judea, who should conquer the world.[4]

In the midst of this expectancy a strange Star[5] shone out suddenly in the eastern sky.[6] The Magi always followed the course of the stars attentively; in the clear nights of the Orient, when the heavens hang out all their glittering lamps, they had remarked this Star, and recognized it as the signal for some great marvel. And at the same time their hearts as well as their eyes were opened to admit the light which heralded the Christ; they recalled to each

---

[1] Danl. v. 11.
[2] S. Epiphanius, *Adversus Hæreses*, lib. iii.
[3] Num. xxiv. 17.
[4] This report had even come to the ears of Suetonius and Tacitus: "Percrebuerat Oriente toto vetus et constans opinio, esse in fatis ut, eo tempore, Judæa profecti, rerum potirentur" (Seutonius, *Vespasianus*, 4; Tacitus, *Historiæ*, lib. v. cap. xiii.).
[5] As to the nature of this phenomenon, see Appendix IV.
[6] Matt. ii. 2.

other the Star of Jacob and of Judea, and three from among them resolved to travel afar in search of Him of whose approach the heavens were telling.

Whether they set out from Babylon, from Persepolis, or from some other city of the Parthian Empire (at that time master of the East), the Magi must have been many long months journeying;[1] and they had proceeded apparently without any further guidance from the Star, since we see them entering Judea quite uncertain as to the spot where the Messiah was to be found, and coming to Jerusalem to clear up all their doubts. The Holy City was accustomed to seeing within her walls caravans from the far distant Orient, with their striking costumes, and long files of camels laden with luggage. But great was the surprise when these strangers were heard to inquire, "Where is the King of the Jews who has been born? We have seen His Star in the East, and are come to adore Him."[2]

This question, flying from lip to lip, came to the ears of Herod. No one could be more disturbed by it than he, conscious that his unhoped-for good fortune and his thirty years reign had not been able to sanctify his pretensions to royalty in his subjects' eyes. In vain had he espoused the daughter of the last kings of Judea, in order to make them forget his origin; none the less did the blood of Ishmael and of Esau flow in his veins; and the Scribes loved to recall that he had been "the servant of the Asmoneäns."[3] Powerless to appease this bitter hatred, the usurper could know no repose; and in his dread of any rivalry, he shed the blood of his family in torrents. No remnant of the race of the Machabees being left alive, he had hoped, at last, to reign without further strife, when the rumor bruited abroad reached his ears, — that certain strangers were seeking in Jerusalem for a new-born King of the Jews. At once the tyrant's jealousy was aroused to a savager

---

[1] They had been travelling for about four months if they came from Persia (Greswell, *Dissertations on a Harmony of the Gospel*, vol. ii. dissert. xviii.), or seventy days if they started from Chaldea (S. John Chrysostom, *Ad Stagir.* ii. 6.)

[2] Matt. ii. 2.

[3] *Sanhedrin*, 19 a, b; *Baba-Bathra*, 3 b.

intensity than ever. So, it was no longer the extinguished race of the Machabees, but that of David, which now threatened him; for this unknown Babe, destined to the throne, could be none other than the Messiah; and it was easy to see from the excitement which pervaded the city that all Jerusalem was reading the occurrence in that light.

Dissembling his fears, in order to strike a better directed blow,[1] Herod convened a council composed of High-Priests and Scribes,[2] and ordered them to declare where the Messiah should be born. The answer could not be misunderstood.

"In Bethlehem of Juda," they said; "for it is written, 'And thou Bethlehem, land of Juda, thou art not the last among the principalities of Juda, for from thee shall spring the Chief Who shall feed the flock of Israel, My people.'"[3]

These members of the Sanhedrin did not so much quote

---

[1] Matt. ii. 4-6.

[2] This does not mean the whole Sanhedrin, which comprised also the Ancients of the people; but it was rather such members of that assembly as had the authority to interpret the Holy Writings.

[3] The citation in S. Matthew is a free paraphrase of that text: "And thou, Bethlehem Ephrata, art too little to form one chiliad of Juda, and notwithstanding out of thee the Prince of Israël shall come forth" (Mich. v. 2). The tribes were divided into Chiliads, אֲלָפִים, or groups of a thousand families, each one having at its head a Chief called אַלּוּף, of אֶלֶף, which in Hebrew signifies a thousand (Keil, Bibl. Archäologie, par. 140). It was this last word which the Jewish doctors consulted by Herod translated בְּאַלְפֵּי, "among the Chiefs," ἐν ἡγεμόσιν, instead of בְּאַלְפֵי, "among the Chiliads," ἐν χιλιάσιν, which we find in the Septuagint. Thus, commenting freely upon the text of the Prophet, they gave it this form, and though it departs from the original text, it renders the thought very clearly: "Thou, Bethlehem, art not as thou seemest, in the lowest rank among the Chiefs of the Families of Juda;" Bethlehem being personified, and taking its rank among the princes of Israël. Micheas had appended to Bethlehem the ancient name of that village, — Ephrata. S. Matthew here substitutes those words, γῆ Ἰούδα, "in the land of Juda," in order to distinguish this Bethlehem from a town of the same name situated in the territory of Zabulon. The last member of the sentence, ὅστις ποιμανεῖ, "who shall pasture My people Israel," is an addition to the text of Micheas, inspired by the words of the Prophet, which follow: "He shall feed the flock of Israel, brought back by Him unto their God."

the words of the prophet Micheas as they interpreted his thought; but Herod saw only too clearly what he had wished to know, and his plans were at once settled.

He resolved to separate the Magi, not only from the Jews, who must naturally be all afire with emotion at this tale, but even from his own associates, who might well have warned them against his hypocrisy. He summoned them to him therefore in secret, and feigning great interest in their quest, he made exact inquiry as to the Star, particularly as to the time when it had made its appearance.[1]

So soon as there was nothing more to learn, "Go to Bethlehem," he said to them, "seek zealously for the child, and as soon as you have found him make it known to me, in order that I may go also to adore him."

And he despatched them on the instant, without guides, without escort, thus giving no time for any warning, in order that no one, either at Jerusalem or at Bethlehem or among the retinue of the Magi, might suspect his intentions and rob him of his Victim. Night had fallen upon the city; Herod saw in all this the very moment adapted to his designs. It was but to result in their confusion.

Scarcely had the Magi passed beneath the gates of Jerusalem, when the Star shone out anew upon their gaze.[2] "This sight filled them with great joy;" for the Star, leading them on their way, preceded them to Bethlehem, and rested above the place where they were to find the Babe.[3]

There they found only Mary and Jesus.[4] Whereupon

---

[1] Matt. ii. 7, 8.
[2] Matt. ii. 9–11.
[3] It would seem that the adoration of the Magi did not take place in the stable where Jesus was born, for (1) the holy record speaks of the house, οἰκία (Matt. ii. 11), where it occurred; and (2) among the numberless monuments of Christian art which have represented this scene, we only find two of an earlier date than the eleventh century in which Jesus is depicted as lying in the manger. In every other picture Mary is seated in her dwelling, holding Jesus in her arms.
[4] From the silence of the sacred text, it appears that Joseph must have been absent when the Magi arrived (Jansenius Yprentius, *Tetrateuchus*, in Mat. ii.).

that holy night witnessed a wondrous spectacle: at the feet of a Virgin, clasping within her arms a young Child, these three sages fell prostrate in the dust, and adored the Godhead enshrined within this poor abode. Round about them, their attendants were eagerly bestirring themselves on all sides; the camels too had bent their knees, while the retainers lightened them of their precious burdens. Then the Magi, opening these treasures, made offering of them to Jesus. There were gold, incense, and myrrh.[1]

Such is the scene in the Gospel. Pious legends there are, which add more details than one. They robe these wise men in the royal purple, set crowns upon their brows, depict their features and their expression; their names even are made known to us.

"The first was called Melchior," says the Venerable Bede. "He was an old man, with white hair and long beard; he offered gold to the Lord, as to his King. The second, Gaspar by name, young, beardless, ruddy of hue, offered to Jesus, in his gift of incense, the homage due to His Divinity. The third, of black complexion, with heavy beard, was called Baltasar. The Myrrh he held within his hand prefigured the Death of the Son of man."[2]

Unhappily, these details have no authority at all; for it is only in the sixth century that Saint Caesar of Arles confers upon the Magi the title of Kings, now so generally attributed to them,[3] and it is in the ninth that we find their

---

[1] This gum, which exudes from the *Balsamodendron Myrrha*, has a somewhat bitter taste. At first it is of yellowish-white color; after a little begins to take on light golden shades, and as it hardens becomes gradually of a deep red (see Winer, *Biblisches Realwörterbuch:* MYRRH).

[2] Bede, *De Collectaneis*.

[3] Everything combines to prove that the Magi were not kings. (1) S. Matthew, whose leading motive is to set the Royalty of Jesus in higher relief, would not have failed to draw attention to these sovereigns bowing their majestic heads at the feet of the Monarch of Eternity; (2) Herod would have received them with much more ceremony; (3) the primitive monuments of Christian art, which show the Magi wearing the Persian cap, never set the tiara over it, although that was the diadem of the Persian kings. The first mosaic in which we see the Magi wearing crowns belongs to the eighth century (Ciampini quoted by Fr. Patrizi); (4) but of this we can feel sure, *i.e.*, that even before the time of Saint Caesar of Arles a certain few of the Fathers regarded the words of Psalm

names cited for the first time.[1] Two points only appear to be certain; these are, that the Magi were three in number and that Persia was their native country.[2]

II. The Flight into Egypt and the Holy Innocents.

Matt. ii. 12–23.

This their pious duty being discharged, the Magi were relieved from the fulfilment of their promise to Herod; for God, Who had been leading them thus far, would still take care for their return. Being warned in dreams not to appear again before the king, they returned to their own country by another road.

As soon as the Magi had departed, the Angel of the Lord appeared to Joseph while sleeping.

"Arise," he said to him; "take the Child and His Mother, and flee into Egypt. There you will dwell until such time as I shall declare to you, for Herod is searching for the Child to destroy Him."

It was still night;[3] Joseph, rising up, took the Child and His Mother, and set forth.[4]

lxxi., "Reges Tharsis et insulæ munera offerent . . . etc.," as in some sort foreshadowing the adoration of the Magi (see Patrizi, *De Evangeliis*, lib. iii. dissert. xxvii. cap. ii. pars. iii.).

[1] Zaccaria, *Annotationes ad Tirin.*, in Matt. ii. 1.

[2] The traditions of the Syrian Church increased this number to twelve; but it has ever been the feeling of the Church that there were but three. To be more exact, S. Leo (440–461) is the first from whom we have any formal testimony on this point; however, we know that this Father followed the ancient traditions, for the monuments in the Catacombs, which are older than his time by two centuries at least, almost always represent three Magi adoring the Child-God. The rare exceptions to this rule can only be traced to the caprice of individual artists (see P. Patrizi, *De Evangeliis*, lib. iii. dissertat. xxvii. cap. ii. pars. ii.; P. Allard, *Rome Souterraine*, p. 329).

[3] Νυκτός (Matt. ii. 14).

[4] We believe that is not at all improbable that the events which S. Matthew relates in verses 12–14 of chapter ii. should have occurred during the space of one night. In fact, the rapid turn of the narrative, the present tense used in the phrase ἰδοὺ ἄγγελος φαίνεται, which follows immediately after ἀναχωρησάντων αὐτῶν, would seem to indicate that there was no

Egypt has ever been the refuge for those unfortunates whom persecution and famine have driven forth from the land of Israel. From the mountains of Juda it only takes a journey of three days to reach Rhinocolura.[1] Beyond that valley, with its narrow water-courses, Herod had no further power; it was Egypt. To all fugitives it offered safety and an assured asylum; and for this reason the Jews of the Dispersion had once spread their colonies throughout all the land of Mizraïm, the ancient abode of their fathers.[2]

The Gospel tells us nothing concerning this flight of Jesus; doubtless this is because nothing occurred worthy of remark. The long stretches of the Desert alone witnessed the passage of the Holy Family; some unknown dwelling sheltered them; while there was nothing of any note about them to betray their own unparalleled distinction. The design of God in sinking these early days in the shadow was thereby to throw out in higher relief the future splendor of the Divine Life, and not to dazzle the gaze by such wonders as are found only in the apocryphal gospels.

All in vain have the great painters of Italy immortalized these legends: the dragons of the desert couchant before their Lord; the lions and tigers bounding forward to adore Him; beneath His feet the sand grows green and flowering

lapse of time between the departure of the Magi and the apparition of the Angel to S. Joseph. And, furthermore, it is enough to recall the circumstances at this crisis to comprehend with what swiftness this incident must have come upon all the actors in it. Bethlehem is but a two hours' journey from Jerusalem; would Herod, consumed as he was by restless suspicions, have allowed anywhere from seven to ten days to elapse (as Fr. Patrizi thinks was the case) before taking action in the premises? The jealousy which devoured his peace of mind would not have permitted him to endure such a long delay. Undoubtedly he had knowledge of the precipitate departure of the Magi on the very next morning, and on the same day ordered the massacre of the Holy Innocents.

[1] To-day called Ouadi-el-Arish, that is, Nachal Mizraïm, the river of Egypt mentioned in Scripture (Num. xxxiv. 5).

[2] From Alexandria and the Thebaïs, whither Alexander had formerly transported them, the Jews spread throughout every known country, from the deserts of Libya on the north as far as the frontiers of Ethiopia (Philo, *in Flaccum*, ii. 523), and their colonies soon covered Cyrenaïca, a part of Libya and the African coasts of the Mediterranean (Josephus, *Antiquitates*, xvi. 7, 2).

as the Field of the Roses of Jericho; while the palm-trees bow down their fronded crests, disclosing their fruits to the Fugitives.[1] All these lovely pictures are but reveries born of a fanciful devotion.

Certain local traditions merit perhaps more consideration. To the east of Cairo a sycamore is venerated as having once overshadowed the Holy Family; and near by there bubbles up a stream whose waters (or so say the Copts) were sweetened beneath the touch of Jesus. This legend points out Heliopolis, the ancient On,[2] as the abode of the Saviour in Egypt; but they cannot tell us what possible reason Joseph could have had for conducting the Mother and the Child so far away, when he might have found a secure shelter on the frontier. Indeed the time of their exile was so short[3] that it was probably here, on the border, that the fugitives remained.

The precipitate departure of the Magi upset all Herod's plans. The morbid jealousy of the tyrant, little used to finding himself thwarted, vented itself in savage fury.

---

[1] *The Arabian Gospel of the Childhood*, xi., xxv.; *The Apocryphal Gospel of Saint Matthew*, xviii., xxiv.

[2] The ancient On (now-a-days known as Matareeyeh, the native country of Asenath, wife of Joseph) received, in the time of the persecution of Antiochus, a Jewish colony, which was conducted by the High-Priest Onias; the Sanctuary built by him in this city rivalled that of Jerusalem in splendor. Of this temple and of the monuments of Heliopolis there now remain but a few scattered signs, — an obelisk, and some crumbling stonework half buried under the green harvest lands of Matareeyah. The tree which is still called "the Virgin's" is better preserved; it towers up majestically in the middle of a garden, now carefully tended by the Copts, and, despite its years, yet retains the verdure of youth. Matareeyeh is only two hours' journey from Cairo; a sightly and pleasant road winds across the fields, overhung with oranges and nopals.

[3] The apocryphal gospels, in order to allow some time for the performance of the numberless miracles recounted by them, suppose that the sojourn of Jesus in Egypt lasted three years (*Arab. Gospel*, xxvi.); S. Bonaventure extends it to seven. But there are much weightier reasons for limiting this exile to a relatively short space of time; for, on the one hand, the massacre of the Holy Innocents took place, as we shall see, only a little before the death of Herod; and on the other hand, when Joseph returned to Judea, Archelaus still bore the title of king, which he assumed at his father's death ($\beta\alpha\sigma\iota\lambda\epsilon\acute{\upsilon}\epsilon\iota$, Matt. ii. 22). Some months later, Augustus obliged him to content himself with the more modest style of ethnarch; hence it could not have been long after the death of Herod that Joseph brought back the Holy Family into Judea.

Lacking any precise information, but only recalling what the Magi had said about the time of the Star's appearance, he concluded from this that the young King must be yet unweaned; and as it is the custom with Jewish mothers to nurse their babies for two years,[1] he ordered a slaughter of all the children of that age and under in Bethlehem and the outlying territory.[2]

This cruel order was executed at once, with a brutality which wrought most horrid anguish in those mothers' breasts; for Saint Matthew tells us of the shrill screams reëchoing round about the mountains. Rachel herself awakes from the tomb, where she sleeps at the foot of Bethlehem,[3] to mingle her mournful cries with those of the afflicted women. Then was accomplished that which had been foretold by the prophet Jeremy, — "A voice has been heard upon the heights,[4] great weeping and an unceasing wail of lamentation: Rachel mourning her children, and she will not be comforted, because they are not."

Certainly, if we take these words in their literal sense, it was over the Jews made captives under Nabuzardan and collected at Rama to go together into exile, — it was over these wretched ones that Judea laments with the voice of Rachel, the beloved spouse of Jacob;[5] but, most

---

[1] *Ketoubot*, 59 : 2 Machab. vii. 27.
[2] '*Ορίοις*, probably the dwellings and hamlets around Bethlehem.
[3] Matt. ii. 17, 18. You pass the tomb of Rachel, Koubbet Râhil, as you descend from Bethlehem, going to Jerusalem, after about a half-hour's journey. In its present form the monument is evidently apocryphal, and probably contains the ashes of some holy Mussulman. Nevertheless, the traditions of Christian and Mussulman alike agree in locating the tomb of Jacob's wife upon this spot, and the place answers very well to all we know of the burial of Rachel (see Guérin, *Judée*, chap. viii.).
[4] Jerem. xxxi. 15. Rama, רָמָה, signifies a High Place, and the Vulgate, in common with the Targum of Jonathas, gives it this sense in the text of Jeremy: "Vox in excelso audita est . . . ." The Septuagint and the Syriac Version, on the contrary, make it a proper name; and the Vulgate in the text of S. Matthew retains the name without translating it: "Vox in Rama audita est . . .," etc. It is difficult to decide where this village was situated, since the geographers have located it in eight different places: but evidently it must have been one of the cliff hamlets which surround the heights of Bethlehem (see Stanley, *Sinai and Palestine*, ch. iv., note *on Ramah*).
[5] Jer. xl. 1, and the Targum of Jonathas on Jeremy xxxi. 15.

reasonably, Saint Matthew sees in this passage a portent of the tears which should be shed over the Holy Innocents. Indeed, nothing had ever occurred to the Israelites which had not some secret reference to the Messiah; sufferings and joys, humiliations and triumphs, each after their own manner, were for a figure of that which should be perfectly fulfilled in Jesus. The bereavement celebrated by Jeremy was thus in reality a prophecy of the moanings and wails which would rise over the first-fruits of our martyrs.[1]

This massacre made little stir in Judea; and Rama alone hearkened to the piercing shrieks of the mothers. In those days what mattered the sacrifice of a few [2] little children to a monarch's caprice? Antiquity had small respect for babyhood;[3] furthermore, the reign, now just at its close, had been nothing but a tissue of murders, tortures, and atrocious cruelties; so that, according to the address of the Jewish ambassadors to Augustus, "the living coveted the lot of the victims."[4] Under such circumstances one can conceive how easily profane historians might pass over a deed so unimportant in their eyes.[5]

---

[1] Moreover, it is enough to read over the entire chapter in order to convince one's self that the Prophet's glance was taking in events far beyond that present captivity of Rama and the return from Babylon, even to the distant days of the Saviour; for he announces that in this same time of which he is speaking there shall be a marvellous Childbirth, a gracious law written deep in their hearts, and a new pledge destined to cast the ancient Testament into the shadow (Jerem. xxxi. 15, 22, 31-35).

[2] The number of the Holy Innocents has been exaggerated; Bethlehem being a mere village, there could not have been any great multitude which would fall under the conditions of Herod's barbarous order.

[3] Suetonius (*Augustus*, 94) tells us that at the time Augustus was born, there was a prediction which announced the near advent of a Child who should reign over the world. In order to preclude any such danger which might menace the existence of the Republic, the Senate ordered all the babies born in that year to be exposed or otherwise left to perish. Happily, those senators whose wives were with child prevented the execution of this decree, each one of them hoping that the prophecy might refer to his own infant son.

[4] Josephus. *Antiquitates*, xvii. 11, 2.

[5] Josephus' silence on this point has nothing surprising about it; it is a well-known fact that this historian and courtier wrote rather for the Romans, and not at all for his fellow-countrymen. This is why he affects such lofty indifference in regard to the religious sects, which were then absorbing the mind of all Judea. If he scarcely deigns to mention the

Nevertheless, Augustus seems to have had some knowledge of the fact, for Macrobius has preserved this characteristic speech of his: "Upon the news that Herod had sacrificed his own son, among the children of two years of age butchered by him in Syria, 'It were far pleasanter,' quoth the Emperor, 'to be Herod's sow than his son.'"[1] This imperial pun supposes a confusion as to the facts, — quite natural on the part of Augustus, who must have learned of this massacre as coincident with the news of the murder of Antipater, who had been the fomenter of a new revolt against his father. It could not have been invented later on, in the Christian centuries; for then the immolation of these first martyrs had attained an unparalleled importance in all minds. At all events, this sally of Augustus is not simply a valuable witness of the fact as recounted by Saint Matthew, but it even enables us to fix the date also, since it was but five days before his death that Herod delivered his son into the hands of the executioner.[2]

Not that God had delayed His visitation of the tyrant until this moment. A horrid disease, which Heaven seems to reserve for persecutors,[3] had been corroding and consuming his body, little by little. Our pen would refuse to copy the picture drawn by Josephus; it is enough to say that the corruption of the tomb devoured him during life itself. A prey to insupportable agonies, he sought some relief in the warm baths of Callirhoë; but he was forced to return to his superb palace, overshadowed by the palm-

name of Jesus, why should we be surprised that he says nothing of the death of the Holy Innocents? (As to this silence of Josephus, see Mill, *Observations on the Application of Pantheistic Principles*, p. 291.)

[1] "Melius est Herodis porcum (ὖν) esse, quam filium (υἱόν)" (Macrobius, *Saturnal.*, lib. ii. 4). It is easy to understand the allusion in this play upon words, if we remember that the Jews could not eat pork. In fact, Macrobius, who relates it, lived in the fifth century of our era; but he drew his matter from much more ancient writings. Mill has learnedly established the authenticity of this fact (*Observations on the Application of Pantheistic Principles*, p. 292).

[2] Josephus, *Bellum Judaïcum*, i. 33, 8.

[3] Antiochus Epiphanes, Maximian, and Diocletian succumbed to *Phthiarisis*.

trees of Jericho, and there stretch himself upon a bed of torture. Vexatious tidings found their way thither to irritate his frenzied spirit. A rumor of his death had reached Jerusalem, and a golden eagle, placed by him over the gate of the Temple, had been torn down. The culprits were two famous scribes, Judas and Mathias. After being dragged to Jericho, with forty of their disciples, they were burned alive;[1] but their death only added to Herod's hideous terrors. Succumbing at last to the extremity of his sufferings, he attempted to shorten their duration, and thereafter recovered consciousness only long enough to order that horrible execution of his son. His last thought was worthy of such a life; he was determined that tears should be shed at his funeral, and, knowing it was impossible to expect those of affection, he collected into the Hippodrome of Jericho the Chiefs of the great Jewish Families, that he might have them butchered at the hour of his death. The order was not executed;[2] but it is well to recall it just here, as it enables us to comprehend how the massacre of the Holy Innocents would be passed over almost unnoticed in the midst of the torrents of blood which the tyrant spilled in the delirium of his last days.

Herod's end was so impatiently awaited that the news must have been carried, far and wide, in a short space; but the Angel of the Lord anticipated its arrival in Egypt.

He appeared to Joseph during his sleep, and said to him:[3] "Arise, take the Child and the Mother, and return to the land of Israel, for they are dead who sought the life of the Child."

Joseph rose up immediately, and set out toward Judea. Saint Matthew, always intent upon setting forth the ac-

---

[1] The date on which these unfortunate Zealots were put to the torture has been fixed as the twelfth of March, in the year 750 of Rome; for Josephus says that on that same night there was an eclipse of the moon (see Ideler, *Handbuch der Chronologie*, vol. ii. p. 28; Wieseler, *Chronologische Synopse*, p. 56).

[2] Josephus, *Antiquitates*, xvi. and xvii.

[3] Matt. ii. 19-21.

complishment of the prophecies in Jesus, upon this event refers to that line from Osee:[1] "I have called My Son out of Egypt," whose terms apply both to the Exodus of Israel and to the return of the Child-Jesus. It was a habit with the Jewish people to consider their very existence and their history as the outlines of the coming Messiah; and this made the connection very striking for the first readers of this Gospel.

Joseph's intention was to settle in Bethlehem; his thoughts often recurred thither; and, more than all else, was it not expedient that the Child, Who was destined to rule over the world, should dwell near to Jerusalem and His Temple? But on the road the Holy Family learned that Archelaus reigned in the place of his father. Judea had only changed the person of her tyrant; for, as his first essay in infamy, the son of Herod had already put to the sword, within the Temple walls, three thousand of his subjects. Joseph dared not expose the Treasure confided to him to such perils. He lifted his eyes heavenwards, and Heaven made answer, in a dream, that he should retire into Galilee. At his death Herod had bequeathed this province to another of his sons, Herod Antipas. Under this ruler, of a corrupt but careless character, the Divine Child would incur fewer dangers; for this reason Joseph returned to dwell in Nazareth;[2] and thus was fulfilled what had been said by the Prophets, — "that Jesus should be called a Nazarene."[3]

This was not so much any particular prediction (as Saint Matthew refers to it), as it was a thought often uttered by the Prophets; the Messiah was to be "The Netzer," that is to say, the Flower, that shall crown the rod of Jesse. On its side, Nazareth took its name from the same stem, in allusion to the beauty of its site — for

---

[1] Matt. ii. 15; Osee xi. 1. "Quod scriptum est: Parvulus Israel, et dilexi illum, et ex Ægypto vocavi filium meum; dicitur quidem de populo Israel, qui vocatur ex Ægypto, qui diligitur, qui eo tempore post errorem idolatriæ quasi infans et parvulus est vocatus; sed perfecte refertur ad Christum" (S. Jerome, *in Osee*, xi.).
[2] Luke ii. 39.
[3] Matt. ii. 23.

"it was the flower of Galilee."[1] We do not know how this word, which from its origin could evoke none but the sweetest reminiscences, in the end lost all loveliness in their eyes; indeed, for the Jews, "the Nazarene" was unmistakably a term of contempt, and apparently it was in order to upraise it to a new dignity that Saint Matthew recalls how Jesus once dwelt in Nazareth, was hailed by its name,[2] and was thus the Flower of Israel.

[1] "Ibimus ad Nazareth, et juxta interpretationem nominis ejus, Florem videbimus Galileæ" (S. Jerome, *Epist.* xlvi.).

[2] Ναζωραῖος. This word does not signify that Jesus was vowed to the Lord by the vows of the Nazarite. In fact, the Hebrew word which is used to designate this consecration is נזיר, a different root from נצר, a bough, a branch, a flower, from which the name of Nazareth was taken. S. Jerome tells us that the first doctors among the Jews converted to Christianity considered that this Prophecy of which S. Matthew is speaking was to be found in all those passages of holy writ where the Messiah is represented as a Branch, bearing fresh flowers and leaves, upon the trunk of Jesse (Isai. liii. 2; Jerem. xxiii. 5; Zachar. vi. 12), and particularly in that figure in the eleventh chapter of Isaiah: "An offshoot shall spring from the stem of Jesse, and over above these roots a branch shall rise bearing its crown of fruit." S. Matthew does not indeed quote any special prophecy, and speaks only in general terms, διὰ τῶν προφητῶν (Matt. ii. 23).

CHAPTER VI.

JESUS AT NAZARETH.

I. THE CHILDHOOD OF JESUS.

Luke ii. 40.

ALL that we know of the Childhood of Jesus is comprised in those words of Saint Luke: "The Child grew, and waxed strong in the fulness of wisdom, and the grace of God was upon Him." There was therefore a transitional period in the life of Jesus, — a period of growth in body, which grew like that of other children, — a period of progress, even "of the soul, which fortified itself," according to another reading of the sacred text.[1]

How are we to understand this interior development of Jesus? The common feeling is that His wisdom and His power declared itself by degrees, although he possessed them in their plenitude even from His Conception; and hence this increase in strength was only an apparent progress. However, we should not forget that the Saviour willed not only to appear, but to be in reality, a Child; now, it is the law of childhood that, just as the organs, at

---

[1] Luke ii. 40. Πνεύματι is an addition which we find in the Alexandrine Manuscript and the Syriac Version; it is very rightly rejected by Lachmann, Tregelles, and Tischendorf, for it has weighty authorities against it, — the Vulgate, the manuscripts of the Vatican and of Sinaï, and the Codex Bezæ. Salmeron gives this interpretation of it: "Hoc ad interiorem hominem pertinet, quod scilicet per ætatis incrementa augebatur." However, this reading is a very valuable gloss, for it fixes the sense of the otherwise vague expression, ἐκραταιοῦτο.

first imperfect, develop little by little, so the intelligence awakes in perfect concord with it.[1] Since Jesus was once a Child, did He too submit Himself to the gentle influences of age and its changeful growth? Yet, if we admit this point, how are we to reconcile that absolute Omniscience possessed by the Man-God in virtue of the Hypostatic Union, with any intellectual increase, however small we may consider it to have been, even were it no more than an experimental knowledge, as many theologians define it?[2] Here there is, we must confess, an inexplicable problem; and it were wiser by far to humble our minds before it, than to insist stubbornly upon a satisfactory solution. We believe, with firm faith, that Jesus is the Son of God, that He is God even as is the Father, and by this He is always infinitely wise, infinitely mighty; on the other hand, we read in the Gospel that Jesus was really a Child, and that He grew, in age, in grace, in wisdom. No one of these truths involves a contradiction; certainly we do not know how they were reconciled in Him; and yet, if it were otherwise, the Incarnation would cease to be — what God has willed that it should forever be — a Mystery, which escapes the grasp of our reason without shocking or contradicting it.

However it may have been with the interior life of Jesus, outwardly at least there was nothing to distinguish Him from the children among whom He lived, and in Mary's arms He appears to us as Bossuet has painted

[1] "Christus non habuit regulariter ullam operationem humanam nisi dependenter ab organis et dispositionibus connaturalibus, sicut alii homines: nec loquebatur ab infantiâ . . . ergo non habuit operationem humanæ phantasiæ ante organum bene dispositum, ergo nec operationem humanam intelligendi, quia hæc tam pendet a phantasiâ, quam phantasma ab organo disposito" (De Lugo, disp. xxi. sect. i. n. 5, 11).

[2] "Scientiam simpliciter acquisitam in Christo fuisse per se clarum videtur, nec apparet quomodo eâ negatâ, præsertim quatenus empirica est, sine specie quâdam Docetismi, infantia, pueritia, tota vita Jesu Christi explicari possit . . . De tempore et modo quo cœperit Christus habere hanc scientiam, valde probabilis videtur sententia Card. de Lugo fuisse paulatim et progressu ætatis communicatam. Cum enim hujus scientiæ usus non sit independens ab organis corporeis, videtur certe Deus initium et incrementum ejus accommodasse ipsi naturali constitutioni organorum" (Franzelin, *De Verbo incarnato*, sect. iii. cap. ii. th. 42).

Him: "Thou lovely Babe! Happy were they who gazed upon Thee, stretching forth Thy arms from out the swaddling bands, lifting up little fingers to caress Thy holy Mother; now, upheld by her firm hands, adventuring Thy first short steps; now practising Thy baby-tongue with stammerings of the praise of God, Thy Father! I worship Thee, dear Child, at every stage of Thy divine growth, the while Thou art nursed at her pure breasts, or while, with feeble wails of infancy, Thou dost call for her, or while Thou dost repose upon her bosom, clasped in her warm arms."[1]

The mysterious tide of this divine Childhood passed away in the obscure village in which Joseph and Mary dwelt. We know already the name of their retreat; it will suffice to describe its site, to make it understood why Jesus loved Nazareth, and preferred it to any other abode.

Judea is scarcely more than a succession of hill-ranges, running from the north to the south, at some distance from the Mediterranean. In the west they slope down to the sea-shore; in the east they are broken suddenly, to leave a passage through which the Jordan flows, hemmed in by their steep walls and that of the mountains of Hauran. Thus four parallel lines of hills make up the whole of Palestine; the plains along the sea-board, the highlands of Juda, the bed of the Jordan, and, beyond that, the hills of Perea. Only one valley, that of Esdralon, breaking through it transversely, cuts the first chain into two parts: one of these stretches north to the Libanus, — this is Galilee; the other extends south as far as the desert, — that is the land of Juda.

Nazareth belongs to Galilee, and nestles down along the mountain-side, shielded from the plain of Esdralon by the many hill-tops which are crossed by those winding foot-paths and steep, hilly roads. On the confines of the village these crests stand apart for a space (as it were), so to encircle with their wooded heights a grassy vale. Some scholars have presumed that this verdant amphitheatre was once the crater of an extinct volcano, and indeed the

---

[1] Bossuet, *Élévations sur les mystères*, xxe semaine, 1re élévation.

fertility of the spot supports their conjecture. In fact, Palestine has no more smiling glade than this little valley of Nazareth. Antoninus the Martyr compares it to a paradise. "Its women are of an incomparable grace," he says, "and their beauty, which surpasses that of all the maidens of Juda, is a gift from Mary. As for its wines, its honey, its oil and its fruits, it yields not the palm even to fruitful Egypt."[1] To-day Nazareth has lost these glories; but it still has its meadows, its shady hollows, watered by cool springs, its gardens of nopal and fig trees, where the olive mingles with orange and pomegranate trees, in fruit and in flower. To the southwest, the village spreads down the slope of the mountain, and the campanile of the Latin Convent marks the location of the abode of Jesus.

Nazareth has no other horizon beside this circle of wooded eminences, which shut it in on every side, but from the brow of the hillside on which the village is built Jesus could in one glance embrace all that territory which He had come to conquer: to the north, the mountain peaks of Libanus and Hermon, covered with eternal snows; to the east, Mount Tabor, like a dome of verdure, then the deep river-bed of the Jordan, and the high table-lands of Galahad; from its southern side, the plain of Esdralon reached from His feet as far as the mountains of Manassah; on the east was the Sea, and Carmel, with its many reminders of Elias.

Galilee of the Gentiles, as its name[2] indicates, did not form a little world by itself, like the land of Juda. Its inhabitants were of various races. Phœnicians peopled the frontier of Tyre and of Sidon; mingling with the Jews were Arabs and Assyrians, who together cultivated the fields of that province; a few Greek colonies occupied the towns of the Decapolis; and, over all, the garrisons of Rome held the whole country in their grasp.

Amid these surroundings the early years of Jesus were passed. Outwardly the same as other children, He received

---

[1] Antoninus the Martyr, *Itinerarium*, v.
[2] Is. ix. 1; Matt. iv. 15.

from Mary and from Joseph the simple lessons which the Law prescribed;[1] at His Mother's knee he learned to read the Scriptures, which only spoke of Him; but Mary knew What He was, and though charged with the duty of instructing Him, she never forgot that He must be the Object of her adoration.

II. Jesus among the Doctors.

Luke ii. 41-50.

Along about His twelfth year,[2] the young Jew found Himself, in a certain measure, exempt from the family government. Having entered the synagogue, He had begun already to bind about His brows the phylacteries, — long bands of parchment, covered with sacred texts, — and was become "a Son of the Law," and so subject to its prescriptions. One of paramount importance was to visit Jerusalem at the Feast of the Pasch. The parents of Jesus acquitted themselves of their duty faithfully; and although custom did not insist upon the presence of the women,[3] Mary accompanied her spouse. The Saviour was

---

[1] Exod. xii. 26; Deut. iv. 9, vi. 7, 20; 2 Tim. iii. 15. Kitto, *Cyclopædia:* EDUCATION. Doubtless it was from this custom that Christian art obtained the idea of representing the Child Jesus learning to read at the knees of Mary. It is a pious fiction which in no wise offends dogmatic truth; for the Saviour, despite His infinite Wisdom, desired to be obedient both to the Law and to His parents, even in the slightest details.

[2] Aben Esra, *in Gen.* xvii. 14 (Jost, *Geschichte des Judenthums,* iii. 3, 1), informs us that having arrived at his thirteenth year, the child was made subject to the Law. According to this, Jesus, being only twelve years of age, simply attended the Feast as accompanying His family. The Fathers held a contrary opinion, and assure us that on this occasion Jesus took His part in the legal ceremonies; for the rest, the rule which obliged the Jews to go up to Jerusalem for the Pasch was probably made to include all the male children: "exceptis surdo, stulto, puerulo; puerulus autem ille dicitur, qui nisi a patre manu trahatur, incedere non valet" (Bartolocci, *Bibliotheca magna Rabbinica,* vol. ii. p. 132; Lightfoot, *Horæ Hebraicæ,* in Luc. ii.).

[3] "Pascha feminarum est arbitrium" (*Kiddouschin,* fol. 61, 3; Schoettgen, *Horæ Hebraicæ,* vol. i. p. 266).

twelve years old when, for the first time doubtless, He made the journey to Jerusalem with His Family.[1]

The pilgrims from Galilee, because they feared the violence of the Samaritans, usually were loath to cross over their country.[2] It may be believed that the hatred of the sectaries was not so active at this moment; for the traditions declare that, both going and coming, the Holy Family followed the direct road, which passes close by Sichem. By this route Nazareth is distant from Jerusalem some thirty-two leagues, and the trip would take a slow-travelling caravan not less than three or four days. To the south of the valley of Esdralon, the springs and groves of En-Gannim afford a first camping-spot for the pilgrims. From thence, after crossing the hill-country of Manassah, on the second evening, the tents are pitched near Jacob's Well, at the foot of Mounts Ebal and Garizim. Beëroth with its fountains was the customary stopping-place for the third day.[3] After this there remained only some three hours' travel, and hence the next morning would find them within the walls of Jerusalem.

In that city the Holy Family passed the seven days of the Passover.[4] And on the day following the caravans were gathered together for their departure; that of Galilee, which was composed of many thousands of persons,[5] was never ready for the start until near mid-day; for tradition [6] points out Beëroth as the spot where, at nightfall, Joseph and Mary were first made aware of the absence of Jesus.

One is at a loss to understand, upon first thoughts, how they were so slow to take alarm; but it must be remembered that Jerusalem, during the Passover Season, was

---

[1] Luke ii. 42.
[2] See in Appendix VI. how the Samaritans formed a separate nation in the midst of Judea, and were the hereditary foes of the people of God.
[3] This route is poetically described by Farrar (*The Life of Christ*, vol. i. chap. vi.), and with more exactness in Murray's *Handbook for Palestine*.
[4] Τελειωσάντων τὰς ἡμέρας (Luke ii. 43).
[5] Galilee was the most densely populated part of Palestine (Josephus, *Bellum Judaïcum*, iii. 3, 2).
[6] This is given by Quaresmius as being a very ancient tradition (*Elucidatio Terræ sanctæ*, t. ii.) (See Guérin, *Description de la Judée*, t. iii. pp. 7–9).

thronged with two or three million pilgrims,[1] and in consequence caravans were formed amidst the greatest confusion. It was only when the long files of travellers with camels and mules had left the city gates far behind them, that it became possible to collect together one's own party, and to keep some order. Kindred and friends were then united, the women and the old people mounted upon beasts of burden, the men on foot, leading the way, while, as they journeyed along, they chanted their sacred hymns.[2] The parents of Jesus not seeing Him, would think that He had joined some other band, and thus they would pursue their way, expecting Him to rejoin them when the Caravan came to a halt at eventide.[3]

But their search for Him then among the crowd was a vain one: Jesus was not to be found; and their anxiety was very great, for Judea was then in an uproar of sedition. The exile of Archelaus, recently deposed by Augustus, had resulted in the reduction of his kingdom into a Roman province and the imposition of additional taxes. At this new badge of servitude the people revolted, and the excitement raised by the insurrections of Sadoc and Judas the Gaulonite was still agitating them. In such troublous times, amid the wild crews which were scouring over the country, what perils might not menace a lost child!

Joseph and Mary returned immediately to Jerusalem.[4] For the space of two nights and two days, all along the wayside and through the Holy City, they continued the fruitless search. Only upon the third day did they discover the Child, "seated in the Temple, in the midst of the Doctors, hearing them and asking them questions, the

---

[1] Josephus, who speaks of them as being an innumerable multitude, also relates that when Cestius issued an order to count the lambs immolated for the Passover, they reported the number as two hundred and fifty-six thousand. Now, as each lamb was eaten by a group of from ten to twenty persons, the number of Jews who took part in this Passover must have been about three millions (Josephus, *Bellum Judaïcum*, ii. 1, 3; vi. 9, 3.)

[2] At such times the Psalms of the Degrees (cxx.–cxxxii.) were chanted.

[3] Luke ii. 44.

[4] Luke ii. 45–47.

while all those who heard Him were astonished at His discretion and at His answers."

How came it that Jesus should be found in this place and in such noble company? The Jewish Doctors were accustomed to meet upon Sabbath-days in one of the lofty halls of the Temple,[1] and would there solve any difficulties occurring in the interpretation of the Law. In the time of the Pasch particularly, when Jews from all over the world flocked to Jerusalem, there were great throngs about these far-famed masters, eager to be instructed by them. The Divine Child mingled among their auditors; those questions of His, so profound in their simplicity, attracted the attention of the Doctors, who were soon surrounding Him, eager to question and to hear Him.[2] And such was the charm of His discourse that it held these sages of Israel fast captives to His voice.

This congregation was not unworthy to hearken to Him, for it was made illustrious by men of most venerable authority; Hillel,[3] revered as the peer of Moses, habited still in all the majesty of a noble old age; the unyielding Shammaï,[4] who bound all that Hillel loosed; Jonathas, son of Uziel, whose speech was so fiery that the birds (says the Talmud), as they passed above his head, were either burned, or were transformed into Seraphim.[5] Grouped about these, the parents of Jesus might have seen Rabban Simeon as well,—he who had foretold to Mary her future griefs; probably there, too, were Joseph of Arimathea, and Nicodemus, whom Grace was shortly to allure.[6] But even more than the aspect of this company

---

[1] The Sanhedrin, together with the Scribes, ordinarily assembled in the Hall of Gazith, a vast basilica built of square blocks of stone erected by Simon ben Shetah (110 B. C.); it was not far from the Priests' Porches and the Court of the Israelites (see Kitto, *Cyclopædia:* SANHEDRIN).

[2] "Interrogabat magistros, non ut aliquid disceret, sed ut interrogans erudiret" (Origen, *Homiliæ*, xix., in Luc.).

[3] According to the dates given by Sepp in his *Life of Jesus*, Hillel, though very aged, would still be living at this time (*Leben Jesu*, B. i. K. xxi.).

[4] "Shammaï ligat, Hillel solvit" (Mischna, *passim*).

[5] *Soucca*, 28; *Baba-bathra*, 134.

[6] Sepp (*Leben Jesu*, B. i. K. xxi.) has collected various details, as abundant as they are curious, concerning these different personages, their manner

did the part played by their Son overwhelm them with amazement. He in Whom, thus far, they had seen only a thoughtful, recollected Child, sedulous to conceal the Divinity inherent in Him,— He now discloses Himself suddenly as a superior Being, overawing by His questions and replies these old men of consummate learning.

Still the marvellous character of this scene could not make Mary quite forget all that she had been made to suffer, and her tremulous heart overflowed in this tender reproach :

" My Son, why treat us thus ? Your father and I have sought You sorrowing."

Jesus was content to recall to Mary's mind that His only Father was in the heavens.

" Why did you seek Me ? " He said ; " did you not know that indeed I must be about My Father's business ? "[1]

But even this reply,— the first sentence from the Saviour's lips which has come down to us, — this His word neither Joseph nor Mary comprehended. The humble Virgin herself makes the avowal by that line in Saint Luke's narrative :[2] " And His parents did not understand what He had said to them ? "

All she could do, then, was to engrave upon her memory everything she saw and heard that day. As for Jesus, He invested Himself again in the same serene silence as of old, and now the veil which had covered His Childhood once more screens from our view the eighteen years which are to follow.

---

of life, their doctrine, and their disciples. The Scribes of the lower class revered them as oracles (Cf. Lightfoot, *Horæ Hebraicæ*, in Matt. xvi. 19; and Jost, *Geschichte des Judenthums*, ii. 3, 13).

[1] Luke ii. 48, 49. That commentary of Euthymius, " Is it not befitting for Me to be in My Father's house, in this Temple which is His abode ! " unnecessarily restricts the deeper significance of those words. The Vulgate leaves them their natural sense by putting it under this general form : " In iis quæ Patris Mei sunt oportet Me esse ; Does it not behoove Me to be about My Father's business ? " — about all things which concern His interests ?

[2] Luke ii. 50.

III. THE HIDDEN LIFE OF JESUS AT NAZARETH.

Luke ii. 51–52.

"Jesus went down to Nazareth with His parents; there He was subject to them, and He increased in wisdom, in age, and in grace before God and before man." Saint Luke here reiterates of the Youth of the Saviour what he had formerly said of His Childhood. He grew in accordance with the laws of that Humanity wherewith He had clothed Himself, and this external life had nothing to the outward view but what was natural and ordinary: only it was an irreproachable life and an unpretentious one. Those who saw Jesus in the days of His hidden life, beheld before their eyes only a poor laborer toiling in his workshop.

Joseph was a carpenter; Jesus was one like him. His countrymen recognized Him as such when He preached in the synagogue of Nazareth.

"Is not this fellow, here, the carpenter, Mary's son?"[1] they cried out.

It was a custom among the Jews for every child, whatever his rank or fortune might be, to learn some mechanical art.[2] It was then doubly necessary for Jesus to work with His hands, for the Holy Family was poor, and their only means of livelihood were drawn from this handicraft of Joseph.

Everything leads us to suppose that the latter died during the hidden life of the Saviour; indeed his name appears no more in the Gospel, neither at the bridal banquet

---

[1] Mark vi. 3.

[2] The dignity of manual labor, its healthful effects upon the body, which is strengthened by it, and upon the conduct of life, which is purified by it, were truths never unheeded by the Jews, as among the Greeks and Latins. S. Paul mended tents; R. Ismaël, the illustrious astronomer and rival of Gamaliel II., made needles (Jerusal., *Berachot*, iv. 1); R. Jose was a tanner (*Sabbath*, 49 *b*); R. Jochanan a shoemaker, etc. "Labor is the workman's honor and dignity," says R. Judah (*Nedarim*, 49 *b*). Hence, all these most illustrious doctors took care to have some mechanical art; having this, they had the means of gaining a livelihood and preserving their independence. (See Kitto, *Cyclopædia:* EDUCATION; Sepp, *Leben Jesu*, B. i. K. xxiii.)

in Cana, nor at the departure for Capharnaum,¹ nor amid any of those other circumstances in which the relations of the Christ are mentioned. Besides this, would Jesus have left Mary to Saint John if her husband had been still alive?² Joseph died in Nazareth, therefore, in the arms of Mary, and with the kiss of peace upon his lips from the Lord Himself. Jesus was left alone to be the support of His Mother; and so He busied Himself in that carpenter's workshop at Nazareth, handling the saw and the plane. In its infancy, the Church was wont to recall, for the reverent remembrance of the faithful, those ploughs and yokes which His divine hands once fashioned from the rough wood.³

It may be that Jesus did not always dwell alone in that quiet home. According to a tradition mentioned by Eusebius, a sister of the Holy Virgin, like her called Mary,⁴ had married a brother of Joseph, named Alpheus or Cleophas.⁵ He too must have died during Jesus' sojourn in Nazareth, for the Gospel observes the same silence concerning him that it does as to Joseph. But for the two sisters, it would seem that they kept together; and the numerous children of Mary, wife of Cleophas, are those brothers and sisters of Jesus of whom the townspeople spoke in these terms: "Are not His brethren named James, Joseph, Simon, and Jude? and are not His sisters all here amongst us?"⁶ It is the usage in Sacred Scripture, and is, in fact, a general custom in the Greek language,⁷ to call even distant kinsfolk brethren. That term, therefore, only refers to these four cousins of Jesus. As for the daughters of Mary and Alpheus, who lived in the household of the Saviour, we know neither their names nor their number. However these words: "Are they not all here among us?" leave it to be supposed that there were at least three.⁸

---

¹ John ii. 1, 11, 12.   ² Mark vi. 8 : Matt. xiii. 55.
³ S. Justin, *Contra Tryphonem*, 88.   ⁴ John xix. 25.
⁵ Hegesippus, apud Eusebium, *Historia ecclesiastica*, lib. iii. cap. xi.
⁶ Mark vi. 3.
⁷ Gen. xiii. 8, xiv. 14 ; Lev. xxv. 48 ; Job xix. 13 ; Xenophon, *Cyropædia*, i. 5, 47 ; Isocrates, *Panegyricus*, 20 ; Plato, *Phædrus*, 57.
⁸ As to these brethren of the Lord, see Appendix V.

Two of their brothers are better known; we shall encounter them shortly among the Apostles. James, son of Alpheus, is that "brother of the Lord" whom Saint Paul wanted to see, together with Peter, and whom he hailed as one of the pillars of the Church.[1] His sturdy virtue got for him the surname of The Just. "Consecrated to God from the womb of his mother, he drank nor wine, nor strong liquor, and abstained from animal food. Never had the razor been passed over his locks, never did he use fine oil to anoint his limbs."[2] Jude, the brother of James,[3] had not, like him, this austerity of the Nazarite; but it was as a tribute to his generosity that he was given the name of Lebbeus (Thaddeus), "the Man of Heart,"[4] by which he is distinguished in the Gospel.

These characteristics were not, however, unfolded until later on, beneath the breath of the Holy Spirit. At Nazareth the kindred of the Saviour had no higher thoughts than such as were common to their contemporaries; all their desires limited to the enjoyment of the good things of this earth. At the outset of the Ministry of Jesus, they understood so little what was His divine Mission that they set out upon a day to bring Him back by force to their home, and to constrain Him to take some nourishment: "He is becoming mad,"[5] they said. Used as they were to see in Jesus one of their own household, the cousins of the Saviour were apparently the last to believe in Him; and if, seeing the marvels worked by their "Brother," they did finally follow Him, it was in the hope of finding the wealth and honors they coveted.

The following fact related by Saint John hardly leaves any doubt about this point.

It was just as the Feast of the Tabernacles was drawing near, in the last year of Jesus; He had not more than six months to live. His brethren came to Him:

---

[1] Matt. x. 3; Gal. i. 19, ii. 9.
[2] Hegesippus, apud Eusebium, *Historia ecclesiastica*, ii. 23.
[3] Luke vi. 16.
[4] Matt. x. 3; Mark iii. 18. לֵב, heart; תָּד, breast.
[5] Mark iii. 20, 21.

"Come out from Galilee,"[1] they cried, "and go into Judea, so that your disciples may see the works which you do; for no man does such things in secret when he wishes to show himself publicly. Since you are doing these things, manifest yourself to the world."

"Even His brethren," adds Saint John, sadly, "did not believe in Him." And still it was in their society that Jesus of Nazareth lived. These laborers, more engrossed in earthly cravings than careful for the things of Heaven, shared in His tasks, gathered around the same family table, sat by the same fireside, were witnesses of His days and nights. And thus Jesus, by partaking of them, has hallowed those daily trials of our daily life, which Heaven mingles with the joys of home and family, and which make for the probation and salvation of so many souls.

[1] John vii. 2-5.

BOOK SECOND.

THE BEGINNINGS

OF THE

MINISTRY OF JESUS.

ΚΑΤΑ ΜΑΤΘΑΙΟΝ.

ά. ις', ιζ'.

Βαπτισθεὶς δὲ ὁ Ἰησοῦς εὐθὺς ἀνέβη ἀπὸ τοῦ ὕδατος, καὶ ἰδοὺ ἠνεῴχθησαν οἱ οὐρανοί, καὶ εἶδεν ΠΝΕΥΜΑ ΘΕΟΥ καταβαῖνον ὡσεὶ περιστερὰν ἐρχόμενον ἐπ' αὐτόν. Καὶ ἰδοὺ ΦΩΝΗ ἐκ τῶν οὐρανῶν λέγουσα · —

Οὗτός ἐστιν Ὁ ΥΙΟΣ μου ὁ ἀγαπητός, ἐν ᾧ εὐδόκησα.

The Testimony of the Holy Trinity.

And Jesus being baptized, forthwith came out of the water; and lo, the heavens were opened, and He saw THE SPIRIT OF GOD descending as a Dove and coming upon Him. And behold a VOICE from Heaven, saying:

"This is My beloved SON, in Whom I am well pleased!"

SAINT MATTHEW.

iii. 16, 17.

Book Second.

THE BEGINNINGS OF THE MINISTRY OF JESUS.

CHAPTER I.

THE EPOCH AND THE LOCALITIES IN WHICH JESUS EXERCISED HIS MINISTRY.

Luke iii. 1, 2.

"In the year fifteen of the reign of Tiberius Cæsar, Pontius Pilate being Governor of Judea, and Herod Tetrarch of Galilee, Philip, his brother, ruling over Iturea and the land of Trachonitis, and Lysanias over the country about Abila, under the Pontificate of Annas and of Caïphas, the word of God was spoken to John, son of Zachary, in the desert." Saint Luke, in using these terms to announce the mission of John the Baptist, has not thought so much of giving us, in this summary of the times, an accurate chronology, as he desires to recall the various circumstances surrounding the appearance of the Precursor of Jesus; nevertheless, he is not so wanting in precision but that we can infer from his words the very year in which the Saviour commenced His Ministry. Indeed, the public life of Jesus was begun by His Baptism; and as this baptism followed close upon the first preaching of John the Baptist, it must have been in about the fifteenth year of Tiberius that the Saviour, leaving Nazareth, descended to the banks of the river Jordan.

But what are we to understand by the fifteenth year of Tiberius? As Augustus died the nineteenth of August, in the year 767 of Rome (14 A. D. of our calendar), would it not seem, at first sight, that this year must be from 781 to 782 (28 to 29 of the Christian era), and that consequently the birth of Jesus took place, at the latest, in 751, since He was "about thirty years old"[1] at the time of His baptism? However, this date cannot be adopted; for we know from incontrovertible testimony, on the one hand, that Herod died in the month of April, 750,[2] and, on the other, that the Nativity of Jesus preceded that event.[3] The fifteenth year of Tiberius must then be computed by reckoning, not from the death of Augustus, but from the year in which Tiberius took active part in the government of the Empire. This way of calculating the reign of their emperors was the common custom in the provinces of the East. Wieseler has demonstrated this fact by the aid of inscriptions and medals.[4]

Adopting this hypothesis, Jesus was born toward the end of the year 749, some months before the death of Herod, and He began His Ministry about 780 (27 of the common era).

One other date, which is preserved by Saint John, supports these conclusions. Some months after His Baptism we find Jesus in Jerusalem for the Passover. Moved to wrath at sight of the hucksters in the Temple,

---

[1] Luke iii. 23.

[2] M. Wallon has established this point in his *La Croyance due à l'Évangile*, c. iv. part ii. A careful study of certain medals of the time of Herod Antipas has led a learned professor, Herr Sattler of Munich, to adopt the same conclusions. These coins, unaccountably neglected hitherto, give the number of years during which the Tetrarch governed Galilee, and have thus determined the exact date of the death of his father, Herod the Great.

[3] Matt. ii. 1.

[4] Wieseler, *Beiträge zur richtigen Würdigung der Evangelien*, pp. 191-194; Comp. Patrizi, *De Evang.* t. iii. diss. xxxix. 45. M. Fillion (*Evang. selon S. Luc.* in loc.) observes that this mode of computation has been adopted by the great majority of modern exegetical critics. It cannot be denied, however, that the contrary opinion is supported by weighty reasons; they are clearly set forth in the scholarly work of M. l'abbé Memain, *La Connaissance des temps évangeliques*, and in the works of M. Wallon.

He whipped them from their stalls with blows from a thong.

The Jews demanded at once, "What warrant have you to show us for such actions as these?"[1]

"Overturn this Temple," said Jesus, "and in three days I will rebuild it once more!"

"What?" they replied, "this Temple was forty-six years in building, and will you raise it up again in three days?"

The restoration of the Temple which is referred to here was commenced by Herod in the eighteenth year of his reign (734).[2] The Passover during which these words were spoken is therefore that of 780. Now, the date of this Pasch being also that in which Jesus began His ministry, His birth, which took place thirty years earlier,[3] must be put about 750 (four years before Christ), or, to be more exact, in the month of December, 749 (year 5 B. C.).[4]

These two dates (749 and 780) settled upon,—the one as fixing the nativity of Jesus, the other that of the commencement of His ministry,—there remains only to be determined the period of His death, in order to arrange the chronicle of His whole life. It took place, as we shall see later,[5] on the fortieth of Nisan (Friday, the seventh of

[1] John ii. 13–25.
[2] Josephus, *Antiquitates*, xv. 11, 1.
[3] Luke iii. 23.
[4] This date is the one most commonly adopted. In fact, Lamy, Usher, Petau, Bengel, Wieseler, Anger, Greswell, agree in setting the date of the Nativity somewhere about the end of the year 5 B. C., or at the beginning of the year 4. Although M. Wallon coincides with San-Clemente and Ideler in favor of the year 747 (year 7 B. C.), he nevertheless confesses that there are no decisive reasons to be alleged against the year 749. So, after all is said on the subject, one is free to prefer either side of the argument: "Whether we should locate the Birth of our Lord at a little earlier or a little later date, and thereby shorten or prolong His life on earth by a short space, is after all a discussion which displays our uncertainty as to the chronology of the world as much as it affects the dates in the life of Jesus Christ. And let the discussion result as it may, the thoughtful reader will have recognized the truth that all this can in no measure affect the ordering or the fulfilment of God's eternal Counsels. Let us scrupulously avoid anachronisms, and the rest we may safely leave for the learned labor of scholars" (Bossuet, *Discours sur l'Histoire universelle*, partie i. époque x^e.).
[5] See Appendix X., The Chronology of the Passion.

April) 783 A. U. C. (the thirtieth year of our era). And hence there must have been four Passovers during the public life of Jesus. That of 780 marks the beginning of His preaching[1] and teaching; a second (781) would seem to be the one referred to by Saint John in his fifth chapter[2] as that in which Jesus cured a paralytic at the Pool of Bethesda.[3] The Saviour did not attend the third (782); it was just about the time when He multiplied the loaves in Galilee, and to His disciples promised a New Pasch; the fourth Passover[4] was that of His death (783).

As for the ministry of John the Baptist, it preceded the first Pasch of 780 by some months. But the period that elapsed between the autumn of 779 and that of 780 had been observed by all Judea as a Sabbatical Year.[5] We know what that term meant in the Mosaic legislation. Every seven years the fields were left fallow; what they brought forth of themselves was divided between the poor, the foreigners and the cattle, while over all Judea there was a full remission of all debts.[6] Is it not most probable that John Baptist appeared at the beginning of this year, when such a protracted period of leisure allowed of the people's listening to his Message, — a Message in which they heard him speak of expiation, mercy, and forgiveness? The Sabbatic Year commenced, like the civil year, in the month of Tishri (September);[7] therefore the ministry of John Baptist preceded the Baptism of Jesus by about three months. A tradition of the primitive Church locates the latter event about the sixth of January, during that same winter.[8]

We may conclude from these facts that the various

---

[1] John ii. 13.
[2] John v. 1.
[3] John vi. 4. See Appendix VIII.
[4] John xiii. 1.
[5] Wieseler, *Chronologische Synopse*, p. 204.
[6] Kitto, *Cyclopædia:* SABBATICAL YEAR.
[7] The Jews commenced their religious year somewhere in the spring equinoctial season, in the month Nisan (April), and their civil year about the autumnal equinox, in the month of Tishri (September).
[8] Patrizi, *De Evangeliis*, lib. iii. dissert. xix.

THE EPOCH AND THE LOCALITIES. 97

events in the life of Jesus Christ may reasonably be connected with the following dates: —

749 A. U. C.,	5 B. C.,	Dec. 25,	Nativity of Jesus;
779 „	26 A. D.,	Sept.,	John the Baptist;
780 „	27 „	Jan.,	Baptism of Jesus Christ;
780 „	27 „	April,	First Pasch (John, ii.);
781 „	28 „	April,	Second Pasch (John, v.);
782 „	29 „	April,	Third Pasch (John, vi.);
783 „	30 „	April,	Death of Jesus Christ.

Whichever view one may choose to follow in this matter of dates, there is no reason for laying any very great stress upon it, after all; for Saint Luke only alludes cursorily to such dates as he gives, and without ever being diverted from his subject. But, on the other hand, he goes into a detailed account of the names of sovereigns and countries, in order to give a survey of the world at the point of time when John Baptist began to preach. He mentions the lands through which the Saviour moved; he tells what princes held sway in each. It is therefore the field of the Ministry of Jesus which is here spread before our eyes.

First of all, let us glance over the regions included in that field. Two of these provinces, Judea and Galilee, are already known to us. However, it may be remarked that this latter comprised also (as belonging to the realm of Herod Antipas) the mountains of Galaad, which the Gospel calls by the name of Perea, "the country on the other side of Jordan."[1]

Below this province begins the domain of Philip, containing the pasture lands of Basan.[2] On the east, "the land of the Trachonites;" and on the north, "Iturea."[3] This

[1] Πέραν τοῦ Ἰορδάνου (Matt. iv. 15; John i. 28, iii. 25; Josephus, passim). This country reached from Hieromax as far as the Arnon.

[2] S. Luke does not speak of the land of Basan; but we know from Josephus that the realm of Philip then comprised the portion of territory known to-day as Hauran, which at that time was divided into four provinces, — Gaulanitis (the present Jaulan), Auranitis (which properly speaking is Hauran), Batanea (Ard-el-Bathanyeh), and Trachonitis (now Lejah). (Josephus, *Antiquitates*, xvii. 8, 1; 11, 4.)

[3] Iturea owed its name to Jetur, son of Ismaël (Gen. xxv. 15; 1 Paral. v. 19).

last-named region, with its rich meadow-country in the south, gradually grows more and more forbidding of aspect the nearer we approach to Damascus. The ground is rugged, strewn with jagged rocks and black bowlders, and the flocks feed within the craters of extinct volcanoes.

Still wilder and more gloomy is the Trachonite country. It lies between Iturea, Basan, and the desert, only elevated some thirty feet above the undulating plains of Hauran, — like a shoal of rocks in a sea of verdure. Any one might imagine, viewing the chaotic condition of these dreary wilds, that some time, long ago, huge waves of basalt had been petrified all at once in the midst of a tremendous tempest. Some violent upheaval must have been the cause of these ugly chasms, dark caves, and deep defiles, which make the waste lands of Lejah[1] an object of wonderment. Such it was in the days of Jesus, and such we find it still to-day; for neither time nor man has changed the character of this strange country. The sixty cities of Argob — "the Heap of Rocks,"[2] as the Hebrews called them — have still preserved intact their rugged walls and their houses with doors made of stone, — all so dark and gloomy that, in the time of Solomon,[3] they were believed to be made of bronze. Abilene, the province ruled by that Lysanias whom Saint Luke puts last in his list, is a country of a more charming complexion. It lies about the base of the Antiliban Mountains. The traveller who leaves Damascus for Baalbek, after a six hours' journey in a gorge made fertile by the waters of Barada, encounters the ruins of ancient Abila (called to-day Souk Ouadi Barada), the many inscriptions found in this locality[4] leaving no doubt as to this point. This city was the capital of a principality which extended

---

[1] The Arab's name for this province, Lejah (The Lair), was given to it because of its being used as a refuge and haunt for the robber hordes; that of Trachon, Trachonitis (τραχὺς καὶ πετρώδης τόπος), as well as the Hebrew word Argob, alludes to the rocky character of the soil. This singular region is oval in form, and is about eight leagues in length by five in width. (See Porter, *Damascus* and *Bashan's Giant Cities*.)

[2] From the root גבב, "to heap together" (Fürst, *Handwörterbuch*).

[3] 3 Kings iv. 13.

[4] Murray, *Handbook for Syria and Palestine*, route 37. There the two Latin inscriptions are cited

from Hermon to Libanus, and of which the origin is very doubtful. Josephus and Strabo speak of a Ptolemy, son of Meneus, who held sway over the plains of the Marsyas, in the mountainous country of Iturea, and counted among its towns Chalcis, at the foot of Libanus, and Heliopolis (Baalbek).[1] This Ptolemy had a son, Lysanias, who was put to death by Antony, at the instigation of Cleopatra, who thus wrested from him his realm.[2] What became of this principality thereafter? Did it pass into the hands of Herod, who, as we know, purchased from Cleopatra a parcel of her domains in Syria,[3] and obtained the remainder from Augustus after the battle of Actium?[4] There is room here for any number of conjectures, since after the death of Lysanias no mention of his kingdom is found anywhere until the time (about sixty years later it was) when Saint Luke mentions this same region in connection with a Lysanias, — no longer as king but tetrarch — of Abila. The division of Palestine and the neighboring country into Tetrarchies did not take place until the death of Herod. Probably during that epoch a prince of the lines of Ptolemy and Lysanias, and bearing the name of the latter king, received from Rome, along with the title of tetrarch, a portion of the kingdom of his fathers, and so made Abila the centre of a new state. The historian Josephus had some knowledge of this tetrarchy, since he takes care to distinguish between the Abila of the second Lysanias and Chalcis, the capital of the first ruler of that name;[5] and, furthermore, we possess inscriptions later than the time of Herod which in like manner make mention of a Lysanias, Tetrarch of Abilene.[6]

The other princes who lived in the time of Jesus were

[1] Josephus, *Antiquitates*, xiv. 7, 4; Strabo, xvii. The Marsyas empties into the Orontes between Larissa and Apamea.
[2] Josephus, *Antiquitates*, xv. 4, 1.
[3] Josephus, xv. 4, 2.
[4] Josephus, xv. 7, 3.
[5] Josephus, *Bellum Judaicum*, ii. 12, 8; *Antiquitates*, xx., 7, 1.
[6] Here we have done no more than give the conclusions arrived at by M. Wallon from his learned researches as to the Abilene of Lysanias (*De la Croyance due à l'Évangile*, partie ii. chapitre v.; compare Kitto's *Cyclopædia:* LYSANIAS).

sons of Herod the Great, and had inherited his estates. It is true that their father's will only designated two among them for the succession, — Archelaus and Antipas ; but in those days everything happened in Judea according to the good pleasure of Rome, and Augustus had little respect for any dispositions made by the old king. Half of his territory — Idumea, Samaria, and Judea — was handed over to Archelaus ; the rest, divided in equal parts, formed two tetrarchies, which, following the proper acceptation of this term,[1] comprised each a quarter of the kingdom of Herod. One such portion fell to the lot of Antipas ; it was composed of Galilee and Perea. The other was reserved for Philip, — the son whom Herod had by Cleopatra of Jerusalem, and who while he was being educated at Rome had won the imperial favor.[2] His tetrarchy extended from the Lake of Genesareth[3] to the sources of the Jordan. It comprised Iturea and Trachonitis, as we have already seen, and beyond this countries much more fertile, — Gaulanitis, Auranitis, and Batanea ; these altogether went to make up his province.[4] During the entire lifetime of Jesus[5] these countries enjoyed peace under the government of a prince who was just, humane, and a patron of the arts.[6] More than once did the Saviour pass along its pleasant paths, whether it was to seek a retreat near Mount Hermon, or

---

[1] The title of Tetrarch properly means the sovereign of a fourth part of any country (Smith, *Dictionary of Antiquities:* TETRARCHA). It was given by the Romans to those tributary princes whose domains were not important enough to merit the name of kingdom; however, the tetrarchy of Antipas and that of Philip were each made up in reality of one quarter of the kingdom of Herod (Josephus, *Antiquitates*, xvii. 11, 4 ; *Bellum Judaïcum,* ii. 6, 3).

[2] Josephus, *Antiquitates*, xvii. 1, 3 ; *Bellum Judaïcum,* i. 28, 4.

[3] The village of Bethsaïda, on the northwestern shore of the lake and near the mouth of the Jordan, was one of his possessions. This Bethsaïda, situated in Gaulanitis, should not be confounded with a village of the same name which we shall encounter later on, upon the western border of the lake. Philip transformed this little hamlet into a superb town, which thus became his favorite residence. He afterwards called it Julias, in honor of the daughter of his illustrious benefactor.

[4] Josephus, *Antiquitates*, xvii. 11, 4 ; *Bellum Judaïcum,* ii. 6, 3.

[5] Philip reigned over this tetrarchy for thirty-seven years (from the year 4 B. C. to 34 A. D.).

[6] Josephus, *Antiquitates*, xviii. 4, 6.

to rest within its fresh blooming valleys watered by the springs of the Jordan.[1]

Of all the regions which we have been naming over, no one listened for a longer time to the teachings of the Saviour than Galilee. Antipas, tetrarch of this province, was an indolent and dissipated prince, entirely engrossed in the pursuit of vicious pleasures and in courting the favor of Tiberius;[2] he was of a nature which would be apt to pay little heed to a matter which appeared so trivial, to his way of thinking, that it need not cause him any uneasiness. His only desire in the matter was to witness some of the wonders concerning which rumor had aroused his curiosity.[3]

As for Archelaus, he could never have been seen by Jesus; for in the tenth year of the Divine Childhood this prince was deposed and exiled among the Gauls. From the outset Augustus had distrusted his weak and passionate nature, and he only vouchsafed to allow him for a time the title of ethnarch, promising him that of king if he proved himself worthy thereof.[4] But the Emperor saw his forebodings amply and immediately justified; for the Jews were shortly stirred to revolt by the tyranny of their new ruler. Hence it became necessary to withdraw what little power had been conferred upon him.

Thus vanished even that poor shadow of independence which had still remained to Judea. Augustus made the country merely an appendage to Syria, the government of which was then in the hands of Publius Sulpicius Quirinius. Nevertheless, the importance of Judea, as well as the necessity of restraining so uneasy a people, made the presence of a procurator invested with almost absolute authority requisite.[5]

[1] Matt. xvi. 13.
[2] Josephus, *Antiquitates*, xviii. 2, 3.
[3] Luke xxiii. 8.
[4] Josephus, *Antiquitates*, xvii. 11, 4; 13, 2; *Bellum Judaïcum*, ii. 6, 3.
[5] The Procurators (procuratores Cæsaris) in the imperial provinces were intrusted with the collectorship of taxes; they exercised functions analogous to that of the Questors in senatorial provinces. Sometimes, however, when the seditious state of the country demanded it, they had

A Roman knight, Coponius, was the first to fill this difficult position. He was obliged to use force to bend this stubborn country beneath his yoke, and impose upon it the tax-levy which had been decreed for the whole empire. It required all the influence that the High-Priest Joazar could exert to prevent a general uprising; but he could not, by any efforts, discourage a certain few fanatics, who revolted at a signal from Judas the Gaulonite and the Pharisee Sadoc. Their attempts were at once suppressed; but the frequent executions only exalted their courage; and, ever after, similar Zealots did not cease to trouble the peace of Jerusalem, still repeating their war-cry: "We have no other Master but God." These seditions, which were continually springing up, exhausted the patience of the first governors promptly enough. In less than ten years we see three Romans, each in turn endeavoring to direct the affairs of Judea, — Coponius, Marcus Ambivius, and Annius Rufus.

With Tiberius Judea entered upon a calmer era, and during the twenty-three years of his reign it received but two procurators, — Valerius Gratus and Pontius Pilate.[1] Of the former, the only fact on record which is remembered of him is the facility with which he deposed the High-Priests; for finding Annas invested with these lofty functions on his entering into office, he substituted Ismael, son of Fabi; then, after him, Eleazar, son of Annas; a little later, Simon, son of Camith; and finally, Joseph Caïphas, son-in-law of Annas.

Pontius Pilate, who succeeded him, has attained a sad renown. In the twelfth year of Tiberius, being charged with the government of Judea, he showed himself, at the outset, such as he was to the last moment, — a man with a predisposition to justice, but rendered unreliable by a combination of ambition and cowardice. One of his first acts was to send a Roman garrison, with their standards, to

still ampler powers, and in particular the right of acquitting or executing the accused party (Pauly, *Real Encyclopædie*: PROCURATORES CUM JURE GLADII).

[1] Valerius Gratus undertook the government of the province in the year 16, and Pontius Pilate in 26.

Jerusalem. His predecessor, more politic than he, had been careful not to intrude within the Temple walls with those Roman ensigns, emblazoned with idolatrous legends and insignia; they even forbore to interfere with the troops of Zealots. But at the command of Pilate legionaries broke down the gates in the night time, and at dawn the populace saw with horror those impure images contaminating the Citadel of God. A suppliant throng was despatched to Cesarea, and during five days kept beseeching Pilate with their clamorous petitions. The Governor, wearying of their persistency, ordered the soldiers to surround the crowd and disperse them by force of arms. At their approach the Jews cast themselves flat upon the ground, preferring to die rather than to endure any violation of the Law. Pilate was compelled to yield to their stubborn resolution, and withdrew his standards.

At another time, a little later than this, he was even less successful in a similar enterprise. He suspended, along the walls of his palace in Jerusalem, golden shields with the names of Pagan divinities graven upon their glittering surfaces. Again the people rose up in revolt, and Tiberius himself ordained the removal of those emblems, which were so abhorred by his new subjects.

It was not merely this vacillation between rashness and timidity which militated against Pilate's authority; even his favors were treated with disdain. Jerusalem lacked a sufficiency of water; he decided to bring the needed supply from a distance of about three leagues, introducing it into the city through one of those majestic aqueducts, such as remain to this day a grand memorial of ancient Rome. But the people, upon learning that the revenues of the Temple were to be devoted to this project, laid hold upon the workmen and put a stop to all labor upon it. Much blood was spilt before the rebels were suppressed.

This persistent hostility put Pilate's capricious nature out of all patience, and he decided to follow the example of his predecessors. He retired to Cesarea, upon the borders of the sea, administered the government while keeping aloof from the people, and contented himself with levying taxes and putting a check upon unruly spirits. It was only during the feasts of the Pasch that he would condescend to occupy the fortress Antonia with a detachment of his troops; for from this seat he could dominate the Temple with its throngs, while he held his forces in readiness to crush out any insurrection.[1]

Of all the members of the Sanhedrin, those who conceived the bitterest animosity against Jesus were the princes of the Priesthood. And so, because they had such a preponderating influence in that Council, Saint Luke mentions this fact at the outset of his Gospel — that Annas and Caïphas were the two leaders of the great Sacerdotal Body during the public life of the Saviour. Annas, it would seem, held the first place there. Although deposed from his office by Valerius Gratus, the predecessor of Pilate, he not only retained enough influence to procure the elevation of his five sons, together with this same son-in-law Caïphas, to the pontificate, but he even managed to maintain a rigorous authority in all the councils of the high-priests who succeeded him. Undoubtedly the Jews, who held the more tenaciously by their theocratic institutions in proportion as the Romans infringed upon them more insolently, in this instance would regard the continual changes imposed upon their royal priesthood as illegal and without force. Exasperated by such sacrileges, they would, to all outward appearance indeed, submit to the pontiff put over them by the will of Rome; but all the same they would look upon one man alone as their legitimate head. This man was Annas, whom, as we shall see, they loaded with attention and honors.[2]

---

[1] In regard to the condition of Judea after it was reduced to a Roman province, and as to the various procurators who administered its affairs, see Milman, *History of the Jews*, book xii.

[2] Probably this is what S. Luke meant to have us understand when he put the title High-Priest in the singular number and next to the name of Annas. In fact, the original text should be translated thus: "Under Annas the High-Priest, and under Caïphas" — Ἐπὶ ἀρχιερέως Ἄννα καὶ Καϊάφα. The Vulgate has given us the reading of the received text: ἀρχιερέων — "sub principibus sacerdotum Anna et Caïpha." The other form, ἀρχιερέως, is supported by the authority of the most ancient manuscripts, — the Alexandrine, those of the Vatican, Sinaï, Ephraim, Beza, etc.

Such was the government of Judea in the time of Jesus Christ, such the circumstances amid which He appeared, and to which Saint Luke has been careful to call our attention. As he was addressing readers who were familiar with the period and the places of which he speaks, a few words sufficed for his purpose; to-day we need to know much more of detail in order to give the words of the Evangelist their original clearness and importance.

CHAPTER II.

THE MISSION OF JOHN BAPTIST.

Matt. iii. 1-17 ; Mark i. 1-11 ; Luke iii. 1-22.

IN a westerly direction from Jerusalem and near the village of Aïn Karim, you will find a cave which still bears the name of John. It is a considerable cavern, difficult of access, and retains no sign of habitation, save a stone bench hewn out of the rock, made to serve for a bed or couch ; a few stunted shrubs surround the mouth, and close by there is a spring, beneath which a basin has been hollowed out. It is here, as the local traditions tell us, the son of Zachary grew to manhood. The solitary reaches round about are called "John's Desert," and some would even go so far as to make this neighborhood the birthplace of the Precursor. We have seen that much weightier evidences have secured that distinction for the region about Hebron. So, then, Aïn Karim is only one of those numerous retreats in which the Prophet passed the solitary days and years of his early life.

From his very infancy, in fact, John had given signs of a strength of soul far from common, and though by right of inheritance he might have claimed the office of Sacrificer, he quitted the Temple to bury himself in the desert.[1] By this term is to be understood the wild hill-country which reaches from Hebron to Jerusalem, being no more than a series of steep ranges, cleft and broken into by a number of parched and arid valleys ; a patch of dry underbrush, here and there, is all that varies the monotony of those chalky stretches, whose glare so wearies one's

---
[1] Luke i. 80.

eyes. Even this dreary undergrowth disappears as you near the Dead Sea; the desolation now comes to be complete, an absolute waste; the sight can descry nothing but an undulating moorland, as it were, made up of gray fields of ashes; while in the distance the attainted lake exhales its noisome breath, recalling the memory of Sodom's awful condemnation.[1] Such is the appearance of the desert where John dwelt until the age of thirty, not as a hermit, but wandering about, like the prophets of olden time, without other shelter than the caverns of the mountains or the scanty foliage of the thickets.[2]

In the midst of this wilderness, blasted by the thunderbolts of divine Justice, John grew to an understanding of his Mission. All things must have revealed it to him, both the wondrous happenings at his birth and the prophecies which foretold his coming. Two of these predictions are mentioned in the Gospel. That of Malachy[3] prophesied that the Lord would send before His Messiah a Messenger, to prepare the way against His coming. In the other, Isaiah tells us to hearken "to the voice of him who cries out in the desert:[4] Prepare ye the way for the Lord; make straight His paths; every deep defile shall be filled up; every mountain and little hill laid low; the crooked paths shall be straightened out, the rugged places become plain, and all flesh shall see the Salvation which

---

[1] The Dead Sea presents this repulsive appearance whenever the strong heat of the sun penetrates to the foul depths of that seething sea of asphalt; but only let the wind blow from the north and sweep away the bituminous vapors, and at once its whole aspect changes. During a fresh, breezy morning in the spring, we have seen the waters of the accursed pool as bright and charming as any lake in Italy; its placid waves ripple softly upon the beach; and until you plunge your hand into the water you would scarcely believe it could be of so repulsive a nature.

[2] 4 Kings vi. 2.

[3] Matt. iii. 1.

[4] Is. xl. 3. The words ἐν ἐρήμῳ, which both here and in the Septuagint refer to βοῶντος, are connected with ἑτοιμάσατε in the Hebrew: "A cry reëchoed: Prepare ye in the desert the ways of the Lord!" S. Luke (iii. 4–6) gives this prophecy more at length than does S. Matthew (iii. 3); but S. Mark (i. 23) gives it preceded by this oracle of Malachy (iii. 1): "Behold, I send My Angel before Thy face to prepare the way for Thee."

cometh of God." These impassable ravines, these mountains rising around him on every side, these steep pathways, forced by the great bowlders and precipices to make innumerable curves and windings,—all these were before the eyes of John; and to him, as to Isaiah, these all only betokened that desolation, midmost the wilderness of souls, which he must needs make ready for the coming of the Messiah. As the Precursor of Jesus, he was to run before Him, just as heralds announce the sovereigns of the East, with trumpet and loud voice, bidding all make clear the thoroughfares to do honor to the royal progress.

John was preparing himself for his ministry, not only by meditating on what Heaven revealed to him, but by the practice of the most austere virtues. Consecrated to God by the vow of the Nazarite, he never tasted either of the fruit of the vine or of strong liquor, nor had his locks ever been shorn.[1] But soon this abstinence seemed to him too common and too slight. All his food, in the desert, was limited to locusts,[2] and the wild honey found among the rocks.[3] His frame became reduced by fasting. Gaunt and half-naked, wearing no other covering than a leathern girdle about his loins, while over his shoulders hung a cloak of camel's-hair.

Therefore, so soon as John entered the valley of Jericho, all eyes were drawn to him, while forthwith they recalled

[1] Luke i. 15; Num. vi.
[2] The Laws of Leviticus made it lawful to eat locusts (Lev. xi. 22), and in Judea they furnished a staple article of diet for the poor. The Ethiopians, the peoples of Libya, and the Orientals generally, made use of them in the same way (Pliny, *Historia naturalis*, vi. 35; *Diodorus of Sicily*, iii. 29; Aristophanes, *Acharnenses*, 116; Niebuhr, *Description de l'Arabie*). Shaw has seen the Moors of the Barbary States making a meal of these insects (*Travels*, p. 164). The locust was served up in various fashions, sometimes ground and mixed with meal, sometimes salted or smoked, sometimes roasted, and dressed with butter. Kitto (*Pictorial Bible*, note on Lev. xi. 21) assures us that the taste of the grasshopper cooked in this style is not unlike that of the shrimp.
[3] Wild honey has always been abundant in Palestine. Long before their entrance into Judea, the Lord had described it to Moses as a land where floweth milk and honey (Exod. iii. 8). All travellers agree in declaring that in this respect it has not changed, and that in the wildest and most deserted spots the bees fill the hollows of the trees and the crevices in the rocks with their waxy combs.

how Elias was caught up in the chariot of fire, from these same fields of theirs.¹ They had always believed that the Thesbite had been but lifted up into the heavens that he might descend again upon some future day. This Malachy had declared. But that famous prophecy, in which he alluded to both precursors, had only perplexed the minds of the Jews. They could not distinguish John, the Herald of the living Christ, from Elias, who was to precede the last coming of the Lord; and as Elias was alone named by the Prophet,² it was to him solely that their hopes had reverted. And hence always, upon the least rumor that God had raised up a new Seer, one single question sprung to the lips of the whole people:—

"Is it Elias?"

On beholding John, their excitement was all the more natural, since in him there was really revived the lofty fervor and austere features of the most illustrious of all the prophets; the same abruptness in manifesting himself, the same ascetic garb, the same strong speech. The resemblance was so perfect that the people were mistaken, and believed that the Thesbite had returned, just as he is painted in the Song of the son of Sirach:³—

He hath arisen, Elias, the Prophet who is as a fire!
His word burns like a torch.
He hath brought down upon Israel a famine,
And, in his mighty zeal, he hath made them very few.
Armed with the word of the Lord, he hath shut up the heavens,
And, from thence, three times hath he drawn down fire.
What glory unto thee, Elias, flash forth these wondrous deeds:
Who then shall equal thy renown?
Thou who hast awaked the dead men from their tombs,
Thou who didst bring them up from Hades by the word of the
    Most High!

---

[1] 4 Kings ii. 1-14.
[2] We have already alluded (page 27) to the fact that Malachy, in the third chapter of his Prophecy, announces the coming of John Baptist as the Herald of Jesus, while in the fourth chapter he speaks of Elias returning at the end of the world : "I will send the Prophet Elias before the great Day of the Lord cometh," etc.
[3] Ecclesiastic. xlviii.

Thou who hast brought down kings, down to perdition,
And the haughty ones from their beds of soft repose!
Thou hast hearkened to the sentence upon Sinai,
And upon Horeb heard decrees of vengeance;
And thou hast anointed kings unto penance,
And the Prophets, that they may come after thee.
Uplifted in the fiery whirlwind's midst,
Upon the chariot with steeds of flame,
Thou art preserved to give us warning of the fateful hour,
And to appease His wrath, ere ever it blaze fiercely forth:
To reconcile the hearts of the fathers unto the children,
And to restore again the tribes of Israel!
Blessed are they who have beheld thee, they that have been
    beloved by thee!

The hope of finding a Prophet so famous thrilled the heart of all Israel, and on every side they flocked to the Jordan. Here it was that John commenced his Mission. "His voice resounded through the desert of Judea," says Saint Matthew;[1] by which we are to understand (following Saint Luke[2]), "throughout all the country which borders upon the Jordan."

In fact this stream bears a singular aspect, because of its flowing along between uninhabited banks. No craft ever furrows its waters; no town is builded along its brink. The valley through which it rushes on its way is called by the Greeks the Channel (The Aulon), and by the Arabs the Gorge (The Ghor).[3] It merits both these names; now extending itself to some width, then again intrenched between the mountain-sides which overhang it. In the middle way lies a long gully, forming the bed of the Jordan, which flows along hidden beneath a leafy screen of willows and azaroles. At a distance this green line, wind-

---

[1] Matt. iii. 1.
[2] Luke iii. 2, 3.
[3] The Jordan (the Iarden, from the word ירד, Iarad, "to descend") well deserved its name; for in its numberless windings it has channelled out a bed which continually deepens as it flows along. Though the Marsh of Houleh lies but a short distance from the sources of the stream, it has, however, at that point reached a depth of eighty-eight metres below the level of the Mediterranean.

ing through the barren pass, is all that there is to indicate the presence of the stream.

The Prophet generally remained near some ford; for he baptized by immersion, and everywhere else the steep river-banks make it difficult of access. John the Evangelist, at this point, speaks of a place named "Bethany or Bethbara, over beyond the Jordan." Both these words signify alike "the House at the Passage,"[1] and hence we know that the river used to be crossed at this spot. The tradition which locates this ford opposite Jericho says that Jesus received baptism here, together with a great number of those who had come from the south. John remained a long time at Bethany, for that route was frequented by the Jews who travelled between Perea and Jerusalem. Only toward the end of his life do we see him ascending the course of the stream, as far as Œnon (The Springs); this was near Salem, and above the Pass of Succoth, over which Jacob crossed on his return from Mesopotamia. So that, with Jericho on the south, Œnon to the north, keeping to the valley of the Jordan, we have marked out for us the region within which John preached and baptized. He exercised his ministrations there with entire freedom, passing from one bank to the other, but without ever withdrawing far from the streams of water, which were necessary for baptism and the symbol of his Mission.

It is often asked whence the Precursor borrowed this

---

[1] The most ancient Manuscripts and nearly all the Versions have Bethany. Origen proposed the reading Bethbara, because in his time there was a village of that name on the banks of the Jordan, while he had looked in vain for one called Bethany. Bethbara, בֵּית עֲבָרָה, the House at the Passage, and Bethany, בֵּית אֲנִיָּה, the Boat or Ferry House, according to him might have been used to designate the same place. But without resorting to this hypothesis, why not admit that in Origen's day the village of Bethany might have disappeared? In a country which for three hundred years was ravaged by fire and sword, such a fact would not be in the least unlikely. The traditions of the Latin Church indicate Bethany as the spot where Jesus was baptized, just opposite Jericho, near the ruined Convent of S. John. The pilgrims who come from the Greek Church hold that the spot is three or four kilometres lower down the stream (Robinson, *Biblical Researches*, t. i. p. 536).

rite, and some believe that it is to be connected with the ablutions which were ordained for Jewish proselytes. But why need we look to an origin so uncertain as this?[1] What moved John with the desire of baptizing was, in the first place, the example of those frequent purifications commanded by the Law; but, most of all, the exhortations of the Prophets,[2] which urged them to wash away the stains of sin from their souls, while they thus purified their bodies. John's Baptism was only figurative of this cleansing of the heart, and, to make it clear that true contrition must penetrate through all secret recesses of the soul of man, the Precursor chose to immerse the whole body of the sinner.

One other ordeal was enjoined upon his penitents by the Baptist, — that of confessing their sins. The sacred text seems to insinuate that he even made it an express condition of baptism.[3] Did it only go so far as an acknowledgment that all men are sinners? Christian antiquity never tolerated any such belief, for it was in remembrance of the Confession prescribed by John that the catechumens made a voluntary declaration of their sins.[4]

And, after all, the persuasions by which John incited them to penance leave no doubt as to the motive animating his thought. It is all summed up in those words: —

"Do penance, for the Kingdom of Heaven is nigh unto you!"

The Kingdom of Heaven, no longer the kingdom upon earth, of which Israel was in expectation. The Jewish doctors, deluded by their own chimeras, had but travestied that expression, "the Kingdom of Heaven," by making it

---

[1] Neither Josephus nor Philo, nor any of the Targumists, make mention of this Ablution of the Proselytes, and the first trace we find of it is in the Gemara of Babylon.

[2] Is. i. 16; iv. 4.

[3] Ἐξομολογούμενοι, Mark i. 5. The present participle would indicate that the penitents received baptism at the moment of their confession, and by this it would seem that John only baptized those from whom he obtained this token of repentance (Fritzsche, *in loco*).

[4] "Cum confessione omnium retro delictorum, ut exponant etiam baptismum Joannis" (Tertullian, *De Baptismo*, 20. See Patrizi, *De Evangeliis*, lib. iii. dissertat. xliv. 6).

portend the temporal triumph of the Messiah;[1] but John restored to it its real significance, and by this proclaimed the divine character of the coming reign.

This Message thrilled them with all the more emotion since everything about the Baptist spoke to their souls so insistently, moving them to true contrition. He was a Voice,—"a Voice crying in the desert, 'Prepare ye the way of the Lord.'"[2] He was listened to by the sons of Israel, who were just then celebrating a solemn Sabbatical Year, and so, during the leisure hours of those holy days of rest, felt their hearts stirred with deeper yearnings than ever before for the coming of the Messiah. More than that (let us never lose sight of this fact), there are certain times when grace moves upon the spirit of this world in more notable abundance; the appearance of John the Baptist was the signal of one such great epoch. The hand of God laid hold upon the agitated throng and bore them on towards the sacred stream. They came from either bank, "from Jerusalem, from Judea, and from the countries lying round the Jordan;"[3] that is to say, from Perea, from Samaria, from Galilee, and from Gaulanitis. Pharisees, Sadducees, priests, publicans, soldiers, courtesans, one and all, hurried to listen to this man's word, so stern and relentless to all imposture, all pride and luxury.

The poor and humble ones were the first to kneel before the envoy of Heaven.[4] One after another they stepped down into the stream of the Jordan, weeping, confessing their sins, and, by their penitence, giving an efficacy to John's baptism which it had not in itself. But when it came the turn of the Pharisees and Sadducees, and when the stern Prophet saw them advancing to play a hypocritical part in the performance of the sacred rite, then rang out those thundering words, bringing them to a halt there upon the bank:—

---

[1] See Schoettgen, *Horæ Hebraïcæ*, dissertatio *De Regno cœlorum*.
[2] Mark i. 3.
[3] Matt. iii. 5.
[4] Matt. iii. 6.

"Breed of vipers,"[1] he cried, "of whom have you learned to flee from the Wrath that is to come?"

These great ones of Judea had never listened to such language as this; they were used to see foreheads bowed down to the ground before them, while all Jerusalem hailed them as her masters. John tore away the mask:—

"Show me some worthy fruits of repentance," was his command, "and do not venture[2] to say among yourselves: 'We have Abraham for our father.' For I say to you, God is able to make these stones give birth to children unto Abraham."

It were impossible to strike these haughty men with a better aimed or a more trenchant blow. It was useless for them to pride themselves upon their ancestry. John had declared that to be sons of Abraham by the flesh was of no avail to them, if they were not the true offspring of his virtue and his faith. The same Hand which had formed Adam out of clay, and brought Isaac from the bosom which was chill and barren as a stone,[3] could likewise bring forth from the very pebbles of this river-bed the seed promised unto Abraham, innumerable as the stars of heaven, or as the sand upon the shores of the sea.[4]

Thus, finally, the ancient alliance was declared to be dissolved, and with it went the loftiest prerogative of Israel, — that ancient privilege which had exalted it above all the nations. For, John added: "Already the axe is at the root of the trees. Every tree which will not bear good fruit shall be cut down and thrown into the fire."[5] And yet this warning was to be of no avail. Humiliated, but not converted, the Pharisees and Sadducees withdrew from the Jordan, while only a very few of their number bowed down beneath the hand of John and received his baptism.[6]

Though he was unsparing, even to harshness, toward these supercilious formalists, the Precursor had only words of mercy and kindness for the common people. When, in

---

[1] Matt. iii. 7–9. "Serpentes e serpentibus" (Lightfoot, *Horæ Hebraicæ*, in Matt. iii. 7).

[2] Μὴ ἄρξησθε (Luke iii. 8): "Do not even begin to say; do not attempt it."

[3] Is. v. 1. [4] Gen. xxii. 17. [5] Matt. iii. 10. [6] Luke vii. 30.

their turn, the crowd gathered around the Prophet, asking, "And we too; what must we do?"[1] John did not tell them to imitate his penitential life; he was content to preach to them the duties of almsgiving and fraternal love.

"Let him who has two coats give to him who has none, and let him who has food use it in like manner."

The publicans drew near as well. Hateful to the Jews from their office as collectors of the Roman tax, they came to seek John, ready to sacrifice everything for this baptism.[2]

"Master, what shall we do?" they asked him.

He did not oblige them to throw up this despised business of theirs; but rising above the narrow views of his countrymen, he recognized that they might serve the public authority without wronging the people.

"Demand nothing," he said, "above that which has been commanded you."

Certain soldiers, upon their march, passed near to where John was preaching,[3] and witnessed some of these scenes of pardon. These also, yielding to grace, questioned the Prophet, and he told them: "Do not do any violence, nor any fraud; be content with your pay."

This was the way he chose to throw open the gates of the celestial kingdom, and thus he prepared them for the coming of Jesus, by preaching, not a visionary perfection, but a godly and upright fulfilment of man's daily duties, and the ordinary virtues of each one's state of life.

Yet, notwithstanding, every day the excitement increased with the growing concourse of people about the Baptist. Very soon it was not only of Elias that they spoke, but the whole country began to cherish the thought that this might indeed be the Christ.[4] John heard them, and his reply came quick and sharp:—

"As for me, I baptize you with water, in order that you may do penance; but after me there cometh One who is mightier than I; I am not worthy to loosen,—to bear

---

[1] Luke iii. 10, 11.   [2] Luke iii. 12, 13.
[3] Στρατευόμενοι (Luke iii. 14): "On their way to the war,—in active service" (Herodotus, iv. 28, etc.).
[4] Luke iii. 15, 16.

His shoes. He it is who shall baptize you with the Holy Ghost and with fire."[1]

No longer a baptism of water, unquickened and lifeless, as was that of the Precursor, but an ablution made fruitful by the Holy Ghost.

These are but fragments recalled from the many sermons which John preached; for "he spoke many other exhortations, evangelizing the people."[2] If that Message of his had come down to us in its entirety, throughout all his speech we should find the same eloquence, alive with the figures of the desert, with its scarped cliffs, hissing serpents, and gnarled tree-trunks, among which he had lived for so long a time.

Yet sometimes, too, he spoke of their fields and harvests, as when he depicted the Messiah as a Thresher, with the huge cradle of the harvester in His hand,[3] throwing upon the air the good grain, mingled with all its impurities, to be winnowed by the wind, even as He does to-day in His Church upon earth; Whose wheat are the elect, whom He receives again purified for the heavenly storehouse; the chaff, those profitless souls which shall forever be consumed. "The fan is in His hand," he said, "and He will cleanse His floor; He will gather together the good grain into His granary, and will burn the chaff in a fire which shall not be extinguished."[4]

He whom John announced under such animated imagery followed close upon the footsteps of His Herald. The

---

[1] Matt. iii. 11; Luke iii. 16.   [2] Luke iii. 18.

[3] In order to understand this figure aright, one needs to recall the manner in which the Jews gathered in their crops. As soon as the mowers had cut down the grain, they arranged the sheaves upon a round platform; then cattle yoked abreast were put to trampling it, until the ears were all crushed and the grain loosened from its envelope. Toward evening, at the time when usually in the East a strong breeze blows up, they toss this compound of grain and loose straw into the air by the aid of a fan (a huge shovel with a very short handle); the grain, as it is the heavier, falls back to the earth, while the chaff and lighter refuse are carried off to some distance by the wind. This is what is meant by purging the threshing floor; after this, all that the harvester had to do was to store his crop in the caverns, which are generally used as granaries in this region. As for the straw and the chaff, they mostly burn it as a fertilizer.

[4] Matt. iii. 12.

Baptist, as we have remarked already, began his ministry in the month of September, with the beginning of the Sabbatic Year; three months after this Jesus appeared upon the banks of the Jordan. According to the primitive traditions they were then in the middle of winter; for the mild climate of Jericho permitted John to pursue his practice of immersion during this season.

Although united by ties of kinship, Jesus and His Forerunner do not seem to have had any intercourse until this time. One had grown up in Galilee, the other in the desert. "I did not know Him,"[1] is said twice, in fact, by John the Baptist, "but He Who hath sent me to baptize with water said to me: 'He upon Whom you shall see the Holy Ghost coming down and abiding with Him, He it is Who baptizeth with the Holy Ghost.'" Watching solely for the fulfilment of this promise, John awaited the covenanted signal from on high.

But even before this marvel did actually take place, the Prophet recognized Jesus. It may have been by revelation from Heaven; it may have been by some divine lineaments making the Master known to His messenger. The Lord had followed the throng of Galileans to the Jordan; He was therefore surrounded by the surging crowds when He was seen by the Precursor. John had thought to finish his ministry when the Christ should appear; so what must have been his awe and wonder when he saw Him descending into the waters of the stream with the penitents, and heard Him ask for baptism at his hands!

"I ought to be baptized by Thee," he exclaimed, "and dost Thou come to me!" and he withstood Him.[2]

"Suffer Me to do this now," said Jesus; "thus it behoveth us to fulfil all justice."

It was indeed the decree of Heaven that the Christ should efface our sins by placing Himself among the ranks of common sinners.

---

[1] John i. 31, 33.
[2] Διεκώλυεν (Matt. iii. 14) is a stronger expression than κώλυω, and well describes how earnestly John at first rejected the idea of baptizing Jesus, and how he withstood Him as far as might be.

John resisted no longer, but immersed Jesus in the Jordan; and lo, at the moment when the Lord arose from the waters, and was in prayer, the heavens were thrown open, the Holy Ghost came down upon Him in the form of a Dove, and rested over Jesus; at the same time a Voice came from the far heights, which said: "This is My dearly beloved Son, in Whom I am always well pleased."

This Vision does not seem to have attracted the attention of the Jews towards Jesus. Without doubt they did not hear the Voice of God, but only, as it were, a noise as of thunder;[1] but John could not have misapprehended the Spectacle which was intended for his eyes alone. In that instant he perceived all that appeals to our reverent thoughts of it, — the Trinity made manifest to man for the first time: the Father in the Voice falling from the heavens, the Son in Jesus, the Holy Ghost in the Dove, symbol of grace, whose reign was now begun in the world. Then, too, he saw the waters of earth sanctified by the presence of the Christ, receiving of Him the power to purify souls in baptism. Then he saw Jesus proclaimed the Son of God, — that Son of Whom the Psalmist sang,[2] begotten in the Bosom of God before the day-star and the sunrise were conceived.

Drawn thither by memories such as these, a caravan of some six or seven thousand pilgrims every year leaves the Holy City, in the Paschal Season, to go down to the Jordan; at its head marches the Pasha of Jerusalem, and a Turkish escort wards off the robbers, who still infest the defiles just as they did in the days of the good Samaritan. These throngs, of most various complexion and costume, make their camp at evening near Gilgal, in the place where the Israelites long since pitched their tents, after having crossed the stream.[3] On the morrow, two hours before dawn, the clang of the kettle-drums awakens the multitude; thousands of torches flare up over the plain, and the crowds are far along on their road before the heat of the day becomes in-

---

[1] S. Justin (*Dialogus cum Tryphone*, par. 88) adds this apocryphal touch to the picture: he says that the Jordan was suddenly changed to a stream of radiant fire.
[2] Ps. cix. 3.   [3] Josue iii.

supportable. The first rays of the sun are just gilding the mountain-tops of Moab, when the great Caravan arrives at the spot where the Jordan is of easy access; horses, asses, mules, camels (which sometimes carry a whole family), pick out a pathway through the brushwood, and so, wading out in the current, the pilgrims perform their pious ablutions.[1]

Formerly, at that place, long marble slabs beautified the banks, and a Cross rose out of the midst of the waves above the very spot where Jesus was baptized. Priests went before the pilgrims into the waters, to sanctify them with solemn prayers, casting balm and flowers on the stream; then only did the faithful step down into the river, clad in a garment which they afterwards took away with them, and in which they were robed in death.[2]

These customs are now but a dim-remembered story. The churches, the monasteries, once so numerous along the banks, to-day only encumber them with their ruins; while the pilgrims who bathe in the stream are no longer sons, as of old, submissive to their Mother. Greeks, Copts, Jacobites, Armenians, all have rent asunder the seamless robe of the Church, and display before the eyes of the Mussulmans those piteous divisions which they have made in the Kingdom of the Christ. Nevertheless they all, by this common homage paid to the Jordan and to Jesus, bear witness to the fact that in these lands the Saviour once besought His Father that the one Baptism and one only Faith might regenerate the world. This Prayer, uttered by Him unto whom the Heavens hearkened "for the reverence which was His due,"[3] may not be denied forever. A time will come — would that it might be soon! — when all Christian peoples will plunge once more into the rivers of Jordan to be made one in Jesus, without a shadow of reserve, in a perfect Unity of faith, hope, and love.

[1] See the masterly description of this scene in Stanley's *Sinai and Palestine*, chap. vii. 3. We could do no more than borrow a few details from that admirable work of art; the picture is too vast for us to reproduce it here in its entirety.
[2] *Itinerarium* B. Antonini Martyris.   [3] Hebr. v. 7.

CHAPTER III.

THE TEMPTATION.

Matt. iv. 1-11 ; Mark i. 12, 13 ; Luke iv. 1-13.

The Holy Spirit had rested upon Jesus, not only to bear witness outwardly to the grace which abounded within Him, but to exercise an active influence over Him. And therefore, so soon as the Christ had received this consecration, He was "led by the Spirit," Saint Matthew recounts;[1] "impelled," says Saint Luke;[2] "thrust out," borne away, driven "into the desert," according to Saint Mark.[3] The energy of the terms chosen by the Evangelists plainly indicates that though the Spirit of God never failed to guide the steps of the Saviour, yet there was, here and now, a more sensible and lively motion than was customary upon the part of the Holy Ghost.

Intrusting Himself to this Divine Compulsion the Lord went up into the desert.[4] By this name all the traditions understand a certain hill to the west of Jericho, which now bears the name of the Fortieth (Quarantine), in memory of the Fasting of Jesus, rising above the Fountain of Eliseus, its sides all honeycombed with caves. Long ago, whole communities of hermits dwelt there, anxious to lead their solitary life in imitation of their Redeemer, in the very spot where He consecrated, by His example, the way of abstinence and prayer.

But no monastic discipline ever equalled in austerity the penance done by Jesus; for it was in the midst of winter that He buried Himself in that retreat — at a time when the wilderness is more desolate than ever, — the

---

[1] Matt. iv.   [2] Luke iv.   [3] Mark i.   [4] Matt. iv.

very skies are pitiless, and the trees are bare of fruit, and stripped of their leafy screens. Here He abode in an entire solitude, "alone with the wild beasts,"[1] surrounded by lions and leopards, which lurk in the thickets of the Jordan,[2] amid the jackals whose mournful howling is still heard along the mountains. And they harmed Him not; for the creatures are but armed against a sinful race,[3] and the Holiness of Jesus held absolute sway over their savage natures.

But it was to attain far other triumphs than these that the Saviour had gone up into the desert. He had come hither that He might be tempted. The New Adam, He was come to take up the combat at the point where the first had failed and fled, and to turn defeat into victory. Yet what manner of trial was this with which He must needs make issue? Must we really, with the rationalists, treat it all as a vision, in which the Christ, like the heroes of ancient fable, was given to choose between the paths of Virtue and of Vice? Did the Saviour, in relating His Temptation to His disciples, represent it as being merely an allegory? There is nothing in the Gospels to suggest such a thought; and it is only by a preconceived idea of stripping the scene of everything marvellous that one can be brought to consider it otherwise than as an actual happening.

However it is a profitless effort at best; for what astounds us in the inspired record is not so much the wonders wrought, then and there, as it is the simple fact of a God being tempted. Theology has no problem to offer us requiring more delicate discrimination in its solution. Could the world have anything wherewith to seduce a Divine Nature? Where was the merit in such a victory for a Soul which could not sin? At every step the mind must halt before the brink of an abyss, and of necessity we must acknowledge that here the mystery of the Incarnation presents one of its features which still remains shrouded in deepest obscurity to mortal ken.

Without pretending to illuminate those infinite depths,

---

[1] Mark i. 13.   [2] Jerem. xlix. 19, l. 44; Zachar. xi. 3.
[3] Rom. viii. 19-22; Wis. v. 21.

we ought to make it clearly understood, however, that the greatest difficulty comes from the idea, ordinarily entertained, that the Temptation of Jesus was like to ours. There is scarcely any appetite for evil in us which does not leave some traces of its passage through our souls. Let the wretched thought be as swift as may be, the first movement of the heart is too often as if she would detain it. There was nought of this in Jesus; for having taken no part in the perversion of our humanity, he could not know those desires which awake within us without our consent, and which are nevertheless our own, because we can detect therein either the promptings of past faults, or the seed sown by inherent concupiscence. Jesus was but tempted outwardly, by an imagery and eloquence appealing most strikingly to the senses, yet without the possibility of such attractions hurting His Soul or staining it. If clear water be absolutely free from all impurity, the rudest shock will not at all disturb or sully its sweet limpidity; yet if it rest upon a miry bottom, the least movement will suffice to drabble it. Thus it is with Jesus and with us; those same storms in which our sinful natures oftenest suffer shipwreck could only assault and buffet Him; they could not soil the purity of the Son of Mary.

Incorruptible in the bosom of corruption, none the less was Jesus made acquainted with the struggles of our daily warfare, even as He tasted all the glories of such victory. His resistance, which was that of a hero in this Temptation in the desert,— which later on in the Garden of Gethsemani was unto the shedding of blood,— this divine hardihood was then, and will ever continue to be, His eternal merit. And that we may better comprehend it, it is important to remember that His time of trial was not limited to the three assaults whose details are known to us, but that it was an issue consuming all of the forty days during which Jesus remained in the desert. During all that time He was tempted:[1] "And now He can have compassion upon our infirmities. for, without sinning, He hath been subject to all our temptations."[2]

[1] Mark i. 13; Luke iv. 2.   [2] Hebr. iv. 15.

It was also a season of penance for the Saviour, through which He passed without eating or drinking. It would seem that during that long fast, wrapped in prayer and inward strife, He remained unconscious of the needs of the body; "but when the forty days were spent,[1] He was hungry," and the Demon profited by that hour of weakness to attack Him in person. Under what semblance[2] did he present himself before Jesus? Was it as a Spirit of darkness, as an Angel of light, or with the features of man? This the Lord did not disclose; and there is little to be gained for us by forming any conjectures.

Not less clouded in obscurity is the character of the conflict in which such mighty powers were brought to battle. Was there only that threefold attack of sensuality, vainglory, and ambition? Surely to concede only such feeble weapons as these to Satan, now in arms against his Lord, were to underrate the artifice and cunning of the Fiend. Though the Saviour passed through all our common trials, yet all that was during the forty days which preceded the last combat; at this hour, wherein the Prince of Darkness entered the lists, it would be only natural to expect that the allurements would take on somewhat of nobility commensurate with Him toward Whom they were directed, and at the same time something super-subtile and strange worthy of the fallen Angel, whose wiles were all exerted then. The aim of the Tempter seems to be betrayed even in his questions. He wanted to know surely

---

[1] Luke iv. 2. The fasting of Moses upon Sinaï (Deut. ix. 9) and that of Elias on his journey toward Horeb (3 Kings xix. 8) lasted the same length of time, and in Holy Writ this number is manifestly held to be the prescribed period of penitence. We find the same in the forty days and forty nights of the Deluge (Gen. vii. 4), in the forty years which Israël passed in the wilderness (Num. xiv. 33), in the forty blows of the thong which the Law inflicted upon the guilty (Deut. xxv. 3), in the forty years of desolation which Ezechiel foretold for Egypt (Ezech. xxix. 11); in a word, everywhere where there is any question of chastisement or of sufferings (S. Jerome, *in Jon.* iii. 4). Thus the Church, inspired by the example of Jesus, every year commands the faithful to observe the forty days' fast of Lent.

[2] The language of Scripture and Tradition do not admit of a doubt as to the fact of Satan having appeared to Jesus under a visible and tangible shape.

who Jesus was;[1] for that keen intellect, which still remained in spite of his overthrow as clear as ever, had seen in the Divine Counsels that his ruin and the salvation of the world would be consummated on the day when the Son of God should become Incarnate.[2]

So then he approached the Saviour: "If you are the Son of God, command these stones to become bread!"

The snare was worthy of the hand that fashioned it. Satan did not offer to those eyes hollowed by long fasting, to the lips parched with thirst, to that famished body, the enticement of luscious fruits or savory meats. He was content to remind Him Whom no lust could have mastered that He, the Son of God, held nature at His beck, and that one word from Him would suffice to change the stones into bread. Was it befitting that the Christ should perish of hunger in this wilderness, where Heaven seemed to have abandoned Him? Was it not high time to have recourse to His almighty Attributes?[3]

But Jesus could not forget that it was the will of His Father that He use this power of miracles, which belonged to Him, not for Himself, but for others. With one word He thrust back the Tempter:—

"It is written: Man does not live by bread alone, but by every word[4] which comes from the mouth of God."

Even as Israel was nourished with Manna during the forty years in the desert,[5] so the Christ would intrust Him-

---

[1] "Dæmon Christum aggressus est, potissimum ut exploraret utrum vere Filius Dei esset" (Suarez, *In tertiam partem divi Thomœ*, quæstio xli. art. i. com. ii.).

[2] Suarez, *In tertiam partem divi Thomœ*, quæstio xli. art. i. com. ii.

[3] "Hac tentatione voluit diabolus Christum allicere ad vanam suæ potentiæ ostentationem, et ad diffidentiam opis Dei Patris; quasi diceret: Pater tuus per quadraginta dies tui oblitus est, nec tibi cibum submisit; tu ergo tibi ipsi consule" (Cornelius a Lapide, *Commentaria in Matthæum*, iv. 3).

[4] Matt. iv. 4; Deut. viii. 3; or more exactly, "of everything which comes from God." In order to give the words the deep significance which they have in the Hebrew, עַל־כָּל־מוֹצָא, they must be rendered "all that which cometh."

[5] "You shall remember," Moses had said to them, "the ways whereby the Lord has led you during these forty years to afflict you and try you, in order that He might lay bare all that was hidden in your hearts, and that

self to the Divine Loving-kindness, seeking above all else that support of the soul, which is the Word of God, His Truth.

Jesus had not responded to that query: "If you are the Son of God;" but the Devil knew that a superior being stood before him, — in all likelihood the Messiah promised to Israel. Thereafter he had but one intention, — to bring the Christ to unveil His Mission, and thereby His nature.[1]

Therefore he transported Him to the Holy City,[2] and placed Him upon a pinnacle [3] of the Temple. Then, point-

---

He might know whether you would be constant or unfaithful to His Commandments. He has afflicted you with hunger, and He has given you Manna, a food unknown to you and to your fathers, to show you that man does not live by bread only, but by all things which proceed from the mouth of God" (Deuter. viii. 2, 3).

[1] The two Evangelists who give the details of the threefold Temptation do not follow the same order. S. Matthew puts the scene on the pinnacle of the Temple second, — in the place where S. Luke has the temptation upon the high mountain. Although the latter is generally more careful than the other in his chronological details, yet S. Matthew, who lived so long with Jesus, and hence gathered his knowledge of the Temptation from His lips, is more likely here to give the actual order of events. Then too, the terms used by him to connect the facts seem to imply as much (τότε "then," πάλιν, "and again"); and further, the words by which both depict the Devil meeting with his repulse upon the high mountain ("Begone from here, Satan!") would lead us to suppose that that was the arena of the final trial.

[2] The thought that that spotless Tabernacle of His body should be not merely touched by the foul fiend, but surrendered to his pleasure, to be borne by him up to the very summit of God's Sanctuary, this has dismayed the loving hearts of many a Christian from the days of S. Cyprian even to to-day, and with him, many interpreters of the text have held that this scene was all a vision; but the more commonly held opinion is that Jesus really submitted to these outrages. He Who delivered over His limbs to the torturers, to be lashed and tortured, to be covered with spittle and stretched upon a cross, may well have permitted the Prince of Darkness to exercise his awful powers upon His sacred Person.

[3] The pinnacle whither Jesus was transported is not clearly indicated in the Gospel; however, it does not seem to mean the summit of the Holy of Holies, for the sacred text does not speak of the Sanctuary proper (ναοῦ), but of the Temple in general (ἱεροῦ). One of the porticos which surround the Holy Place seems most likely to have been the spot; perhaps the Royal Portico to the south of the sacred edifice; or it may have been Solomon's Portico, which bordered the torrent of Kedron on the east. The roof of this lofty gallery projected out over the Courts of the Temple (πτερύγιον= ἀκρωτήριον, Hesychius); it was from this point that James, the brother of the Lord, preached to the people, and was precipitated thence to the pave-

ing to the crowds which thronged its courts, He insinuated that the Saviour might well perform some notable prodigy in the sight of His people.

"If you are the Son of God," he said, "cast yourself below; for it is written that He hath given command to His Angels to keep guard over you,[1] and they shall bear you up in their hands, for fear lest your feet should strike against a stone."

To descend encircled by Angels, to appear before the upturned eyes of men in this celestial pomp, would not this be to compel their wondering worship and to draw all hearts unto Him?[2] Satan could not have conceived a temptation more alluring to the Messiah than was this, and that he might render it irresistible he fortified it by the very language of Scripture.

Vain and useless wiles; for Jesus was come to irradiate the eyes, not of the flesh, but of the spirit, and to conquer souls by a grace unknown to the haughty. So He was content to add: "It is written also: Thou shalt not tempt the Lord thy God."[3]

"Then the Devil transported Him to the top of a tall mountain, whence he showed unto Him in an instant all the empires of the world and their glory.

"I will give you all this power," he said, "and the glory of these kingdoms; for I have them in my dominion, and I distribute them to whom I will,— all these things shall be yours, if, falling down before me, you will adore me."[4]

---

ment below by the furious Scribes (Hegesippus, apud Eusebium, *Historia Ecclesiastica*, ii. 23; Epiphanius, *Adversus Hæreses*, xxix. 4), and from here too Satan could propose that Jesus should descend in the midst of the astounded people.

[1] Matt. iv. 6; Ps. xc. 11.

[2] "Si Filius Dei es, mitte te deorsum,— ut te templi et altaris quasi domus tuæ dominum Deumque sacerdotibus et laïcis ostendas, atque ab eis jus adorationis et sacrificii tibi debitum reposcas" (Cornelius a Lapide, *Commentarii in Matthæum*, iv. 5).

[3] Matt. iv. 7. These words are to be found in various parts of the Old Testament, but particularly in Deuteronomy (vi. 16), where it is added, "As you did once in the place of temptation," that is, at the encampment in Raphidim, when the people, dying of thirst, reproached Moses with having brought them out from Egypt (Exod. xvii. 1-7).

[4] Matt. iv. 8, 9; Luke, iv. 5-7.

We would not attempt to imagine what the surroundings of that last scene in the Temptation were like; for from the summit of the Quarantine, pointed out by the primitive traditions as the locality, the view only extends from Libanus to the desert of Tekoa; while of course it were useless to look for any height whence in the twinkling of an eye one can embrace all the kingdoms of the world. But if we are to see in the very high mountain only a figure of that power over the whole face of the world which the Demon arrogates to himself, still we may ask what is the nature of this his empire, whereof we see to-day only too signal proofs,[1] and what object had he in view by thus tendering it to the Christ? Did he hope to see Him prostrate Himself at his feet? Such blindness as this can hardly be attributed to Lucifer. In this assault of the Tempter, there is evidently nothing but despair at seeing himself overcome by a man, though it be the Man-God;[2] and hence we have this cry of rage and madness. Satan asked no more: "Art Thou the Son of God?" For him there was no longer any room left for doubt; but now, made certain of his downfall, he sought at least to gratify his hate, and so blasphemed openly before the Presence. His last speech upon the mountain is but an echo of that cry of revolt which of old he had flung in the face of Heaven itself. "I will ascend," he had said long since, "and I will be like unto the Most-High!"[3]

At sight of this monster of pride, Jesus, so calm until then, might well have felt a movement of horror.

"Begone, Satan!" He said to him; "for it is written: Thou shalt adore the Lord thy God, and Him only shalt thou serve."[4]

[1] Bossuet, *Élévations sur les mystères*, xxiiie semaine, v^e élévation.
[2] It is the teaching of very famous theologians that the fall of the Angels had its origin in the revelation (vouchsafed to them long ages before the fact) of the Mystery of the Incarnation. The thought that God should ever become Flesh and Blood shocked the haughtiest of those Spirits, and with disdain they refused to adore the high counsels of God, and thus their mad pride hurled them down to the depths of Hell (Suarez, *De Angelis*, lib. vii. cap. xiii. 13).
[3] Is. xiv. 13, 14.
[4] Matt. iv. 10; Deut. vi. 13.

The Demon had discharged his last darts. "All the Temptation being accomplished, he departed from Him for a time,"[1] — until the hour of the Passion, until that desolation upon the Cross, when for the last time he was to attack Jesus with all the fury of despair. During the public life of the Saviour we shall see him retaining such a vivid memory of this first defeat that he is fain to fly distraught from His Presence, now grovelling at His feet, while he confesses His Divinity, now crying out to Him in his terror: "Wherefore comest Thou to destroy us before the time?" now beseeching Him for the bodies of swine, as a last and only refuge.[2]

After the tempest, sweeping wildly over the Mount of the Temptation, suddenly, after the storm was spent, there came a great calm; "the Angels drew nigh unto Jesus, and they served Him."[3] Jewish legends tell how Moses, during his forty days of fasting on Sinai, was nourished by a wondrous harmony, — the hymning of the spheres.[4] Of yet more celestial concord was the banqueting of the Saviour, since He had for ministers unto Him those Spirits of light before whom the stars of the firmament wax pale and wan, and are hushed in silence.

[1] Luke iv. 13.
[2] Mark iii. 11; Matt. viii. 29; Mark v. 11.
[3] Matt. iv. 11.
[4] Schœttgen, *Horæ Hebraicæ*, t. i. p. 87; Philo, *De Somniis*, L 6.

CHAPTER IV.

JOHN BAPTIST'S TESTIMONY, AND THE FIRST DISCIPLES OF JESUS.

John i. 19-52.

ALL the while that Jesus was sustaining that struggle in the desert John continued to preach along the banks of the Jordan. The gatherings grew every day greater, the enthusiasm more intense. Very soon it was spread abroad that a heavenly Voice had marked out One from among the penitents, and that the Baptist had cried aloud to the multitudes: "Behold Him of Whom I have said: 'There cometh after me a Man Who hath been set over me, because He was before me.'"[1]

So, though they had been for a long time indifferent to anything said by this rude preacher, who vouchsafed only anathemas and rebuffs to the princes of Israel, yet at last the members of the Sanhedrin were aroused by these rumors which arose from all round about him. Ablution was to be one of the tokens of the Mission of the Christ.[2] They began therefore to question whether John might not be the Messiah, or at least one of the Prophets who were to announce Him. In order to clear up this doubt the Supreme Council despatched some of its members to the Precursor. Those chosen for this office were priests;[3] because all that pertained to the ablutions lay within the province of the sacerdotal body;[4] and the delegates were also taken from the sect of the Pharisees,[5] noted for their scrupulous respect for all such observances. Certain of

---

[1] John i. 15.   [2] Ezech. xxxvi. 25 ; Zachar. xiii. 1.   [3] John i. 19.
[4] Lev. xii. 6 ; xiii., xiv., xv., etc.   [5] John i. 24.

the Levites[1] acted as a sort of escort in order to enhance the dignity of the embassy.

"Who are you?" asked the ambassadors.

"John confessed it, and denied it not; and he confessed that he was not the Christ." The Evangelist by this repetition shows with what insistence the Precursor reiterated his testimony before the Sanhedrin's envoys: 'I the Christ! I am not; no, I am not He.'

"What, then?" was the response; "are you Elias?"

"No," answered John.

"Are you the Prophet?" they said thereupon, making allusion to the Seer of whom Moses had told them.[2]

"No," replied John.

"Who are you, then?" persisted the members of the Sanhedrin,—"in order that we may render an account to those who sent us here. What do you say of yourself?"

"I am the Voice[3] of one who crieth in the desert: 'Make straight the ways of the Lord!' as hath said the Prophet Isaiah."

This response, far from touching the Pharisees,[4] seemed to them incompatible with the right of preaching and of purifying by ablution, which John claimed for himself.

"Why do you baptize," they said, "if you are neither the Christ, nor Elias, nor the Prophet?"

John replied: "As for me, I baptize in water; but there has been One in your very midst Whom you knew not. He cometh after me, He who hath been set above me;[5] and I am not worthy to loosen the latchet of His shoes."

---

[1] John i. 19.   [2] Deut. xviii. 15.

[3] "What do we mean by a voice? What is it but a breath which fades upon the air? I am a Voice, or, if you will, a Cry. Even to this extent would S. John annihilate his own personality." (Bossuet, *Élévations sur les mystères*, xxive semaine, 1re élévation.)

[4] John i. 25-27. The corrections with which the Manuscripts are covered make it hardly possible to decide whether ἀπεσταλμένοι ought to be read with or without the article. Either way the sense is clearly fixed by the Vulgate: "Et qui missi fuerant, erant ex Phariseis." And thus there is no reason for regarding this as a new embassy of Pharisees which succeeded the first.

[5] The Alexandrine Manuscript, the Peshito, and the Vulgate keep this incidental phrase, which is omitted in the Syriac of the Cureton, the MSS. of Sinaï and the Vatican.

Such steadfastness and humility before one greater than himself disconcerted the councillors of the Sanhedrin, who turned away, disdaining to interrogate him any further. "These things took place at Bethany, on the other side of the Jordan, where John was baptizing,"[1] — that is to say, opposite Jericho, as we have seen, and at one of the fords which allow of the stream being crossed near that city.

The Saviour, on His descending from the Mount of the Temptation, would find His way naturally to this same spot. Indeed, upon the morrow John saw Him coming toward him.[2]

"Behold[3] the Lamb of God!" he said; "behold Him Who beareth the sins of the world!"

This was enough to recall to the minds of the Jews who surrounded him the oracle uttered by Isaiah:[4] "The lamb standing dumb before his shearers, the Man of Sorrows, Who shall bear the sins of the people."

"Look," continued the Precursor, "see, and behold Him of Whom I have said: 'There cometh after me a Man Who hath been set above me, because He was before me.' And I knew Him not; yet I am come, giving you the baptism of water, that so He may be made manifest in Israel."[5]

Plain as these words were, they did not impel any one of those who heard them — on that same day at least — to follow Jesus. The impression which they produced was soon effaced; only a certain few souls cherished the presentiment that salvation was close at hand, and began to turn their eyes to the Saviour. As for the Baptist, he was so

---

[1] John i. 28.
[2] John i. 29–31.
[3] Ἴδε; this word was not addressed to Jesus, but to the multitude: "ἴδε, though in the singular, is often used of many persons."
[4] Is. liii. 7.
[5] This testimony seemed of such importance in the eyes of the Evangelist that he repeats it under another, longer form, as if he regretted having related it too briefly in the former instance: "Then it was that John bare witness: I have seen the Holy Ghost descending from Heaven in the form of a Dove and abiding upon Him; and I had not known Him, but that He Who sent me to baptize with water said to me: He upon Whom thou shalt see the Spirit descending and abiding upon Him, He it is Who baptizeth with the Holy Spirit; and I have seen Him, and I have borne witness unto Him, that He is the Son of God" (John i. 32–34).

used to waiting the divine action that he left all for grace to operate upon the people, contenting himself with simply showing them the Lord, Who must needs call unto Himself those whom He willed, and at what hour He willed to have them come.

On the following day John was walking with two of his disciples when Jesus passed on before them.[1] The Precursor, casting upon Him a glance of infinite meaning,[2] in which shone deep love as well as wondering awe, thus gazing after Him, exclaimed:—

"Behold the Lamb of God!"

Then these two disciples yielded to the prompting of those words, which had touched them so nearly the night before, and they parted company with John to go after Jesus. The Saviour very soon turned about, and seeing that they were following Him, He said: "Whom are you seeking?"

"Rabbi,[3] where do you dwell?" was their reply.

The title they gave the Unknown and this demand of the disciples both declared what hunger and thirst for the truth filled their hearts.

"Come and see," said Jesus. And they went with Him and saw where He dwelt.

The Lord was living in one of the huts which were then built along the banks of the Jordan; perhaps it was merely one of those shelters woven from the boughs of turpentine and palm trees, beneath which the traveller spreads his mantle of hairy skins. It was about four in the afternoon (the tenth hour[4]) when the disciples entered the

---

[1] John i. 35–40.

[2] Ἐμβλέψας (John i. 36. Compare Matt. xix. 26; Luke xx. 17; Mark x. 21).

[3] "Rabbi;" רַבִּי, from the root, רַב, great, corresponds exactly to *Magister* in the Latin tongue, taken from the words *magnus*, *magis*. This title of honor was given to the most famous doctors, to those whose fame consisted not only in forming a school about them, but who were also potent enough to attract the multitude as well (Lightfoot, *Horæ Hebraicæ*, in Matthæum, xxiii. 7).

[4] John i. 39. The Jews computed the twenty-four hours of the legal day as beginning at sunset,—from evening to evening. After the Captivity, although the more ancient custom still existed, they had also

abode of Jesus, and "they passed the rest of the day with Him." The Evangelist does not tell us of their conversation, which was doubtless prolonged until it came to be one of those intimate communions most dear to holy souls, and from which they issue forth filled with new strength and light, with the unassailable certitude that God has revealed Himself to them. When night came on the two disciples were gained unto Jesus; they had recognized in Him the Prophet,— a greater than Moses, Him for Whom Israel had been waiting for so many ages.

One of these young men who in this way came to be the first to attach themselves to Jesus was Andrew, the fisherman of Galilee, born on the shores of Lake Genesareth. The second was no other than John Evangelist. It is easy to divine this fact from his characteristic modesty, which makes him here, as elsewhere, conceal even his name; beside this, there is the minuteness of the narrative, which enters into the slightest details, even to making note of the hour in which Jesus drew these first disciples to Him.

Simon, Andrew's brother, and a fisherman like him, had also quitted the Lake of Genesareth to go down to the Jordan. Andrew came across him.[1]

"We have found the Messiah," he said (that is to say, the Anointed, the Christ), and he brought him to Jesus.

The Saviour looked long upon him. In this Galilean He saw the immovable Rock on which he would build His Church.

"Thou art Simon, son of Jonas," he said to him; "hereafter thou shalt be called Kephas." And this signifies, translating the Hebrew names of which the Lord makes use: Thou art Simon,— child of a dove,[2] feeble and tim-

---

conformed to the method of the Chaldeans, who reckoned the day as commencing at sunrise (six o'clock in the morning). This is what S. John ordinarily does; iv. 6, 52; xi. 9; xix. 14, etc. Consequently there is no reason for adopting Wieseler's theory that the Evangelist here counts the hours starting at midnight.

[1] John i. 41, 42.
[2] Jonas; יוֹנָה, the Dove; or from the root יָנָה, to be feeble; lowliness, weakness (Fürst, Handwörterbuch).

orous as she, but hereafter thou shalt be impregnable as the cliff[1] in which she finds her hiding-place; or again: Thou art the son of feebleness; hereafter thou shalt be firm as a rock, — a play of words made sublime by their depth of meaning, and by the effects which followed upon their utterance; for from that same hour there began the slow working of a wondrous change within the son of Jonas, which was to discover itself to the whole world shortly.[2]

The Church, at its birth, numbered already three members eager to spread abroad their faith. Not far from this spot there was still another Galilean, named Philip;[3] "he was of Bethsaïda, the village of Andrew and Peter." The Lord encountered him on the morrow, when he was preparing for his departure to Galilee.

"Follow Me!" He said to him, thus inviting him to share henceforth His life and His sufferings.

Philip only vaguely understood what was implied in this vocation; notwithstanding, so docile was he that he abandoned himself to grace and followed Jesus.

There were two ways of returning to Nazareth open to the Saviour. The one made its way through Scythopolis and by the sea of Tiberias, keeping to the banks of the Jordan; but the Galileans only took this road, which wound along the river banks, when they wanted to avoid the territory of the Samaritans; whenever the animosity of this people had for a time subsided they preferred a shorter road, which ascends by Bethel, and thence by Sichem and En-Gannim, coming out upon the Plain of Esdralon. A few months later we shall see Jesus taking this direction on His return to Jerusalem, and stopping at Sichem, close by Jacob's Well; but outside the season of Israel's feasts this route was fraught with no perils, and

---

[1] Κηφᾶς, in Aramean, כֵּיפָא; כֵּף, in Hebrew, signifies a stone.

[2] By changing Peter's name in this manner, Jesus, at the very outset, performed an act which declared His authority over His disciples; for the right of imposing a new name, or even of giving it a different meaning by some slight alteration, was a power reserved by law to the magnates and masters of Israel (Gen. xvii. 5, 15; Dan. i. 7, etc.).

[3] John i. 43-45.

the Saviour would therefore choose it for their journey from Jericho to Cana.

Having reached the heights of the hills of Ephraim the little company were passing through Bethel and the meadows which had once witnessed the Vision of Jacob,[1] when they perceived a Jew seated beneath a fig-tree. It was Nathanaël,[2] the friend of Philip, who was to become the fifth disciple of the Saviour.

The son of Tolmaï (Bar-Tolmaï),[3] this newly elect, was of a lineage more noble than the other four,[4] and apparently he always retained something of an air of distinction in the midst of the rest; just as he is represented, in the paintings of the Middle Ages, with his purple mantle broidered with precious stones. He was versed in sacred literature,[5] and perhaps he was meditating there beneath the fig-tree; for the Jews were wont to seek the shade of this tree at the "Hour of Prayer."[6]

---

[1] That allusion to Jacob's Ladder which Jesus makes just a little after this, seems to us to indicate that in the meanwhile they were crossing the heights of Bethel, where everything would recall that famous Vision.

[2] John i. 45–52. Nathanaël; נְתַנְאֵל, God-given. This name, which corresponds to that of Theodore, Θεόδωρος, is found in the Old Testament (Num. i. 8; 1 Paral. ii. 14).

[3] In fact, everything leads us to believe that this new disciple made one of the number in the Apostolic College, and so is no other than Bartholomew. The synoptic writers, it is true, make no mention of a Nathanaël; but, in their lists of the Twelve Apostles, one of them is always inscribed under his family name only, Bartholomew, Bar-Tolmaï, that is, son of Tolmaï. Now it has been generally held that this Bartholomew is the same disciple whom John mentions by his proper name of Nathanaël, and there are numerous reasons for considering this a justifiable hypothesis, — the circumstances under which Nathanaël was called, which are in no way different in solemnity from those connected with the most illustrious Apostles; his presence as one of their number after the Resurrection (John xxi. 2); the place which the name of Bartholomew occupies in the various lists of the Twelve, always in company with Philip, and next after him, so preserving to each their rank in the order of their separate vocations.

[4] "Non Petro vili piscatori Bartholomæus nobilis anteponitur, imo piscatori totius mundi monarchiæ traditur principatus" (S. Jerome, *Epistola ad Eustochium*).

[5] S. Augustine, *in Joan*, i.

[6] R. Hasa et discipuli ejus . . . summo mane solebant surgere et sub ficu studere" (*Bereschith*, fol. 62, 2. See Winer, *Real Wort.*, FEIGENBAUM). Nowadays the country-folk in these parts avoid even the shadow

Philip called to him, telling him: "We have found Him Whom Moses in the Law,[1] and the Prophets, have announced; 't is Jesus, the Son of Joseph of Nazareth!"

Of Nazareth! This name awoke at once in the mind of Nathanaël an invincible objection. Was it not written that the Messiah would be born in Bethlehem?[2] What was to be expected of a man hailing from an obscure village, of ill repute, and in Galilee?

"Of Nazareth!" he replied; "can anything good come from there?"

Philip still believed that Nazareth was the birthplace of Jesus, and of Joseph, His father; he did not know how to respond to the difficulties made by his friend; but with unshaken faith, all he could say was: "Come and see!"

They were indeed the very words of the Master which he repeated then; for he knew what had been their power over Andrew and John, and availed himself of them as though they were some divine charm to lure Nathanaël.

So soon as the Saviour saw the latter coming toward Him: "Behold a true Israelite,"[3] He said, "a man in whom there is no guile!"

What a meed of praise those words bestow! What is there more to be desired than to recognize within one's

---

of this particular tree, declaring that it breeds sickness. Such a complete revolution of feeling in any matter of sentiment is rarely to be found in the East.

[1] Gen. xvii. 7; xlix. 10; Deut. xviii. 15.

[2] The difficulty before which Nathanaël halts now a little later presented itself to the minds of the Jews; but, less docile than he, they let it become a source of scandal and infidelity for themselves. "What, then," they said, "shall the Christ come out of Galilee? Does not the Scripture declare that He shall be born in Bethlehem, the city of David?" And then they turned away in great contempt of the Saviour (John vii. 41, 42).

[3] The Jews preferred this name of Israelite to any other; for, if they must needs share the glory of being the children of Abraham and Isaac with the sons of Ismaël (the Arabs) and of Esaü (the Idumeans), on the other hand they were the sole descendants of Jacob, and this his name Israël, as it was got by conquest in a struggle where the faith of their common father had triumphed with God, so it ever remained in their eyes as their most splendid title of national glory (Gen. xxxii. 24-31).

self this true righteousness, and know that one is "of that Israel which is not of the flesh, but of God?"[1]

Nathanaël, in his surprise at seeing himself already known, replied with quiet candor: "How do you know me?"

"Before Philip called thee," said the Saviour, "when thou wert under the fig-tree, I saw thee."

Evidently Jesus then made an allusion to something that had occurred under the tree, before Philip called to him, — some action which must be still a secret to us, but one which was as well known to Him as it was to Nathanaël. By recalling it, the Lord revealed Himself as the Divine Seer, Whose glance pierces all mysteries.

"Master," cried out Nathanaël, "You are the Son of God, the King of Israel!"

These two titles explain each other. Nathanaël did not make use of the first as meaning that Jesus was the Son of God by nature, equal and consubstantial with His Father; but he recognized in Him the object of His nation's vows, the Son of God, the King of Israel.[2]

---

[1] 1 Cor. x. 18; Gal. vi. 16.

[2] The Jews only needed to meditate upon the inspired sayings of Scripture, in order to be convinced that in God there are several Persons (see Appendix II.), and that the Messiah was to be God (Ps. ii. 7; xliv. 8; Is. ix. 6; Jer. xxiii. 5; Mich. v. 2, etc.). Nevertheless, they habitually used the term "Son of God," as though it meant sonship by adoption, and hence they attributed this title to the Angels (Job i. 6; ii. 1), to the princes of Israel (Ps. lxxxi. 6) and to men distinguished for their pious or noble natures (Gen. vi. 2). This ignorance as to the Mystery of the Trinity, and their attachment to the dogma of the Divine Unity, prevented most of them from believing that the Messiah could be God, as is He Who sent Him; and so we see them, even in the time of the Saviour, welcoming mere individuals as Christs, only asking that they free Judea from her yoke, without troubling themselves at all whether they were the sons of God. Nay more, this title which Jesus took as His Own was a most scandalous act in the eyes of His contemporaries. When they accused Him of blasphemy, when they would have liked to stone Him, it was always when the Lord declared Himself the Son of God, equal to His Father and One with Him (John v. 18; viii. 58, 59; x. 30-36). And when the Sanhedrin passes sentence upon Him, they give as their reason, "that in accordance with our Law He ought to die, because He made Himself the Son of God" (John xix. 7). The Jews generally did not expect a Divine Messiah, and there is very little likelihood that Nathanaël,

Jesus followed out the thought: "Because I have said to thee that I saw thee beneath the fig-tree, thou dost believe; thou shalt see things greater still. Of a truth, ay, of a truth," He repeated, "thou shalt see the heavens opened,[1] and the Angels of God ascending and descending upon the Son of Man."[2]

As we have hinted, the hills of Bethel undoubtedly suggested this allusion to the Lord. Therefore, that which Israel had once beheld in this very land on which they now trod, but had seen only in a dream, this it was given to Nathanaël, the true Israelite, to contemplate in reality: the heavens thrown open, to shower down grace divine; Jehovah, no longer afar off, on the cloud-hung apex of the celestial ladder, but pitching His tent[3] in the midst of us; earth united to Heaven, by ties not visionary but everlasting, by the communion of those Angels who ascend to God, bearing unto Him the prayers of men, and again descend to us, the bearers of His blessing. And this saintly commerce was no far-away hope held out to their longing hearts; for from that very hour[4] Jesus commenced His Office of Mediator. He has given us assurance of this by the affirmation — the form of which Saint John

before being instructed by the Saviour, would have recognized him as the Son of God, by Nature consubstantial with the Father.

[1] In the Holy Books "the heavens opened" was always a figure of the overflowing of God's grace upon man (Gen. xxviii. 12; Is. vi. 1; Ezech. i. 1; Mal. iii. 10).

[2] This name, which recalls those humiliations which the Incarnate Word suffered for our sakes, is found for the first time in the famous Vision in which Daniel describes the glory of the Messiah (Dan. vii. 13). The Prophet, in order to make the contrast more striking, does not make use of the term Ben-Ish or Ben-Adam, but calls Him Ben-Enosh, that is, man in all the weakness inherent in our humanity. It is proper to remark here also that Jesus habitually takes this title just when He has called Himself the Son of God (Matt. xxvi. 64); or when He asserts some of His divine powers, as the right of working miracles (Matt. xii. 28-32; xiii. 41): or of forgiving sins (Matt. ix. 6; xvi. 27; xix. 38). In this manner He proposed to proclaim His human nature and Divine Nature at one and the same time.

[3] Ἐσκήνωσεν (John i. 14).

[4] Ἀπ' ἄρτι is omitted in most of the versions, and in the ancient manuscripts. Still we think that this reading ought not to be overlooked, out of respect for the Syriac Versions and the Alexandrine Manuscript.

has preserved for us, and which so well befitted Him Who is the eternal Amen: "Amen, Amen,[1] I say unto you: You shall see the heavens opened, and the Angels of God ascending and descending upon the Son of Man."

[1] This double Amen occurs here for the first time, and, in its twofold form, is only mentioned by S. John; the other Evangelists content themselves with putting the word "Amen" once in reporting the Saviour's language. We are surely warranted in believing that the beloved disciple would have remembered the words of his Master more faithfully than did any others, and hence we may think that it was a custom with Jesus to reiterate this solemn affirmative, so to add importance to the Truths which He wished to impress on their minds.

CHAPTER V.

THE WEDDING FESTIVITIES AT CANA.

John ii. 1–11.

WITH these five disciples Jesus kept on along the road northwards. As they were journeying without any train or beasts of burden, they were able to make their camp at Sichem on the first night, taking En-Gannim for the second; and from this point, after crossing the plain of Esdralon, they soon reached Nazareth. On their arrival they did not find Mary; for "on the third day[1] there was a wedding celebration at Cana of Galilee, and the Mother of Jesus was there." As He also was invited to take part in their merry-makings, Jesus, in company with His disciples, pushed onwards to Cana[2]

---

[1] John ii. 1. The memory of every hour that he had spent with Jesus was so fresh in the memory of John the Evangelist, that it is enough for him to jot down this detail of time. But with us that "third day" has been construed in several different ways; some by dating from the arrival of Jesus in Cana; others take it to be from the calling of Nathanaël; sometimes it is reckoned from the day following His departure for Galilee; finally it is thought to mean the third after His leaving this first point; and the last opinion strikes us as the most natural supposition.

[2] Kefr Kenna is, in fact, only a league from Nazareth to northward. This poor little village still possesses the ruins of a church which was erected over the very spot where the wedding was celebrated, and they show you the very fountain which undoubtedly supplied the water for the Miracle, since it is the only one in the town. Robinson contends that Kana el-Jalil (located some three hours' journey from Nazareth toward the northeast) ought to have the glory of being the ancient Cana; but all the traditions are against this hypothesis, and they have always pointed out Kefr Kenna as the scene of the Miracle, while the absence of any ruins at Kana el-Jalil is also against it, for all the travellers of olden days speak of the churches and convents which were raised in this hamlet as a witness of the marvel. Hence there is only the closer similarity in the names, which might lead us to prefer Kana el-Jalil. Robinson attached great

that same evening.¹ It was just at the hour when the ceremonies of the marriage were about to commence, and the Lord, on His arrival, could assist as a guest at the most brilliant spectacle of all, — the procession formed by the bridal couple, surrounded by the whole family.² Sacred writers allude so often to the nuptial festivals, that it would suffice merely to collect the words in which they have referred to them, in order to restore for us the bright pageant which was enacted before the eyes of Jesus.

The bride's preparations for this great day were matters of the weightiest moment. From the instant she stepped from her perfumed bath,³ she shed around her such a wealth of fragrance that Solomon compares her, wrapped in her long veils, to a cloud of incense floating over the earth.⁴ These veils are a distinctive feature of the betrothed maiden; not only covering the head, but enwreathing the whole body,⁵ and concealing from sight the white and gold-embroidered robe,⁶ her jewels,⁷ the virgin's girdle (which no one might unclasp save only the joyous spouse),⁸ and the crown of myrtle that encircled her brow.⁹

---

importance to this double name, which is exactly translated in Arabic as "Cana of Galilee." But various travellers who are conversant with that language have since questioned the inhabitants of this region, but without avail; for they all call the village of which Robinson is speaking by the name of Khourbet Kana, and the addition el-Jalil would seem to be a mistake of the learned American. (See Thomson, *The Land and the Book*, p. 425.)

[1] It was very likely of a Tuesday evening, or, to speak more precisely, at an early hour of Wednesday, since it was an ancient custom among the Jews to calculate the day from night to night; it was by the order of Esdras (*Ketoubot*, i. 1) that the marriage feast must commence on this day when the bride was a maiden, and on a Thursday if she were a widow.

[2] Although the oath taken by the bridal pair (Ezech. xvi. 8; Mal. ii. 14), and the blessings which they then received (Gen. xxiv. 60; Ruth iv. 10; Tob. vii. 15), gave to the marriage its sacred character, yet the splendor of the nuptial procession was so notable a feature, that this latter ceremony was popularly regarded as the principal event of a Jewish wedding.

[3] Ruth iii. 3; Ezech. xxiii. 40.
[4] Cant. iii. 6.
[5] Gen. xxiv. 65; xxxviii. 14.
[6] Apoc. xix. 8; Ps. xliv. 10, 14.
[7] Is. xlix. 18; lxi. 10; Apoc. xxi. 2.
[8] Jer. ii. 32.
[9] *Ketoubot*, ii. 1.

The young maid, thus attired at the hands of her girl companions, awaited the arrival of the bridal retinue. By her side the paranymph, or bridesmaid, kept watch with the ten virgins, who must needs accompany her with lamps in their hands. It was generally at a late hour that the cry rang out: "Behold the bridegroom is here! Come ye out to meet him!"[1] In those lovely nights of the Orient, which well-nigh surpass anything our days can boast in the way of soft splendor and delicious balminess, the procession advances, led first by a troop of singers, their voices mingling with the notes of the flute and the clash of tambourines;[2] while, last of all, comes the bridegroom, gorgeously clad, his forehead wreathed with a golden turban entwined with myrtle and rose. About him march his ten friends, called "Sons of the Groom,"[3] holding palm branches in their hands;[4] while his kinsmen, acting as his escort, bear lighted torches,[5] and the daughters of Israel greet him on every hand with their laughing compliments.[6] The bridegroom and his companions enter within the dwelling of the young maiden, and, taking her by the hand, he leads her toward the threshold; and here he receives the tables of stone on which is inscribed the dowry;[7] whereupon, in merry marching train, the guests retrace their way back to the house of the fortunate youth.

A banquet is there made ready,[8] which always lasted for many a long hour, enlivened by gay enigmas and bright sallies of wit.[9] A whole week, sometimes even two, slipped by amid such rejoicings;[10] and so, to put somewhat of a check on this immoderate joy, and to recall their minds to thoughts of graver things, it was the custom, from time to time, for some one to shatter the wine-glasses of the happy

---

[1] Matt. xxv. 6.
[2] Gen. xxxi. 27; Jer. vii. 34; xvi. 9; 1 Mac. ix. 39.
[3] Jud. xiv. 11; Matt. ix. 15.
[4] *Ketoubot*, 16, 17; *Sabbath*, 110 a; *Sota*, 49 b.
[5] Matt. xxv. 7.
[6] Cant. iii. 11; Ps. xliv. 15; *Ketoubot*, 15 b.
[7] *Ketoubot*, 1, 2.
[8] Matt. xxii. 1–10; Luke xiv. 8; John ii. 2.
[9] Jud. xiv. 12.
[10] *Ibidem*, xiv. 12; Tob. viii. 23.

pair.¹ This was indeed to show forth in action that thought of the ancient mime: "Fortuna vitrea est, tum quum splendet frangitur."²

> Toute notre félicité,
> Sujette à l'instabilité,
> En moins de rien tombe par terre ;
> Et comme elle a l'éclat du verre,
> Elle en a la fragilité !³

In the time of Jesus, were there the same symbolic rites performed which to-day are peculiar to Jewish marriages, beside the ceremonies already mentioned, — the long white napkin stretched over the head of the newly wed, who sit with their hands clasped under the veil, while the ring is slipped upon the finger of the bride in token of their indissoluble union.⁴ The sacred writings make no mention of these; they only tell how the guests conduct the lady to the nuptial chamber,⁵ where her couch was set in state beneath a canopy,⁶ sometimes even (if we may credit Jewish authorities)⁷ under a bower of blossoms.⁸

Such were some of the ceremonies at which Jesus was a Guest upon "that evening of the third day." In this instance the pomp and splendor were indeed of a somewhat modest degree; for everything seems to indicate that the family which had bidden Jesus as one of their friends

---

¹ *Berachot*, f. 31, 1.
² Publius Syrus.
³ Corneille, *Polyeucte*, acte iv. scène ii.
⁴ These ceremonies are also found in Christian marriages, and we are justified in believing that the primitive Church borrowed them from the Ritual of the Synagogue.
⁵ Jud. xv. 1 ; Joel ii. 16.
⁶ Ps. xviii. 6 ; Joel ii. 16.
⁷ *Ketoubot*, 4, 5.
⁸ On the morrow, if no cloud had appeared to obscure their happiness (Deut. xxii. 13–21), the "Friend of the Bridegroom" returned thanks to God, in the name of all. "Lord God," he said, "King of the Universe, Thou Who hast set a place in Thy Paradise for this sweet-kernelled nut, this rose of the dales, so that no stranger may ever hold domain o'er this sealed fountain — wherefore it is that this fair form of love hath never proven false to her plighted faith: Blessed be Thou forever, O Lord ! O Thou Who hast chosen Abraham and his seed to be Thine own !" (*Halecholh gedoloth*, 51 b.)

was of as humble a station as He: the fact of the wine
having given out so early in the feasting; the air of authority with which Mary, the wife of a carpenter, gives
her orders; the respect shown her Son, who is invited,
although at the time absent from home. The apparent
luxury in the details of the banquet do not really contradict this conclusion; for everything which they might
stand in need of, — ornaments, rich furnishings, service of
all kinds, — these even the poorest people could always
borrow of their neighbors.

Mary, who had preceded her Son to Cana, had betaken
herself thither undoubtedly in order to lend her aid in the
necessary preparations; thus she was able to notice how
little wine her friends had to dispose of; and so too she
was the first to perceive that it was falling short in the
very middle of the repast. It was the unlooked-for arrival
of the five disciples which had brought down this disgrace
upon the young couple; for (according to an ancient witness on this point) "it happened that the wine gave out
in consequence of the great number of guests."[1]

Mary was distressed, and betaking herself to Jesus:
"They have no wine," she said.

Used as she was to seeing her Son anticipate her least
wishes, she continued to treat Him as she had always
done hitherto, still bearing herself as a Mother who is
all-powerful and always to be obeyed.

But now the times were changed. In order to show
Mary that He had ceased to belong to her (yet only that
He might be entirely at the will of His Heavenly Father),
Jesus refused to pay any heed to her appeal.

"Woman," He said to her, "what matters it to you and
to Me? My hour has not yet come."

This answer, which sounds so harshly to our ears, has
not the same meaning in the Aramean tongue. It is in
frequent use among sacred writers, sometimes to denote a
lively objection, sometimes only a simple dissent; both,

---

[1] "Et factum est per multam turbam vocatorum vinum consummari."
(Another reading found in the Italic Version. Codex Rhedigerianus,
vii. century.)

however, were in perfect consonance with the forms of highest courtesy.[1] As for the title "Woman," that was, indeed, a term of respect.[2] In making use of it, Jesus rendered filial homage to her, whom He loved beyond all other creatures, and whose prayer it cost Him so dear to deny.

And, furthermore, we must needs supply to this bare refusal some words which John Evangelist either did not hear, or at least has omitted to report; for we see in the sequel that the response of the Saviour, far from disheartening Mary, gave her yet fuller assurance.

On the instant she gave orders to the servants to hold themselves in readiness at His word: "Anything that He may say to you, do it."

They had not long to delay. The last drops of wine had been poured out; there was nothing now left for the young couple except to make a humiliating avowal of their insufficient stores. Now there were standing close at hand six great urns of stone, covered with branches, as is the custom in the East, in order to keep the water cool and fresh. These vessels, each containing two or three firkins,[3] were kept in readiness for the guests, who were required not only to wash their feet before touching the linen and drapery of their couches, but even during the meal frequently to purify their hands. Already there had been many of these ablutions performed, and the urns were being rapidly emptied. At a word from Jesus, the servants filled them with water to the brim.

"Draw out now," said the Lord, "and bear it to the Master of the Board."[4] This was one of the guests, selected

---

[1] Jos. xxii. 24; Jud. xi. 12; 2 Kings xvi. 10; 3 Kings xvii. 18; 4 Kings iii. 13.

[2] This is the very style in which Augustus salutes Cleopatra (Dion Cassius, *Historiæ*, li. 12). In a Chorus of Æschylus, it is the title given to the Queen, Clytemnestra, and it is a word often used of princesses by the tragic poets.

[3] The metrix : $\mu\epsilon\tau\rho\eta\tau\acute{\eta}s$, so called because it was the standard measure of capacity among the Greeks; it was the cubic foot of twenty-seven litres. But the Roman amphora, which contained but nineteen litres, was also known by the name of a metrix, and it may have been this latter measure that S. John had reference to here.

[4] Some have thought that this master of the feast was a higher servant, hired to overlook the arrangements for the banquet, and to set in order

to preside over the feasting and to keep watch so that there might be nothing lacking. The serving-men presented him with the drinking-cup. He tasted the water changed to wine, without knowing whence it came. Those who had drawn it out were not ignorant; but even so, the stupor that had fallen on them at sight of such a prodigy now enchained their tongues.

The master of the festal board called to the bridegroom: "Every man," said he, "serves the good wine first, and when some one has over-drunk, then he serves up what is not so good. But you — why, you have kept the best until this hour!"

This bantering allusion to drinkers who dull the edge of their taste by over-much indulgence, — the familiar hint anent the usual excesses at other wedding banquets, where there is not (just as here there was) permeating the feeling of all a sense of some Divine Influence present amongst them, — all this shows that the supposition arrived at by the master of the entertainment was that the young host had wished to surprise the company agreeably. But at once, to his amazement, the latter was made aware that a wondrous deed had been accomplished. His eyes turned to the servers, to Mary. Then in a few words all was disclosed. Jesus had performed His first Miracle.

He did it to console a few Galileans, whose very names still remain unknown, and in order to sanctify the bond of Marriage, which was to become, in His Church, a sacramental union. He did it to teach the world, which gives its best at first and leaves the dregs at the bottom of the cup, that the Christ would not so deal with us, — that He

---

the wines and the meats. It is true the ancients had some such butlers, or, as the Latins called them, "Tricliniarchæ" (Patronius, *Satyricon*, 22 ; Heliodorus, vii. 27) ; the Greeks called him τραπεζοποιοί (Athena, 170 d) or τραπεζοκόμοι (Diogenes of Laërtes, 9, 80). In this case, was he not rather the συμποσίαρχος, " the arbiter bibendi," who was chosen from among the guests (Hermann, *Lehrbuch der griechischen Privataltertümer*, par. 28, 29). A passage in Ecclesiasticus (xxxii. 1, 2) shows us that that office was in use among the Jews, and the familiar freedom with which the governor of the feast addresses the bridegroom gives us a good reason for thinking that he could not have been his servant, but his equal, and consequently one of the invited friends.

would reserve for eternity that wine of the elect which will inebriate us with holy raptures. And finally, He did it at the prayer of Mary, whose faith, thus tested by a first refusal, shone out in its strength only the more triumphantly.

"Here then took place," the Evangelist adds,[1] "the first sign given by Jesus, being given at Cana in Galilee; and thus He manifested His glory, and His disciples believed in Him." This word "sign"[2] tells us what the Miracles of the Saviour were for John, — the manifestation of His Divinity. Elsewhere he goes so far as to call them the "works"[3] of the Christ, as if prodigies were but the natural Attribute of Him, in Whom resideth almighty powers, and that the real miracle would be, not for God, whose name is Wonderful, to do wondrous things, but for Him not to do them. And so the miracles which Jesus will work beneath our eyes should only be for us as signs and tokens, as the lustrous rays of His Divinity piercing through the veils of the flesh. In those moments which will sometimes come upon us, when the humiliations of the Word Incarnate do well-nigh shake our faith, and force from us that cry of bewilderment: "Why, what is there Godlike in all this?" then at once the answer should spring to our lips: "His Miracles declare His might; and in these flashes of power He stands forth revealed, as in the fierce white glare of the lightning, the almighty Son of God."[4]

[1] John ii. 11.
[2] Σημεῖα.
[3] Ἔργα (John v. 36, vii. 21, x. 25, etc.) The Synoptical writers, who have most in mind the amazement which overwhelmed the witnesses of these extraordinary deeds, speak of them as "prodigies" (τέρατα).
[4] Pascal, *Pensées*, art. xxv. 95.

CHAPTER VI.

GENESARETH.

WHAT was it that occurred at Nazareth when Jesus returned thither? The Gospel does not tell; but apparently something happened which rendered any tarrying in this village either painful or perilous for the Saviour, since Saint John adds immediately: "After that, He descended to Capharnaum with His Mother, His brothers, and His disciples."[1] The uncouth violence of the Nazarenes was proverbial.[2] Perhaps they refused to see anything but a clever imposture in the miracle of Cana, and so would force this "son of Joseph" to take Himself out of their country.[3]

From Nazareth to Capharnaum is about a day's journey, which, as indeed may be inferred from Saint John's expression, is only a long descent[4] down the slopes of the hills of Zabulon. The traveller reaches the end of his road, when, on coming out of the Valley of Doves (Ouadi el-Hamâm), he beholds at his feet the Sea of Galilee. The long and narrowing outlines of the lake's formation, with the rippling of its waters, suggested the idea of a harp, from which the Hebrews gave it the name Chinnereth.[5] In the time of Jesus it was oftener called the Sea of Tiberias; or again, the Lake of Genesareth, from the plain, which bloomed and flowered like a garden-bed,[6] encircling

---

[1] John ii. 12.   [2] John i. 46.   [3] Luke iv. 22.
[4] κατέβη (John ii. 12).   [5] Num. xxxiv. 11.
[6] Genesareth, according to some authorities, is merely an altered form of the Hebrew פָּרֵיה, the פ being changed to ג, and the ם inserted into the body of the word. But it would appear to mean rather the Valley of Flowers, from גַּיְא, "valley" and נֵצֶר, "a flower" (S. Jerome, *Opera*, t. xvii. p. 103 *b*, Migne Edition); or again, it may mean the Garden

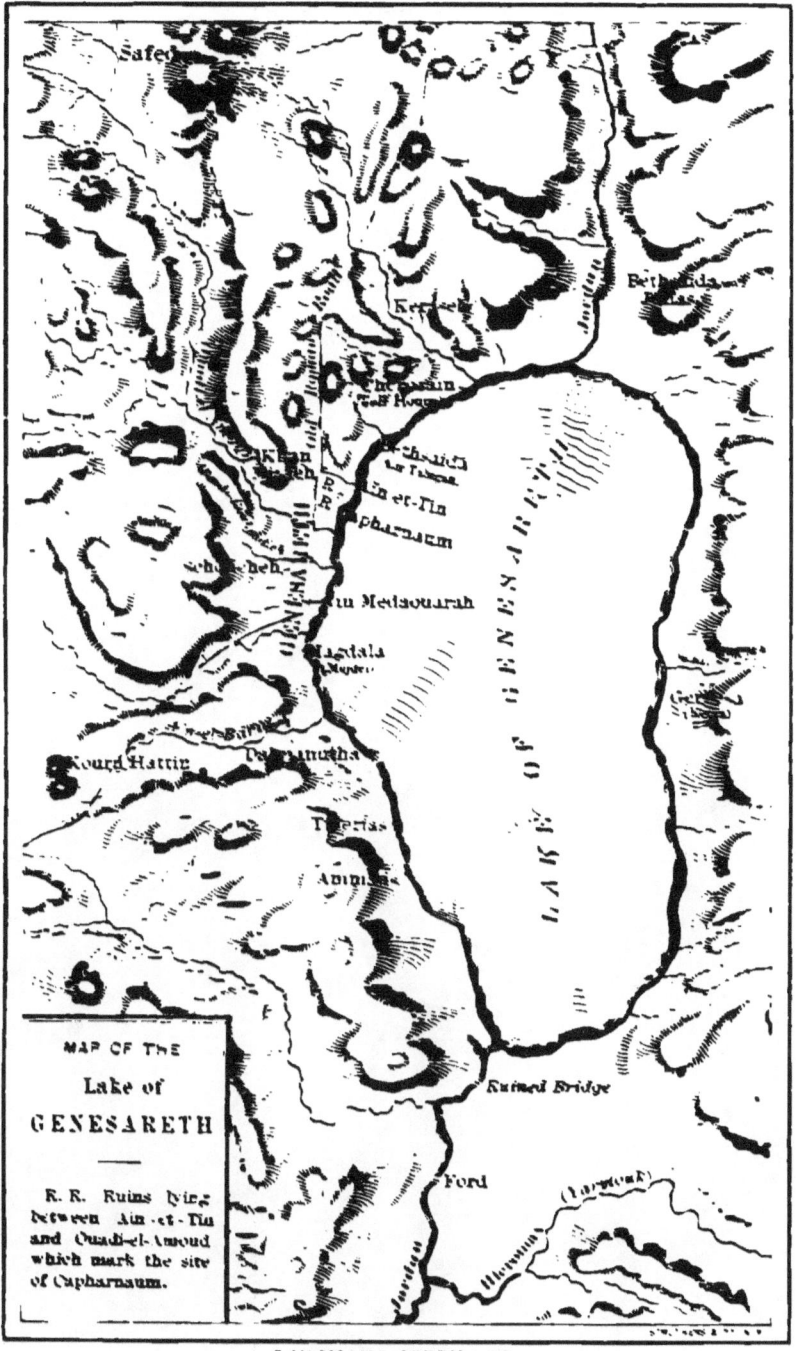

its shores. The Jews, in their admiration for this beautiful sheet of water, hold that the Lord once said: "Seven lakes have I created, yet but one of them have I reserved unto Myself, — the Lake of Genesareth."[1] But the renown of this lake rests not so much upon its beauty as upon our memories of Jesus. Here everything recalls the Master, — the waves over which His bark furrowed its way; the fertile banks along which He wandered; the rich harvest-fields; the sea-beach where He was so often to be found seated, sometimes in solitude, sometimes surrounded by the listening throngs. In the distance you may still see those same bleak, bare mountain-peaks which were the lonely watchmen at His hours of prayer. There is no region which was witness to a greater number of His prodigies, nor one that hearkened for a longer period to His heavenly accents; thereby it is too endeared to all Christian hearts to pass over without striving to bring up a picture of it in our minds.

The Lake of Genesareth is one of the three deep basins which are filled by the waters of the Jordan, on its course to the south. Though it stretches out to a greater width than the Marsh of Houleh, yet it has not the dimensions of that sea of pitch into which the Jordan empties its waters;[2] but in the epoch of the Christ, the two lakes formed an astonishing contrast. Everything round about the one was teeming with life, — its clear depths so well stocked with fish, its outlying lands lovely with flowers and fruit; while over and about the other there lay a horror as of death, — with its sluggish sulphurous flow, with no living creature in its floods of bitumen, with its blasted and riven banks. Nevertheless, each of these wide expanses of plain and water, now so different of aspect, had once rivalled one another in fertility. When

---

of the Princes, if with Lightfoot we derive it from נא, "valley," and שׂר, "a prince."

[1] *Midrasch Fillim*, f. 4, 1.

[2] The Lake of Genesareth is about five leagues long by two in width. The dimensions of the Dead Sea, which vary with the different seasons, have never been taken very exactly; generally it is given as being twenty-five leagues long by four leagues in its broadest part.

from the highlands of Bethel Lot looked down on the Lake of Sodom[1] and the Vale of Siddim, he found them both equally grateful and pleasant to the sight, even as the gardens of the Lord and the banks of the Nile.[2]

There were, in fact, the same causes which could not but have produced an equal fertility; for indeed these two seas are nothing but craters of extinct volcanoes, sunken so far within the burning soil that the Jordan, after entering the Lake of Genesareth, ranges to a depth of a hundred and ninety-one metres below the level of the Mediterranean.[3]

In such low-lying lands the earth, warmed by a sky of fire, while it is refreshed with abundant waters, clothes the fields with every variety of plant. "The walnut, a tree of colder regions, here springs up majestic, while the palm-tree bends beneath its load of fruit, as in the torrid zones. At their side products of the temperate climes here thrive and flourish, — the grape, the fig, and the olive. It seems as if Nature had reversed all her laws to gather together in these places everything she has to offer which could present the most striking contrast, — those which in their native habits are the most opposite. The different seasons here dispute with one another for the sway, and exert their influence simultaneously. Figs and grapes ripen, without intermission, during ten months, and the other fruits never are damaged by any season of the year."[4]

In this picture it is easy to recognize the touch of a Galilean, proud of his fatherland and its beautiful lake. There is not a particle of exaggeration in it, however; for even in our days, only let the Bedouins cease from their ravagings for a season, and the traveller will still find the

---

[1] Those twin cities of vice and sin stood in that southern part of the peninsula of Lisan, in the region around the Dead Sea that sunk in the fearful catastrophe in which Sodom was involved; in our times the foul waters which cover it are but a few feet in depth. The primitive lake lay in the northern part of the present basin; in fact, soundings made there have shown very great depth (three hundred and fifty metres in certain spots).

[2] Gen. xiii. 10.

[3] The depression of the Dead Sea is twice this, — three hundred and ninety-four metres below the level of the sea.

[4] Josephus, *Bellum Judaicum*, iii. 10, 8.

palm-trees overshadowing the Lake of Tiberias; in the meadows of Magdala he will see the indigo, the lotus, and sugar-cane, while all around the lake still gleams a crimson girdle of laurel-roses.[1]

With no less complacency does Josephus boast of the fecundity of the waters. The fish were so abundant that the fishermen living along its banks could be counted by the hundred; there were even two villages bearing the name of Bethsaïda (The Fishery House). Therefore, ever since the partition of Judea among the sons of Israel, the right of casting nets into the lake had been reserved, as the common privilege of each and every inhabitant, by a law of Moses.[2] In the time of Jesus thousands of bright sails sparkled over the sea: there were Roman galleys, Herod's fine fleet, and fishermen's craft in plenty. To-day there are only three boats, which lie almost unused by the indolent seamen of Tiberias and Mejdel.[3]

So it was, too, with the cities of the lake; to-day lying in ruins, formerly so busy and populous. They were mostly dotted in a close line along the western shore; for on the eastern side the scarped and steep cliffs, rising from the water's edge, make the shore inaccessible, except by way of the gorges, through which rush the mountain torrents in the winter season. Of all these towns the city of Tiberias was the most famous. Herod Antipas had only recently founded it, in honor of his protector Tiberius, and with such sumptuosity of architecture and ornament as the tastes which he had cultivated during his sojourn in Rome now prompted. However, in his contempt for all Judaic customs, he had erected his Capitol upon the site of an ancient cemetery; and by so doing had closed its portals so far as the Jews were concerned, for they could not enter therein without contamination.[4] It was useless for him to

---

[1] Kitto, *Cyclopædia:* PALESTINE; Murray, *Handbook for Syria and Palestine*, route 28, Magdala.
[2] *Baba Kamma*, 81, 1, 2.
[3] Two of these barks were put in use by us when we sailed over the lake in 1879, and the third followed in our wake. If what our rowers told us was true, there was not another boat on the lake at that time.
[4] Num. xix. 11; Josephus, *Antiquitates*, xviii. 2, 3.

multiply his solicitations, his favors, his privileges: he never triumphed over the scruples of his people. Tiberias still remained, for the most part, a city of foreigners, — Greeks and Romans, who were charmed with a residence more Pagan than Jewish in tone and aspect, with the gilded palace of Antipas, his amphitheatre, and the warm baths of the ancient Ammaüs.[1] It is more than probable that Jesus never entered the gates of this city, and only from afar did He look upon its snowy ramparts and palaces of marble.

To the north of Tiberias the hill-ranges approach nearer to the shores; and the highway, climbing along a cliff, follows its trend for an hour or so, until it comes out upon the Plain of Genesareth. There the heights, sweeping back from the sea once more, form a natural amphitheatre encircling those fields, which the Talmud calls the Paradise of Earth.[2] Genesareth is no longer the fair and fragrant garden[3] through which Jesus wandered long ago; yet now, in its desolation, it still bears delicate traces of its former fertility, — in the spring-time covered with flowers, with thickets of laurel-roses overshadowing its brooks, while the thistles round about grow to be a veritable coppice, through which it is with difficulty that the traveller can tear a passage-way.

It is to the streams of water which have been so lavishly granted it, that Genesareth owes her garment of flowers. In the south there is "Round Fountain" (Aïn Medaouarah); in the north, the Spring of the Fig-tree (Aïn et-Tin); in the centre, a stream (which is, in fact, a river) falls sparkling from the mill-wheel of Shoucheh, and gliding through a thousand channels, moistens the fields along their course to the lake. It seems as if even this wealth of waters was not thought sufficient to freshen Genesareth, for athwart the barrier cliff which rises over

---

[1] Probably Emath, spoken of in the Book of Joshua, xix. 35 (Josephus, *Bellum Judaïcum*, ii. 21, 6).

[2] *Eroubin*, f. 19, 1.

[3] "Quare vocatur Gennezar? Ob hortos principum." (Lightfoot, *Horæ Hebraïcæ*, Chorographical Century, chap. lxxix.)

the northern part of the plain an aqueduct[1] has been channelled out to divert this way the waters of Aïn-Tabigah.

Still farther on the banks present a different scene: here the hillsides slope gently down to the lake, while all strong winds are warded off by the thick clumps of caper-trees, tamarisks, and laurels. But on the summit of the hills and on the farther side of these mountains, there is nothing beside barren and scant pasturages, where a stony surface of basalt stares one in the face.

Such is the general landscape of the country bordering the western shores of the lake. From Tiberias to the outlet of the Jordan, it forms a curve of nearly four leagues; and it is here that the towns made famous by the Gospel are to be found, — Magdala, Capharnaum, Bethsaïda, and Chorozaïn.

The first named is the only one of these cities which can be easily located. The desolate little village of Mejdel,[2] situated at the southern extremity of the plain of Genesareth, still retains the name of Magdala, — the native place of the Magdalene, from whom Jesus drove seven devils, and who in gratitude for her deliverance followed Him even to the foot of the Cross.

It is more difficult to discover any traces of Capharnaum, "the city of Jesus."[3] Geographers sometimes locate it to the south, in the Plain of Genesareth, close by Round Fountain (Aïn Medaouarah); sometimes in the north, in the vicinity of the Fig-tree Spring (Aïn et-Tin); sometimes even in Tell Houm, near the outlet of the Jordan. The latter is only chosen for the reason that in its neighborhood are some beautiful ruins, and in its name is contained the last syllable of Capharnaum.[4] Aïn

---

[1] Murray, *Handbook for Syria and Palestine*, route 28, Site of Capernaum.

[2] Mejdel still preserves the half-ruined tower to which it owed its primitive name, — Migdal, כִּגְדָּל, "The Tower."

[3] Matthew, ix. 1.

[4] Capharnaum (Kaphar Nahoum), "The Village of Consolation." In order to believe that this is the same name as Tell Houm, we must assume that Nahoum has been abridged into Houm, and that the ancient city,

Medaouarah,[1] on the other hand, is too distant from the lake to be regarded as the site of Capharnaum, "on the sea-shore;"[2] and furthermore, in the neighboring parts there are no remains of any such ruined town. While, on the contrary, to the south of Aïn et-Tin rise two masses of ruins, one of which gives certain indications of being a tomb, while far and near as far as Ouadi el-Amoud the ground is strewn with stones and ruins. It is in this locality that, in harmony with the most ancient traditions,[3] we have placed Capharnaum; for this position alone (or so it seems to us) answers to the descriptions of it in the Gospel, — lying in the Plain of Genesareth, close by

---

after its destruction, was no longer called the Village (Kaphar, Kefr), but the Wilderness, the Tell; hence, Tell Nahoum, Tell Houm. Such an alteration as this, where not only the vowels but the consonants also are different, seems little likely to us. As for the traditions cited by Frère Liévin, since they are more recent than the evidence of Willibad, of which we shall speak shortly, they are naturally of much less value.

[1] Some geographers believe that Aïn Medaouarah is the fountain of which Josephus speaks in these terms: "All the land of Genesareth is watered by a full-flowing well-spring, which those living in the country call Capharnaum" (Josephus, *Bellum Judaïcum*, iii. 10, 8). This description does not answer either to the Round Fountain (Aïn Medaouarah) or to that of the Fig-Tree (Aïn et-Tin); for the former only waters the fields in the neighborhood of Mejdel, and the other bubbles up close by the lake. May it not be that under this name the Jewish historian referred to the abundant streams that separate from beneath the great mill at Schoucheh, which lies midway between the hills encircling the plain? And, in fact, Josephus does not say merely that the fountain of Capharnaum rises somewhere in the land of Genesareth; he states that it waters this whole region. Now the current of water rising from Ouadi Rouboudieh grows to the size of a river before it reaches Schoucheh, and after falling from the big mill-wheel it is distributed over all the plain, from Ouadi el-Amoud to Aïn Medaouarah; that is to say, over the whole plain of Genesareth properly so called. This very natural supposition came to my mind at once when I saw the innumerable little rivulets which, starting from Schoucheh, water all the fields down to the lake-side; the more I have studied this point, the more plausible I consider the supposition to be.

[2] Matt. iv. 13.

[3] S. Jerome and Eusebius simply state that Capharnaum was near the lakeside; next to them, the most precise evidence we have comes from Willibad, who visited Palestine in the beginning of the eighth century (722). Starting from Tiberias on his way north, he came to Magdalum (Mejdel), next to Capharnaum, then to Bethsaïda, finally to Chorozaïn, where he formed a Christian church; and after this he encountered the mouth of the Jordan. From his description, it appears manifest that the pilgrim was following the shores of the lake, and in this way that he met

the lake, within the borders of Zabulon and Nephthali,[1] and upon the highroad of the caravans which, coming from the East and from Damascus, would descend by this route into Egypt.[2]

Yet, after all, it matters little enough what opinion one may cherish as to these geographical questions; for, however uncertain we are as to the precise spot whereon the Christ made His abode, at least we know in what places He dwelt. It is with perfect assurance that we hold the Plain of Genesareth in veneration, since Jesus once trod its paths; here His bark came to land when He left the opposite shore; just here too the little boat was pushed out from land at that time when, the crowds becoming so great about Him, the Master would so order it that all

with Capharnaum before any of the other cities of the lake; now the first ruins which you pass after leaving Mejdel are those which lie between Ouadi el-Amoud and Aïn et-Tin; hence, according to all appearances, this is the spot where Willibad locates Capharnaum (see Robinson, *Biblical Researches*, iii. 347-360).

[1] Matt. xiv. 34; Mark vi. 53; John vi. 17.
[2] This is the way S. Matthew describes the situation of Capharnaum: "Jesus quitted Nazareth, and came to Capharnaum by the sea, on the frontier of Zabulon and Nephthali; then was fulfilled that saying of the Prophet Isaias: Land of Zabulon and land of Nephtali, the way of the sea from beyond the Jordan, Galilee of the Gentiles" (Matt. iv. 13-15). These words can only mean that Capharnaum was situated upon the highway which stretched along the sea of Tiberias and led up into the Galilee beyond the Jordan, following along the frontiers of Zabulon and Nephthali. Now the boundary lines of these two tribes are known to us (Caspari, *Einleitung*, par. 64). Zabulon extended to the valley of Esdralon, along the hills which surround Nazareth, and eastward from Genesareth to the Mediterranean. Nephthali, lying nearly in the middle of Zabulon, was bounded on the south by the frontiers of the latter Tribe; but the western bank of the Jordan and the lake also belong to it, and from Safed its territory reached as far as the highlands of Thabor. This last line of partition indicates quite exactly the direction followed by "the way of the sea" of which S. Matthew speaks; and indeed this was none other than the great high-road between Damascus and Jerusalem. One of the first achievements of Van der Velde was the discovery of this ancient pike beneath the débris of the old Roman Road, which still exists. From Thabor it descends to the plain of Genesareth, then to Khan Minieh, one of the great Khans of the journey; then, mounting along the hills which border the lake, it at last reaches the Bridge of the Daughters of Jacob, and there crosses the Jordan. So then, being located near to Khan Minich, between Aïn et-Tin and Ouadi el-Amoud, we find that Capharnaum answers perfectly to the description in S. Matthew, "upon the road by the sea," and "upon the frontiers of Zabulon and Nephthali."

might hear some one of those Parables over which the world will meditate to the end of time. Somewhere, too, above those meadow-lands which to-day lie untilled, stood in those days the synagogue where Jesus healed the Demoniac; there too was the residence of Jaïrus, with that of the Centurion to whom He gave back his faithful servant; the dwelling where Simon's mother-in-law lay in all the languors and pains of fever.[1] Matthew the publican had his toll-gatherer's office on "the highway which skirts the sea,"[2] close by that caravansary whose ruins are still visible at Khan Miniëh.

Past the promontory which shuts in the Plain of Genesareth on the north, crossing over a sandy beach strewn with sea-shells, Jesus would find Bethsaïda, the native-place of His disciples Peter, Andrew, Philip, James, and John. Aïn Tabigah to-day marks its site for us; for Saint Matthew speaks of this village as being on the border of the lake, between Capharnaum and Chorozaïn;[3] and Saint Mark,[4] adds that it was near Genesareth. Now Aïn Tabigah is separated from the Plain only by a little headland; further on, along the shore, there are no traces of any habitations until we come to Tell Houm, and we are presuming that Tell Houm is Chorozaïn. While, furthermore, there is no position which could have answered better for a fisherman's hamlet. Here they had a bay sheltered from the winds; there are the mouths of numberless little streams also, whose fall would draw thither great runs of fish; and there was too a smooth strand, on which they could beach their boats. It was here that Jesus was walking when he called the sons of Jonas and Zebedee to Him; it is here that He went aboard of Simon's bark, and miraculously filled his nets to overflowing.[5]

We have said that Tell Houm appears to locate the

---

[1] Mark i. 21-26. v. 22-43; Luke vii. 1-11, iv. 38.
[2] Mark ii. 13, 14.
[3] Matt. xi. 21-23. Willibad's Itinerary agrees perfectly with this testimony from S. Matthew, for he places Bethsaida between Capharnaum and Chorozaïn.
[4] Mark vi. 45, 53.
[5] Matt. iv. 18-22; Luke v. 1-11.

whereabouts of Chorozaïn.[1] This region, in fact, is where we find the ruins most numerous, — great columns lying along the ground, the remains of a synagogue which was without a rival in all Palestine. Big blocks of stone whereon the eyes of Jesus rested once are still scattered about the foot of the hills, which, from Aïn Tabigah to the outlet of the Jordan, form a graceful border about the Sea of Tiberias.

Genesareth, Capharnaum, Bethsaïda, Chorozaïn, — or, in a word, the western shore of the lake, in length about three or four leagues, formed therefore the field chosen for the Ministry of Jesus. This region was the most populous of all Palestine, and nowhere else would the Saviour have found that commingling of races, manners, religions, sects, which made it well deserve its name of Galilee of the Gentiles. Officers of the court of Herod, Greeks from Decapolis, countrymen, fishers, Galileans, courtesans whom contact with the Pagan cities had corrupted, Syrians, Phœnicians, Orientals, whose caravans were following down "the road that runs along the borders of the sea," soldiers, Roman centurions, set to watch over these tumultuous lands, publicans seated by the highway to collect taxes,[2] — made up of such a motley multitude was the populace through which Jesus passed, and which He was soon to draw after Him.

Then too, as there was no one central point from which His renown could have spread abroad so swiftly throughout all Syria, so also there was no place which offered Him more secure retreats in seasons either of weariness or of danger. In a few hours a boat could bear him to the mountain fastnesses of Gaulanitis, amid whose solitudes He often consecrated whole days and nights to prayer. A three hours' walk from the lake in a northerly direction

---

[1] Some recent explorers have thought they could decipher the name of this city from that of Keraseh, a village lying to the north, about an hour's walk from Tell Houm ; but S. Jerome says that Chorozaïn was on the borders of the lake, and but two miles from Capharnaum. So then Keraseh is too far from the shore and the Plain of Genesareth to be confounded with Chorozaïn (see Murray, *Handbook for Syria and Palestine*, route 38).

[2] Matt. iv. 24.

would bring Him into the kingdom of a just and mild prince, the Tetrarch Philip. Jesus had only to cross the frontier, should it be needful to shield Himself from any blow from Herod; and He did more than once take this precaution, for that listless monarch had intervals of bloodthirsty activity. On these occasions we shall see Jesus taking refuge near to the other Bethsaïda-in-the-North where Philip had taken up his abode.[1] But these periods of absence were of short duration; as soon as Herod had fallen back into his usual indolent mood Jesus would return to His chosen land of Genesareth.

Thus from the testimony of olden times we have tried to rehabilitate that country-side just as it was when long ago Jesus saw and loved it. To-day the traveller coming down to the border-lands about the Sea of Tiberias, with his fancy filled with such memories as these, would be sadly undeceived. The green pastures, the vines, and the orchards have disappeared; the flourishing towns are only heaps of ruins; jackals slink about the synagogue of Tell Houm, where Jesus taught; the few thorny thickets do not suffice to temper the great heats within these hollow spaces, and the air which one breathes fairly burns with the dry glow. The lake indeed still shimmers in the sunlight between the long lines of hills, as clear and as calm as it was of old; it reflects the same horizon and the same sky. And yet all that the scene has lost in grace and in beauty it has gained in savage majesty, nay more, in eloquence, in sooth; for this sea aforetime so brilliant with life, and now doomed to the desolation of death, must recall great thoughts to all who wander about the solitary stretches of sand along its shores to-day,—thoughts which remind us how terrible it is to reject the word of God and incur His Anathemas.

"Woe to thee Chorozaïn![2] woe to thee, Bethsaïda! for if Tyre and Sidon had beheld such miracles wrought among them as have been worked in your midst, they would have done penance long since in sackcloth and ashes. This is why I say to you that Tyre and Sidon in the Day of

---

[1] Matt. xiv. 12, 13; Luke ix. 10.   [2] Matt. xi. 21-24.

Judgment shall be dealt with more mercifully than shall you. And thou, Capharnaum, wouldst thou lift thyself up to the heavens? Thou shalt be humbled down to Hell; for if the miracles which have been done in thee had been wrought in Sodom, she would perchance be living even to this day. This is why I say to thee, in the Day of Judgment, the land of Sodom shall be dealt with more mercifully than shalt thou."

BOOK THIRD.

FIRST YEAR

OF THE

MINISTRY OF JESUS.

ΚΑΤΑ ΙΩΑΝΝΗΝ.

δ'. κθ', μβ'.

Δεῦτε ἴδετε ἄνθρωπον, ὃς εἶπέν μοι πάντα ἃ ἐποίησα· μή τι οὗτός ἐστιν Ὁ ΧΡΙΣΤΟΣ;

... τῇ τε γυναικὶ ἔλεγον· Οὐκέτι διὰ τὴν λαλιάν σου πιστεύομεν· αὐτοὶ γαρ ἀκηκόαμεν, καὶ οἴδαμεν ὅτι οὗτός ἐστιν ἀληθῶς Ὁ ΧΡΙΣΤΟΣ, Ὁ ΣΩΤΗΡ ΤΟΥ ΚΟΣΜΟΥ.

The Schismatics' Testimony

"Come, see a Man Who has told me everything that I have done! Is not this THE CHRIST?
... And they said to the woman: "Not because of your tale do we now believe; for we ourselves have heard Him and know that this Man is truly THE CHRIST, THE SAVIOUR OF THE WORLD."

SAINT JOHN.
iv. 29, 42.

Book Third.

FIRST YEAR OF THE MINISTRY OF JESUS.

CHAPTER I.

THE FIRST PASCH IN THE MINISTRY OF JESUS.

I. The Hucksters Driven from the Temple.

John ii. 12–25.

The first sojourn of Jesus at Capharnaum was of short duration.[1] However at that time He manifested His power by the tone of authority which thrilled in His speech and by His miracles, insomuch that only a little later we shall hear the Nazarenes uttering their reproach: "Do some of the great works like those which you performed in Capharnaum here in your own country!"[2] We do not know what deeds these were, whose renown had been spread throughout Galilee; no one of the Evangelists has given us any particulars in regard to them, and we are forced to

---

[1] John ii. 12.
[2] Luke iv. 23. The fellow-citizens of Jesus addressed this remark to Him upon His return to Nazareth from Judea; hence the miracles to which they alluded were those performed by Him during his first stay in Capharnaum. These, then, were some of the marvellous deeds which were so numerous (according to S. John's evidence, xxi. 25) that the Evangelists could not recount them all.

resign ourselves to the bare knowledge of their occurrence, as must be inferred from Saint Luke's allusion to them.

Hardly had the Saviour awakened Capharnaum to a knowledge of His presence by these miracles when He withdrew from their country-side. The caravans which go up to the Pasch were being formed just at this time, collected from all the lands bordering on the lake. Jesus joined company with the pilgrims of Galilee.

Apparently they took the route through Perea, and arrived in Jerusalem by way of Bethany and the Mount of Olives. There was nothing at that time to distinguish Him from the crowd of Jews about Him, — neither the testimony of the Precursor, which was almost forgotten by this, nor the miracles wrought in Capharnaum, since no report of them had up to this date reached Jerusalem; the Saviour entered the holy City unknown, unnoticed, and with nothing to mark Him out from the throng. His first act was to go up to the Temple to pray; but it was useless for Him to seek any place on the Holy Hill for silent adoration; for He, being a Son of Juda, might not penetrate within the porches of the Levites; He must remain with His tribe without in the lower courts; but just now and all during the feasts this part of the Sanctuary was given over to the merchants, and was thus profaned by an unhallowed traffic.

This abuse, unheard of before the Captivity, had crept in since the period when the Jews, who had been dispersed over the whole world, thronged into Jerusalem for the Passover. As they could not bring with them from those far distant lands the animals necessary for the sacrifices, it happened that for a long while the small number of victims was in disgraceful contrast with the multitude of worshippers. To guard against this dearth of oblations, one of Herod's favorite courtiers, Bava, son of Bota, gathered thither great flocks of sheep, and generously offered them to the sons of Israel.[1] What he had done prompted by

---

[1] Coming into the Temple (says the Talmud of Jerusalem), He found it destitute of any sort of offerings. "Oh, may desolation," He cried, "befall the household of those who have so despoiled the dwelling-place of Jeho-

liberality others continued to do from motives of selfish interest. The priests were greatly in favor of these enterprises, whence they derived numerous perquisites.[1] Protected by their political influence, the sellers soon slipped into every avenue of the Temple and all through the Porches of the Gentiles, turning that vast court into a market, where was set out for sale every requisite for the service of the altars, — cages full of doves intended for the offerings of the poor; herds of cattle and flocks of sheep, for richer customers. Indeed, it was not alone the paschal lamb which had to be immolated at this season; the Jews of the Dispersion, since they came to Jerusalem but once a year, were obliged to wait until this visit to make presentation of such victims as were required of them, either according to the prescriptions of the Law, or in fulfilment of some pious vow.[2] And it must be remembered how innumerable these sacrifices were[3] in order to conceive a just idea of the tumult, which was aggravated by the presence of the money-changers. Seated at their tables, these bankers of the lower classes provided every one with the half-shekel which he must pay "as the price of his soul;"[4] and this because the greater part of the visiting Jews, having come from Roman provinces, would have in hand only moneys stamped with idolatrous images, and therefore unworthy of being offered to the Lord.

Necessary as this traffic may have seemed, it profaned

---

vah!" Straightway he caused a great search to be made, as far as Araby and through the pasture-lands of Cedar, until he had three thousand head of cattle: of these he chose out the unblemished ones, and brought them to Mount Moriah: "Ye Israelites, my brethren," he said, "let those among you who propose to make a Holocaust or any acceptable Sacrifice, offer it forthwith unto the Lord" (Lightfoot, *Horæ Hebraicæ*, in Mat. xxi. 12).

[1] S. Jerome, *in Mat.* xxi.
[2] Lightfoot, *Horæ Hebraicæ*, in Mat. xxi. 19.
[3] It was the spectacle of the Hecatombs presented by the Jews during the Pasch which moved Herod to make the Altar of the Holocausts of such huge dimensions. It was fifteen cubits (7 m. 87) in height, and formed a square, whose four sides were fifty cubits (26 m. 25), while a long ascent with a gentle slope gave access to the top (Josephus, *Bellum Judaïcum*, v. 5, 6).
[4] Exod. xxx. 11-16. In accordance with the order given them by the Lord, this money was reserved for the Temple.

the House of God. Certainly the victims were always immolated and the rites celebrated upon the topmost terraces; but the chanting and the prayers were no longer audible in the lower courts; shrill cries, incessant bellowings, coin rattling upon the trays of the noisy brokers, a confused rabble of pilgrims and hucksters, with their beasts lying about the mosaic pavement of the porches as though it were the litter of their stables. This was what Jesus must needs hear and see within the very shadow of the Sanctuary.

The spectacle aroused His wrath; seizing a handful of those flexible rushes which Orientals plat together like cords, He twisted them into a whip, and advanced, all suddenly, with uplifted arm, beating before Him both buyers and sellers, cattle and sheep.[1] Nor were the coin-changers spared; He put them all without the gates, overturning their tables and scattering their piles of money upon the ground. The sellers of doves were less rudely treated; forasmuch as they sold the offerings made by the poor, they merited the Saviour's pity; therefore he did not touch their cages, but was content to say, simply: "Take all these away from here, and do not make a house of traffic out of My Father's House."[2] What must have been the astonishment of the first disciples at the sight of Jesus in His indignation and the multitude flying before Him! Yet some of them remembered that it was written: "The zeal of Thy House hath eaten Me up."[3] Thus their faith was only the more strengthened.

As for the throng, it offered no resistance at all, but scattered like the startled sheep before the lash of Jesus. More than once in the annals of Israel the Prophets had disclosed themselves in like manner, clad in shepherd garb,

---

[1] Πάντας appears to include everything which was to be found in the Temple, the peddlers as well as their animals; however, some learned critics have held that πάντας only refers to the cattle and sheep, of which mention is made directly after (Meyer, *Kommentar über das Neue Testament*, in Joan. ii. 15; Alford, *Greek Testament*, ibidem). In their opinion, the words τά τε πρόβατα καὶ τοὺς βόας are to be taken in apposition to πάντας, and as limiting its meaning.

[2] John ii. 16.   [3] John ii. 17; Ps. lxviii. 10.

or as a hardy mountaineer, or other such man of the people; and further, all the while they were dishonoring the Holy Places the Jews knew themselves guilty of sin, and hence they were the more disposed to receive this Voice, ringing out in denunciation of their disorderly conduct, as inspired of God. Though the usurers and merchants may have cursed the Vindicator of the Temple's sanctity in secret and cast upon Him dark scowls of hatred, still none of them dared to face Him, Who had driven them out in the Name of Jehovah.

Much less could the Scribes, or even the priests themselves (however much to their interest it was to condemn the Galilean), much less could they summon up the necessary courage, so conscious were they of the righteousness of His rage. But as soon as they had recovered from their surprise they came to the Christ and demanded: "What sign He had to show as His warrant for an action of this sort?"

"Overthrow this Temple," Jesus answered, "and in three days I will raise it up again."[1] The thought concealed under these words escaped them; they only understood them in their literal signification, and thus saw simply an announcement of the destruction of this sanctuary, whose splendor was one source of their overweening pride. The enormous blocks of stone, the tessellated mosaics, the precious metals, the silver, the gold, the brass, now blended in beautiful brilliancy before their eyes, — in a word, their Temple, the wonder of the world, a Galilean dared to talk to them of levelling and rebuilding this splendid fabric with so much ease! The work which Herod, having at his disposal all the treasures of Judea, was forty-six years in constructing, this royal task a poor Artisan boasted that he could accomplish in three days! The saying made such an impression upon the Jews that ever after they kept repeating it; in the last hours of Jesus' life they related it before the Sanhedrin, as a blasphemy and the capital crime of the Saviour; but not content with making a simple accusation of it, they took care to distort

[1] John ii. 18.

it after this fashion : "I can destroy this Temple of God, and in three days I will rebuild it."[1] Now note what Jesus really said : "Destroy this Holy of Holies"[2] (as you have done by your faithlessness and corruption), "and in three days I will reëstablish it." "He spoke of the Temple of His body," the Holy of Holies of the New Testament, which after three days He would rescue from the tomb. In His wording He merely made use of the enigmatic spirit so familiar to the Oriental thought when they wish to give only a hint of their real meaning.

No one understood Him then. "What!" cried out the Jews, "Forty-six years[3] has this Temple been a-building, and you say that in three days you will reconstruct it!" and they retired in impatient contempt of such presumption. The disciples themselves, without partaking of the Jews' incredulity, did not comprehend all that this response of the Master implied ; " but after the Resurrection, they remembered what He had said, and they believed in the Scripture,[4] and in the word of Jesus."

---

[1] Matt. xxvi. 61.   [2] Τὸν ναὸν τοῦτον (John ii. 19).

[3] Josephus, in his *Antiquities*, dates the construction of the Temple from the eighteenth year of Herod (*Antiquitates*, xv. 11, 1) ; and again, from the fifteenth year of the same reign, in his recital of the wars of the Jews (*Bellum Judaicum*, i. 21, 1). This apparent contradiction comes from the two ways by which he calculates the years of Herod's reign, sometimes taking the time when Rome invested this prince with the royal power, sometimes making the death of Antigonus the initial event. Now, if we reckon the forty-six years of which the Jews are speaking here by making the fifteenth year of Herod the starting-point, we shall find we have twenty years up to the birth of Jesus Christ and thirty after ; and in fact the Saviour was about thirty years of age at the time of the Pasch here in question (Luke iii. 23). The sum of these two numbers is fifty instead of forty-six ; but from the former we must subtract four, our common reckoning being set backward by four years, and thus we have the forty-six years of which S. John was speaking. The Temple was not finished until 64 A. D. under Herod Agrippa II. and the Procurator Albinus ; hence, οἰκοδομήθη here means "is in building." The Greek Aorist has this sense in the following passage from the First Book of Esdras (v. 16) : Τότε Σαβανασὰρ ἐκεῖνος ἦλθε καὶ ἔδωκε θεμελίους τοῦ οἴκου τοῦ Θεοῦ ἐν Ἱερουσαλήμ, καὶ ἀπὸ τότε ἕως τοῦ νῦν ᾠκοδομήθη καὶ οὐκ ἐτελέσθη.

[4] John ii. 22. Τῇ γραφῇ here refers to the Old Testament ; indeed there are many passages in the New Testament which affirm that the Resurrection, that unparalleled Prodigy in the life of Jesus, was foretold in the ancient Scriptures (John xx. 9 ; Luke xxiv. 26, 27 ; 1 Cor. xv. 4 ; Psalm xv.).

"While He was"[1] at this time "in Jerusalem, for the festival of the Passover, many believed in His Name, seeing the signs which he did. But Jesus did not confide Himself to them, because He knew them all, and because He had no need that any one tender unto Him the testimony of man; for He, of Himself, knew what there is in man." The Gospel does not declare what prodigies the Saviour performed during those days. Certainly they must have been of a striking character to attract to Him suddenly such a host of disciples; but their faith was only rooted in self-interest and ambition, and thus the Lord "did not intrust Himself to them" as he did to the Galileans. Having read their hearts, He put no confidence in these new-comers.

II. Nicodemus.

John iii. 1-21.

Among the Jews, attracted at that time by the word of the Lord, there was a member of the Sanhedrin named Nicodemus, a rich man, influential in Jerusalem, who was possessed of a high order of intelligence as well as the distinction of noble rank.[2] He, without doubt, had been one of the few Pharisees who had humbled themselves before John the Baptist and received his ablution;[3] for we shall hear Jesus reminding him "of that Baptism of water and the Spirit" foretold by the Precursor.[4] However, it was not what he had seen on the banks of the Jordan, but the wondrous deeds done in Jerusalem, which had decided him to believe in Jesus.[5] Prompted by grace, he was made desirous of a closer intimacy; and as he dared not take any

---

[1] John ii. 23-25.
[2] Certainly he could not have been unaware of the embassy which the Sanhedrin sent to the great Prophet, and he himself, being a distinguished Scribe among the Pharisees, would be very likely to be chosen as one of that deputation (John i. 19-24).
[3] Luke vii. 30.
[4] John i. 33, iii. 5.
[5] John iii. 2.

such step openly, he stole by night to the house where the Lord was to be found.

Nicodemus opened the conversation [1] with a tribute to Jesus: "Rabbi," he said, "we know [2] that you are a Master come from God, for no man can do the prodigies which you do if God be not with him."

However respectful he was in tendering this acknowledgment, the Scribe only rendered it to Jesus as to a man and a doctor like himself; but the Saviour knew Nicodemus's heart. He saw that the man was secretly stirred by strong feeling, eager to be enlightened as to that Kingdom of Heaven which John Baptist had announced; and so, without prolonging his suspense, He made known to him at once that the reign of the Messiah so far transcends all human understanding that nothing less than the putting on of a new life can enable man to have part in it:—

"Of a truth I say to you, if a man be not born anew [3] he has no share in the Kingdom of God."

The idea of the new birth, in the spiritual sense, was no novel or unheard-of conception in the doctrine of the

---

[1] It is quite evident that S. John does not report this conversation in full or at length, for in the form we have in hand it could not have lasted over a few minutes; and it is hardly to be believed that the Scribe would have quitted the divine Master so brusquely. It is difficult to discover the connection between the different thoughts at first, and this fact alone indicates that the entire dialogue is not reproduced here, but that we have only the headings of their long conference.

[2] John iii. 2. Some critics have supposed that Nicodemus came on the part of a majority in the Sanhedrin to get information as to the ulterior designs of Jesus. So far as we can see, there is nothing to indicate that he had been charged with any such commission.

[3] Ἄνωθεν (John iii. 3). S. Cyril and many of the Greek Fathers translate this word "from Heaven, from on High;" but S. John Chrysostom, the Vulgate, and the Syriac Version render the meaning more exactly by "anew, a second time," "denuo." And so Nicodemus certainly understood it; for at once he urges the impossibility of any one who has come to man's estate becoming subject to a second birth. Of course, as the theme under discussion was the Kingdom of God, there would be nothing improbable in itself in taking ἄνωθεν to have this two-fold meaning, and thus signify both the being born again and that by a celestial interposition; but Grotius calls our attention to the fact that neither the Hebrew nor the Aramean tongue have any words which could comprise both these meanings. The Apostles seem to have understood ἄνωθεν in the sense of "a second time," for the idea of a new birth occurs frequently in their writings (1 Peter i. 3, 23; Tit. ii. 5; Gal. vi. 15).

Scribes; for they had often compared the proselyte to a new-born child.[1] That a Pagan must first take upon himself a new life in order to be of the seed of Abraham,—no idea could be more in conformity with their beliefs than this; but that this obligation extended even to the sons of Israel was indeed a strange and new thought to Nicodemus.

"How," he exclaimed, "can one be born again when he has already grown old? Must he reënter the womb of his mother to emerge thence once more?"

The Saviour proceeded to explain His thought so badly comprehended: "Of a truth, aye, of a truth,"[2] he repeated, "if he be not born again of water and the Spirit, he cannot enter into the Kingdom of God."

To be immersed in water in token of purification was a rite known among the Jews; and John had already proclaimed that though he plunged them in water, which was without virtue in itself, yet after him there was to be an ablution of the Holy Ghost; that is to say, the Spirit of God would vivify this water of ours, that thus it might renew the heart of man. Therefore it was not within the womb of his mother, but into the streams of sanctifying grace, that Nicodemus must enter in order to attain unto the Life which is from on High.

Jesus did not stop there; from this baptismal regeneration He stripped away whatever the carnal fancy might suggest: "That which is born of the flesh is flesh," He proceeded;[3] "that which is born of the Spirit is spirit; be not astonished, therefore, if you "— born according to the flesh and dead through sin — " if you must be born again." Then, in order to give Nicodemus some idea of the workings of the Holy Spirit, the Saviour added: " The wind blows where it wills, and you hear its voice, but you know not whence it comes nor whither it goes; so it is with him who is born of the Spirit."

This similitude was wonderfully apt; for the wind is akin to the Spirit, of which it is the symbol. It may be at that very hour, while Jesus and Nicodemus were con-

---

[1] Lightfoot, *Horæ Hebraïcæ*, in Joan. iii. 3.   [2] John iii. 5–7.
[3] John iii. 6–8.

versing there, the murmuring of the night-wind made itself heard; or it may be that the Saviour had in mind those light airs[1] which spring up even at mid-day in fine weather. No one knows aught of their origin; you can scarcely feel their soft breath on your cheek. They only betray their presence by a gentle rustling amongst the leaves. Most like to this is the action of the Holy Ghost in the supernatural life. It bloweth where it listeth; without hindrance it worketh, nor is it subject to fixed times nor to constant laws. At its first touches we do not know whence it comes nor whither it goes; only it makes us feel its nearness, makes us hear its voice, then suddenly it departs, and leaves behind it within our hearts nothing but languor and silence, and thus it goeth and returneth by secret ways. All that the soul may know of it is that sometimes she feels its Presence near her, and then she rejoices; sometimes she must weep its absence.

These workings of the Spirit of God could not have been unknown to Nicodemus. He himself without doubt had had experience of them in his inner life, and he had found them written down in the Psalms and the sapiential writings, where so many pious souls have recounted the ways of God within them. Therefore when Nicodemus answered once again: "How can this be done?" Jesus showed some surprise.

"Are you a master in Israel,[2] and yet you are ignorant of these things? Of a truth, I say unto you: We speak[3] that which We know, We give testimony of the things

---

[1] The term used by S. John, πνεῦμα, appears to have reference to the breeze, the gentle and regular breathings of the air. Whenever they speak of high winds the Evangelists make use of the word ἄνεμος (Matt. vii. 25, 27, viii. 26, xiv. 30, 32; Mark iv. 37; John vi. 18, etc.).

[2] John iii. 9-12. The article gives σὺ εἶ ὁ διδάσκαλος τοῦ Ἰσραήλ the meaning, "You, above all others, are a master in Israel" (Winer, *Grammatik*, p. 161).

[3] It is hardly probable that by the use of this plural Jesus meant to designate the Galilean disciples who were with Him. The faint-hearted Doctor of the Sanhedrin, who durst not come save at night and unbeknown to all, would not have conversed so freely before witnesses. In οἴδαμεν, λαλοῦμεν, etc., we have simply the plural form, as used in emphatic and elevated diction.

which We have seen, and Our testimony man is not willing to receive. If you believe Me not when I speak of the things of earth, how will you believe Me of the things of Heaven?"

By "the things of earth" Jesus referred to all that He had been saying regarding Baptism; since the sacred rite, so far as its external forms are concerned, has a terrestrial side which appeals to the senses. By "the things of Heaven" He alluded to the lessons that still remained to be given to the world,—His celestial Origin, His Cross, raised aloft like the Serpent in the wilderness [1] in order to save men, the salvation promised to those who believe in Him, the judgment and condemnation of the unbelieving.[2]

"And behold," the Saviour concluded, "the cause of this judgment! It is because the Light is come into the world, and men have loved darkness better than the Light, because their works were evil. For he who does evil hates

---

[1] John iii. 13-18. The Saviour set forth the reproach of the Cross under imagery which was already familiar to this Scribe, and He chose His words so well that the likeness between the reality and the figure was made more striking. Moses lifted the Serpent high in air, in order that they who looked upon it might live again; thus the Son of Man must be lifted up on high upon His Cross, and so also He will restore life in those who believe in Him. The Brazen Serpent was but made in the image of those which had stung the Israelites; it had no poisonous sting, and only by its form did it recall the creatures which had spread death in their members. So too Jesus had only taken upon Himself "the likeness of our sinful flesh" (Rom. viii. 3); "He hath been made sin for us, though without knowledge of evil" (2 Cor. v. 21). In Him, nevertheless, was crucified all that He represented in His Humanity, our original sin and the death in our members being thus done away with, He having taken it upon Himself, nailing it to the Cross (Rom. vi. 6; Coloss. ii. 14).

[2] John iii. 19-21. Very many critics, looking at these last words as only a commentary of the Evangelist, would have the dialogue proper end at verse 16. In order to support this hypothesis, they allege (1) that after this there is no further allusion made to Nicodemus; but what more natural result than that the Scribe, struck with the lofty language of the Lord, should have ceased his questioning to listen more intently? (2) They refer to the constant use of the past tense, from now to the end of the chapter; but here, as in many other places, the Saviour is speaking of the work which He is to accomplish as though it were already finished and completed (John v. 24, xvii. 4, 11, etc.). (3) The term μονογενής they say is an individual phrase peculiar to S. John, and yet we find it in these last verses; but may it not be that the Evangelist's fondness for this word rose from the fact that he learned it from his Divine Master?

the Light, and he comes not near it, for fear lest his works be discovered. But he who does the truth comes to the Light that his works may be made manifest, because they are done in God."

Uttered, as apparently they were, upon the threshold of the dwelling, just at the moment when Nicodemus was taking his leave, while already the dawn was lighting up the eastern sky, these words sound like a last exhortation, whereby Jesus would conjure this doctor of the Sanhedrin not to draw away from Him. But the Rabbi, though qualified to discuss with the Christ upon such lofty themes, was yet of a cowardly soul: he would rather steal away from the insistent promptings of grace within; and though he believed deep down in his heart, he would still strive to let nothing be seen. During the whole period of the Saviour's Ministry we shall look in vain for Nicodemus in the number of the disciples; only once [1] we shall hear him in the Sanhedrin essaying a timid speech in favor of Jesus, then, as if this feeble effort had exhausted his courage, he disappears, until amid the shadows of Calvary we meet him again, at the very last, close by the lifeless Body of his God.[2]

[1] John vii. 50, 51.   [2] John xix. 39.

CHAPTER II.

JOHN BAPTIST'S LAST TESTIMONY

John iii. 22–36, iv. 1–2 ; Matt. iv. 12, xiv. 3–5 ; Mark i. 14, vi. 17–20 ;
Luke iii. 19–20.

THE interview with Nicodemus is the only one among all the incidents of this Passover as to which we have any particulars. The faith of the Jews of Jerusalem, so ready and strong in outward seeming, was not to bear any fruit; this Jesus well knew. And so, quitting the town shortly, He went with His Galilean disciples into "the land of Judea."[1] This name was assigned to all the outlying territory about Jerusalem, and especially to the mountainous country which extends to the south. In fact, in a northern direction, it is but a few hours' walk to the confines of Samaria; to the east and west the city is surrounded by wild and rocky ravines, which on one side are channelled down to the shores of the Mediterranean, and on the other, straight to the uninhabited banks of the Jordan; so then it is principally to the south that we must look for the Judea to which Jesus consecrated the first year of His ministry.[2]

During eight months He travelled over this region; indeed, He went even as far as Idumea, whence, as Saint

---

[1] John iii. 22.
[2] From April to the month of December. In fact, we shall soon hear Him saying to His disciples, as He is passing by Sichem, on the way back to Galilee, "Four months more, and the harvest will be upon us" (John iv. 35). Now in Palestine the first crops are taken in during the month of April; hence Jesus must have prolonged His stay in Judea until December.

Mark relates, He drew after Him some faithful disciples.[1] However, it does not follow that we are to conclude that the Saviour penetrated into the mountain-districts of that land; for the *ouadis* with their valleys, which reach from the Dead Sea to the Elanitic Gulf, Mount Hor, Petra, and its tombs,—these were now no longer in the land of Israel, but in that of Esau. The Idumea of the Gospel, doubtless only included that part of Judea which extends south of Hebron, and which had belonged since the time of the Machabees to the kingdom of Edom.[2] We do not know through what various ways Jesus journeyed in that southern land, but He could not have failed to visit ancient Hebron, where the Patriarchs were buried; nor the great oaks of Mambre beneath which Abraham pitched his tent, and there knew the Presence of Jehovah near unto him; nor the birth-place of His Precursor, the humble village of Youttah; nor Kerioth, from which came Judas who betrayed Him.[3]

However arid and mountainous were these countries, still Jesus could find there the water necessary for the immersion of His penitents; for "He baptized,—not Himself, but by the ministrations of His disciples."[4] For many a day has the discussion been prolonged as to the nature of this Baptism. Some of the ancient Fathers, assimilating it with John the Baptist's ablutions, consider it as a mode of initiation, the ordering of which the Christ intrusted to His faithful Galileans. But for the most part commentators concur in regarding it as the Sacrament which regenerates the soul; and they believe that if Jesus did not administer it Himself, it was to denote that the Sacred Rite has in itself a divine efficacy.[5]

[1] The crowds which assembled round Him on the banks of Lake Genesareth had followed Him (says the Evangelist) "from Jerusalem, from Judea, and from Idumea" (Mark iii. 8).

[2] 1 Mac. iv. 15, v. 65; Pliny, v. 13; Ptolemy, v. 16; Josephus, *Antiquitates*, xiii. 9, 1.

[3] Judas Iscariot, the Man from Kerioth, קְרִיּוֹת אִשׁ. The village of Kerioth is mentioned by Joshua (xv. 25), and lies a little to the south of Hebron.

[4] John iv. 2.

[5] It may be too that in this way Jesus sought to put Himself in the foreground as little as possible, and by this means meant to pro-

Remembering what was the prize which they of this New Birth attained unto, we may not suppose that the Saviour would make use of it so freely as did John with his ablutions in the Jordan. He enlightened these first converts as to the virtues of Baptism,—demanded of them an uprightness of heart, and unlimited self-sacrifice, and faith in the truths He had revealed to them; but there these first teachings stopped, for though before this Jesus had unfolded the plan of Redemption to Nicodemus, as yet He did not deal after the same manner with the common people. We know from Saint Matthew and Saint Mark what was the burden of His sermons at this period, and we hear, as it were, an echo of the Message which John had brought them: "Do penance, for the time is fulfilled and the Kingdom of God is nigh."[1] The design of the Christ, by at first simply repeating the words of His Precursor, was to confirm the mission of His Prophet, waiting the time to disclose His whole doctrine, when He could do so freely in Galilee. Therefore, as He was even then an object for the Scribes' jealous suspicions, He was content to purify the hearts of numberless sons of Juda, by gaining them unto the Kingdom of the Messiah which was so near at hand.

In this same interval, apparently, occurred "that difference upon the subject of the purification"[2] which Saint John recounts. The heats of summer had so far shrunken the waters of the Jordan that it became difficult to perform any ablutions along the banks of the stream. So John Baptist withdrew from Bethbara, and ascending the valley as far as the ford of Succoth tarried there, near by the village Salim, at a place called Œnon, because of its copious springs.[3] Beyond the necessity of seeking a spot better

---

long the period of His preaching in Jerusalem and Judea as long as He could.
  [1] Matt. iv. 17; Mark i. 15.
  [2] John iii. 22, 23.
  [3] Αἰνών. Ænon is the Greek translation of the Aramean word עֵינָיִן, "The Springs." S. Jerome locates this place about eight miles from Scythopolis toward the south, and his testimony is confirmed by Eusebius, S. Epiphanius, and the Samaritan Chronicle entitled *Abul Phatach*.

adapted for baptism, there was also, animating his thought in seeking this retreat, a desire to yield place to Him for Whom the Precursor had come to prepare the way.

But although they flocked around Jesus, they still came to John; and the latter continued to baptize, joyfully gleaning after the footsteps of the Saviour in fields where hitherto he had harvested all alone. But his disciples, on the contrary, incapable of such self-forgetfulness as this, saw with secret vexation that their master's glory was being obscured just as that of the New-Comer increased. Something soon occurred to make them give vent to their envy.

It was but a little while before the imprisonment [1] of the Precursor: "They had entered into a dispute with a Jew [2] upon the subject of purification." Undoubtedly the latter, enlightened by Jesus, refused to admit the efficacy of the earlier baptism. Up sprung at once a contest which gave John's disciples an occasion of manifesting their jealousy. They referred to the Baptist finally, and said to him:

There are some weighty reasons for taking the ruins lying along the foot of Tell Ridghah to be the ancient Salim, for there are fine springs bubbling up all around the spot, and the tomb of a holy Mussulman thereabouts bears the name of Sheik-Salim (see Van der Velde, *Memoir*, p. 345). The only objection to it is that if so Salim would be located in Samaria, and it is hardly probable that John would have retired into any territory hostile to Judaism. This difficulty has seemed so serious to some scholars that they have been moved to look further afield for Ænon and Salim, among the mountains of Juda to the north of Hebron. Among the twenty cities which were in the neighborhood of this latter city, Joshua (xv. 31) mentions Salim and Aïn, of which we have discovered some vestiges in the ruins of Beit Ainun and in the name of Ouadi Salim; however attractive this hypothesis may seem at first sight, it has all the traditions against it (Sepp, who adopts it, has set it forth in poetical language in his *Life of Jesus*, vol. iii. chap. xix.).

[1] John iii. 24–26. It is not certain at what date John Baptist was taken prisoner; however, it seems more than likely that the Forerunner was seized a little while before the Saviour departed for Galilee, that is, about the month of December, and that he was kept in confinement until Paschal Time, in the second year of the Ministry of Jesus.

[2] The Italic, the Vulgate, and the Syriac of Cureton have the reading μετὰ ’Ιουδαίων; the other Syriac versions and the oldest manuscripts (the Alexandrine, those of the Vatican, and Sinaï) give μετὰ ’Ιουδαίου, and this modern editors generally have adopted. S. John would seem to infer that the discussion was set on foot by the disciples of the Baptist: Ἐγένετο οὖν ζήτησις ἐκ τῶν μαθητῶν.

"Rabbi, he who was with you beyond Jordan, and to whom you rendered your testimony, behold now he baptizes, and all men are coming to him."

What sadness underlies these complaints,—the very name of Jesus suppressed designedly, as though they remember how the Christ had been drawn from obscurity by this very man whose brilliant renown He now has eclipsed! Overcome with envy, and valuing not at all the penitents that were still attracted to Œnon: "All men are going to him!" they said. But John, while mitigating the bitterness of their feeling, did not fail to render homage to the divine Master once more, by setting forth more clearly the limits of his own Mission, marked out for him from on High.

"Man," he said, "can have nothing which is not given him from Heaven. You yourselves bear me witness that I have said: 'I am not the Christ, but I am sent before Him.'"[1]

Then, in order to explain better what his true position was in relation to Jesus, he borrowed from the Prophets the figure by which he compared the Saviour to a Bridegroom, of whom Israel is the Spouse. What Jehovah had been unto His chosen people, this the Word, from that hour, has become for all faithful souls.[2] The advent of the Messiah the throngs following after Him, typify the marriage festival, and the wedding procession which joyously conducts the Spouse unto Christ. But as for him, the friend of Jesus, he must needs be glad and rejoice in His glory. "He Who hath the bride[3] is the Bridegroom," he

---

[1] John iii. 27, 28. Some Fathers apply these words to Jesus Christ alone: "If His works are more wondrous than mine, if all go to Him you need not be amazed thereat; this is in the order of the divine decrees" (S. John Chrysostom, *in loco*). We believe that the phrase has a deeper significance, and refers equally to the Mission of Jesus and that of His Herald.

[2] Ezech. xvi. *passim*; Jerem. xxxi. 3; Osee ii. 19, xi. 4.

[3] John iii. 29. "Who can fathom the graciousness of these last words? S. John herein reveals a new beauty in the character of Jesus Christ, tenderer and more lovable than any other; it is that of the Spouse. He has espoused our human nature, Who was altogether the opposite of it, yet He has made it all as one with Himself; in this union He has espoused His holy Church, the immortal Bride who hath nor spot nor wrinkle. He hath

said "but the friend of the Bridegroom, who is by His side, and listens to all, is transported with delight at the voice of the Bridegroom; and thus it is that my joy is fulfilled. It is fitting that He should increase, and that I should diminish."[1] Thus the Baptist concludes; and then dwelling upon that brief sentence, he proceeds to compare himself to the Saviour, that so he might the more humble himself before Him.

Jesus comes from on high; John is of this earth.[2] He, John, has not seen that of which he beareth witness: he but accepts and delivers the Message with which he is intrusted. Jesus has Himself seen all things, has heard all things, in the heavens; therefore He testifies nothing upon the belief of another; and nevertheless His testimony is not received, or rather, so pitiful is the number of those who accept it that the Baptist, kindling under the passion with which the vision stirred him, held this poor handful of souls as of no account! Then, reverting to his own Mission,[3] severely straitened, like that of the ancient

---

espoused the holy souls whom He hath called, not only to the commonwealth of His Kingdom, but even unto His Royal couch; pouring out His largesses upon them, all His chaste delights; rejoicing with them, and being glad in their company; giving them not simply all that He hath, but all indeed that He is, His Body, His Soul, His Divinity, and preparing them for a Communion incomparably more great in the everlasting life of the future" (Bossuet, *Élévations sur les mystères,* xxive semaine, viiie élévation; furthermore, read his admirable *Discours sur l'union de Jésus-Christ avec son épouse*). We will only add one remark to this comment, and that is that we are indebted to the most austere of all the Prophets for the loveliest imagery under which pious souls have ever delighted to contemplate the Lord Jesus, — those two greatest types, the Lamb of God and the Spouse.

[1] John iii. 30. Here many expounders of the text would terminate the discourse of the Forerunner, and consider the rest as a commentary by the Evangelist; this they do upon the assumption that the ensuing thoughts are of too lofty a tone to come from John Baptist. To sever the connection between the words, which are evidently meant to form a perfect whole, would be to surrender the text to any arbitrary division whatever, inasmuch as these verses, which they regard as an addition on the part of the Evangelist, are simply the natural development of the thought which precedes it. The mighty enthusiasm of this Poursuivant of the Godhead grows in intensity with the bold imagery wherein he depicts the bridal festivities of the Word and Humanity, until it attains to that great Vision of the Son as He abides in the Bosom of the Father.

[2] John iii. 31, 32.   [3] John iii. 34-36.

prophets, John contrasts it with the Mission of the Christ, which is all-divine, sweeping over and beyond all bounds; for God, meting out His gifts unto His Son in the measure of His love for Him, has lavished all things upon Him. "The Father loveth the Son, and placeth all things within His hands. He that believes in the Son has eternal life; he that believes not in the Son shall not see life, but the wrath of God abideth on him."

That Wrath, whose thunders now threaten these disciples of the Baptist, reverberated more terribly still over the heads of haughty sinners. John never suppressed these outbursts. We have seen with what hardihood he menaced the great men of Israel at the outset of his ministry; and since then his zeal had been only the more aroused. No grandeur, no rank nor dignity, could act as a shield against his just rebukes. Herod Antipas very soon made proof of this.

By ascending the Valley of the Jordan, the Precursor had drawn near to Galilee; scarcely had the licentiousness of its prince been made known to him before he bestirred himself to stigmatize it.[1] We know to what a pitch this tyrant had already carried his scandalous disorders. Casting aside his legitimate wife, daughter of Aretas, king of Petra, he lived with Herodias, the wife of his brother Philip.[2] This princess, famous among the descendants of Herod, was the daughter of that Aristobulus who was strangled at Sebaste by his father's orders; she was granddaughter of Mariamne, whose execution had ever after haunted the old king with bitter remorse. Being married to her uncle Philip, she found in her husband merely a disinherited son of Herod, living like an ordinary

---

[1] Mark vi. 17, 18.
[2] The Herod Philip here alluded to should not be confounded with Philip, Tetrarch of Iturea, whose character and kingdom we have discussed elsewhere. This latter was the issue of Herod's union with Cleopatra of Jerusalem; while the mother of Herod Philip was Mariamne, daughter of the High Priest Simon. As for Antipas and his brother Archelaüs, Ethnarch of Judea, they were sons of Malthace the Samaritan, one of the many wives of Herod. The following table, while it contains only the most celebrated names among the wives and children of this

private personage.¹ Such a common-place condition as that to which this union reduced her seemed insupportable to her brilliant nature; beautiful, fiery, imperious, holding Judaism and its observances in supreme contempt,² she was one who would rule at any cost.³ And so when Antipas, during a visit he once made with his brother, saw her and became enamoured of her, he had only to promise her his throne in order to ensnare her.⁴

The daughter of Aretas, being warned that Herod was about to repudiate her, anticipated his action by retiring to the fortress of Macheronte, then among the possessions of her father, lying to the east of the Dead Sea. But it was all in vain that the king of Petra took up arms to avenge the wrong done his daughter; in vain also that his troops routed those of the Tetrarch:⁵ the monstrous and unnatural union of Antipas and Herodias was consummated, despite all obstacles.⁶

prince, will enable the reader to take in just so much of this genealogy at a glance:—

HEROD THE GREAT had as wives:

1. DORIS | ANTIPATER (put to death during Herod's last moments)

2. MARIAMNE (the Asmonean) { ARISTOBULUS (put to death) { HEROD AGRIPPA / HERODIAS, married { 1. to HEROD PHILIP / 2. to ANTIPAS } ALEXANDER (put to death)

3. MARIAMNE (daughter of Simon, the High Priest) } HEROD PHILIP (first husband of Herodias)

4. MALTHACE (the Samaritan) { ARCHELAUS (ethnarch of Judea) / ANTIPAS (tetrarch of Galilee, second husband of Herodias)

5. CLEOPATRA (of Jerusalem) } PHILIP (tetrarch of Iturea)

¹ Josephus, *Bellum Judaïcum*, i. 30, 7.
² Josephus, *Antiquitates*, xviii. 5, 4.
³ Josephus, *Antiquitates*, xviii. 7, 1; *Bellum Judaïcum*, ii. 9, 6.
⁴ *Antiquitates*, xviii. 5, 1.
⁵ *Antiquitates*, xviii. 5, 1.
⁶ This union was a double crime. In point of fact, Philip, the husband of Herodias, was still living (Josephus, *Antiquitates*, xviii. 5, 4), as was

So shocking a transgression of the Law could not fail to excite the mind of all Galilee. Did Herod, startled as he was, and fearful of some disturbance among his people, come to John the Baptist, thinking to obtain from him some words of approval and commendation? Some writers have so interpreted the facts. Yet it is more probable that the Precursor himself at once took the initiative. Pushing his way straight into the palace of the Tetrarch, — as of old Elias came before Achab, — he made the gilded halls reëcho with those words which the Church has so often since repeated to guilty princes: "It is not lawful for you to have your brother's wife."[1] And then John reproached him for all the evil deeds committed by him; whereupon having fulfilled his mission, he departed, leaving in Herod's heart a rankling memory, an incurable wound. The prince dared not arrest the Prophet on the instant, for he feared the people, who still thronged about him;[2] but he was only waiting some favorable opportunity for laying hands upon him. As soon as it presented itself, he had him seized by his satellites, and from the Gospel account we may infer that the members of the Sanhedrin, always the secret enemies of the Baptist, were not entirely unconcerned in this act of violence.[3] The prison in which John the Baptist was thrown was that same fortress of Macheronte where the daughter of Aretas had taken refuge.[4] Josephus has described its strange appearance,[5] also the legitimate wife of Antipas; hence both adultery and incest were here involved; for Herodias, who was sister-in-law to Antipas, had a daughter by Philip, named Salome; now this circumstance rendered any union with her brother-in-law unlawful, even after the death of her first husband (Lev. xviii. 16; Deuter. xxv. 5, 6).

[1] Mark vi. 18.
[2] Josephus, *Antiquitates*, xviii. 5, 1.
[3] S. Matthew (iv. 12) relates how, when Jesus was informed that John had been thrown into prison, He retired into Galilee, or in other words, to the realm of Herod Antipas. If the Saviour saw reason to fear this prince less than He did the members of the Sanhedrin, was it not because He had seen how they had plotted the downfall of John, and in this way He would Himself ward off their fanatical persecutions for a time?
[4] Josephus, *Bellum Judaicum*, vii. 6, 1, 2.
[5] Before the time of Herod, Alexander Janneus had built a stronghold upon these rock-bound heights; but it was destroyed by Gabinius during his war against Aristobulus.

erected upon one of the mountains which border the Dead Sea, while on the east it is surrounded by gorges so deep that the eye can scarcely fathom their dark chasms. Herod struck with the value of such a coign of vantage,[1] had encircled the cliff with enormous ramparts, and raised upon the heights a town and a palace. Tales of unhallowed deeds gave the deep defiles which environ it an evil renown. The popular imagination, deluded by the volcanic phenomena which are of so frequent occurrence in this region, conjured up numberless prodigies which were to be beheld in these parts. The smallest plants (they said) here grow to the size of the fig-tree; great twisted roots, red as fire, sending out flames at evening, glide away from the profane hand that would grasp them, or strike him down in death. From the depths of the valleys, and from the summits of the mountains, there burst forth springs of most various flavors, — sometimes boiling with heat, sometimes pouring out at the same time, as from a double vessel, icy streams mingling with the warm.[2]

Such is the fantastic neighborhood in which Josephus locates the prison of the Precursor. Although held within these fastnesses, the latter retained his liberty so far as to be able to receive his disciples, and to charge them with divers messages.[3] Herod himself, during his sojourns at Macheronte, sought converse with the captive; for "he feared him, knowing that he was a just and holy man, and although he kept him in prison, he listened to him willingly."[4] Thus he came "to do[5] many things by his counsel;" and at the last did really halt for an instant,

---

[1] We are not told what were the circumstances under which this property of Herod passed into the hands of Aretas; but it did not long remain with its new owner, for Josephus tells us that, after his unlucky campaign against the king of Petra, Antipas was, at all events, once more master of Macheronte (Josephus, *Antiquitates*, xviii. 5, 2).

[2] Josephus, *Bellum Judaicum*, vii. 6, 3.

[3] Matt. xi. 2 et seq.; Luke vii. 18.

[4] Mark vi. 19–20.

[5] Πολλὰ ἐποίει. This reading is sustained by quite an array of authorities: the Alexandrine Manuscript, the Codices of Ephrem and Beza, and nearly all the versions (Syriac, Vulgate, Gothic, Ethiopian).

undecided,[1] in the downward path of sin on which he had so far proceeded. But his wicked paramour was ever on the watch: she felt that the influence of John was ruinous to her own, and so, making a vow of merciless vengeance upon him, she went about procuring his death. For a long time Herod protected the Forerunner; for he was attached to him, and feared the people, who venerated John as a Prophet. Such half-hearted resistance as this was however powerless to withstand Herodias. We shall see very soon how, in a night of debauchery, she snatched her victim from the hands which so feebly defended him.

[1] Πολλὰ ἠπόρει (Mark vi. 20). "He hesitated much." This is the other reading found in the manuscripts of the Vatican and Sinaï, and in the Coptic Version as well.

CHAPTER III.

THE SAMARITAN.

Luke iv. 14; John iv. 4-42.

JESUS having learned of the imprisonment of John Baptist, retired into Galilee, not of His own desire, but "by the power of the Spirit;"[1] apparently this interior Guide revealed some impending danger to Him, for John Evangelist states that the Saviour was not free to choose what way He would take: 'He was of necessity," he says, "to pass through Samaria."[2]

The frontier of this country was soon crossed, and toward the middle of the day[3] Sichem appeared on the left, surrounded by rich meadow-lands and gardens. Jesus did not push on as far as this; tired after the long foot-travel, He Himself rested at the entrance of the valley wherein the town is situated, and hard by the Well of Jacob. The disciples, however, proceeded on their way toward Sichem; for in the haste of their setting out not having made any provisions for a long journey, they now found themselves obliged to buy the necessities of life from Samaritans.

Jesus, left alone, sought shelter beneath the archway overhanging the Well,[4] and from this spot, as He sat gazing out over the valleys spread before Him, the scene may

---

[1] Luke iv. 14.
[2] John iv. 4.
[3] It was about the sixth hour, that is to say, high noon (John iv. 6).
[4] Almost all the wells in the East have an overhanging hood, with benches ranged beneath.

well have brought up memories of many ancient happenings in Israel. Here, under the oaks of Moreh,[1] Abraham had pitched his tent, and raised the first Altar to Jehovah. Jacob, on his return from Mesopotamia, had bought this very land which Jesus now trod, and here too he had dug this well,[2] although there were fountains of water round about him, because he wished to be free from any subjection to the neighboring domains. Still later, when his sons had rashly wiped out the dishonor of Dina in the blood of the Sichemites, the Patriarch, though obliged to flee, yet always retained such tender recollections of this valley that he bequeathed it to his dearly-loved son.[3] Here also was the spot where Joseph was to be endowed with every blessing, showered upon him from the heavenly heights and rising from the depths below, while he himself would be upheld by the blessings of his fathers, whose God was forevermore to be his helper.[4] Here Ephraim, mindful of this same precious heritage, laid to rest the embalmed body of Joseph,[5] and so for centuries made Sichem the principal city of all Judea. Over yonder, upon the opposite slopes of Ebal and of Garizim, the eleven tribes, with solemn anathemas against all transgressors, had once vowed eternal fidelity to the Law.[6] At the foot of these very hills, for many long years, Israel had held her councils and courts of law; and when Sion

---

[1] עַד אֵלוֹן מוֹרֶה : "near the oaks of Moreh" (Gen. xii. 6), words which the Septuagint translates by : ἐπὶ τὴν δρῦν τὴν ὑψηλήν, and the Vulgate by : "usque ad convallem illustrem." The name Moreh, which has been preserved by the Targum of Onkelos, is apparently that of some Chanaanitish Chieftain, who owned this grove of oaks.

[2] Gen. xxiii. 18-20.

[3] Gen. xxxiv. The Old Testament, without stating the fact of this donation in specific terms, gives us to understand that it was made to Joseph. In Genesis (xxiii. 19), indeed, we find Jacob buying a field near Sichem, to which the body of Joseph was afterwards translated (Josue xxiv. 32), because this region was now part of the territory of his son. The version of the Septuagint leaves no doubt upon this question : "Joseph was buried in the parcel of ground which Jacob purchased from the Amorrheans of Sichem, which he afterwards gave to Joseph to be his portion," Καὶ ἔδωκεν αὐτὴν Ἰωσὴφ ἐν μερίδι.

[4] Gen. xlix. 25.

[5] Josue xxiv. 32.

[6] Deut. xxvii. 12, 13.

was become the capital of Judea, we still find Roboam inaugurating his reign at Sichem.[1]

But what was there now remaining of these olden splendors? The hills and valleys of Ephraim had forfeited their ancient renown by taking the name of Samaria,— a new town of schismatic tribes. The Field of Jacob was now an unhallowed region, through which travellers passed in haste lest they should come in contact in any way with its inhabitants.[2] How deeply must not Jesus have grieved over such sad changes of faith as these! Thus, in weariness of body and of soul, He sank down upon the low curb of the well; a divine despair which Saint John pictures in one word, which it is impossible for us to translate: "He was seated after this manner[3] by the well." The Church standing above the graves which she has blessed, loves to recall that mysterious lassitude:—

> Quærens me sedisti lassus.
> Redimisti crucem passus:
> Tantus labor non sit cassus!

And very shortly there came up from the little city of Sichar[4] the woman whom Jesus had come to seek at the

---

[1] Josue xxiv. 1-25; 3 Kings. xii. 1.

[2] As to the Samaritans, their origin, worship, and traditions, see Appendix VIII.

[3] John iv. 6. In the opinion of Winer (*Grammatik*, par. 69, 9), οὕτως does no more than recall the idea expressed by the participle: κεκοπιακὼς ... οὕτως: "because of this fatigue. He was seated." Meyer objects with good reason that in that case οὕτως would not be placed after the verb, but at the beginning of the phrase, as in the passages of the Acts where it has this meaning (Acts xx. 11; xxvii. 17). Hence we rather prefer to follow the interpretation of S. John Chrysostom ἁπλῶς, ὡς ἔτυχε, "naturally, even as He might," upon the bare stonework around the margin of the well.

[4] Sichar appears to be derived from a corruption of the name Sichem, which is the modern Naplouse (Neapolis, New Town). Indeed Naplouse is a half-hour's walk from Jacob's Well, but we are free to suppose that the ancient Sichem was still farther removed from this spot. Probably the term λεγομένην is used to indicate that S. John regarded the word Sichar as a nickname: "the City of Untruth" (Scheker, שקר), in allusion to the schismatic worship of Garizim; or the "City of Drunkenness" (Shikhor, שכר), in memory of the anathema uttered by Isaias: "Wo to the haughty crown of the wine-bibbers of Ephraim! Wo to the fleeting

cost of so great a weariness. She was a Samaritan, of evil life. With her slender jar poised upon her shoulder, she passed by all the springs nearer the town, and wandered up to Jacob's Well,—drawn thither by the freshness of its limpid supply, and by something perhaps of traditional respect for the Patriarch. In fact, women of the East do not often go out to draw water in the middle of the day; fearing to encounter some insult, they are never seen around the fountains, except in little companies, and at sunset. But this one had long since lost all timidity and reserve, and she approached the well without concerning herself about the presence there of a man.

"Give Me to drink,"[1] was Jesus' quiet request of her.

The Samaritan[2] looked at the Stranger; by His apparel and His accent she recognized a Judean.

"How," she said, "do you, a Jew, ask a drink of me, who am a Samaritan? The Jews have no dealings with Samaritans."

It was a refusal, rendered the more offensive by its ironical tone; and to appreciate its harshness it must be remembered with what readiness even Bedouins proffer this blessed service to the thirsty traveller. Nothing could show plainer to what extremes the animosity of the two nations had been pushed.[3]

---

flowers which enwreathe with glowing radiance the brow of that rich valley, where their feet stumble mid the thick fumes of wine!" (Is. xxviii. 1.) Those who regard Sichar as another village, distinct from Sichem, lying between this town and Jacob's Well (πλησίον τοῦ χωρίου), suppose that by the expression λεγομένην, "the spot called Sichar," S. John wished to imply that this place was little known.

[1] John iv. 7-9.

[2] Ἡ Σαμαρεῖτις. This word indicates clearly in what sense we are to take the expression: γυνὴ ἐκ τῆς Σαμαρείας, employed above by S. John: that is, a woman, not of the town of Samaria, situated some two hours' walk from Jacob's Well, but of the country which bore that name.

[3] Elsewhere in the Rabbinical literature we find innumerable traces of this rancor. Therein the Jews freely expressed their implacable hatred of the Samaritans; launching curses upon them before all the congregation of the synagogue; refusing them the privilege of becoming proselytes, and denying them the hope of a resurrection; treating them as idolaters and devils; heightening the insult by teaching that their bread was to be regarded as much unclean as the flesh of swine. On their side, the Samaritans sought every possible means to wreak vengeance

To this unmannerly reply Jesus only uttered a gentle objection.

"If you knew[1] the gift of God," He said, "and Who it is that says to you: 'Give Me to drink,' perchance you would have asked of Him, and He would have given you living water."

This gift of God was grace, but the Samaritan did not understand; the thought of living water turned her mind to the streams she had often seen sparkling in the depths of the well.[2]

"My Lord," she said, "you have no vessel,[3] and the well is deep. Whence will you draw this living water?"

Her language had become respectful; for by the majesty of Jesus, and by the nobility of His utterance, she divined somewhat in Him above any ordinary Jew.

"Are you greater," she continued, "than our Father

upon all Jewry; maltreated every Jew caught passing through their territory; defiled the Temple by throwing the bones of dead men within its precincts; disturbed all Judea by lighting, ahead of time, the watch-fires on Mount Garizim, intended to announce the new moon. Josephus relates a fearful example of this animosity. Some of the Jewish and Samaritan colonists of Alexandria, after many long disputes, finally appealed to Philopator for his decision, stipulating that the vanquished faction should be executed; and when Philopator pronounced in favor of the Jews, the partisans of Garizim were forthwith put to death (Josephus, *Antiquitates*, xiii. 3, 4).

[1] John iv. 10-12.
[2] M. V. Guérin has given such a perfect description of this ancient memorial that we could not do better than refer the reader to his Work. An attentive examination led him to the discovery that the Well is not sunk in the solid rock, but built with stones of small size, regularly arranged, very narrow at its upper orifice, but growing somewhat larger as it descends. Its actual depth is about twenty-four metres; it was formerly much deeper, for pilgrims have indulged in an immemorial habit of dropping stones to the bottom, to see if there be any water still left. As to the authenticity of this trophy of antiquity, no geographer has ever thought of contesting it (V. Guérin, *Description de la Samarie*, t. i. p. 376; Robinson, *Biblical Researches*, t. ii. p. 283).
[3] Ἄντλημα does not refer to the cruse which the Samaritan had come to fill, but the leathern bucket which served to draw up the water. All wells in Judea are furnished with one of these vessels, and a long cord, woven out of goat's hair. The Samaritan's words seem to indicate that these were lacking at Jacob's Well, and that therefore she had brought them with her. The fountains round about Sichem were so plentiful that it is very likely this distant water was used only on occasions.

Jacob, who has given us this well, and who drank thereof,
— he, and his sons, and his cattle?"

"He who drinks of this water,"[1] answered the Saviour,
"shall thirst again; but he who drinks of the water which
I will give him shall never thirst. The water which I
will give him shall become in him a fountain springing
up[2] to eternal life."

Jesus evidently did not speak of the springs which
water the earth, but of those which are opened up in the
heart, making it pure and fruitful. Under this figure He
would typify His grace, and show her how man may find
in it all that he can desire, without fearing that this
bounteous repletion should ever turn to satiety.[3]

Not grasping at all the deep significance of the words
she heard, the Samaritan besought Jesus to disclose the
whereabouts of this spring of life, as she conjectured it.

"Lord," she said, "give me this water, that I may no
more thirst, and that I may be no more obliged to come
here to draw water."

The Master was not disheartened; in the sinful nature
of the Samaritan he saw only an illustration of the truth
He had taught to Nicodemus,[4] that the soul which is as
yet in bondage to the flesh is incapable of conceiving
things divine, and hence the surest way to enlighten the
mind is to purify the heart; therefore He at once turned
aside the current of her thought, that He might recall this
woman to a sense of her sins.

"Go," he said, "call your husband, and come hither."

"I have no husband," she responded instantly.[5]

"You are right in saying, 'I have no husband,'" replied

---

[1] John iv. 13–15.

[2] Ἁλλομένου, "salientis. Emphasis est in voce saliet. Solent enim aquæ salire ad altitudinem usque originis suæ" (Grotius, in loco).

[3] It was in one such moment of overflowing gladness of soul that David sang: —
> "As the thirsty hart panteth after the water-brooks,
>   so panteth my soul after Thee, O, my God!
> My soul is athirst for God, —
>   for the strong living God."
>   (Ps. xli. 2. 3.)

[4] John iii. 20.   [5] John iv. 17, 18.

Jesus; "for you have had five such, and he whom you have now is not your husband; indeed, you have spoken very truly."

So it had been useless for the Samaritan to seek shelter behind that ambiguous answer of hers, "My husband! I have no husband." Jesus swept aside her feeble defences, and throwing open the gates of her soul, He laid bare its ill-gotten stores, all the accumulations of a guilty past,— divorce, and not death, that had freed her from each of her five husbands in a shameful succession; a faithlessness which soon degenerated into debauchery, into scandalous connections, no longer protected by any thin veil of legal formalities.

The Samaritan, in her confusion at finding herself so easily exposed, now ceased from any further feigning.

"My Lord,"[1] she said, "I see that you are a Prophet."

Then, immediately turning the conversation from this humiliating theme, she took refuge in a question of doctrine, such as she thought would be likest to divert the mind of a Rabbi of Israel. She recalled the rival pretensions of Sion and of Sichem; their own traditions, which told how the ancient Prophets were the ancestors of the Samaritans, and so represented them as sacrificing upon Mount Garizim.

"Our Fathers," she said, "have worshipped upon this mountain, and do you say that it is at Jerusalem we must worship?"

Jesus, satisfied with having awakened something like penitence in the heart of this sinning woman, would not refuse to follow her thought upon this new track.

"Woman," he said to her, "believe Me: the hour is coming when you will no longer worship the Father, either upon this mountain or in Jerusalem. You worship that which you do not know: as for Us, We worship that which We know, because Salvation cometh of the Jews."

By those last words Jesus recognized the Primacy of Juda: to Juda alone belonged the Promises, the sacrifices acceptable to the Lord, the revealed Law, and the Ark of

[1] John iv. 19-24.

Alliance, overshadowed by the Glory from on high, in token of the presence of Jehovah; but at the same time He announced the end of these prerogatives.

"The hour cometh, and it is already here, when the true worshippers shall worship the Father in spirit and in truth; for it is this that the Father wishes of those who worship Him. God is a Spirit, and those who worship Him must worship Him in spirit and in truth."

The Samaritan, drawn to Him by something she dimly discerned shining through these words, but dazzled and lost in this strange new world of thought, was now vaguely reminded of the Messiah, of Whom her fellow-countrymen were in expectation, Who was to be unto them for a Guide.[1]

"I know," she said, "that the Messiah, the Christ, is to come, and at His coming He will teach us all things."[2]

Jesus made answer to her, "I am He; I, who am speaking with thee."

He went no further at that moment; for the disciples were coming up towards them; but the woman, forgetful of all else beside, leaving her jar lying there at his feet, hastened back to the town,[3] calling to every one she met, "Come, see a Man who has told me everything I have done. Is He not the Christ?" And the latter were so

---

[1] This name is that which the modern Samaritans give their Messias: El-Muhydi (Robinson, *Biblical Researches*, t. ii. p. 278). Their ancestors had designated Him under other names also: as the *Converter*, the *Restorer*. They were far from having any precise ideas of the Messiah, such as the Jews had imbibed from the Prophets; since the Pentateuch, the only part of the Sacred Books in their possession, only furnished them with certain vague foreshadowing in His regard (Gen. xlix. 10; Num. xxiv. 17; Deuter. xviii. 15. See Gesenius, *De Samaritanorum theologia*, and especially De Sacy, *Correspondance des Samaritains, Notices et extraits des manuscrits de la bibliothèque du roi*, vol. xii.).

[2] John iv. 25, 26. Many scholars regard the words: ὁ λεγόμενος Χριστός as introduced by the Evangelist to explain the Hebrew word Messiah, מָשִׁיחַ. However, there is nothing to prevent one looking upon them as the actual language of the Samaritan. In fact, just below, S. John once more puts this word in her mouth: Μήτι οὗτός ἐστιν ὁ Χριστός; the Greek language was at that time so commonly spoken throughout Judea that the word Χριστός may have easily passed into the popular speech.

[3] John iv. 27-30.

thrilled by her words that they hurried out from Sichar in throngs, taking the way which leads up toward Jacob's Well.

But the disciples had returned, just on the closing words of this interview, and great was their surprise at seeing the Master in private conversation with a woman,[1] — and, of all things, a Samaritan! Nevertheless, none of them said to Him, "What were you asking of her? Why were you talking with her?" They offered Him the provisions they had brought.

"Master," said they, "eat." But Jesus' mind was filled with gladness at having garnered the first-fruits from among the Gentiles, in the person of this poor Samaritan; and so deeply replenished with delight was His heart that it caused Him to forget all other hunger.

"I have a food to eat," was His response, "of which you know not."

The astonished disciples murmured to each other, —

"Has any one brought Him food?"

"My food," Jesus replied, "is to do the will of Him Who sent Me, and to accomplish His work."

Thus then the work of God was the conversion of the Samaritans, who were now advancing toward Him. The swaying crowds, with their white garments fluttering through the fields of the valley below, which in four months more would be ready for the reapers,[2] now gave them somewhat of the appearance of a harvest ripe for the sickle. The Saviour, with a glance, pointed them out to His disciples.

"Were you not just now saying:[3] 'Four months more and the harvest time will be here'? And now I say to you: Lift your eyes, and look over these plains; they are already white for the harvest."

---

[1] John iv. 31-34. The Rabbis were so excessively scrupulous upon this point that they would not converse in public with their own wives (*Berachot*, f. 43, b).

[2] In Judea the sowing is done in the month of November, and the harvest is at the full in May; four months before this, in December, the fields are already green.

[3] John iv. 35.

Those words, "four months more," had doubtless been pronounced by some one of the disciples, looking at the fields lying around Jacob's Well. Jesus, taking up the simple words, turned them in harmony with His thought; imaging to their minds a harvest which was ripening more rapidly than any of this earth, — the harvest of souls, now coming toward Him from Sichar, who were to find a resting-place in the storehouses of Heaven. And from this, using the occasion to compare the Apostles' duties with the toils of those who reap, Jesus proceeded to utter some instructions to His disciples, of which (it would seem) Saint John only retained the memory of a few detached sentences.[1]

He explains how[2] "he who harvests" in the field of the Gospel "receives a wage, and garners in fruit which is life eternal." Far different is it here upon earth, where frequently before the time of reaping, the sower is in the tomb; whereas that Festival in the heavens "shall unite in one common gladness both sower and reaper."

Again Jesus recalled the proverb: "One man soweth, and another reapeth;"[3] showing them how perfectly applicable this was to the Evangelical ministry. "I have sent you to reap where you have not labored: others have labored and you have entered into their labors." By this is to be understood not only the Prophets, who had prepared Israel for the coming of the Messiah; but it also refers to the Christ and His teachings, of which the Apostles were to reap the fruits.

"However, the inhabitants of Sichar[4] were now gathered round the Saviour; they begged Him to tarry in their town, and He abode there two days." Many believed in Him, upon the word of the woman who had given that testimony, "He has told me everything that I have done;"

---

[1] This supposition seems to us to savor more of respect for the sacred text than the violent efforts which some critics would have us make in order to wrest some connection from out the various divisions of this discourse.
[2] John iv. 36.   [3] John iv. 37, 38.
[4] John iv. 39–42.

but a far greater number believed because of His own teachings. And these said to the woman,—

"We believe now no longer because of your story. We have heard, and we now know of ourselves, that He is verily the Christ, the Saviour of the world."[1]

Thus the divine Master needed but two days to capture the heart and the faith of the Samaritans; and this is to be explained not merely by their docility, but rather by the idea they had formed of the Messiah. Though much less complete than those of the Jews, their notions of Christ's Kingdom were purer by far; they were not, like the latter's, all directed to the realization of fleshly desires and carnal hopes, such as the end of all foreign rule and the restoration of the royalty of Israel. Hence, so long as He was in Judea, fearing they would make Him King against His will, Jesus concealed this dignity of the Messiah.[2] But in Samaria, on the contrary, He proclaimed it without reserve, and freely revealed Himself both as the Christ and the Saviour of the world.[3]

[1] The Vulgate does not set this first title "Christus" before "Salvator mundi," and this omission seems to be legitimate; for we find the same text in the manuscripts of the Vatican and Sinaï, as well as in most of the Versions. We have introduced the other reading notwithstanding, out of respect for the Alexandrine Manuscript.

[2] John vi. 15; Matt. xvi. 20, xvii. 9; Mark ix. 8.

[3] This title of Saviour of the World, which we so often use to designate Jesus, is only found in this one passage of the Gospel and on the lips of these Samaritans; this indeed is due to the fact that the idea of the Christ's having come to save not the Jews only, but all peoples, was one of those thoughts which were most shocking to Israelitish notions. But for the Samaritans it was altogether different; spurned and execrated by the Jews, and yet powerfully attracted by the law of Jehovah and believing in His promises, they joyously cherished this assurance that Jesus had brought salvation, not to Israel alone but to them likewise, sons of Gentiles though they were. It was the new dawn of hope for their whole race, and in like manner unto the entire world.

CHAPTER IV.

JESUS DRIVEN OUT OF NAZARETH.

John iv. 43-46; Luke iv. 15-30; John iv. 46-54.

AFTER two days spent in Samaria, Jesus resumed the journey to Nazareth, but He lingered in many places along the road. Saint Luke shows Him "teaching in the synagogues;"[1] and Saint John says "that the Galileans welcomed Him because they had seen all He had done in Jerusalem during the Feast."[2] "He was extolled by all men, and His fame was spread throughout the whole country."[3]

Jesus knew "that no Prophet is honored in his native land,"[4] and that He had nothing to expect from His own home; but He would wait until such time as His Heavenly Father saw fit to make known His desires, before He would quit it forever. He returned therefore to the little town "where He had been bred," and once more appeared before the eyes of the Nazarenes, just as formerly had been His wont,— outwardly, with the same simplicity of demeanor and garb as of old; wearing a long tunic,[6] girt about His loins with a leathern belt; sandals upon His feet; a cloak drawn about Him; for head-covering, a loose

---

[1] Luke iv. 15.   [2] John iv. 45.   [3] Luke iv. 14, 15.
[4] By this remark, S. John evidently alludes to the expulsion of Jesus from Nazareth; the episode is recounted by S. Luke (iv. 16-30).
[5] Luke iv. 16.
[6] From S. John's report, we know that this tunic was without seams, "and of the same weft from top to bottom," while the mantle was in four pieces, which were afterwards divided among the soldiers (John xix. 23). According to all the testimony left us, these garments were white (see Martigny, *Dictionnaire des Antiquités chrétiennes*, p. 391).

veil bound about the forehead by a cord.[1] Nor was there anything in His features which should startle the beholder; it was such a countenance as we may trace out among the paintings of the Catacombs,[2] — an oval face; the beard scanty and very fine, ending in a double point; the complexion of austere whiteness; the eye dark and burning; His long hair parted over the brow and falling upon the shoulders; the expression one of gentleness habitually veiled in sadness. Although the exterior of Jesus was so familiar to His fellow-citizens, none of them had as yet any knowledge of the power of His Word, for always in His youthful days He had been one who rather sought retirement and silence. All were then eager to hear Him, and they gave Him a warm welcome, when, on the Sabbath following, He came to the religious services of Nazareth.

We shall so very often find the divine Master in the synagogues of Judea, that we shall surely be pardoned for delaying the narrative an instant, if by so doing we may give some idea of those edifices, and of the ceremonies which were conducted therein.

Of different degrees of richness and grandeur, that varied according to the importance of their respective towns, the synagogues were, however, built all upon the same plan, — a long hall extending between two porticos, and terminating in a Sanctuary. Here there was neither image

---

[1] Artists always represent the Saviour with His head bared; but as it is impossible for any one to expose himself in this fashion without risking great injuries from the sun in Judea, Jesus doubtless conformed to the customs of the country, and covered His head with a veil ample enough to protect the brow and the neck. This head-dress, called Couflieh, is still in use throughout the East.

[2] We have sketched the figure of the Saviour from a painting in the cemetery of Domitilla; it certainly dates back to the third century, and it may even belong to the second. This portrait, which was the first to reproduce the features of the Master, came finally to be the hieratic type; for we find it in the principal sarcophagi of the fourth century, in the mosaics of Ravenna and of Rome, in the Letters attributed to S. John Damascene (ninth century), and to Lentulus (twelfth century). From age to age it passed down to Giotto and the artists of the Renascence. Northcote gives two drawings from this painting in the last edition (1879) of his *Roma sotteranea* (pp. 216-220). (Consult Martigny, *Dictionnaire des Antiquités* (1877), p. 387).

nor altar to be seen, but only a casket of wood, covered over with a veil and enclosing the Sacred Books of Israel.¹ This part of the structure was held in the highest honor.² It was there were to be found "the first seats," much sought after by Scribes and Pharisees,³ and the places of distinction, to which were conducted such of the faithful as were renowned for their wealth.⁴ Near the centre there was a raised platform upon which the Reader of the Holy Books would ascend, with the Rabbi who was to exhort the gathering. As to the faithful, they kept to the nave of the edifice; this was divided by a balustrade into two parts,⁵ one of which was reserved for the men, the other for the women.⁶

Every synagogue had at its head a Chief,⁷ who was assisted by Elders and Pastors.⁸ This body presided over

---

¹ This object, which by its form would remind them of the Ark of the Covenant, occupied the place of honor in the Synagogue; so for a long time the Church herself placed the Holy Books within the Tabernacle alongside the Eucharist. "In olden times, according to S. Paulinus, they used to have two tiny cupboards side by side within their tabernacles, in one of which was the Blessed Sacrament and in the other the Holy Scriptures; thus one enclosed the Word Divine confined under the sacred species, the other held the Divine Word as manifested to us outwardly, whereby He hath given us to understand what He Himself hath said" (M. Olier, *Mémoires*).

² To draw their eyes, and their hearts as well, toward the one spot above all others upon earth where Jehovah wished all men to adore Him, they took care to make this their sanctuary face toward Jerusalem; consequently all the synagogues of the West were "orientées." Very likely, too, this is one of the reasons why our churches have been given the same position.

³ Matt. xxiii. 6.
⁴ James ii. 3.
⁵ Philo, *De Vita contemplativa*, ii. 476.
⁶ The Jewish synagogue (as is plainly to be seen) in many points resembled our Christian Basilicas. Like them it had a sanctuary, a tribune for the officiating ministers (the $\beta\hat{\eta}\mu\alpha$, or ambon of the ancients), and a nave for the faithful. There was a lamp burning night and day before the ark which held the Holy Books; the roof-tree of the edifice must overtop all the dwellings of the town, or at least should have a high spire (much like the campanile towers on our churches or the minarets of the Orient), which should rise above everything round about it. We even recognize our modest poor-box hanging close beside the doors.

⁷ The ἀρχισυνάγωγος (Luke viii. 41, xiii. 14; Acts xviii. 8, 17).
⁸ These officers of the synagogue, if not by their duties, from their names at least, recall the Hierarchy of the primitive Church: Πρεσβύτεροι

the religious exercises, passed judgments, decreed punishments, excommunicated guilty parties, or sent them back in chains to the Sanhedrin. The most active of its members was the Angel or Legate of the Synagogue,[1] who read the prayers and was the representative of the assembly abroad. Below all the various dignitaries was an inferior minister, the Chazzan,[2] who presented the Reader with the Holy Books, guarded the doors and was a general care-taker.

As to the order of the services, it was fixed by rules most scrupulously observed.[3] To the chanting of the Psalms succeeded the Prayer, taken from Deuteronomy and called, from its first word, the Schema[4] (Hearken): "Hearken, Israel, the Lord thy God is the One and only God: thou shalt love the Lord thy God with all thy heart, with all thy soul, and with all thy strength." Then came the eighteen Benedictions,[5] followed by the Instruction, which held

(Luke vii. 3) (זְקֵנִים), also called pastors, ποιμένες (Eph. iv. 11); chiefs and leaders of the flock, πρεστῶτες, ἡγούμενοι (1 Tim. v. 17; Hebr. xiii. 1).

[1] Very different though this office was from the ministry of our Pontiffs, it may be, however, that S. John had the Angel of the Synagogue in mind when he gave to the bishops of the greater Sees of Asia that title, "Angels of the Church" (Apoc. i. 20, ii. 1, etc.).

[2] חַזָּן; spoken of by S. Luke (iv. 20) as ὑπηρέτης, "the attendant."

[3] In the ritual of modern Jews it is difficult to distinguish just how much they have preserved of the primitive worship; but certain usages of the Christian liturgy in the first three centuries must have been borrowed from them, — the ablution before entering the sanctuary, the custom of standing during the prayers with outstretched arms, the Amen with which the whole congregation responded to the invocations of the Elders.

[4] The Schema, properly speaking, comprised the three following passages from Numbers and Deuteronomy: Num. xv. 37–41; Deut. vi. 4–9, xi. 13–21.

[5] "Blessed art Thou, O Lord God, God of our fathers Abraham, Isaac, and Jacob! . . . Lord, Thou art almighty; Thou dost recall the dead to life in Thy great tenderness; Thou dost raise up those that fall; Thou healest the sick, nor hast Thou forsaken them that sleep in the dust. Who is there like unto Thee, O Mighty God? . . . Thou art holy, holy is Thy Name, and none but the holy do praise Thee every day. . . . Blessed art Thou, O Lord, Whose Name is goodness, and unto Whom all praise is due!" (*Rosh-haschanah*, iv.; *Berachot*, iv. 3, etc.) The invocations just cited were certainly in use in the days of Jesus, for they are taken from the three first and the three last benedictions, which, as all the critics agree, are of the greatest antiquity. (See Kitto, *Cyclopædia:* SYNAGOGUE.)

a high place in the religious service of the synagogue. From the evidence of Saint James we learn that "Moses was read every Sabbath, from the most ancient times;"[1] and as this reading was given in Hebrew, which the people no longer understood since the Captivity,[2] an interpreter repeated the Sacred Text, phrase after phrase, in the vernacular.[3] He did the like for the reading of the Prophets, which succeeded that of the Pentateuch. Ordinarily it was read by a Rabbi, who made a running commentary upon it, and addressed to his listeners "the Word of Consolation." But when some stranger or some Jew distinguished for his doctrine happened to appear in the assembly, they would press him eagerly to mount the platform, so that they might profit by his instructions.[4]

The renown which had now begun to surround the name of Jesus merited such honors for Him. The moment of His rising to speak was just as the reading of the Law was concluded. The care-taker of the synagogue handed Him the Oracles of Isaias. The Saviour, unwinding the long scroll of papyrus, rolled about a wand of wood or ivory, found[5] the Lesson marked for the day, and read these prophetic words: —

[1] Acts xv. 21.

[2] The popular tongue in the days of Jesus was the Aramean; it was a dialect which had sprung up during and after the Captivity, as the result of alterations grafted upon the Hebrew language.

[3] The five books of Moses were divided in such a way that the reading would extend over the whole year; now-a-days, the Hebraic bibles divide the Law (that is, all the Pentateuch) into fifty-four sections called Parshioth (plural of Parshah : פָּרָשָׁה = "Part"). Beside the fifty-four Parshioth there were a corresponding number of Lessons taken from the Prophets, and called the Haftaroth, a name of very obscure derivation. This division of the Pentateuch into fifty-four parts was already commonly accepted at the opening of the Christian era; however, in more remote ages the Law was probably divided into one hundred and fifty-five sections (the Sedarim of the Massorites), and then it took three years to read the whole matter. (See Kitto, *Cyclopædia*: HAPHTARA.)

[4] As to the Jewish synagogues, see Vitringa, *De Synagoga vetere.*

[5] Εὗρεν. The Law was read from end to end without any transpositions in the order, and the manuscript was wrapped about two rods. Each Sabbath the "Angel of the Synagogue" unwound one of the rollers for the lesson of the day, and wound up the other as fast as the reading progressed; upon the Sabbath following he would take it up at the page where they had left off. But from the Prophets the lessons were selected here and

"The Spirit of the Lord is upon Me; therefore it is He has consecrated Me by Anointment: He hath sent Me to bring good tidings to the poor, to heal the afflicted hearts,[1] to announce to the captives their deliverance and to the blind recovery of their sight, to bring back, as free men, those who be broken beneath their fetters, to publish forth the Year of Pardon of the Lord, and the Day of His Justice."

Jesus could not have happened upon a more favorable theme. His comments were made upon the Hebrew text, whose full force we may well recall here.[2] "The Spirit of the Lord Jehovah is upon Me; therefore it is He hath anointed Me,[3] to announce the Good News to the meek;[4] He hath sent Me to heal the broken hearts, to announce freedom to the captives, to give unto the prisoners once more to see the light,[5] and to proclaim the Year of Pardon of the Lord." The Vulgate adds the words of the Prophet, which are not given in the Greek text of the Gospel: "And to announce the Day of His Justice." The Saviour could

---

there, and the Volume was wrapped about one single cylinder; hence they were obliged to look for the place indicated by the rules of the Synagogue.

[1] Is. lxi. 1, 2. The phrase ἰάσασθαι τοὺς συντετριμμένους τὴν καρδίαν, which is wanting in many of the versions and manuscripts, is omitted by Tischendorf and Alford.

[2] S. Luke, who always has his Greek readers in mind, is quoting freely from the version of the Septuagint.

[3] Anointed, not by any corporeal unction, but by the Divinity of the Word, which has thus made the Christ our King and Pontiff, — our Monarch and High Priest.

[4] עֲנָוִים: "the meek," that is, those who do not withstand outrages, but suffer all things and are despoiled of all things in this world; this is why S. Luke and the Septuagint call them the poor, those who are stripped of everything.

[5] This meaning is the one adopted by Delitzsch, *Biblischer Commentar über den Propheten Jesaia*. S. Luke felt that the translation of the Septuagint did not convey the force of the Hebrew word פְּקַח־קוֹחַ (as to this word, see Fürst, *Hebräisches Handwörterbuch*); but that here it meant, not merely to open the eyes of prisoners seated in the gloom, but to reach their ears and their hearts, making their shackles to fall from off their limbs. So, too, he adds these words, borrowed from another saying of Isaias (lviii. 6): ἀποστεῖλαι τεθραυσμένους ἐν ἀφέσει: "He hath anointed Me that I may bring them that lie broken under captivity into the fulness of freedom."

not, indeed, deliver the lowly and the desolate, save by humbling those who oppress them.

The reading finished, Jesus rolled up the manuscript, handed it back to the servant, and, according to the custom of the Rabbis, seated Himself and began to exhort the faithful. "The eyes of all were fixed upon Him,"[1] and we may easily fancy what emotion thrilled the audience on hearing Him declare "that on this day this same Scripture is found to be fulfilled." They were the poor, the captives, the blind, the sorrowful hearts, to whom He was bringing salvation; and in their own times they had seen "The Year of Pardon,"[2] the Jubilee of the Lord, above all others. His language, so full of grace, amazed them at first; it sounded in their ears with all the weight of one having authority in the synagogue. "All were delighted with the words which fell from His mouth, and they said: "Is not this the son of Joseph?"[3]

But this wonderment soon turned to suspicion. "The son of a mechanic, a carpenter himself, whom they had seen so many a day working with his hands in their midst, could he be a Prophet, unless indeed he could prove his mission by some prodigy, at least? Certainly he had spoken 'of healing souls,'[4] and there were gossips who said that elsewhere he had done such miracles; then why does n't he begin now and here among his fellow-citizens?"

"Physician, heal thyself!" a mocking voice cried out at Him, as though it would say: "Do for yourself and your own that which you have procured for others!"

With perfect sweetness Jesus put aside this attack.[5] "Of a certainty," He said, "you may apply to Me the proverb: 'Physician, heal Thyself. The great things done at Capharnaum which we have heard spoken of, do the same in

---

[1] Luke iv. 20.
[2] Luke iv. 19. This expression gave rise to that misconception on the part of certain Greek Fathers, who inferred from this that the Ministry of Jesus lasted only one year (Clement of Alexandria, *Stromata*, lib. 1, cap. xxi. p. 885; Origen, Περὶ ἀρχῶν, iv. 5, etc.).
[3] Luke iv. 22.
[4] Luke iv. 18.
[5] Luke iv. 23–27.

Thy native land.' But in truth, I say to you, a Prophet is not received in his own country. There were many widows in Israel in the time of Elias, when the heavens were closed during three years and six months,[1] and there was a great famine over all the earth, and Elias was not sent to any one among them, — no, not to any, but only to a widow woman of Sarepta,[2] a city of the Sidonians. So also there were many lepers in Israel, under the Prophet Eliseus, and not one among them was purified save only the Syrian Naaman."[3]

At these words a sudden access of fury brought the assembly to its feet: "Dares he compare them, the sons of Abraham, with Pagan women and lepers!"

There were now no longer the mutterings of a few dissatisfied hearers, but cries of rage against Him. All surging forward together, they seized Jesus, and swept Him along up to the summit of the mountain on which their town was built, thinking to cast Him headlong over the heights into the rocky hollows below.[4]

But His hour was not come; although it was permitted to the Nazarenes to push and thrust Him before them, to heap blows and abuse upon Him, yet, when they had reached the edge of the precipice, some superhuman Power held their arms fast. Helpless, speechless, transfixed, they saw Jesus pass through their midst and go upon His way, leaving them spell-bound with a sudden stupor.

He withdrew from Nazareth as He had done from Jerusalem. In great sadness and weariness He climbed the

---

[1] 3 Kings xvii. 9. S. James mentions the same duration for the period of dryness in the days of Elias (James v. 17), while the Book of the Kings says that on the third year the Prophet announced the return of the rain to earth. Undoubtedly both the Apostle and the Evangelist had found some more precise evidence as to the length of the drought among the traditions of Jewry, and these they preferred to the vague expression used in the Book of the Kings.

[2] Now called Sourafend, a village lying between Tyre and Sidon.

[3] 4 Kings v. 14.

[4] Luke iv. 28-30. It is not likely that the Nazarenes would have carried Jesus so far along as to the hilltop pointed out by a certain tradition; for this eminence is an hour's walk from Nazareth, and far beyond the distance which the Jewish law allowed them to travel on the Sabbath day.

hill which separates it from Cana,¹ and from the wooded ridge cast one last look upon the peaceful valley where His youthful days had been passed, on the house which had sheltered Him during those thirty years, and where as a poor Laborer He had toiled and suffered, and lived out this every-day existence of ours. It had mattered nothing, after all, that this village and this people were indeed His own, by so many ties of kinship and acquaintance, — "His own received Him not;"² He must depart to bear unto strangers the Salvation which these Nazarenes disdained; now, at last, He must go forth, not having where to lay His head.

Jesus, driven out of Nazareth, dwelt for a certain length of time at Cana, — long enough for the news to be spread through all the cities around the lake. We do not know His reasons for remaining in this village, but we still find Him there when one of the king's officers³ hastened to Him from Capharnaum, beseeching Him to cure his son who was dying.

Although little was known of Jesus among Herod's courtiers, His Name was always regarded with something of respect and awe among them, and cherished with longing hopes as well, by such as admired Him in secret. The Saviour greeted the Jewish nobleman, not without pity;⁴ and yet, comparing His self-seeking supplications with the

---

¹ John iv. 46. We must suppose that this journey spoken of by S. John took place just here and in this order; for the Evangelist, after alluding to the turbulent outburst of the Nazarenes (iv. 44), proceeds at once to say that Jesus, on account of this expulsion, withdrew for a second time to Cana: ἦλθεν οὖν πάλιν εἰς τὴν Κανᾶ.

² John i. 11.

³ John iv. 46, 47. Βασιλικός signifies either a person of royal blood or an officer of the king. Here the latter meaning is to be preferred, for the historian Josephus, our surest guide in everything that involves Jewish customs, employs this term to distinguish Roman magistrates, the courtiers and officers of the kings of Judea, but never to designate a member of the royal family (*Bellum Judaicum*, vii. 5, 2; *Antiquitates*, xv. 8, 4).

⁴ The Evangelist does not give the name of this personage. Some critics have suggested that of Manahen, son of Herod's nurse, who, in the Acts, is placed in the ranks of the first Christians (Acts xiii. 1). Others, with perhaps better reason (for we know that the officer's entire family believed in the Saviour), have fancied he might be that same Chuza, the tetrarch's Intendant, whose wife, Joanna, we find among the Galilean ladies who were the first to follow Jesus (Luke viii. 3).

generous forgetfulness of self shown by the Samaritans, it made Him grieve the more over the incredulity of Israel.[1] "If you do not see signs and prodigies,"[2] He said, "you do not believe." In uttering this reproach, it was not His intent to repulse the supplicant, nor to extinguish the glimmering spark of faith which He saw in his heart. This the officer must have gathered from the compassionate glance of the Master and from the tones of His voice, for he redoubled his urgent suit: —

"Lord, come down before my poor little one[3] dies."

What a note of terror is sounded in this prayer! — in the touching terms in which he mentions the son whom he fears he may never see again; but, too, how great was his mistake when in his anxiety and alarm he dreaded lest Jesus Himself would be rendered powerless if death were to anticipate and prevent Him! This man did not know that it is no more difficult for God to resuscitate the body than to cure it, and that neither time nor space can impose limits upon His power. The Divine Master took compassion upon this father's blindness, distraught with grief as he was.

"Go," he said; "your son lives."

And at that same moment wherein He healed the body of the child He worked so powerfully upon the heart of the father that the latter rose up to return home, filled at once with glad hope and confidence.

It was one o'clock in the afternoon[4] when the officer parted from Jesus. Even in the shortest days of winter he could have reached Capharnaum by nightfall, since Cana is not more than a six hours' journey; but some obstacle delayed him upon the road; he slept at some posting-place on the way, and did not arrive until the morrow.

---

[1] John iv. 48–51.

[2] Σημεῖα καὶ τέρατα. As to the different meanings of these words, refer to page 147, and to Trench, *Synonyms of the New Testament*, p. 230.

[3] Παιδίον. This diminutive denotes either the extreme youth of the child, or, more likely still, the great love of the father. S. John ordinarily employs this word when he wishes to use a term of endearment (John xxi. 5; 1 Ep. John ii. 13, 18).

[4] "The seventh hour" (John xiv. 52. See p. 132, note 4).

As he neared his mansion the servants hurried out to greet him with the announcement that his son was living.

Immediately he asked them at what hour the child had begun to revive.

"Yesterday," they replied,[1] "at the seventh hour, the fever left him."

He knew then that it was the very moment in which Jesus had said to him "Your son lives." And he believed, he and all his household.

"This was the second miracle which Jesus had performed thus far upon His return from Judea into Galilee."[2] By adding these words the Evangelist does not mean to ignore the wondrous deeds done at Capharnaum,[3] but he is thinking only of the miracles done by Jesus at Cana, and his intention is simply to connect two facts that took place in the same locality. The changing of the water into wine was the first manifestation of the Saviour made by Him on His return from the banks of the Jordan into Galilee. The healing of the official's son was the second sign, not less striking than the other, and destined indeed, as well as its predecessor, to mark the beginning of a new period in the Ministry of Jesus.

[1] Hengstenberg thinks that the officer reached home on the evening of the same day, but so late at night that the servants would naturally say "yesterday," meaning the day which had just terminated at set of sun.
[2] John iv. 54.
[3] Luke iv. 23.

CHAPTER V.

THE FIRST ACTS DURING THE MINISTRY OF JESUS IN GALILEE.

I. The Calling of the First Disciples.

Matt. iv. 13-22; Mark i. 14-20.

Cana, though more hospitable than Nazareth, was not to be the centre from which Jesus would extend His labors throughout Galilee; this glory was reserved to Capharnaum; and Saint Matthew, studious as ever to trace throughout the life of the Saviour the fulfilment of Prophecies, quotes here the famous oracle: [1] —

"Land of Zabulon and Nephthali! Border-land of the sea! Country beyond the Jordan! Galilee of the nations! The people that abode in darkness have seen a great Light. The Light has arisen upon those who were seated in the region of the shadow of death."

It was the arena of the Ministry of Jesus which Isaias had here before his eyes: the Sea of Tiberias, lying along

---

[1] Matt. iv. 13-16; Is. ix. 1, 2. This difficult text of Isaiah has been variously construed. In describing the site of Capharnaum, we gave the ingenious interpretation of Caspari (p. 155): here we follow the commoner opinion, which makes דֶּרֶךְ = via, an adverb signifying, "toward, in the direction of," and then understands אֶרֶץ, land, before the two members of the sentence, which in the Greek are translated by these words: ὁδὸν θαλάσσης and πέραν τοῦ Ἰορδάνου, "the land lying seaward," or (in other words) the western banks of the Sea of Galilee; "the land beyond the Jordan" (that is to say), Perea. The last expression, "Galilee of the Gentiles," in a single phrase embraces all the different countries of which the Prophet is speaking.

the confines of Zabulon and Nephthali; the western shore, where the Christ ordinarily sojourned; upon the opposite side, and beyond the Jordan, the Greek colonies of the Decapolis,[1] — a mingling of races [2] well described by the name Galilee of the Gentiles. The first Israelites who were carried off into Assyria had been snatched from this pleasant "land of Zabulon and Nephthali;" so to comfort them the Prophet tells how a Youthful Liberator shall rise up, like a great Light; and how Galilee, the first to be plunged in the dark night of slavery, is destined to be the first to view the New-born Star.[3]

This prediction, the theme of long-cherished hopes, was accomplished on the day when the Christ took up His abode upon the shores of the Lake and made Capharnaum "His own city."[4] He came thither accompanied doubtless, as at the beginning of His public life, by His Mother, His

[1] We shall see later on (vol. ii. p. 12), that the word "Decapolis" does not designate any particular country, but a confederation of ten free cities, situated to the east of the Jordan, between Damascus and the Mountains of Galaad.

[2] Teglath Phalasar, after carrying away the Israelites from out of Galilee, filled all their holdings with Assyrian colonists; in like manner the Greeks, after the conquest of Alexandria, had spread through the whole country; hence, as it came to be more and more monopolized by Gentiles, it naturally became an object of scorn for all patriotic Jews (John i. 46; vii. 52; Matt. xxvi. 69).

[3] The Prophecy from which S. Matthew cites a few sentences is the one which precedes that foreshadowing of the Messiah: "A little Child is born to us, unto us a Son is given ... Wonderful Councillor, Mighty God, Father of Eternity, Prince of Peace" (Is. ix. 6). Here Isaiah deplores the impiety which plunged the Israelites into the abyss of darkness: their country he represents as a land without any sunrise, desolated by famine, sunk in dark shadows whence arise only curses against Achab and against God. Still, Assur is only the scourge of Jehovah; his mission of vengeance once fulfilled, he shall fade away before the coming of Emmanuel. Then "there shall be no longer any dimness over the land which is now grievously vexed. For indeed Jehovah hath loaded the lands of Zabulon and Nephthali with afflictions at the first, yet afterwards He will bestow honors upon them, ay, even on them, the land lying to seaward, on the further bank of the Jordan, Galilee of the nations. The people that abode in darkness have seen a great Light; the Light hath risen over them that dwell in the land of the shadow of death." The text of the Prophecy was so familiar to the readers of S. Matthew that the Evangelist knew it would be enough to quote a few words, to remind them of the perfect correspondence between the prediction and the reality.

[4] Matt. ix. 1.

VOL. I. — 14.

brothers, and His disciples.[1] However, the foremost among the latter, Peter, Andrew, James, and John, whom He had chosen upon the banks of the Jordan, are not now found with their Master; and that we know so little of the doings of the Lord in Judea is due probably to the fact that they did not follow Him into that country. John the Evangelist seems to be the only one who made the journey through Samaria with the Lord;[2] but he did not go on as far as Nazareth; for the Saviour, upon coming down to the shores of the lake, found him again at Bethsaïda, in the boat of his father Zebedee.[3]

It was Jesus' first care to go to this village, that He might gather together the Princes of His Church. He was walking along the strand when he saw some fishermen busy casting their nets from out their boat;[4] they were the two brothers Simon and Andrew.

Jesus spoke to them: "Come with Me, and I will make you to become fishers of men."

At once dropping everything, they followed Him. Having advanced a little further, He saw two other brothers, James and John; these also were in a boat, with their father Zebedee. Some accident had caused a breakage in their nets, and they were busy mending them. The Lord would not wait for the work to be finished; He called them, and upon the instant they followed Him, leaving behind them their father Zebedee, with his hirelings, in the fishing-smack.

It was not that the Christ chose these humble fishermen at random, but it was because the Divine Handiwork must needs be supreme in the work of our Redemption; and therefore it was needful that the ministers of Jesus, though unfitted by nature for such great designs, should nevertheless be so devoid of self-confidence, so free from self-love, as to let themselves be guided by grace. The first dis-

---

[1] John ii. 12.
[2] The precise manner in which all the details set down in this fourth chapter are recorded makes it necessary to infer that the narrator was an eye-witness (John iv. 6, 8, 28, etc.).
[3] Mark i. 19.
[4] Ἀμφιβάλλοντας ἐν τῇ θαλάσσῃ (Mark i. 16).

ciples were men such as this Mission required, — simple, upright of heart, and of generous inclinations. At the call of Jesus, they followed Him without hesitation and without casting a glance backwards; all that they left behind was little enough doubtless, — a fishing-craft and a few nets; but that little was their all, and in sacrificing it they showed what docile instruments Jesus was to find in them.

Furthermore their trade could not fail to have developed in them such qualities as are most suitable to the Apostolic Ministry, above all the religious spirit, natural to those who live by the sea; the life of these men, always exposed to perils, their powerlessness to contend with the great tempests, with that Breath from on High which stirs up storms and calms them again in an instant, — all these things combine to keep before their mind the feeling that they are in the hands of God; at the same time, because they are thus inured to danger, their courage is of the hardiest, and self-denial and devotedness become as habitual to them as sturdy prudence. These simple virtues were sufficient for the Master; surely they were as nothing in comparison with the sublime Work which He had in mind; but thus to construct an Edifice upon nothing is manifestly a work of Creation; it is to perform an Act of God. This indeed is why the Saviour, instead of calling to Himself the wise and great ones of Israel, chose rather for the foundation-stones of His Church four fishermen of Bethsaïda, — Peter and Simon, James and John.

II. A Sabbath Day at Capharnaum.

Luke iv. 34-43; Mark i. 21-38; Matt. viii. 14-17.

The first Sabbath after the return of Jesus to Capharnaum is an exceptional day for us; perhaps it is the only one during which we are able to follow the Saviour from early morning until evening, and even as far as the dawning of the next day; and so this detailed account shows us how, for the most part, Jesus was wont to spend His days.

The religious service commenced in the morning at the synagogue;[1] there the Lord found an attentive throng about Him, for His wondrous deeds were well known in Capharnaum; and moreover He could count among that gathering some faithful hearts, — Mary His Mother, the sons of Zebedee and of Jonas, the disciples who had followed Him from Judea, the officer of the court of Herod with his family, who were eager to hear the Prophet whose word had already worked such marvels.

When the prayers were finished the Master ascended to take the chair. There He bore Himself very differently from the Scribes and the Doctors,[2] who were only accustomed to cite certain texts which would confirm their teaching by the authority of ancient traditions, or perhaps explain those of other famous Rabbis. But Jesus taught as one having power; He spoke in His own name, interpreted the Scripture with authority, not merely stirring over the surface of the soul by subtile reasonings, but plunging deep down into the hearts of men, so that they felt themselves penetrated with His persuasion.

"All were in admiration of His doctrine," when a scream rent the air of the place; it was a demoniac in the throes of horrid frenzy. He had crept through the crowded doors, and at the first had experienced a strange rapture while listening to the Divine Word; but unable any longer to withhold the foul spirit which held him in its clutches, he burst into shrieks of horror, perhaps even into unclean actions.[3] "Let be!"[4] he cried. "What is there between us and

---

[1] Mark i. 21.   [2] Mark i. 22-26.
[3] "Ἄνθρωπος ἐν πνεύματι ἀκαθάρτῳ (Mark i. 23). These words seem to imply that the unclean spirit had fastened its hold upon the miserable victim so completely that this element of impurity became the sole vital and active principle of his being. Some scholars do not coincide with this opinion; to their mind, the term "impure" applies to all the fallen Angels, and as used here merely reveals the burning thirst they feel for whatever is unchaste, since they know uncleanness is of all things most hateful in God's sight; that it is more than any other vice contrary to the angelic purity from which they have fallen, and more terrible in its effects upon man, since it degrades him, blinds him, dulls and hardens his heart.
[4] Luke iv. 34. "Ea (translated as "Sine!" in the Vulgate) is probably but a cry of fear and horror, the exclamation, in Hebrew, אָחָה.

Thee, Jesus of Nazareth? Art Thou come to destroy us? I know Who Thou art,— the Holy of God!"

What are we to see in this confession of the Demon? Was it a ruse whereby Satan meant to interrupt the discourse of Jesus and publish prematurely His title of the Messiah, or was it an avowal wrung from the terror of the fiend,— the fawning of a slave that trembles before the lash and seeks to mollify the master about to inflict well merited punishment? Whatever may have been the motive of this homage, Jesus disdained it; at once He stood over the possessed, and threatening the devil which was torturing him,

"Be silent,"[1] He said to it, "and depart from this man."

Satan obeyed: one last cry escaped the breast of the demoniac, who flung prone upon the ground for an instant writhed in terrible convulsions; then rose up before the eyes of all, free once more, completely calmed.[2] His body, which had served as a dwelling-place for the infernal powers, now showed no trace of their awful assaults.

At this sight fright and wonderment quite overwhelmed the crowds; for man can never feel the nearness of the invisible world without a stronger sense of emotion. And yet it was not so much the suddenness of the cure which astonished the Jews; indeed they were accustomed to the performance and the effects of various Exorcisms, which were in fact much like the tedious ceremonials of their magicians.[3] But that Jesus, without sprinkling of water or

---

[1] Φιμώθητι (Luke iv. 35), or, giving the full force of the literal meaning, it might be translated: "Put bridle and curb upon thy jaws."
[2] Luke iv. 35; Mark i. 26.
[3] S. Justin tells us how the Jewish exorcisms, though lawful at first, came to degenerate into superstitious rites (*Dialogus cum Tryphone*, 85). Josephus reports an example of this sort of witchcraft, as in vogue among his fellow-countrymen; it is enough to compare the scenes which he witnessed with the quiet manner in which Jesus dealt with the demons, to realize how entirely at variance are Truth and Error. The thing was done, says the Jewish historian, under the eyes of Vespasian, Titus, and the whole army. A Jew, named Eleazar, drove a devil out of a man, making it proceed from the nostrils of the possessed creature by means of a ring and a magic root. The demoniac was thrown on the ground. Eleazar adjured the unclean spirit, in the name of Solomon, and with sundry other incantations, to torment his victim no longer, and bade him,

any mystical rite, could expel the demon with a word,— it was this that overwhelmed them with wonder. Hitherto they had only experienced the eloquence of the Christ; this prodigy declared the invincible might of His word; and now their souls must needs tremble in His Presence as before the Supreme Majesty.

"What is this?" they whispered among themselves; "what new and all-powerful Doctrine is this?[1] He commands the spirits, and they obey!"

In these sayings there is no trace of that bitter spirit which, in a short time, would try to brand the Miracles of the Saviour as a violation of the Sabbath, or as a proof of a compact with the fiends. The Galileans harbored no such suspicions as these; they saw, they believed, and their faith, spreading ever further and wider, finally penetrated throughout all the country-side.

The marvellous deeds of that Sabbath were by no means ended now. Leaving the synagogue, Jesus entered the dwelling of Simon.[2] The son of Jonas the fisherman was married to a woman of Capharnaum; thus he had in this city, as well as at Bethsaïda, both family connections and a home. Here the Divine Master found the mother-in-law of the disciple sinking under a raging attack of fever,[3] her anxious kinsfolk grouped about her bed. At once all eyes were turned towards the Saviour; every voice was raised to implore His aid.

Jesus drew near, and rebuking the fever[4] with the same authority which He was only a little later to display in quelling the rebellious powers of nature, He now

---

in token of obedience to this dismissal, to overturn a basin of water set at some distance from the spot (Josephus, *Antiquitates*, viii. 2, 5). When describing the site of Macheronte we spoke of a root with stems of flame-color, which was thought to work many wonders. But in order to pluck it a man must resort to certain practices of such an extraordinary nature that we refrain from mentioning them here. They are detailed at length by Josephus (*Bellum Judaïcum*, vii. 6, 3).

[1] Mark, i. 27. Καινή may be joined with κατ' ἐξουσίαν, when it will mean "an utterance of new and hitherto unknown efficacy," or it may form a distinct attribute of κατ' ἐξουσίαν; "a new and powerful teaching."

[2] Mark i. 29.   [3] Luke iv. 38.

[4] Luke iv. 39.

bade the disease to depart; and then, taking the hand of the sick woman, He gently raised up her shattered body, by the simple contact infusing a plenitude of health and life into her aged body. The fever disappeared, and that without leaving behind it any weakness, which is its usual sequel. On the instant the mother of Simon's wife arose, then, as it was the hour at which they usually dined, — for on the Sabbath it was customary to have a noonday meal,[1] — she herself made ready what was needed for Jesus and His disciples, set the dishes in order, and herself served the guests.

Capharnaum was still talking of the miracle in the synagogue when the report of this other prodigy was noised abroad; the excitement became general, and nothing but the inviolable quiet of the Sabbath could have held the ardor of the multitude in check. But as soon as the rays of the setting sun along the distant hills marked the end of the Holy Day,[2] the throngs came hurrying through the streets, some bringing the insane and possessed folk to the Divine Healer, others bearing pallets, on which were laid those too ill to move themselves; soon the whole town had collected about Simon's door, displaying before the eyes of Jesus every form of wretchedness known to poor human nature, — madness, deformity, and every hideous disease.

Not one of those who besought His help was rejected by the Saviour, but without distinction laying His hands upon them, He healed them. As for the possessed, one word from Him was enough to deliver them; trembling at the sound of the Master's voice, the devils fled away, crying aloud, "Thou art the Son of God."[3] But with threatening words Jesus forbade them to say that He was the Christ.

The Saviour's ministrations were prolonged far into the night, and to all He showed such touching compassion, that in the wonders of that day's doings Saint Matthew sees the fulfilment of the words of Isaias:[4] "He hath taken

---

[1] Josephus, *De Vita Sua*, 54.   [2] Luke iv. 40.
[3] Luke iv. 41.   [4] Is. liii. 4.

upon Himself our weaknesses and hath borne our infirmities." None ever understood so clearly as Jesus did how disease and death have entered into the world through sin;[1] no one consequently has ever been so keenly struck with horror at sight of them. Hence arose that great pity in Him predicted by Isaiah; hence came His tears before the tomb of Lazarus;[2] and so too, His sighs of sorrow at sight of the deaf-mute.[3] His Heart could never view the depth of our woes without strong throes of sympathy, and without reaching out His healing hand to dispel even the sin itself, which is its source.

The last sufferer did not quit the house of Peter until the dawning of another day.[4] Without giving a moment to sleep, the Lord rose, and went out into the morning streets. The little city of Capharnaum was still all silent and at rest when He passed along its narrow ways, and reached at length the desert place wherein He wished to pray alone.

But this holy solitude was soon to be broken in upon; the crowds, surprised at not seeing the Saviour upon their awakening, set to work seeking Him on every side. Peter and His companions were most noticeable in their eagerness;[5] they found the Divine Master absorbed in God.

"Every one is looking for You." they said to Him.

"Let us go elsewhere," replied Jesus, "into the neighboring towns, and into the cities, so that I may preach there also; it is for this that I am come."[6]

The throngs were coming up, close after the disciples; they wished to keep the Saviour among them; but He withstood them,[7] and told them, as He had told the rest, that His Mission compelled Him to depart for a time, that He might carry unto others the Good Tidings of the Kingdom of God.

---

[1] Rom. v. 12.   [2] John xi. 35.   [3] Mark vii. 34.
[4] Mark i. 35.   [5] Mark i. 36-38.
[6] Ἐξῆλθον (Mark i. 38), the general term: "I have come forth," out of Capharnaum, out of My native land, from My hidden and obscure Existence, from the Bosom of God, My Father, that so I may fulfil My Mission.
[7] Luke iv. 42, 43.

III. THE MIRACULOUS DRAUGHT OF FISHES. — HEALING OF A LEPER.

Luke iv. 44, v. 1–16 ; Mark i. 39–45 ; Matt. iv. 23–25, viii. 1–4.

On going out of Capharnaum, Jesus followed the borders of the lake, and striking out toward the North, He stopped again at Bethsaïda, the village-home of His first disciples.

So the sons of Jonas and of Zebedee once more launched their little barks, and were out fishing all night long;[1] for they were poor, and the necessity of getting something wherewith to buy bread for the morrow forced them back to their old occupation. But it was all a useless toil dredging and hauling over the sea; until finally the sun rose, and the morning heats put an end to their hopes. They had taken nothing, even during those hours most favorable for their work.[2]

Greatly discouraged, they returned to the shore just as Jesus was coming down thither; there were glad crowds surrounding Him, eager to catch His words. But though they pressed closely about Him, He straightway espied the two boats, and His disciples, who, having landed upon the beach, were washing their nets. At once He went on board of Simon's boat, and desired Him to draw a little away from the land; then, seated in this first Chair of Peter, He began to instruct the people.

But His longing to spread the Good News did not prevent His feeling a keen sympathy for the useless and tedious toils and disappointment of the fishers; so when He had ceased speaking to the people, He said to Simon, " Push out into the deeper water; " and to His companions, " Cast over your nets for the fish."

"Master," Simon responded, "we have labored all the

---

[1] Luke v. 1–11.
[2] Indeed, we know that it is toward sunset, and just before sunrise, that the fish run the freest and are most easily taken in nets (Aristotle, *Historiæ animalium*, viii. 19 ; Pliny, *Historia naturalis*, ix. 123).

night without taking anything, but at Your word I will cast the net."

They dropped it over the side, and thereupon drew up such a great quantity of fishes that the cords were breaking. As they were separated too far from the others to be heard in the neighboring bark, they made signals for their companions to come to their aid.[1] When these were come, the draught of fishes filled the two boats to such a degree that they were almost submerged.

Seeing this, Simon Peter threw himself at the feet of the Christ: "Depart from me, O Lord," he said, "for I am a sinful man."

By this miracle Jesus revealed Himself as Lord and Master over Nature and her resources. And so Peter only yielded to a feeling of terror which was common to all Jews, since they believed that to see God was to die; the same dread fell also upon those who were with him, and on the sons of Zebedee.

Jesus reassured them, one and all,[2] saying, "Be not afraid! hereafter you shall be fishers of men."

It was the second time the Saviour had spoken these words to the disciples, and He showed them, by the miraculous draught of fishes, how fruitful the power which He would confer upon their souls was to be. This prodigy was therefore a figure of their Ministry; thus they were to come out from the plain of Genesareth to launch upon the stormy sea of events, to live in labor and trouble without ceasing, tossed about upon waves more restless than those of their little lake. Yet if their duties, hitherto so peaceful, were henceforth to be fraught with trials, by a just recompense there were the most glorious rewards assured to them: they were to exchange their rude trade for a celestial Mission; instead of the rough meshes of their old torn and mended nets, they were to have the lovely snare of the Gospel, "which kills not that which is taken in it, but protects it, and brings up to the sweet light of Heaven that which it has rescued from the depths of the abyss."[3] Had the fishermen of Bethsaïda any such

---

[1] Luke v. 7.   [2] Luke v. 9.   [3] S. Ambrose, *in Lucam*, lib. iv. 72.

full comprehension of this symbol of which He made use? We think not. God, however, let them catch some glimmerings of the light; for their fright gave place to confidence. They no longer prayed the Lord to depart, but rowed their boats back to the shore, and threw everything aside, once for all, to go and follow Him.

Surrounded by these companions, Jesus traversed all Galilee,[1] " teaching in the synagogues, preaching the Gospel of the Kingdom, and healing all the ill and infirm among the people." The very poorest villages, even those which had no synagogues, were not forgotten. The Lord bore to all the Good Tidings; not waiting, like John the Baptist, for them to come to Him, but seeking out such as He could save. The days of the Divine Master among these little hamlets were passed much like that Sabbath-day at Capharnaum; the places and the times were different, but always with the same patience and never-wearying tenderness He lavished His good deeds upon all; with inexhaustible compassion He cured their souls and bodies, healed every malady, and departing, left behind Him, as it were, the perfume of His Presence.

Of that first mission in Galilee we know but one single event.[2] Jesus had come to a town whose name is un-

---

[1] Luke iv. 44; Matt. iv. 23; Mark i. 39. The passage in S. Luke which mentions this preaching offers one serious difficulty; the reading εἰς τὰς συναγωγὰς τῆς Γαλιλαίας, which is given in most of the versions (Latin, Peshito, Gothic, Armenian, Ethiopian), is not contained anywhere else except in the Alexandrine Manuscript, and the Codex Bezæ. The others, and notably the manuscripts of the Vatican and Sinaï, as well as the Palimpsest of Ephraem, read Ἰουδαίας. From this it seems only natural to conclude that Jesus extended the field of that first Mission to embrace all Judea. To choose between these two readings, supported as both are by such weighty authorities, seems a difficult task. Is it not practicable for us to accept the two readings as having come from the pen of S. Luke? May it not be that the Evangelist, when writing for the Greeks, who were more or less strangers to Palestine, thought it unnecessary to be so precise in the marking out of localities, and was content to use the vaguer term "in the synagogues of Judea," but that afterwards, in response to the questions addressed to him, he changed the word Judea to the more exact term Galilee?

[2] Luke v. 12–16; Mark i. 40–45; Matt. viii. 2–4. Here we follow SS. Luke and Mark. S. Matthew puts the healing of the lepers after the Sermon on the Mount: " When Jesus came down the mountain

known, when a man, running toward Him, threw himself
at His feet, and implored His mercy. The unfortunate
well merited pity; leprosy had consumed his whole body.
The scourge when it reaches this stage becomes an object
of horror, for the corruption of death has then actually
taken possession of a living body. No plague was dreaded
more by the Jews; they called it the Finger, or the Hand-
writing, of God; and in its ravages they saw the counter-
part of that sin which fastens upon the soul and poisons
the very well-springs of life within it. The funereal tokens
always surrounding lepers still further fortified them in
this feeling. Banished from home, and not allowed to
enter beyond the city gates, their garments tattered and
torn to shreds like those of mourners, their heads shaven,
and their lips covered with a veil,— thus they were nothing more to the eyes of their fellow-citizens than living,
moving sepulchres, obliged at every approach of man to
send forth that lugubrious cry,

"Unclean! Unclean!"

Although the leper of the Gospel had infringed this law [1]
by overstepping the limits of the city's enclosure, his
misery was so piteous that at the first glance Jesus
thought of nothing except to assuage it.

"Lord," [2] cried the wretched creature, "if You will, You
can heal me!"

Immediately the Master stretched out His hand, laid it
upon his body with its repulsive sores.

"I will," He said; "be thou healed."

And on the instant the leprosy disappeared. It was
because of the sufferer's faith that Jesus granted him so

---

side, a great throng followed him, and lo! a leper came," etc. (Matt.
viii. 1). This would be to grant that the expression "and behold, . . ."
Καὶ ἰδού, so often employed by S. Matthew, is used by him consistently to
mark the order of events: on the contrary, in the majority of instances it
is used with no idea other than that of bespeaking our attention for what
follows. Hence we are perfectly free to separate these two phrases,—
looking upon the first, "Jesus, on coming down, was followed by the
multitude," as being the conclusion of the Sermon on the Mount; and
taking that which follows, "And lo! a leper cometh," as the beginning
of another tale.

[1] Lev. xiii. 46; Num. v. ii.   [2] Luke v. 12.

prompt a hearing, but it was also owing to his sad condition. No leper ever invoked His aid without being heard; the Lord always had compassion upon their desolate lives, and at once purified them.

However, after having yielded to the first movement of pity, Jesus now saw in this man only a law-breaker. He reproached him severely,[1] and bade him go out of the city which he had presumed to enter unsanctioned.

"Be careful," He said, "to tell no one of this; but go, show yourself to the priest, and offer in return for your cure that which Moses has ordained, in order that it may be a testimony unto them."[2]

By this command Jesus not only testified His respect for the legal ordinances; He wished also to cover over in silence an act which revealed in Him the Supreme Lawgiver, able to touch the most dreaded and most noxious impurities without being contaminated, and thus working a cure reserved to the power of God alone.[3] A marvel so manifestly divine could not fail to excite unbounded hopes in the multitudes, hopes which would be likely to interfere with the Saviour's Mission. Therefore He spared neither commands nor threats in order to insure the silence of the

---

[1] Ἐμβριμησάμενος (Mark i. 43). Ἐμβριμάομαι, to be indignant, to chide one sharply (Wahl, *Clavis Novi Testamenti*). Ἐμβριμώμενος μετ' ἀπειλῆς ἐντελλόμενος: issuing a command in a threatening manner (Hesychius).

[2] Leviticus furnishes us with the details of this Purification of Lepers. The priest must go with the sufferer outside the town, and there sacrifice a sparrow in an earthen vessel, over a running stream; then taking a living sparrow, a little cedar wood, some scarlet and hyssop, he dips them in the blood of the immolated bird, and seven times sprinkles the sick. The living sparrow was then set at liberty. But for the leper, he must change his garments, shave all his body, and wash in water; thereafter, for a week, he remained in seclusion; on the eighth day, after again shaving, having washed his clothes and his body, he was to make offering of two unblemished lambs, with a quantity of fine flour and oil. Taking the blood of the victims and the oil mingled with flour, the priest, following the mystic ritual, would then touch the right ear of the leper, the thumb of his right hand and the great toe of his right foot, and after pouring what remained of the oil upon his bare head, proclaimed that the sick was at last purified (Lev. xiv.).

[3] At least, this was a general feeling among the Jews. At the sight of Naaman, who besought him to cure him, Joram cried out, "Am I then a God, to take away and to restore life? Wherefore hast thou sent me a man that I should heal him of his leprosy?" (4 Kings v. 7).

man whom He had just healed. But these precautions were all thwarted by the indocility of the leper, who, remembering nothing but his debt of gratitude, went forth and published the news on every hand.[1]

What the Saviour wished to prevent now occurred; the excitement among the people was so intense, their enthusiasm was so overpowering, that He could not enter publicly into a town any longer, but was compelled to remain outside the cities, in the wilderness.[2]

Thither they flocked from all parts, and there Jesus pursued His ministry in perfect freedom; for at such a distance from the crowded centres He had not much cause for anxiety lest His hearers' ardor should call down upon His labors the vengeance of Herod.

IV. Healing of a Paralytic.

Luke v. 17-26; Mark ii. 1-12; Matt. ix. 1-8.

The precautions taken by the Saviour had not been unnecessary; not many days after the healing of the leper, on returning to Capharnaum, He found numbers of Pharisees and Scribes gathered together there,—not only from Galilee, but from Judea and from Jerusalem.[3] The hatred shown Him by the Sanhedrin, which had been the cause of Jesus' departure from Judea, leaves hardly any doubt but that these doctors were commissioned to spy upon the new Prophet, in order to detect Him in some offence, as well as to try and discover His ultimate designs.

Accordingly as soon as rumors of His arrival began to be circulated through the town we see them hurrying along with the populace, and the first to enter the house where the Saviour was; there they seated themselves within the inmost circle of those about him, bent upon hearing and observing everything.[4] A crowd of citizens, which on this day was denser than ever, had filled the dwelling,

---

[1] Mark i. 45.   [2] Mark i. 45.   [3] Luke v. 17.   [4] Luke v. 17-19.

and kept surging about the outer doors; so that it was now quite impossible to find access to any part of it. Jesus, Who had remained seated, was teaching them according to His custom, when suddenly, above their heads, hands were seen making an opening in the ceiling of earthen clods (of which the roofs of houses in the East are often composed), and then four men proceeded at once to let down a pallet, on which a poor invalid was lying.[1] It was a paralytic, who had seized upon this expedient so to reach the great Healer. Those who were carrying him, losing all hopes of forcing an entrance through the multitudes, had drawn him up to the roof, and tearing away the rafters with the clay tiling, had by this means managed to deposit their burden at the very feet of Jesus.

This deed, more eloquent than any words, and their faith, which would not stop to consider any obstacles, touched the heart of the Divine Master, and He granted to the sufferer even more than he had dared to hope for.

"My son,"[2] He said, "take courage; your sins are forgiven you."

The sufferings of the paralytic were doubtless the result, or perhaps the punishment, of past wrongdoing; and Jesus, by His divine power penetrating to the very root of the evil, worked the cure of soul and body at one and the same time.

This speech scandalized the Scribes, seated about the Saviour; for the power of remitting sins, which He assumed, belongs only to God. Jesus saw their glowering countenances and the menace that gleamed in their eyes. In the bottom of their hearts, perhaps even upon their lips, He could easily hear their mutterings, "What does

---

[1] Some critics suppose that Jesus was sitting in the upper story, in one of those high-studded halls which the wealthy Jews used for their frequent gatherings, and that the bearers reached the flat roof above by an outside stairway. This conjecture seems to us rather superfluous, for the poorer dwellings in Judea are generally very low, and nothing would be easier than to climb upon their house-tops; even to-day, when the farmers of Galilee wish to house their crops, they make an opening in the dry earthen tiling of their roofs.

[2] Mark ii. 5.

this man mean to say?[1] He is blaspheming. Who can remit sins except God?"

"Why do you think evil things in your heart?" He answered them, "Which is easier to say to a paralytic, 'Your sins are forgiven you,' or to say to him, 'Rise up; take your bed, and go into your house'?"

The question left them no room for evasion; for if upon the first of these claims He could not be convicted of imposture, still they thought it might not be the same as regards the second, although it would require a miracle to sustain it. Yet to make this avowal before Jesus might even be to furnish Him with another weapon against them, and they would thus expose themselves to be brought to confusion upon the spot.

The Scribes perceived this, and mistrustful as to what might be the power of the Christ, they remained silent.

Knowing their thoughts, He proceeded:—

"Now, that you may know the Son of Man has power on the earth to remit sins,"[2] He turned to the paralytic, "I say to thee: Arise; take up thy bed, and go into thy house!"

The sick man rose up directly, took the pallet on which he had been lying, and threading his way through the swaying masses of people, returned to his home, glorifying God.

Those who witnessed the miracle were at first as if struck dumb with amazement; but their wondering delight soon found tongue and voice, and they said to each other, with tremulous lips and bated breath,

"We have seen marvellous things to-day!"[3]

While others began to glorify God, acknowledging in this deed a prodigy such as never before had greeted their eyes, and they praised the Lord God for having bestowed such power upon man.

---

[1] Mark ii. 6, 7.   [2] Luke v. 24.   [3] Luke v. 25.

V. THE CALLING OF LEVI.

Luke v. 27, 28 ; Mark ii. 13, 14 ; Matt. ix. 9.

Of the six disciples Jesus had chosen on the banks of the Jordan, only four were now with Him constantly; and all of these were equally poor and of a like simplicity of mind and soul. But now it was to be from a class which the Jews looked upon as the vilest and the hatefulest in society, that the Lord would select His fifth companion, in the person of Levi the publican.[1]

We know in what esteem that title was held in Latin literature of this age. It was the name employed to designate those knights who were engaged in farming out the tax-revenue of the provinces.[2] These opulent citizens should not be confounded with the publicans of the Gospel. The latter were merely agents, of the lowest class, who collected taxes in the name of the great Roman companies; for in the course of time these enterprises had become too considerable for one knight to undertake the responsibility of discharging the duties. And so an administrator, residing at Rome, represented his associates, and directed the subalterns whom he employed to supervise the incoming and outgoing of merchandise, and to compute more or less justly the value of the same. Naturally they preferred to appoint to this latter office native residents of the conquered

---

[1] The first Gospel gives this publican the name of Matthew, while the two other Synoptics have that of Levi. The most ancient Fathers agree in regarding Levi as the same person as S. Matthew, and everything goes to support their opinion : (1) The circumstances which surround the calling of the two are so exactly similar that we naturally regard it as the story of one man's vocation. (2) The name Levi is not found in any list of the Apostles; while, on the other hand, all give that of Matthew. Probably it was Jesus who changed the name of this publican, whom He then called, from Levi to Matthew (מַתִּתְיָה, Gift of God, Theodore).

Nothing was of commoner occurrence among the Jews than this taking or giving of a new name in token of some memorable event, and Jesus acted in like manner with Simon. By the word λεγόμενον (Matt. ix. 7), Matthew seems to imply that the name which he takes in the history of his vocation is not that which he was known by at this time.

[2] Pauly, *Real Encyclopædie :* PUBLICANI.

provinces, whose familiarity with the language, manners, and resources of their native land, would make them much fitter for such difficult functions than any foreigners could be.

The disrepute attached to this career was enough to prevent men who were held in any esteem in the community from embracing it; and the Roman collectors were compelled to take their agents from among the lower classes of the populace. Delivered into such hands, the power delegated to these men by the great syndicates degenerated naturally into abuses and exactions, which finally rendered the name publican synonymous with that of robber.[1] Cicero does not hesitate to call them the vilest of men;[2] Stobæus looks upon them as the wolves and bears of the human race.[3]

Beside the general aversion felt for such a trade, there was, in Judea, an additional reason for holding it in abhorrence.[4] Every payment of tribute to foreign masters was, in the eyes of the Israelites, a forbidden act, a transgression of the Law of Jehovah; the publicans, by helping to consummate this sacrilege, were therefore regarded not only as traitors to their country, but as infidels and apostates, and for this reason quite as despicable as any criminals, courtesans, or pagans.[5] It was, then, from among the outcasts of society that Jesus picked out this new disciple.

Capharnaum, situated just where the great highways of Damascus, Tyre, Sephoris, and Jerusalem meet, and through which caravans were continually passing, had grown to be one of the central points best adapted for the handling of custom-duties;[6] hence there were to be found here great numbers of publicans. Jesus, as He was threading his way down toward the shore of the lake, saw one

---

[1] Xeno, *Apud Dicæarch. de Vita Græc.*; Meincke, *Frag. com.* iv. 596.
[2] Cicero, *De Officiis*, i. 42.
[3] Stobæus, *Serm.* ii. 34.
[4] Matt. xviii. 17 : Deut. xvii. 15 ; Josephus, *Antiquitates*, xviii. 2, 1.
[5] Matt. ix. 11, xxi. 31, xviii. 17.
[6] It was probably from the fact of Capharnaum's being a centre for so much trade that the name of this town was commonly taken to mean a place where great quantities of goods are stored up.

of them named Levi, the son of Alpheus,[1] sitting at his toll-office.

"Follow Me!" He said to him.

The publican arose, left all, and followed the Lord.

We are amazed at this prompt obedience; but Levi knew Who He was Who called him. He could not have been all this time an indifferent spectator, since every day he must have listened to the travellers repeating, or even heard himself, the noble utterances of the new Prophet, who was now stirring up all Galilee to higher thoughts; surely his heart must have been already touched, and all his thoughts attracted to Jesus. So when the divine Master, far from drawing away His garments in fear of any contact with the publican, as was generally done among the Israelites, addressed to him that quiet appeal: "Follow Me!" Levi, who until now had never met with anything but contempt, yielded to the grace which had been long time moving within him, and joined the little band of followers around the Saviour, never afterwards to be separated from Him.[2]

---

[1] Mark ii. 13, 14. This Alpheus, father of Levi, should not be confounded with another Alpheus who married the sister of the Blessed Virgin, and had many children who are called in the Gospel the brothers and sisters of Jesus.

[2] S. Luke and S. Mark proceed to relate the incidents of the banquet to which Levi invited the Saviour immediately after the history of his Vocation; S. Matthew connects the two latter events, but he does not mention them until later on, after the Sermon on the Mount. Following the example of the most ancient commentators, we shall separate the Calling of the Apostle from his great dinner-giving. This festival certainly took place at the time marked for it by S. Matthew, because this Evangelist (and he is the only one who describes it) connects this fact with the raising of Jaïrus' daughter, and that with details of so precise a nature as to make it impossible to reject his evidence. So far as his vocation is concerned, we may retain the order indicated by SS. Luke and Mark; indeed it is hardly probable that the publican would have prepared a grand repast and invited a crowd of friends on the day when he quitted all to follow Jesus. Furthermore, all the Evangelists put the selection of the Twelve Apostles before the Sermon on the Mount; so then, in mentioning his own calling at a later date, S. Matthew, as usual, simply disregards the chronological order of events.

BOOK FOURTH.

SECOND YEAR

OF THE

MINISTRY OF JESUS.

ΚΑΤΑ ΛΟΥΚΑΝ.

δ'. μά.

Ἐξήρχετο δὲ καὶ δαιμόνια ἀπὸ πολλῶν, κράζοντα καὶ λέγοντα ὅτι σὺ εἶ Ὁ ΥΙΟΣ ΤΟΥ ΘΕΟΥ. καὶ ἐπιτιμῶν οὐκ εἴα αὐτὰ λαλεῖν, ὅτι ᾔδεισαν ΤΟΝ ΧΡΙΣΤΟΝ αὐτὸν εἶναι.

The Testimony of the Devils.

And Devils went out from many, crying out and saying: Thou art THE SON OF GOD! And rebuking them He suffered them not to speak, because they knew that He was THE CHRIST.

SAINT LUKE.
iv. 41.

Book Fourth.

SECOND YEAR OF THE MINISTRY OF JESUS.

CHAPTER I.

THE SECOND PASCHAL SEASON IN THE MINISTRY OF JESUS.

I. THE POOL OF BETHESDA.

John v. 1–47.

ABOUT this time[1] the Saviour was minded to go up to Jerusalem for the approaching festival season. The Gospel does not mention this celebration by name; but the most ancient Fathers looked upon it as being the second Passover in the Ministry of Jesus,[2] and we entirely coincide with their conclusions. It was to be the last in which He could take part without hazard of His life; and so He interrupted His mission in Galilee, joined company with one of the caravans of Pilgrims, and ascended with them

---

[1] Just here we have placed the Feast mentioned in the fifth chapter of S. John because we look upon it as another Passover, and because in Judea the Paschal Season is coincident with that of the harvest. Now S. Luke, who is as usual our guide in these matters, after relating the vocation of Levi, goes on to speak at once of the ripe grain which the disciples gathered as they wandered through the fields; therefore, they must have been on the verge of harvest-time.

[2] As to this question, see Appendix VII.

to the Holy City. He went thither in obedience to the commands of His Father, that He might once again offer His ungrateful city the Salvation which they had disdained; and so His first thought now, as it had ever been, was to seek out the desolate and distressed that He might comfort and relieve them.

"Now there is at Jerusalem,[1] hard by the Gate of the Flocks, a pool called in Hebrew Bethesda" (The House of Mercy).[2] It was a huge basin, "with five sides surrounded by porticos.[3] Here, lying upon the ground, was a great multitude of infirm, blind, lame, and men with withered limbs, waiting for the water to be set in motion. For an Angel of the Lord descended at a certain moment into the pool and stirred the waters, and the first to enter therein after that he had moved upon them was cured of whatsoever malady he lay under."

In the shadow of these porches a man was stretched, who had lain there for now thirty-nine years. He had always been expecting to be cured; but because he had no one to help him, each time was doomed to see some other of his fellow-sufferers forestall him. He was so lonely and desolate, his hopes had been disappointed so many times, that the wretched fellow was quite cast down and discouraged.

Jesus perceived him lying upon the ground, and knowing that he had been ill for such a long time was filled with pity for him.

"Do you wish to be cured?" He said to him.

The paralytic scarcely grasped the meaning of this question; but he felt that it was a compassionate offer from a Stranger, who would perhaps be willing to aid him at the favorable moment.

---

[1] John v. 2–9.

[2] בֵּית חַסְדָּא, "The House of Grace," the Place of Mercy, Βηθεσδά. We have kept the name which the Received Text gives for this spot. The Manuscript of Sinaï has Βεθζαθά; that of Cambridge, Βελζεθά; the Manuscript of the Vatican, the Vulgate, and some other versions have another form: Βηθσαιδά.

[3] As to the location of Bethesda and the healing powers of its waters, see Appendix VIII.

"Sir," he said, "I have no one to carry me to the pool when the water is troubled, and the moment I reach there another goes down ahead of me."

"Arise!" said Jesus; "take up your bed, and walk."

Instantly the poor creature arose, caught up the mat on which he was lying, swung it over his shoulders, and started to walk. Beside himself with joy, he looked about him to thank his Benefactor; but Jesus had disappeared in the shadows under the crowded galleries.

It was on a Sabbath-day that the Lord performed this cure. The witnesses of the miracle were too astounded to hinder the paralytic from carrying his bed off with him; but the elders of the people,[1] whom he met on the road, were horrified at this violation of the holy repose.

"It is the Sabbath!" they exclaimed; "it is not lawful for you to carry your bed."

"He who cured me told me himself: 'Take up your bed and walk,'" was his response.

"Who is the man," they demanded, "who said to you, 'Take up your bed and walk?'"

The poor paralytic did not know; but the councillors of the Sanhedrin, whose deliberations were now constantly concerned with the doings of Jesus, detected His handiwork in this new prodigy, and they betrayed their hatred and their suspicions at the same time by their manner of questioning this man, — not wanting to know "Who has healed you?" but, "Who told you to carry your mat?" or, in other words, to break the Law?

And so they let the humble offender go, whom under other circumstances they would have punished severely, and turned their whole attention to the fact that Jesus was present in their city. However, the delighted cripple, who had been made whole after so wonderful a fashion, wished at least to return thanks to God, and at once went

---

[1] John v. 10–13. "The Jews," says S. John. By this name the Evangelist generally designates the enemies of Jesus, and particularly the Scribes, the prominent Pharisees, and others of the Sanhedrin who were the prime movers in the opposition which the Saviour encountered in Judea from the very commencement of His Ministry. (See Smith, *Dictionary of the Bible:* JEW).

up to the Temple for this purpose.¹ There Jesus encountered him; always careful to renew the soul at the same time as the body, He said to him:—

"I have given you back your health; hereafter guard against sin, for fear lest some worse evil should happen to you."

The man forthwith went in search of the Jews, and told them that it was Jesus Who had healed him.

By this act he did not mean to betray his Benefactor, but on the contrary to glorify Him, and give some token of his own gratitude.² The result was not such as to gratify his desires; for this news only increased the anger of the Sanhedrin by confirming its suspicions. In that same hour they resolved to put down this Man, who violated their observances.³ We do not know whether it was in the Temple or in Jerusalem that they found Him; but wherever it may have been, they were overcome with astonishment, when they heard Him, Whom they had come to rebuke, declare in their presence that, as He was the Son of God, He had all power over the Sabbath.

To the casuists who accused Him with having broken the Law, Jesus replied,⁴ therefore, that the repose of the Sacred Day is not the inertia of death, but a suspension of corporal labor, whose excess does indeed wither and destroy the soul; but that it is at all times lawful to

---

[1] John v. 14, 15.

[2] S. John Chrysostom remarks with perfect justice that if the paralytic had cherished any malicious designs he would have said to the Sanhedrin, "It was Jesus who bade me carry my bed and desecrate the Sabbath." On the contrary, he thinks only of acknowledging Him as his Benefactor; "It was He who cured me!" is what he really says.

[3] John v. 16.

[4] John v. 17. The Evangelist gives the Saviour's reply in this concise form: "My Father ceaseth not to work, and I likewise work." Did Jesus merely utter these words and no more? We cannot think that that was all He said, for although the Jews were accustomed to speak of God as their Father (Is. lxiii. 16, lxiv. 8; Jer. iii. 4; Mal. i. 6; Wis. xiv. 3; Eccl. xxiii. 1, 4), they at once comprehended that the Master did not use this Name with the meaning they usually gave to it: "He has said that God was His own Father, making Himself equal to Him." From this speech we must presume that Jesus set forth His meaning without any equivocal expressions, giving them the full development of this Truth.

do good, and that if God, after the Creation, has made His habitation within an everlasting Sabbath, this His Attribute is not, so to say, the offspring of sterile sloth; but rather He thus conservates the indwelling life of all creatures by continuing to be, what He is in His Essence, the Life eternal, the eternal Quickener unto life. In like manner He, being the Son of God, and God even as is His Father, could not know any surcease of activity in His operations: "My Father ceaseth not to work," He said, "and I work likewise."

This response incensed the Sanhedrin Councillors, who saw nothing in the Christ but an impious fellow and a blasphemer. Henceforth they were determined to compass His death,[1] "not only because He had broken the Sabbath, but also because He said that God was His own Father, making Himself equal to God." But for the present moment, not daring to proceed to extremities, they submitted to listen to His word, which like a sword of fire cleaved their spirit, piercing to the inmost recesses of the soul;[2] for Jesus, far from concealing His office in the presence of the princes of Israel, proclaimed openly Who He was.

Declaring that He is God as His Father is God,[3] the Saviour added, moreover, that He possessed three divine Attributes of the Godhead, — the power of restoring spiritual life to those dead in sin,[4] the power of judging, and the power of raising up from the grave unto life all flesh, at the last day. To establish such lofty prerogatives as these, the testimony of John was not enough, being that of man.[5] Jesus appeals to three Witnesses which come of God, — His Miracles, the unmistakable sign of His Mission;[6] the

---

[1] John v. 18. [2] Hebr. iv. 12. [3] John v. 19-30.
[4] The allusion here is to verse twenty-five. Here it is the death of sin which is referred to, since Jesus said that the hour has already come when the dead are to hearken to the call of the Saviour; and He adds that only those shall receive life who listen to the voice of the Son of God. In verse twenty-eight, where the general Resurrection is announced, He tells us that all those that lie in the grave shall hear the voice of the Christ, which recalls the dead to life; yet it is not said that the hour of the Resurrection is already present, but that it is to come.
[5] John v. 31-35.
[6] John v. 36.

Voice of the Father which at the Jordan had proclaimed Him His well-beloved Son;[1] finally, the Authority of the Scriptures.

"Search them,"[2] He said, "since you think you find eternal life therein; they themselves give testimony of Me. And you will not come to Me that you may have life! . . . I know you; I know that you have not the love of God in you. I am come in the Name of My Father, and you receive Me not. Let another come in his own name, him you will receive."

These reproaches show that the Saviour was not content to enlighten the Sanhedrin as to the Truth, but he sought to move their hearts as well. Yet this effort was to be all in vain; the great men of Judea were too haughty to adore the Son of a carpenter as the Christ. Though they did not dare to give vent to their hatred and contempt, they preserved a perfect secrecy as to what He had said to them; for His claim that He was the Son of God, confirmed and justified as it was by so many miracles, would have caused the people to proclaim Him as the Messiah. On the other hand, as Jesus had transgressed the Pharisaic precepts by healing a man within the limits of the Sabbath, they directed all their public attacks upon this one point, and accused Him of contemning the Day of the Lord, assuring themselves that the people would side with them in any quarrel which involved the sanctity of the Day of Rest.

Indeed there was no institution more holy in the eyes of the Jews. They looked upon it as the one individual characteristic which distinguished them from all other nations, and esteemed themselves as chosen by Jehovah solely to guard its observance.[3] The ancient directions were far from satisfying their scrupulosity. After the Captivity, the Great Synagogue had drawn up a list of Thirty-nine Articles, called "Aboth,"[4] or Principal Prohi-

---

[1] John v. 37, 38.
[2] John v. 39–47.
[3] We know that they went so far in their fanaticism as to submit to be slaughtered rather than defend their life on the Sacred Day.
[4] Literally, the "Fathers," Aboth, from the Hebrew, אָב "father;" and the "Descendants," from תולדות "generations, descent."

bitions. These, in turn, had given birth to an infinite number of "Toledoth," or descendants; and these secondary restrictions, embracing every detail of daily life,[1] did, so to speak, really render any action impossible during the Sabbath Day.

We can see how the Pharisaic customs must have hindered and hampered the ministry of Jesus; and how easily the Sanhedrin, by exaggerating each least infringement upon its edicts, gradually so prevailed over the general mind that at last popular indignation demanded its Victim that had been thus made ready for the Sacrifice.[2]

II. A Sabbath Walk through the Fields.

Luke vi. 1-5; Mark ii. 23-28; Matt. xii. 1-8.

As we proceed hereafter, we shall find the hatred of the princes of Israel evermore pursuing and annoying the Saviour. Everywhere — along the roads, in the fields,

---

[1] There was a law which forbade the blind man to use his staff on the Sabbath day; every Israelite was forbidden to carry even the smallest article, were it only a fan, a false tooth, or a ribbon not sewed to the garment. There was a law which forbade the writing of two letters of the alphabet in succession; or the killing of an insect which worried one with its sting; the rubbing of a rheumatic limb; or to bathe an aching tooth with vinegar, unless one swallowed the liquid immediately afterwards. They forbade one to throw any more grain into the poultry-yard than the fowls could eat, for fear that the rest might sprout and take root that same day; forbade the belated traveller, whom Saturday night overtook on the roadside, to pursue his way, even were he in the woods or in the open fields exposed to winds and rain and the attacks of brigands. Shammaï, that strict Rabbi and Formalist, who has left the imprint of his character upon many of these prescriptions, — Shammaï durst not entrust a letter to any heathen after a Wednesday, for fear it might not be delivered before the Sabbath; moreover he spent all his time in meditating further regulations by which he might observe the sacred repose more rigorously. These pharisaic customs are detailed more at length by Otho (*Lexicon Rabbinicum*: Sabbathum), and by Buxtorf (*De Synagoga Judaica*).

[2] A glance over the public life of the Saviour is enough to demonstrate that the unjust complaints made against Him and the opposition which He met with, not only in Judea, but in Galilee and Perea, are oftenest to be laid to the fact that He had neglected some Pharisaic Law concerning the Sabbath (Matt. xii. 1, 2; Mark ii. 24, iii. 2; Luke xiii. 14, xiv. 1; John vii. 23, ix. 14, etc.).

and in the wilderness, even when He seemed to be alone with His disciples — He was shadowed by spies who were stirring up the crowd against Him. From the first day, we find traces of this persecution. The Lord, as He was returning to Galilee, on the Sabbath which followed the Passover,[1] happened to be walking through a corn-land, now ripe for the harvest. The disciples, moved by hunger, broke off some ears of wheat;[2] rubbing it in their

---

[1] Luke vi. 1. "On the Second-First Sabbath," says S. Luke. This singular expression is not found in any passage of the Gospel other than this; the most various interpretations of it have been proposed. Grotius looks upon it as the second of the Great Sabbaths; that is, the great Feasts of the year, which were the Pasch, Pentecost, and the Feast of the Tabernacles. Wieseler takes it to mean the first Sabbath in the second year of the septenary cycle; as the Jews counted by weeks of years (Dan. ix.), the learned Chronologist supposes that the first Sabbath of the first year was called "the *first First* Sabbath;" the first Sabbath of the second year, "the *second First* Sabbath," and so on. The most likely hypothesis, to our thinking, is that of Scaliger and Father Petau, who regard it as a time-hallowed phrase used to designate the first Sabbath which followed the second day of the Pasch, sixteenth of Nisan. This day was the starting-point from which Leviticus commanded that they should compute seven full weeks unto the Feast of the Pentecost (Lev. xxiii. 15, 16). The Sabbath of the first of these weeks was called the *second First* because at once the first Sabbath of the seven weeks and the second Sabbath as regards the Sabbatic day of the Passover, which was used as the point from which they counted those same seven weeks; indeed we know that the first two days of the Festival were regarded as Sabbaths. Caspari has proposed a new solution too clever for us to pass it over in silence. He recalls the state of uncertainty wherein the Jews were as regards the exact duration of their lunar months, which contained sometimes twenty-nine, sometimes thirty days; and hence he would have us suppose that, in order to assure for the holy month of Nisan its full complement of days, they celebrated two Sabbaths in succession, one being called *First Sabbath* and the other *Second First Sabbath* (Caspari, *Einleitung*, par. 102). The word δευτεροπρώτῳ is omitted in some versions, and in the manuscripts of Sinaï and the Vatican.

[2] Meyer translates the words of S. Mark thus: "The disciples began to clear a way across the corn-fields by plucking away the ears." We could not adopt this interpretation; for (1) ὁδὸν ποιεῖν does not necessarily mean "clear a path," but often means "to make one's way." The Septuagint makes use of it in translating the Hebrew, עָשָׂה דֶרֶךְ, "iter facere;" and although the Greek of the classics in this case would be more likely to read ποιεῖσθαι, the active ποιεῖν is still in common use. (See examples quoted in the lexicons of Wahl and Robinson.) (2) By this interpretation Meyer deprives the rest of the narrative of any intelligible meaning; for if this be so, what is the upshot of that reply of Jesus: "Have you never read what David did when he was put to it by necessity and when he was

hands and blowing away the chaff, they began to eat the grain. In this there was nothing which was not lawful. Moses had permitted it in definite terms;[1] and from age to age in the Orient the custom has always been cherished of never refusing the wanderer this charity, which costs so little. But although the Law allowed one to take a few ears, it forbade all reaping and gathering and threshing of the harvest on the Sabbath Day; but the Scribes had decided that to pluck an ear, and to bruise the grain between your palms, was the same as "to reap, to gather in, and to thresh the crops."[2]

Some Pharisees who were following the little band had no mind to let such an infraction of their Rules pass unnoticed. They approached the Saviour, and said to Him:—

"Look! your disciples are doing that which is not allowed upon the Sabbath day."

Jesus walking before His disciples, had taken no heed of their action, nor participated in it; but far from disowning the responsibility, He covered their innocent indulgence with the mantle of His benign approval. To these Councillors who reproached Him with having broken one of the Precepts, He quoted the Law as opposed to them, and with something of irony confessed His surprise that men so deeply versed in the Scriptures should be ignorant of their teaching on this point.

"Have you never read, then," he said,[3] "that which David did when he was compelled by necessity and urged on by hunger, he and those who were with him? How he entered the House of God, in the time of the High-Priest Abiathar,[4] and ate the Loaves of Propo-

a-hungry? . . ." and that memorable addition found in S. Mark: "The Sabbath is made for man."

[1] Deut. xxiii. 25.
[2] "Vellere spicas est species messionis" (Maimonides, *in Shabb.* cap. 7). Certain Pharisees went to the absurd extreme of teaching that to walk upon the grass was to perform the act of threshing grain, and to catch a fly was an illegal sort of hunting.
[3] Mark ii. 25, 26.
[4] The Book of the Kings calls the Pontiff who harbored David, Achimelech, and not Abiathar; the latter was the son of Achimelech, and dwelt with him (1 Kings xxii. 20). In the family of the High-Priests the father

sition,¹ which it is not permitted to any one to eat except the priests, and gave to those who were with him?"

If David, in his extreme need, might lay hands upon the Sacred Bread, and so transgress the precepts of the Law, how could they hold it criminal for His hungry disciples to have pulled a few handfuls of wheat, that they too might sustain their strength? Furthermore, the Pharisees themselves acknowledged that the Sabbatical observances must have their exceptions; for this maxim was generally received among them: "In the Temple there is no Sabbath." Even on this Day of Rest, the Priests might cut the wood, kindle the altar-fires, replace the Loaves of Proposition, and sacrifice a double holocaust;² the sanctity of the Temple itself kept them blameless.

Jesus pleaded with them for this generous reading of a law which His adversaries insisted upon as being so inflexible, and He admonished them that their exceptions applied to Him as much as to the Temple. Indeed, had He not just now proclaimed before the Sanhedrin that He was the Son of God made man, and hence rightly to be revered as a Sanctuary of Jehovah? These lawyers who were hounding His steps must certainly have known this;

---

did not necessarily exercise the supreme functions; hence it is very probable that even during the life of Achimelech his son Abiathar was High-Priest; and in this case the Book of the Kings would mention Achimelech because he was the head of the Sacerdotal Family, while Jesus speaks of Abiathar because he was actually invested with the Sovereign Priesthood. This hypothesis has been learnedly supported by P. Patrizi (*De Evangeliis*, lib. iii. dissertatio xxviii. 38–40). Other critics prefer to admit that both father and son bore the two names together (a common occurrence among the Hebrews), or finally, that there has been some confusing of the names in the Book of the Kings.

[1] We know with what veneration they preserved these loaves. They were ranged in order upon a table of acacia-wood overlaid with gold, and set in the Holy Place, where, by their number, they represented the twelve Tribes of Israel; by the incense with which they were covered they figured forth the perpetual consecration of the Jews to their God. Wherefore when the priests came to put fresh loaves in place of those which had lain all the week in the presence of the Lord (for this was done each Sabbath), they must needs regard the offerings which they took away with them as hallowed, and must consume them in the Sanctuary itself.

[2] Num. xxviii. 9, 10.

but once more He recalled it to their mind in these words: [1] —

"But I say to you, there is here a greater than the Temple."

The Master longed to gain his persecutors to the Truth, much more than He desired to confound them. Therefore He sought to enlighten their minds by showing that "the Sabbath is made for man, not man for the Sabbath." [2] The Sabbath instituted by God to lighten the burden of man's labors, the offspring of his sin, is, in the divine order, for a pledge of a never-ending rest and peace. During this day of mercy, to forbid the hungry from gathering a few grains of wheat were to change our heavenly Father into a Tyrant, and to turn His loving commands into hateful restrictions. Jesus mourned over these blind and stolid interpreters of the Law.

"If you but knew," He concluded, "what is the meaning of those words: 'I love mercy better than sacrifice,' you would never have condemned the innocent." [3]

This response scarcely touched these men, stubbornly clinging to their mistaken views; and though at this moment they did not venture to move against the Divine Master, they decided to scrutinize His actions more narrowly than ever.

---

[1] Matt. xii. 6.
[2] Mark ii. 27.
[3] Matt. xii. 7 ; Osee, vi. 6. By defending His disciples the Saviour did not intend to authorize every violation of the Sabbath, and if we may credit a curious reading in the Manuscript of Beza (Luke vi.), on that same day Jesus explained His thought beyond the reach of misunderstanding: "On that very Sabbath," we read in this ancient Codex, "He passed an Israelite who was laboring at some handiwork ; 'O man,' he said to him, 'if thou knowest what thou art doing now, thou art blessed ; but if thou dost not know, thou art condemned, for then thou dost transgress the Law.'" That is to say, if you understand how far I transcend the Law, you are not blameworthy in acting as you are doing ; but if indeed self-interest or caprice alone have moved you to this, you have drawn down on your head the divine anathema. This reading, which is not found in any other manuscript, is evidently apocryphal ; still it shows in what sense Antiquity interpreted this answer which Jesus made to the Pharisees.

III. THE MAN WITH THE WITHERED HAND.

Luke vi. 6-11; Mark iii. 1-6; Matt. xii. 9-21.

It was on the journey from Jerusalem into Galilee that the incident of the plucking of the wheat occurred. The Evangelists do not tell whereabouts on the journey Jesus tarried; but on one of the Sabbaths following[1] they make mention of His being in the synagogue of a little town. Now there was a man present whose right hand had all shrunken away. According to the "Gospel of the Nazarenes," it was a poor mason, who had been hurt in some accident.[2]

I beseech you, he said to Jesus, restore me to health, so that I need no longer beg my bread in shame and sorrow.[3]

His prayer was overheard by the Pharisees, who were sharply watching these deeds of the Christ, "that they might have cause to accuse Him." They whispered among themselves these words, which came to the ears of the Master:[4] —

"Is it lawful to heal on the Sabbath-day?"

Jesus did not keep them long in uncertainty. "Arise," He said to the cripple, "and stand there in the midst."

Then turning to the Pharisees, seated, as was their wont, in the Seats of Honor,

"I ask you," he said,[5] "Is it allowed upon the Sabbath-day to do good or evil, — to save or to destroy a soul?"

---

[1] Μεταβὰς ἐκεῖθεν, says S. Matthew (xii. 9); ἐν ἑτέρῳ σαββάτῳ, according to S. Luke (vi. 6). All the testimony seems to us of too precise a nature for us to allow that the man with the withered hand was healed at the same time, and on the very spot where the Apostles plucked the corn.

[2] Ἐξηραμμένην (Mark iii. 1); "non ex utero, sed morbo aut vulnere: hæc vis participii" (Bengel, *Gnomon*, in loco).

[3] "Cementarius eram, manibus victum quæritans. Precor te, Jesu, ut mihi restituas sanitatem, ne turpiter mendicem cibos." Fragment from the Gospel of the Nazarenes, quoted by S. Jerome (*in Matt.* xii. 13).

[4] S. Matthew says that the Pharisees put this question: ἐπηρώτησαν (xii. 10); S. Luke, on the contrary, says that the Saviour knew it because He fathomed all their thoughts: ᾔδει τοὺς διαλογισμοὺς αὐτῶν (vi. 8). The most natural solution of this difficulty is to suppose that the question, though uttered in a low tone, came to the ears of Jesus.

[5] Luke vi. 9.

Such questioning as this disconcerted them; they had only come to listen to His discourse in order to surprise Him in some error; confused at being anticipated in this way, they held their peace.

The divine Master attempted to draw them out of their silence by recalling their own teachings on the subject. "What man is there among you," He pursued, "who owns only one sheep,[1] if it fall into a pit on a Sabbath-day, will he not take hold on it and draw it out?[2] But how much more is a man worth than a sheep! Therefore it is lawful to do good on the Sabbath-day."

His reasoning admitted of no reply; this the Pharisees saw clearly enough, and they closed their lips the tighter. The Lord waited for their response; as His glance passed[3] from one face to another He saw reflected there nothing but dumb rage, obstinate dislike, and bitter spite. At the sight His heart swelled with deep indignation; it seemed to all the by-standers that in another moment He would surely overwhelm these hypocrites; but almost immediately He recovered His habitual tone of compassion, and, grieving for their blindness, He merely said to the cripple, "Stretch out your hand."

The man obeyed. At the word of the Saviour life revived in the withered limb, and at once it was become whole like the other.

Thus, not content at having discomfited His enemies in argument before the whole synagogue, the Lord would also manifest His power before their eyes; without handling, even without touching, the cripple, without performing any external act, one single word had been sufficient to effect this prodigy. Would they dare to say that one

---

[1] Πρόβατον ἕν (Matt. xii. 11). Ἕν is here taken in an emphatic sense, and signifies "only."

[2] In the event, the Rabbis did not accord this permission save only when the animal was in danger of being drowned; in default of such extreme peril, it was enough to lay a plank for it, or to throw it some food. In like manner, a man's life must be actually threatened before one could offer him any assistance: "Periculum vitæ tollit sabbatum" (*Joma*, vii. 6. See Reland, *Antiquitates Hebraicæ*; Lightfoot, *Horæ Hebraicæ*, in Matt. xii. 11).

[3] Καὶ περιβλεψάμενος (Mark iii. v).

word, one single word spoken in kindness, was a violation of their Sabbath?

That they were so powerless against Him was a maddening thought for them; they went away from the place, beside themselves with rage, and took counsel together " as to what they might do to Jesus."[1]

But nowhere else were their evil plottings destined to encounter so many obstacles as in Galilee; for the people of this Province, upon whom the Saviour had lavished every good gift, drawn to Him by His gracious doctrine, and much less imbued with the Pharisaical superstitions than were the Jews of Jerusalem, would not have permitted any assault upon their Prophet. More than this, the Sanhedrin had only a limited authority in this land, for here it could not stir without the sanction of Herod.

It was necessary, then, in the first place, to come to an understanding with the ministers and partisans of that prince.[2] Hitherto the Pharisees of Jerusalem had displayed the most insulting scorn for these courtiers, alluding to them as " Herodians," and " the Apostates," taunting them with having borne the Roman yoke quite willingly, and with imitating the manners of Gentiles, as well as the impiety of the Sadducees. But with their hatred of the Christ they now brushed aside every one of their scruples, and the emissaries of the Sanhedrin only considered how they might lure their former enemies into these schemes of vengeance.

In this they succeeded without any trouble; for the austere morality which Jesus taught, the mastery He held over the hearts of the people, His claim that He was the Son of God, — all these seemed to this king, so jealous of his authority, a perpetual menace.

The Saviour, seeing so formidable a storm brewing over Him, sought the other side of the lake, which is close by the territory of Philip, in order to evade His pursuers if they should become too relentless in their attacks.[3] These safeguards having been taken, He did not cease to receive kindly those who followed Him into this retreat, and to

[1] Luke vi. 11. [2] Mark iii. 6. [3] Mark iii. 7.

heal the sick; but He did not do so without caution, warning them not to make it known.¹ So He waited, before taking up His ministry again openly, until Herod's changeable nature should be diverted to some other more absorbing subject.

The obscure existence which for prudence' sake Jesus led during this threatening period astonished and shocked the first converts among the Jews. Doubtless they recoiled from the idea that the Messiah should be forced to hide Himself and to work in the darkness; for we find Saint Matthew reminding them that these humiliations had been long since set down in the oracles of Isaiah:[2] — "Behold My Servant, whom I have chosen, My Beloved, in whom My Soul hath been well pleased! I will send My Spirit to rest upon Him, and He shall publish My judgments[3] unto the Nations. He shall not be contentious, He shall not cry aloud, and no man shall hear His voice in the open streets; the bruised reed He shall not break, and the smoking flax He shall not quench, until He triumphs in the strife."[4]

---

[1] Matt. xii. 15, 16.
[2] Matt. xii. 17-21; Is. xlii. 1-4.
[3] מִשְׁפָּט: righteousness, law, judgment.
[4] Even such would He be, so gentle, meek, and silent, until the day wherein He would cease to strive that He might show Himself victorious; then He would bear the brunt of the battle right onward unto triumph: ἕως ἂν ἐκβάλῃ εἰς νῖκος τὴν κρίσιν. In his usual style, S. Matthew quotes the Prophet very freely.

CHAPTER II.

THE TWELVE APOSTLES.

Mark iii. 7–15; Luke vi. 12–19; Matt. x. 2–4.

During this retirement of the Lord the fury of His pursuers slackened; soon He was free to appear openly among men. "A great throng followed Him out of Galilee, Jerusalem, Idumea,[1] and from the country beyond the Jordan; and others from round about Tyre and Sidon, having heard what things He did, came to Him in great numbers. Then He told His disciples to have a boat ready for Him, so that He might not be overwhelmed by the multitudes; for He had healed so very many that it resulted in all those who had any illness pressing upon Him to touch Him; and the unclean spirits when they saw Him fell at His feet crying out: "Thou art the Son of God!" And He charged them, with great threats, that they should not make Him known."

Here we find the Lord in His Ministry bearing Himself just as we have seen Him hitherto at Capharnaum, consecrating His days by turns to the instruction of the people, to the healing of the sick, and to the deliverance of the possessed.

After one such day of wearisome labor, Jesus 'withdrew to a mountain, and there spent the whole night in prayer."[2] Certain traditions single out a hill lying between Caphar-

---

[1] Mark iii. 7–12. Here S. Mark means to remind us of the many countries from which the various disciples now gathered about Jesus had come. We have seen (p. 176) how He evangelized Judea and Idumea during the first year of His Ministry. Since that time, some of the dwellers in those regions had followed the divine Master.

[2] Luke vi. 12.

naum and Tiberias as the scene of this night-watch and of the Sermon which follows upon it. The Christians call it the Mount of the Beatitudes; the Arabs' name for it is Kourn Hattin (The Horns of Hattin), in allusion to the two peaks which rise above the village of that name. To the west the hillside slopes gently up from the rolling meadows; to the east, on the contrary, its steep cliffs overlook a level stretch of ground, big and wide enough to hold a great multitude.[1] In the hill-country bordering this side of the Lake we might seek in vain for any other highlands worthy the name of mountain. So, then, this is the spot to which we must follow the Lord.

At all times Jesus loved the lonely heights, the quiet of evening, the midnight sky with its glittering array of heavenly hosts; in the stillness His glance could pierce the depths until it was absorbed in the Vision of the Father; here unhindered His soul could taste of that mysterious rest which is born of prayerful ecstasy. Yet this one night out on the hill-tops had, in truth, something of a more solemn glory in it; we feel by the very words in which Saint Luke speaks of it that it was to be the forerunner of a great day. In the dawning light Jesus called to Him His disciples, who were slumbering, as we may fancy, at no great distance, and "from among them He chose out twelve, to whom He gave the name of Apostles."[2]

The Master by this act, to all outward seeming so simple, there and then laid the massive foundations of a Work which was destined to be seen of all men and to withstand the fiercest onslaught of the foe. Growing ever more majestic upon our vision as we watch her progress down through the ages, we must recall to mind the while how this Heaven-sent Church, built up under the Master-Workman's hand, had for its mighty base simply these Twelve Apostles. At that time there was nothing about

[1] Luke vi. 17.
[2] Luke vi. 13; Mark iii. 14. S. Matthew does not record the election of the Twelve Apostles, properly speaking; he contents himself with mentioning their names when he is giving an account of their mission (Matt. x. 2-4). SS. Mark and Luke, on the contrary, agree in putting this solemn selection after the healing of the man with the withered hand.

them to mark them from the masses; we have seen, and we have still to see for a long time to come, how ignorant they were, how ambitious, so much more engrossed in the things of the flesh than in the things of the Spirit. But the Hand which had gathered together from out the dark quarries of Earth these rough and heavy blocks by the same supernal strength could cut and polish them. So Saint John once saw in the bulwarks of the Heavenly Jerusalem just such huge bulks of stone, hewn from the shapeless rock; and these same were become twelve precious stones,[1] whose glowing depths of color now uphold the glorious city of our God, our holy Habitation in the Heavens.

Was there any thought in Jesus' mind of the symbolic significance in the number He had chosen? Did He mean in this way to recall those Twelve Tribes of Israel, just as the High Priest used to bear upon his breast twelve great gems as a memorial of them? Many such conjectures have been hazarded,[2] and indeed there is good ground for similar concepts when we think how much stress was laid on the hidden meaning of numbers in olden times. The Pagans were not alone in their belief that strange properties were to be found in such combinations; the Jews, and the first Fathers of the Church as well, scrutinize them with careful curiosity; and it is impossible to deny that very many of the numbers in Scripture itself have a mystic purport.[3] So that we have in this way really a secret language, highly prized by those who are versed in its unique charms, — like the full harmony which sustains the song by setting its pure melody in higher relief. Why should Jesus have scorned this feeling? Rather He deigned to make use of it; and thus, in this point as in so many others, He availed Himself of every usage of the world about Him. We may willingly grant, not only that He did not choose this number without a purpose, but that

---

[1] Apoc. xxi. 19–21.
[2] See Cornelius a Lapide, *in Matt*. x.
[3] This fact is incontestable, so far as the Apocalypse and numerous passages in the Prophets are concerned (see Smith, *Dictionary of the Bible:* NUMBER).

THE TWELVE APOSTLES. 249

He attached so much importance to it that His disciples felt that their first duty, after the Ascension, was to complete the roll of the Apostolic College by the election of Saint Matthias.[1]

Of the twelve Apostles seven had been chosen already. These were: Peter and Andrew, the two sons of Jonas; then the sons of Zebedee, James and John; Philip, who came from Bethsaïda, like the first four; Bartholomew,

[1] Acts i. 15-26. The Gospels themselves, in giving the names of the Apostles, observe such an unvarying and precise order as to suggest the idea that everything about their vocation was symbolic, — the rank of each, as well as the whole number. As a matter of fact, we possess four lists of the Apostles; now all have this much in common, that they distribute them in three series, in each of which the names are always the same, though here they differ somewhat in arrangement; but, in all of them, three Apostles invariably occupy the same position. The first group has Simon Peter at its head; the second, Philip; the third, James, son of Alpheus. In the last place, in all the lists, we find Judas Iskarioth.

		Matt. x, 2-4.	Mark iii. 16-19.	Luke vi. 14-16.	Acts i. 13.
I.	1.	SIMON PETER			
	2.	ANDREW	JAMES (son of Zebedee)	ANDREW	JOHN
	3.	JAMES (son of Zebedee)	JOHN	JAMES	JAMES
	4.	JOHN	ANDREW	JOHN	ANDREW
II.	5.	PHILIP			
	6.	BARTHOLOMEW	BARTHOLOMEW	BARTHOLOMEW	THOMAS
	7.	THOMAS	MATTHEW	MATTHEW	BARTHOLOMEW.
	8.	MATTHEW	THOMAS	THOMAS	MATTHEW
III.	9.	JAMES (son of Alpheus)			
	10.	LEBBEUS (surn. Thaddeus)	THADDEUS	SIMON (the Zealot)	SIMON (the Zealot)
	11.	SIMON (the Cananean)	SIMON (the Cananean)	JUDE (bro. to James)	JUDE (bro. to James)
	12.	JUDAS ISKARIOTH.	JUDAS ISKARIOTH	JUDAS ISKARIOTH	Vacant

We shall not look for the mystic purport of these divisions, since the sacred writers have not divulged it; we simply call attention to the fact as one of the interesting peculiarities of the Gospel.

from Cana in Galilee;¹ and Matthew, the Publican.² Jesus now called five others: His two cousins, James the Less and Jude (Lebbeus, or Thaddeus); the Galileans, Thomas and Simon the Zealot; finally, the traitor,—the man from Kerioth in Judea,—Judas, son of Simon. For the most part we know little enough of these Apostles,—their names, some few words spoken by them, certain deeds of theirs mentioned in the Gospels or the Acts, a number of traditions as to their after life,—altogether hardly enough to furnish us with materials for a sketch of each one of them.

Bartholomew is the least known of all. It has been agreed upon that he is the Nathanaël whom Philip found meditating under a fig-tree, and led to his divine Master.³ Truthfulness and godliness were the keynotes of his character; undoubtedly with these he combined modesty, for from the hour in which he obeyed the call of God we never see or hear anything more of the son of Tolmaï. There is a tradition which tells of his having evangelized the Indies; that he was burned alive, and crucified with his head downwards.⁴

His friend Philip was among the first of the Galileans who were moved to seek John the Baptist, hoping to find in him the longed-for Messiah. The Gospel speaks of his gentle spirit, readily responding to Jesus' appeals,⁵ sympathizing with the distress of the throngs that followed the Master into the desert, but slow to believe that a few loaves would be enough to satisfy them;⁶ slower still to fathom the Mysteries of faith, for even at the Last Supper he begs the Saviour to let him see the Father, of whom He is always speaking.⁷ Polycratus, Bishop of Ephesus, informs us that Philip had been married; his daughters were numbered among the first Virgins; and he himself slept in the Lord at Hierapolis, in Phrygia.⁸

---

[1] John xxi. 2.   [2] See p. 225.   [3] John i. 47. (See p. 135.)
[4] Eusebius, *Historia ecclesiastica*, v. 10; S. Jerome, *De Viris illustribus*. Assemani, *Bibliotheca Orientalis*, iii. 2, 20.
[5] John i. 43.
[6] John vi. 7.
[7] John xiv. 8.
[8] Eusebius, *Historia ecclesiastica*, iii. 31.

As to Simon, we merely know that he was called the Cananean, a name which Saint Luke translates as the Zealot;[1] and this term was also used to distinguish him from Simon Peter. Can it be that this Apostle belonged to that famous Sect which revenged every transgression of the Law, not simply with burning reproaches, like the Prophets of old, but like Phineas, with unsheathed sword?[2] We know what part these Zealots played in the last days of Jerusalem; how they became the terror and scourge of the whole country-side, making it reek with blood, spreading ruin and death on every hand. Would Jesus have called one of these fanatics to Him; would He have thought it wise to admit into equal fellowship this Jew, Simon, who rebelled against every tribute extorted by the hated foreigners, and Levi, collector of the Roman taxes? Yet in this there would be nothing repugnant to the plans of the Master, for He made little account of human prudence in His works, and "chose that which is foolishness in the world's eyes to confound the wise, so that no man should glorify himself before Him."[3]

Matthew has left behind him more than a name,—a divine Book, his Gospel. In it he speaks in one single instance of himself, and that is only to tell us that he was a Publican, a butt for the contempt and hatred of Israel, but that nevertheless Jesus chose him.

Thomas's character[4] may be more clearly deciphered. With a frank, practical spirit, which was easily bewildered by the Mysteries of faith, he declared with perfect sim-

---

[1] Luke, vi. 15. From the Hebrew קנאה, zeal. The real reading, both in S. Matthew and in S. Mark, would seem to be Καναναῖος, and the form of this word indicates that it refers to the member of a Sect. Ewald calls our attention to the fact that if Cananean meant one who lived in Cana, we should have the formation Καναθαῖος.

[2] Num. xxv. 7.

[3] 1 Cor. i. 27.

[4] Thomas, in Hebrew תאמא, means "a twin," and is so translated in S. John's Gospel; Θωμᾶς ὁ λεγόμενος Δίδυμος (John xxi. 2). Eusebius says that his real name was Judas (*Historia ecclesiastica*, i. 13). According to Tradition he was born at Antioch, and had a twin sister named Lydia (*Patres Apostolici*, Cotel. edrs., pp. 272, 501).

plicity, even in the very midst of the Last Supper, that he could not understand the words of the Lord.[1]

"Master," said he, "we do not know where you are going, nor which way the road lies."

After all Jesus' Ministry was finished, after all His miracles, Thomas had not become grounded in the firm faith that He was God; after the Resurrection we see him still unable to put trust in this new wonder, — dejected, despairing, demanding that the Master permit him to touch His wounds with his hands before he would believe.[2] And notwithstanding, he had a generous heart; for when Jesus braved the wrath of the Jews face to face, that He might raise up Lazarus from the dead, it was Thomas who incited the Apostles with those words which all our Martyrs have repeated after him: —

"Come, let us also go and die with Him!"[3]

James and Jude, the two sons of Alpheus and Mary, we have already seen at their home in Nazareth.[4] Throughout the whole ministry of Jesus they continued to be just what they were then, — hard-working mechanics, whose minds were filled with longings for earthly goods. It needed the descent of the Holy Ghost upon the day of Pentecost to transform these kinsmen of the Lord into Apostles, to inspire Jude with that mighty Epistle of his, and to make of James the Less one of the most illustrious Bishops of the new-born Church.

As Pastor of Jerusalem during nearly thirty years, the latter fostered and strengthened the perfect good-will which bound the Pagan and Jewish converts together; at the first Council he suggested the wisest resolutions, and it was he who protected Saint Paul against the unreasoning and fanatic partisans of Judaism. All Jews who became Christians held this servant of God in veneration as their leader, and cherished with deep respect his Epistle, addressed "to the twelve tribes dispersed throughout the world,"[5] in which the Apostle scourges the vices of his fellow-countrymen, their strifes, their haughty and grasp-

---

[1] John xiv. 5.   [2] John xx. 25.   [3] John xi. 16.
[4] See page 87.   [5] James i. 1.

ing character. The later years of James were passed in prayer; kneeling whole days and nights together in the Temple, he delayed by his intercession the ruin which overhung Jerusalem like a dark storm-cloud; indeed, he was "the Rampart of his People,"[1] according to a common saying among his contemporaries. His death was worthy of such a life. At the Festival of the Pasch, the High Priest Ananias and the Council of the Sanhedrin commanded him to exhort the Jews to give up their faith in Jesus. The holy old man allowed them to lead him out upon one of the galleries of the Temple, and promised them he would speak to the people, but it was only that he might seize one last chance to glorify his Master.

"Wherefore would you question me concerning Jesus?" he cried out. "He is seated at the right hand of the Almighty, and will appear again upon the clouds of Heaven."

His furious persecutors fell upon him and threw him down upon the pavement below, and there they stoned him. As he was dying, the aged Apostle drew himself up, and remained kneeling long enough to beseech God to forgive his executioners; whereupon a man who had armed himself with a fuller's mallet strode up and put an end to his sufferings. His people buried him close by the Temple. Eight years later, Jerusalem was only a charred heap of ashes.[2]

And now we have still to speak of the most illustrious of the Apostles, — Simon and Andrew, sons of Jonas; James and John, the sons of Zebedee. These four fishermen of Bethsaïda form a group by themselves, and at their head we always find the Prince of the Apostles, Simon Peter. The least known one among them is Andrew, whose personality is, as it were, overshadowed by his brother's brilliant renown. After having brought Simon to Jesus,[3] he disappears in the background. But if his life

---

[1] "His rare virtues had won for him the surname of Oblias ('Ωβλίας), the Rampart of the People," יְפָל־עָם (Eusebius, *Historia ecclesiastica*, lib. ii. cap. xxiii.).

[2] *Fragmenta Hegesippi* (Migne, *Patrologie grecque*, t.v. p. 1307).

[3] John, i. 41.

was hidden, his death shed such radiance about it, that the priests and deacons of Achaia sent tidings of the glorious event to the whole Church. Their narrative enables us to follow, step by step, every act of the Martyr,—the examination, the replies of Andrew, and his protracted tortures. He died upon the cross, uttering such cries of love for Jesus as thrilled the hearts of those through whose soul the sound reëchoed, while they wept in silence.[1]

Beside Andrew, there are Peter, James, and John, who are always the chosen ones among the chosen few, the intimate companions whom the Master admitted to His confidence and familiar friendship. We see them, the only ones present at the raising of Jaïrus's daughter; the only ones at the Transfiguration; the only ones at the Agony of the Saviour. Jesus has told us what made Him so particularly attached to the two sons of Zebedee; it was because their great hearts burned in fierce flashes, like the lightning; whence it was that He gave them that beautiful name,—"Sons of the Thunderbolt,"—Boanerges.[2] They had something of its resistless rush, and sometimes, too, its destructive wrath. Witness the day when they called down the fire of heaven upon a Samaritan village which refused to harbor them. They had inherited this unbounded zeal from Salome, their mother. Having devoted herself to the Saviour's cause, faithfully following Him even to His Cross, the wife of Zebedee the fisherman dared to dream of a place for her sons at the side of the Christ, and upon His Throne.[3] Jesus tried to curb this ambition by reminding them that His glory was to be bought at the price of suffering.

"Can you drink of My Chalice?" He asked.

"That we can," instantly replied the sons of Salome.

This confidence touched the Lord; and it was then He

---

[1] In the *Patrologie grecque* of M. Migne; see *Acta et Martyrium S. Andreæ, Apostoli* (t. ii. p. 1217).

[2] Mark iii. 17. בְּנֵי רֶגֶשׁ. The *Scheva* is changed to *Oa* in the Aramean tongue: Βοανηργές.

[3] Matt. xx. 22, 23.

granted to James that, before all others, he should not only drink this cup of sorrow, but that he should drain it in a single draught. His zeal marked him out for a victim to the sword of Herod Agrippa, and he in fact was the first of the Apostles to meet the Martyr's death.[1]

The other son of Salome was to survive them all. Soaring above the earth, to the inaccessible heights of his heavenly home, he led a hidden life so long as Peter and Paul held the Christian world in the bonds of faith. But at the end of the first century, when the Witnesses of the holy Word had vanished one by one, and when heresy threatened the youthful Church, the voice of John pierced the cloud. His Gospel, the Epistle which announced it, and the Apocalypse, were like so many sheets of lightning, now dazzling our sight, now thrilling us with peals of thunder, now blinding our eyes when we would descry the outlines of his awful visions: the showers of fire and of blood; the Cups of gold overflowing with Wrath; the Steeds, with serpents for their manes and tails, having breastplates of fire, breathing out flame and brimstone; the Red Dragon, with the seven heads and the ten horns, drawing together with his tail a third part of the stars of the sky, and hurling them down upon the earth.[2] Thus it was, with a loud voice, that the Seer of Patmos was constrained to reveal the great matter of his ecstasies. Christian Art has been prone to sink these raptures of the Apostle into the shadow, and so we are too apt to forget them; painting has rather accorded him every grace of youth, with his eyes lifted up to the heavens, often with an almost virginal timidity. Undoubtedly "the disciple whom Jesus loved"[3] had great tenderness of heart, but it was a heart which throbbed in unison with a soul of fire; and it was this latter trait which won for him the Master's love when He called him, "Son of the Thunder;" and in like manner it moves us most strongly when we see the Apostle drawing away in horror from the heretic Cerinthus, and filling the Apocalypse with those terrible and

---

[1] Acts xii. 2. [2] Apoc. viii. 7; xv. 7; ix. 17–19; xii. 3, 4.
[3] John xiii. 23.

mysterious images. John's rightful emblem is not the Dove, but the Eagle. This passionate ardor, penetrated with deepest tenderness, drew to him the Heart of Jesus, and made John the Beloved Disciple.

The character of Simon, son of Jonas, presents no such opposite traits. It is all summed up in the name which Jesus bestowed on him: "Thou art Peter, and upon this Rock I will build My Church."[1] The great Apostle, therefore, was to serve as the Foundation of the Church, — was to be for his brethren as a Guide and infallible Head. And after the election of the Twelve, the Lord made known these prerogatives of Peter so publicly and so emphatically, in order that all might bow before him. Ever after this day we find him speaking and acting in their name. At Capharnaum, when the Master demanded sadly, "And you, — will you too go away?"[2] it was he who responded, in the name of all the rest, —

"Lord, to whom should we go? You have the words of eternal life!"

It was he who, at Cæsarea, in the land of Philip, once again proclaimed the faith of the Apostles, —

"Thou art the Christ, the Son of the living God."[3]

This lofty dignity conferred upon him became the occasion of his fall; it puffed him up with vain-glory, turned his energy into presumption, his firmness into blind obstinacy; it went so far as to make him openly contradict his Master, and drew down upon him that severe reply, —

"Get thee gone, Satan! thou art a scandal unto Me, for thy thoughts are not of God, but of man."[4]

At the close of the ministry of Jesus, Simon, son of Jonas, is not any longer the immovable rock, but like a loose stone in the road, which a woman's hand may fling aside into the ditch. Yet even then it was not all over with Peter, since after his overthrow he but made for himself a surer abiding place, and in his sorrow found firmer foundations. Overwhelmed with his humiliation, he nevertheless rose up in "the greatness of the power of God."[5]

---

[1] Matt. xvi. 18.   [2] John vi. 68–70.   [3] Matt. xvi. 16.
[4] Matt. xvi. 23.   [5] 2 Cor. iv. 7.

Henceforth, neither his faith nor his mighty courage were ever to fail him; we encounter him everywhere at the head of his brethren, the first to grope his way within the tomb of Jesus, and to gaze upon his Risen Lord; the first to get into the little ship at that last miraculous draught of fishes; the first to cast himself into the sea, to go to meet the Saviour; first, too, to drag up on the shore the net, which had not broken beneath the weight of its one hundred and fifty-three fishes.[1]

Before He went away from their sight into the skies, Jesus laid upon Peter the Charge of pasturing His flock, to feed His sheep, as well as His lambs.[2] The Apostle fulfilled the command of the Lord, stood at their head, ordered their manner of teaching and the form of their government, and by stamping the new-born Faith with his seal, gave it the character which it was to bear unto all future ages, making the first acts of the infant Church the Acts of Peter.

In the Apostolic College there is still one gloomy figure left, which each of the Evangelists thrusts down to the lowermost rank, — Judas, son of Simon, the man from Kerioth. Jesus asked only one Apostle from Judea, and Judea gave Him a traitor. All that we know of him, apart from the tale of his treachery, is that his skill in the management of money won him his position of trust as Treasurer of the Apostles.[3] Hence he must have gained their confidence from the outset; and indeed he retained it up to that last Passover, for it was at his instigation that they murmured against the Magdalene, as she poured out her perfumes upon the head of Jesus. Though he grew ever more depraved and desperate, the man from Kerioth had always succeeded in blinding their eyes; so that on the night of the Last Supper, when the Lord foretold the crime in whose shadow they sat, no one dreamed of charging Judas with it; only the calm glance of Jesus could read the heart of the thief. How many were the words spoken by the Saviour to the multitude which in

---

[1] John xx. 6; Luke xxiv. 34; John xxi. 1-11.   [2] John xxi. 15-17.
[3] John xii. 1-7.

the ears of this faithless follower must have resounded in tones of appeal or reproach! Now He is urging them to true charity: "Do not heap up treasures upon the earth. . . . There, where your heart is, there is your treasure also. . . . You cannot serve God and Mammon."[1] Now He gives utterance to His feeling of horror: "Have I not chosen you Twelve? And there is one among you who is a devil!"[2] The divine Master could not resolve to abandon "this son of perdition."[3] At Gethsemani, once more, He kissed him, and called him His friend.[4]

Composed of such different characters, the College of the Apostles stands before us, from all we can know of its members. Henceforward they were to form a little band of chosen ones about the Saviour, journeying with Him throughout Judea, sharing His labors and His repasts; like Him, they had not where to rest their head, and often laid themselves down by His side without other roof than the starry heavens, with no shelter save the providence of God their Father.

[1] Matt. vi. 19, 21, 24.   [2] John vi. 71, 72.   [3] John xvii. 12.
[4] Matt. xxvi. 50.

CHAPTER III.

THE SERMON ON THE MOUNT.

Matt. v., vi., vii. ; Luke vi. 20-49.

CHRISTIAN orators have always delighted in contrasting Moses upon cloud-capped Sinai with Jesus promulgating the New Law upon the Mount of the Beatitudes. On the one hand we see Jehovah wrapped in dazzling mists, that flash and thunder before His awful Presence ; and on the other, in the quiet of early morning, we hear a Voice whose beloved accents thrill the people's heart. Of old there was the dread hush of the desert ; no water was there, nor any green thing, — only the red-litten peaks rising high above desolate mountain crags ; but here we have every charm of a spring-time in Galilee, the soft slopes of a little hill looking down upon sunny pasture-lands, while the sparkling lake of Genesareth ripples along the shore ; in a word, yonder was the Law of death, delivered to a disobedient and awe-struck nation ; here the law of grace is announced to the believing and joyous throngs.

Beneath such poetic parallels is there really any underlying truth ? Can the Sermon on the Mount be set side by side with the Tables of Stone, graven by the hand of Jehovah, or in point of fact, did Jesus actually present it to us as a Code of Christianity ? There is nothing to prove that this discourse, as preserved by Saint Matthew, had any such distinctive character; that the Evangelist made choice of this one in particular was because no other seemed to him better fitted to convey an idea of the Master's teaching. Indeed Jesus could not have found any more favorable opportunity for disclosing His doctrine.

Up to this time He never had had gathered about Him an audience having knowledge enough of heavenly things to enable them to understand Him; later on, being surrounded by spies, He had not the same liberty, and was often forced to use mystical language and to speak in parables. But at the time of the Sermon on the Mount the Saviour's enemies were not tracking His footsteps so closely as to hound Him through every secluded spot like this; they were content to keep watch upon Him in the towns and synagogues. Freed for the time being from the hunter's pursuit, and speaking to people who were wholly devoted to Him, Jesus could ease His overflowing heart, and reveal in its fulness the light He had brought into the world. The Sermon on the Mount, although quite similar in form to other of the Saviour's instructions, has been chosen, however, for very good reasons, as being the completest expression of the doctrine of Christianity and a brief epitome of the Gospel.

We possess two accounts of it,[1] — Saint Luke's summary, written for the Pagan converts, which contains no allusion to Judaic customs;[2] and the text of Saint Matthew, in which

---

[1] We connect the Sermon reported by S. Matthew (v., vi., vii.) with the one which S. Luke (vi. 20–49) summarizes after the calling of the Apostles. This conjunction, though rejected by certain commentators, appears perfectly legitimate to us. In fact, the renown of Jesus, which seems now to have spread throughout Syria, the multitudes coming from far-away places, all the facts recited at the close of the fifth chapter of S. Matthew, would imply that His work was already far advanced. Further on, in the body of the Sermon, these words of the Saviour: "Do not believe that I am come to abolish the Law . . ." would also infer that His preaching already had excited some suspicions. Hence Jesus did not deliver this discourse at the beginning of His ministry. But then, why need we distinguish between this and the one we find in the sixth chapter of S. Luke? They have many manifest and indisputable points of similarity, — the same opening, the same sequence of ideas, the same illustrations, the same conclusion. The principal variance between the two is in that the discourse was delivered upon a mountain according to S. Matthew, in a plain and smooth place according to S. Luke. To do away with this difficulty, we only have to suppose that, on the mountain side, there was a lofty plateau, and that Jesus came down from the higher peaks above to speak to the people who were gathered in this place. And indeed this is precisely the configuration of Kourn Hattin, where, if we are to believe Tradition, the Lord pronounced the Sermon on the Mount.

[2] "Lucas in transcribendis Christi sermonibus et orationibus, quas habent priora Evangelia, ea quæ in ceteras gentes dicta esse videntur,

the Master's words are reflected as in a clear and spotless mirror. In the latter record the whole scene about Him as He preached lives again before our eyes: the meadows dotted over with brilliant lilies, the thornbush thickets, the rich greenery of the vines, fig-trees growing alongside the thistles, birds flitting across the clear blue sky, while over yonder, around the doors of those humble cottages, you can see the cattle grazing, or at rest; there are fishermen coming up from the neighboring shores of the lake, — men who would be horrified at the thought of giving their children a serpent instead of a fish.[1] From the highlands of Kourn Hattin, at one time, the Saviour could point out on the distant horizon some city built upon a hill;[2] then again, close at hand, in the little hamlets among the mountains, He could remind these village-folk how the savorless salt is thrown out into the street,[3] or He would picture them a scene within the walls of their farm-houses, recalling the single flaring torch which they were accustomed to light at evening, hanging it over the heaps of grain so as to measure them off bushel by bushel; and from this He took occasion to say: "You are the light of the world; no one lights a lamp in order to put it under a bushel, but to set it within its socket, so that it may illumine the whole house; thus let your light shine before men."[4]

By describing time and place so minutely Saint Matthew lets us know that he was one of the listeners to the

---

prorsus resecat, aut eorum severitatem mitigat aliquo modo" (Patrizi, *De Evangeliis*, lib. ii. cap. iii. 51).

[1] Matt. vi. 28, vii. 16, vi. 26, vii. 6, vii. 9, 10.

[2] Matt. v. 14. The town to which Jesus pointed would appear to be Safed; indeed it can be seen very clearly from the Mount of the Beatitudes, and its ruins attest that it existed in the time of the Christ. The fact of a town being built upon the heights is of as rare occurrence in Galilee as it is common in Judea; it would be very natural for Jesus to use it as a striking figure of the Church and the influence which she was to exercise upon the world.

[3] Matt. v. 13. Thomson chanced to see a merchant in Sidon whose stock of salt had lost its flavor from being left on the ground; the man got rid of it in the same fashion as is here mentioned in the Gospel, — scattering it under the feet of the passers by, and beneath the beasts of burden (Thomson, *The Land and the Book*, p. 381).

[4] Matt. v. 15, 16.

heavenly discourse on this occasion; but need we conclude from this that he has given us every word uttered by the Lord on that great day? The most learned expounders have always held the opposite opinion,[1] and everything sustains their theory,— the concise expression of the ideas, the abundance of maxims, the brusque transitions, the parables and the similitudes but barely suggested; indeed, the divine Master was not accustomed to speak in such style. Suiting His words to the comprehension of the simple, earnest minds of His hearers, He would repeat one thought over and over again, putting it before them under a new form each time until it was fully grasped; thus He followed no order, save only such as was prompted by a Heart which would sacrifice everything to its one longing to be known and loved. For Saint Matthew to recount these Homilies word for word would have been to go beyond the scope of his Gospel, since we know that Jesus was never too tired to prolong His instructions while there were souls who needed His help. The Evangelist has chosen rather to select such sayings of the Master as he deemed best adapted to represent His teaching.

Of all the words that fell from His lips on that day none were more strange and surprising in their tenor than the Beatitudes proclaimed by the Saviour; for every prejudice of Israel was overthrown by them. In truth, Moses, by making use of material images to move this worldly minded people, had thought to reach their hearts by setting before their eyes the earthly rewards of righteousness, and had promised Israel that its glory or its shame would finally depend upon its faithfulness to Jehovah. The Jews had concluded from this that prosperity always attends

---

[1] "Ego jam monui non esse anxie quærendam in evangelistis sententiarum connexionem, quia res non eo ordine scribere voluerunt quo factæ a Christo vel dictæ sunt. Quod præcipue in ejus concionibus observatur, in quibus nec omnia quæ dixit, nec eo quo dixit ordine recensent, contenti præcipua ejus doctrinæ capita commemorare" (Maldonatus, *in Mat.* vii. 1). "Compertum habemus ab evangelistis, quum alicujus dicta litteris consignabant, non ipsa verba, sed verborum sensum relatum esse quam sæpissime. Sic verba quibus Christus Eucharistiam instituit, aliter Matthæus, aliter Marcus, aliter Lucas retulere" (Patrizi, *De Evangeliis*, lib. iii. diss. xlvii. 22).

upon the godly man; that wealth being a mark of God's favor, sorrow and trouble are sure tokens of His wrath. Hence arose, despite the spirit of charity which breathes throughout the Law, that scorn of poverty and their harsh usage of the unfortunate and sick, whom they regarded as sinners meeting with a just punishment; hence too they imbibed their mistaken ideas as to the Messiah, who was to raise up their nation to the pinnacle of glory and riches.

Few were the words which Jesus used to dispel such dreams as these. Instead of wealth He set before these Jews the happiness of the poor; to the passionate spirits whose visions are all of great victories He speaks of meekness; tells the hearts in love with pleasure that there is joy in the gift of tears; to the hungry and thirsty He says that righteousness shall sustain them; preaches mercy to the pitiless natures, the loveliness of purity to the sensual man; teaches the blessedness of the peaceful and long-suffering to a people writhing beneath their yoke. What a disenchantment for the mighty ones of this world! But for the poor and the lowly of earth was there ever revelation so unhoped for? Only consider for a moment how dreadful their destitution was, even here in Israel; think of the oppressions endured by the weak and gentle; imagine the despair of those whom misfortune had overcome, who had no one to wipe away their tears; and remembering this we can understand the joy of wretched and weary souls when they heard the Christ speaking these words to them:[1] —

"Blessed are the poor in spirit,[2] because to them belongeth the Kingdom of Heaven.[3]

[1] Matt. v. 3-12.

[2] That is to say, happy are those hearts which are not bound down by the care of riches, who, if they have wealth love not vain pomp nor overbearing conduct, and do not crave to get everything for themselves! Happy too are the poor, who, though actually despoiled of all, are resigned and murmur not!

[3] The Kingdom of Heaven is the name which the contemporaries of Jesus always used in alluding to the reign of the Messiah; in the Rabbinical language the word "Heaven" is frequently used as a synonym for "God." So in places where S. Matthew, writing for Jewish readers,

"Blessed are those who weep, because they shall be comforted.¹

"Blessed are the meek, because they shall possess the land.

"Blessed are they that hunger and thirst after justice, because they shall have their fill.

"Blessed are the merciful, because they shall obtain mercy.

"Blessed are the peace-makers, because they shall be called the Children of God.

"Blessed are those who are pure of heart, because they shall see God.

"Blessed are those who suffer persecution for justice' sake, for the Kingdom of Heaven is theirs." ²

Seeing the Master destroy so many of their illusions, the Jews might well believe he wished to revolutionize all Israel; and indeed this is why He was so careful to add that His Mission was not to abolish the Law, but to elevate it to the point of perfection.³ Moses had said: Thou shalt not kill; Jesus would even forbid angry words and feelings of hatred.⁴ Moses denounced adultery; Jesus condemned an

---

employs this phrase, with which they were all familiar: "The Kingdom of Heaven;" S. Luke prefers to give a form which would be clearer to the minds of the Gentiles, — "The Kingdom of God."

¹ The Vulgate and the Syriac of Cureton place the beatitude of the meek before that of the sorrowing; they are supported by the authority of the Codex Bezæ. But a majority of the manuscripts (notably those of Sinaï and the Vatican) and numerous versions (Peshito, Coptic, Ethiopian, etc.) invert this order.

² It would seem as though the Lord feared that He might not be clearly comprehended; for we learn from S. Luke (vi. 24–26) that He reinforced His blessed promises with these terrible anathemas: "Wo unto you that are rich, for you have your consolation! Wo unto you that are filled, for you shall hunger! Wo unto you that laugh now, for you shall weep and mourn some day! Wo to you when all men shall praise you, for it was thus that their fathers did to the false prophets!"

³ Matt. v. 17–19.

⁴ Matt. v. 21–26. To give some idea of the punishments which God has reserved for cruel and merciless men in the other life, Jesus recalled the three forms of capital punishment then in vogue amid the Jews. The sword was the weapon of the legal tribunal which was established in every city ($\kappa\rho\iota\sigma\epsilon\iota$); stoning was the penalty inflicted by the Sanhedrin ($\sigma\upsilon\nu\epsilon\delta\rho\iota\wp$), burning was reserved for notorious criminals ($\tau\dot{\eta}\nu$ $\gamma\acute{\epsilon}\epsilon\nu\nu\alpha\nu$). Therefore angry feelings will deserve the first degree of punishment, which was death

impure glance or an evil thought.[1] Moses tolerated divorce; Jesus restored Marriage to its primitive sanctity.[2] It was written in the Law, "Thou shalt not perjure thyself, but thou shalt perform thine oaths unto the Lord."[3]

"And now," spoke the Christ, "I say to you: Do not swear at all, neither by Heaven nor by the earth, nor by Jerusalem.[4] Let your speech be: 'This is so,' 'That is not so,' — 'Yes,' 'No.' Everything which is more than this comes from an evil source."

"You have heard that it has been said: 'Eye for eye, tooth for tooth.'[5] And now I say to you, Do not withstand

by the sword. If they go further than this, — if this hatred displays itself outwardly by some furious expression, as it would be to treat one's brother as an "empty-headed fellow" (Raca, רָקָא), — this would be to draw down upon the speaker a sentence as stern as that of the Sanhedrin, — the Supreme Tribunal from which there was no appeal; but for him who would go further in his wretched passion, so far as to treat his brother as a "fool" (Μωρέ) or "infidel" (כרה, Num. xx. 10), upon him would befall a fearful visitation, which Jesus compares to the abomination of Gehenna (Ge-hinnom: גי הנום), thus they had named the low-lying valley which surrounds Jerusalem to the south and west, where the corpses of condemned criminals were abandoned without burial, and the great fagots consecrated to Moloch had once smouldered and failed to burn.

[1] Matt. v. 27–30.
[2] Matt. v. 31, 32.
[3] Matt. v. 33–37.
[4] The Law forbade perjury; but the Jewish doctors evaded this prohibition by teaching that one was not bound by his word unless he fortified it by an oath in the Name of God Himself. To call Heaven, earth, and the holy City to witness one's fidelity was not an oath, they said, and so they took advantage of this technical distinction in order to deceive the Pagans. Jesus restored to Truth its sacred rights. He declared that in every promise there is something of the divine which may not be despised. Surely the heavens are the throne of Jehovah; the earth is His footstool, and Jerusalem the city of the Great King. Then, lifting the minds of His hearers to a higher plane of thought, He reminded them that sin alone has begotten lying upon the earth; sin has imposed upon us the humiliating necessity of calling on God's Holy Name if we would have our word accepted as sacred and inviolable instead of doubtful and untrustworthy. Man, in his natural state of rectitude would be believed upon his simple affirmation, and the Christian's first duty is to recover that primitive sincerity.
[5] Matt. v. 38–42. This was the spirit of the ancient Covenant, as it was the Rule laid down in the tribunals of Judea. There was a certain kind of justice shown in this desire not to go beyond the measure of exact retribution, and to proportion the punishment to the actual injury done by the crime.

violence; but if any one strike you on the right cheek, turn to him the other.¹ And if any one wish to enter into judgment with you, and contend with you for your tunic, let him take your mantle also.² And if any one force you to go one mile,³ go with him two miles more. Give to whoever asks, nor rebuff him who would borrow of you."

Still these divine instructions lacked somewhat of fulfilling the ancient Law in its perfectness. To completely develop its germ of life, and to make it bear the fruits of grace, it was necessary that Jesus should shatter the close and narrow circle within which the Jews had confined it; therefore He must first work a change in their feelings toward other nations. Moses, knowing the weakness of His people, had prohibited any commerce with Idolaters; the Jewish Doctors had turned this precaution into an odious precept, looked upon every foreigner as an enemy,⁴ and wrote down such ruthless dicta as were afterwards to find a place in the Talmud: "Have no pity upon Gentiles."⁴ "The Pagan is not our neighbor."⁵ Against this Law of

---

¹ Here it is not so much a literal precept that Jesus would have us follow: rather, He is urging us to show that willingness of heart which is glad to endure all things out of the pure love of God. Discretion, prudence, charity itself, often compel us to rebuke those who attack us, and even to withstand them. Jesus and His Apostles have given us sundry examples of this (John xviii. 22 ; Acts xxiii. 3).

² If a creditor would seize his tunic as a pledge, he must abandon not only this less costly garment to his greed but the outer mantle as well, which was more valuable, and served for a covering in the night-time (Exod. xxii. 26); that is to say, he must suffer himself to be robbed of all rather than indulge in petty recriminations or harbor a spirit of ill-will and retaliation.

³ Ἀγγαρεύσει; from "Angar," a Persian word which is defined as a "Courier." Herodotus records (viii. 98) that the kings of Persia, in order to insure the efficiency of their postal service, had decreed that no individual should withhold his horses at the demand of these Messengers of State; from Persia this law passed into all the Oriental Codes. Among the statute labors which were laid upon the Jews by their Roman taskmasters, it would seem that this was one of the most repugnant to the vanquished people; for Demetrius, hoping to pacify their uneasy spirit, promised that no forced levies upon beasts of burden should be made among the inhabitants of Judea (Josephus, *Antiquitates*, xiii. 2, 3)

⁴ "Apud ipsos (Judæos) fides obstinata, misericordia in promptu, sed adversus omnes alios hostile odium" (Tacitus. *Historiæ*, v. 5); "Non monstrare vias eadem nisi sacra colenti" (Juvenal, *Satiræ*, xiv. 103).

⁵ See Lightfoot and Schœttgen, *Horæ Hebraicæ*, in loco.

Hate Jesus pleaded for Charity, which finds its brothers in all mankind, and in God their common Father.[1]

"Love your enemies; do good to those who hate you; pray for those who maltreat you and slander you, in order that you may be the children of your heavenly Father, who makes His sun rise upon the good and upon the bad, and sends down rain upon the just and unjust. For if you love those who love you, what reward shall you merit? Do not the publicans as much? And if you greet your brethren only, what more are you doing? Do not Pagans the same? Be you therefore perfect as your heavenly Father is perfect."[2]

How differently the Law sounded, listening to the Lord's simple reading of it, and contrasting it with the hypocritical practices which the Pharisees had miscalled the Law! Jesus denounced these sectaries, zealous to preserve a decorous outside, but caring naught for the corruption and malice seething in their own hearts,[3] sounding trumpets when they gave alms to publish their virtues before the world,[4] disfiguring themselves to make a show of their fasts before men, haughtily standing up and praying with a loud voice in the synagogues and on the corners of the streets.

---

[1] Matt. v. 43–48.

[2] We have only to compare the accounts of S. Luke and S. Matthew to note how the Saviour, in order to make Himself more clearly understood, repeated the same thought under various forms: "Do to another as you would have him do to you.... And if you lend to those from whom you hope to receive a return, what thanks do you deserve? Sinners too, lend to sinners, in order to receive as much in return. But as for you, love your enemies; do good and lend, hoping for nothing in return. And your reward shall be great, and you shall be called the children of the Most High; for He is kind to the thankless and the wicked. Be merciful, therefore, as your Father is merciful" (Luke vi. 31–36).

[3] Matt. vi. 1–8.

[4] Some commentators suppose that the Pharisees did really blow upon a trumpet to gather the poor about them, and so distribute their alms in this ostentatious fashion; but Lightfoot, who is so perfectly conversant with Rabbinical literature, declares that he has not been able to find the slightest sign of any such usage. Hence, we can only regard this as part of the figurative language of His discourse: "Ils sont eux-mêmes leur trompette, tant ils craignent de n'être pas vus" (Bossuet, *Méditations sur L'Évangile:* SERMON SUR LA MONTAGNE, xxe journée).

"Do not imitate them," said the Saviour, "for your Father knows of what you have need before you ask it of Him. As for you, pray thus:[1] —

"Our Father Who art in Heaven, hallowed be Thy Name;

"Thy Kingdom come;

"Thy will be done on earth as it is in Heaven;

"Give us this day our daily bread;[2]

"And forgive us our debts,[3] as we forgive our debtors;

"And lead us not into temptation;

"But deliver us from evil."[4]

Nothing could show better than this prayer how Jesus would change the sons of Israel into a new people by diverting their desires from earth and raising them to Heaven, by proposing nobler ends as the rewards of right-

---

[1] Matt. vi. 9–13.

[2] Ἐπιούσιον. This word is peculiar to the Evangelists (Matt. vi. 11; Luke xi. 3). It may come from ἐπὶ ἰέναι, or, to be more exact, from the feminine participle ἡ ἐπιοῦσα, with ἡμέρα understood, "the coming day." Ἡ παροῦσα, ἡ προσιοῦσα are in fact phrases commonly used by the Septuagint as well as by Josephus to designate the morrow, and S. Jerome found "Mahar: מָחָר, quod dicitur crastinus," instead of ἐπιούσιον in the Gospel which was written for the Hebrews. Τὸν ἄρτον τὸν ἐπιούσιον, therefore, may be construed as meaning "Our bread for the morrow." Still, this interpretation seems difficult to reconcile with the precept uttered by Jesus immediately afterwards: "Be not anxious about the morrow." Hence it seems more natural to think that this word comes from ἐπὶ εἶναι, ἐπὶ οὐσία, "the bread from which we have our being," which is our subsistence, our bread of each day; and this would imply not only the food of the body, but all things which in like manner nourish the soul, such as the divine word, the Sacraments, and above all things else the Holy Eucharist. This is the thought of very many Fathers, and S. Jerome was moved thereby to alter the Vulgate (Matt. vi. 11) which had "quotidianum" in the ancient version, placing in its stead the word "supersubstantialem," "the Bread that is above all substance." However, in S. Luke (xi. 3) he has left "quotidianum."

[3] Ὀφειλήματα, "our debts," our omissions, our sins, as well as what we have left undone; ὡς καί . . ., "even as," not "in the same measure as . . ." (Hartung, Partikellehre, i. p. 460).

[4] Lightfoot has collected from the Rabbinical writings all the formulas of prayer which correspond in any way to the "Our Father." Such a comparison makes us realize more keenly, if possible, how original and veritably divine is this Prayer which our Lord has taught us. So for the prayer of man Jesus did what he had done for the whole Law of God. — He completed it, and bestowed upon it the perfectness of an altogether heavenly grace.

eousness. Undoubtedly Heaven existed for the Jew just as it does for us to-day, yet he never lifted his eyes on high, but looked for his recompense here below. The disciple of Jesus, taught to long after celestial goods, spurns such as are the creatures of time; for his thoughts are all fixed on incorruptible and eternal things. In this new realm of the Spirit he does not fail to fulfil all the duties of life, nor to endure its trials. He fasts as formerly,[1] but with a serene countenance, seeking to attain by mortification to a real detachment from worldly feelings, and to a completer union with God. He prays, but it is in secret he communes with the Father; he distributes alms, but without letting the left hand know what the right hand is doing. With toil and trouble he seeks his daily bread, yet without uneasiness or anxiety, without clinging to the treasures which rust can corrode and thieves filch away; not, like the Jews, seeking to share his heart between God and Mammon,[2] but rather putting all his trust in the Providence of the Father, he relishes, through all their loveliness, something of the holy Truth of his Master's words:[3] —

"Be not harassed about your life, what to eat or what to drink, nor for your body as to how you shall be clothed. Is not the life more than the food, and the body more than the raiment?

"Look up at the birds in the sky: they neither sow nor reap nor gather into granaries, and your heavenly Father feedeth them. Are not you much more than they?

"And which one of us by disquieting himself can add another moment to his life's allotted span?[4]

---

[1] Matt. vi. 16–24.
[2] Μαμμῶνα, from the Chaldean כָּבוֹן, "riches." "Congruit et punicum nomen, nam lucrum punice Mammon dicitur" (S. Augustine, *in loco*).
[3] Matt. vi. 25–34.
[4] Ἡλικίαν may mean the length of life or that of the body. The Vulgate takes it in the latter sense, "Quis potest adjicere ad staturam suam cubitum unum?" but for the most part modern critics have, for very good reasons, preferred the first construction. Indeed, Jesus intended in this manner to remind man of his powerlessness to do any stint by himself, howsoever small it might be; now a cubit (two feet and a half) added to the height of a man would surely be something great and unheard of. So

"Why are you solicitous as to your raiment? Consider the lilies of the field,[1] how they grow. They toil not, neither do they spin, and nevertheless I say to you not Solomon himself in all his glory was ever arrayed like one of these wild flowers.

"If then, this grass of the fields, which is to-day, and to-morrow will be cast into the oven,[2] God doth attire after this sort, how much more shall He do unto you, O ye men of little faith?

"Do not be troubled therefore, saying, 'What shall we eat?' or 'What shall we drink?' or 'Wherewith shall we be clothed?' The Pagans seek after these things, but your Father knows that you have need of them.

"Then seek first the Kingdom of God and His justice, and all these things shall be given you, added unto them.[3]

"Be not anxious concerning the morrow. The morrow shall be anxious for itself. Unto each day its own evil suffices."

To these instructions, which were the striking features of the discourse, Saint Matthew adds certain precepts, given by the Saviour at the same time. It is difficult to find the link which bound together these thoughts and images of widely different nature; probably it is useless to

---

then, it behoves us to understand "the duration of life" by ἡλικίαν, and then translate πῆχυν ἕνα as "a moment." The Greeks in order to measure time, often made use of ideas and images which properly belong to considerations of space. Πήχυιον ἐπὶ χρόνον ἄνθεσιν ἥβης τερπόμεθα (Mimnermus; see Stobæus, xcviii. 13).

[1] By these field-lilies we are not to understand the flower which we call by that name, but rather the anemones and tulips which in springtime brightly bespread the meadows of Judea. During this season we have strolled over the Phœnician country-side, and across the foot-hills of Galilee, and, very often, all about us we saw the fields fairly covered with these "lilies" of the Gospel, whose shades of crimson and gold might well recall the splendid vestments and regal purple of Oriental monarchs (Judges, viii. 26; Cant. vii. 5; Esth. viii. 15; Dan. v. 7, 16, 29).

[2] An Eastern oven is no more than an earthen vessel in which they enclose their bread, spreading over it dry herbs, which, while blazing, produce an intense heat.

[3] There is a saying which Tradition attributes to Jesus, in development of this thought: "Ask for the greater things, and you shall receive the less together with them: ask for heavenly things, and the things of earth shall be given you beside" (Fabricius, *Codex apocryphus*, i. 329).

seek any connection of the kind, the design of the Evangelist being, not to present us with a body of doctrine, but to preserve such few sentences as still lingered fresh in his memory.

"Judge not, and you shall not be judged.... Give, and it shall be given to you; a good measure, pressed down, shaken together, running over, they shall pour into your bosom."[1] Hereupon the Lord speaks of the two blind men, one of whom cannot lead the other without both falling into the ditch; of the mote and the beam;[2] of the pearls put before swine;[3] of the Door opening wide to whosoever knocketh earnestly. "Who is the man among you who gives his son a stone when he asks for bread? And if he ask for a fish, will he give him a serpent? If you, then, wicked though you be, willingly give to your children of the good things which are given you, how much more will your Father who is in Heaven give truly good gifts to them that have recourse unto Him!"[4] Then, as the Master's thoughts follow one upon the other in swift sequence, we see the smooth and spacious highroad which sweeps on to perdition; the little gateway and the narrow path[5] which

---

[1] Matt. vii. 1-2; Luke vi. 38.
[2] Matt. vii. 3-8.
[3] Pearls have something of the appearance of lintels, which make the usual food of swine; yet because these beasts are unable to guess the worth of pearls, and are enraged at not being able to turn them to their own base uses, they trample them under foot, and turn to rend those who offer them a nourishment so little suited to their nature.
[4] Matt. vii. 9-12.
[5] Matt. vii. 13, 14. Was the Door of which Jesus speaks the gate of entrance, or the goal of the journey? It makes little difference which hypothesis we may adopt, for in either case the real significance of the figure remains. In the famous Cebes' Tablet we find an allegory very like to this, and there the gateway lies at the end of the road: "Do you not see a small door-way and a path leading up to this door? it is not much frequented, few wander that way.... It is the way which leadeth unto True Knowledge" (chap. xvi.). This thought is not the only one of the maxims uttered by ancient philosophers which greatly resemble the words of the divine Master; but does that warrant us in believing that His doctrine was borrowed from them? Long ago S. Augustine eloquently refuted this opinion, which has been repeated by the incredulous of all ages: "Dixit hoc Pythagoras, dixit hoc Plato.... Propterea si inventus fuisset aliquis eorum dixisse quod dixit et Christus, gratulamur illi, non sequimur illum. Si quis vera loquitur, prior est quam ipsa Veritas!

lead to life; there are the false prophets clad in sheep's clothing,[1] whom you may recognize as you test a tree by its good or bad fruits. Finally we find the true and the false disciples of the Christ,—"All those who say, 'Lord! Lord!' shall not for that reason enter into the Kingdom of Heaven; but he who doeth the will of My Father who is in Heaven he shall enter into the Kingdom of Heaven."[2]

Jesus terminated these teachings with a striking figure. He had before His mind one of those sheltered ravines which had cut deep into the flanks of some mountain-side, while its floor is strewn with rocks and sand. For the Oriental there is every temptation to build here in the bed of dried-up torrents: he has little more to do than to stoop and collect together the smooth stones; it costs but a little labor after that to level away the sand and erect his home. And yet, woe to the imprudent fellow who lets himself be seduced by the seeming security and safety of this sheltered spot, where no toil is needed to the making of his dwelling! Beneath those southern skies storms burst forth in an instant, emptying streams of water down upon the mountain-tops; then of a sudden these parched channels which wind through the gorges are transformed into raging torrents once more. Before the mighty on-rush of the waters everything is crumbled, crushed, and whirled away in confusion. It were wisdom to dig one's solid habitation deep and strong among the higher rocks; there, raised upon its firm base, his home can defy the fury of tempest and floods.

"Whoever," said the Lord,[3] "hears these My words and puts them in practice I will show you to whom he is like.

O homo, attende Christum, non quando ad te venerit, sed quando te feccrit" (*Enarrationes in Psalm.* cxl. 6).

[1] Matt. vii. 15-20. This may be an allusion to the customary garb of Prophets, whose outer garment was the skin of an animal hung over their shoulders; however, in all probability, Jesus wished to remind them that the false prophets, the better to deceive them, would bear the outward semblance of a lamb.

[2] Matt. vii. 21-23.

[3] Matt. vii. 24-27.

"He is like to a man who builded a house, and having dug deep beforehand, sets its foundations upon the rock.

"The rains fall, the floods come, the winds blow and beat about this house; but it has not fallen, because it is founded on the rock.

"And he who hears these words which I speak and does not put them in practice is like a foolish man who has built his house upon the sand.

"The rain falls, the floods come, the winds blow and beat about this house, and it has fallen, and its ruin has been great."

Such was the Sermon on the Mount. With deep respect we may thus gather together all that Saint Matthew and Saint Luke have remembered and recorded; but there is that which they were unable to set down here, — the heavenly accents of the Master and the grace which exhaled from His lips. The listening throngs were touched with wondering rapture.[1] That which charmed them more than all besides was that He spoke and "taught as one having authority, and not as their Scribes." Never before, indeed, had Israel hearkened to language like this; they no longer heard teaching like that of their Doctors, — a dry and heartless code of ethics, unending disputes about trivial subjects; here was no strained or tedious interpretation of the Law, no slavish attachment to the dead letter. Everything about Jesus bespoke the sovereign Master of the hearts of men, lifting them up toward the Truth, yet without wrenching them away from earth; the loftiest subjects were set before them in such homely phrases that the lowly folk and their little ones could grasp His meaning. He spoke to the villagers of life in the open fields, of trees in fruit or with barren boughs, of wildflowers and of the mountain-torrents; to the fishermen He spoke of their lake or of their nets; to all He told of what they knew and loved, and they all, bending forward with rapt and breathless interest, followed the Word in wonder and delight.

[1] Matt. vii. 28, 29.

CHAPTER IV.

CAPHARNAUM AND NAÏM.

I. THE CENTURION OF CAPHARNAUM.

Luke vii. 1–10; Matt. viii. 1, 5–13.

ACCOMPANIED by a great concourse, Jesus descended the mountain and returned to Capharnaum.[1] He went thither to experience the joy of welcoming the first Pagan who was to come to Him, — one of the noblest souls of whom the Gospel makes any mention. He was a Roman Centurion, commanding the detachment of legionaries stationed upon the borders of the lake.[2] Galilee, though it was under Herod's rule, remained nevertheless under the overlordship of vigilant Roman governors; and Capharnaum was too important a position for the masters of the world to neglect to occupy it. The officer charged with representing the Empire here was worthy of that trust, — resolute in his biddings, keeping his soldiers under perfect discipline, at the same time he was not so much the overseer as he was the protector of Capharnaum. We know that he had been more than a little drawn toward the worship of Jehovah; for this Pagan, who had remained upright and clean of heart in the midst of Roman corruption,

---

[1] Matt. viii. 1 ; Luke vii. 1.
[2] Some scholars interpret this as meaning that the Centurion was one of the Samaritan officials under Herod Antipas; but the Samaritans, though of Gentile origin, were not, properly speaking, Pagans: they worshipped Jehovah, and possessed a portion of His Law. Furthermore, the high esteem in which the Centurion was held at Capharnaum can hardly be reconciled with the mortal hatred which the Jews cherished against the schismatics of Samaria.

could not have known the religion of the Jews without being touched by its pure morality, and to this he had himself borne witness publicly, by having a synagogue built in the town.[1] With this high tone of mind he combined certain feelings of humanity, which were certainly rare enough at that period. There is no one who does not know what sort of a position the slave held in ancient days; he was a machine with a human voice, — a beast of burden, taken care of only in order to obtain a few years' longer services.[2] Should he grow old and sick, it were the wisest course, according to certain most illustrious philosophers, "to sell him along with the old cattle and rusty scrap-iron."[3] Yet this Centurion, when we see him first, is leaning over the pillow of his old servant, watching and weeping; "for he loved him much."[4]

His grief, being known throughout Capharnaum, had moved his numerous friends to come to him, and they were gathered about the sick man, who was now racked with fierce agonies;[5] death was drawing near. In this extremity the Centurion learned of Jesus' return, and recalled all he had heard said of Him; yet, not daring to hope that Israel's Benefactor would listen to a Pagan, he turned toward the Ancients of Capharnaum,[6] and asked them to intercede for him.

The latter, remembering only their debt of gratitude, set out in search of the Saviour, and besought His aid.

"This man deserves that you should assist him," they said, "for he loves our nation, and has built us a synagogue."

[1] Luke vii. 5.
[2] "Instrumenti genus vocale" (Varro, *De Re rusticâ*, i. 17); "Servus vel animal aliud" (Ulpian, *Digeste*, vi. 1, 15, par. 3).
[3] Cato, *De Re rusticâ*, iii.
[4] Luke vii. 2.
[5] This "paralysis" (Matt. viii. 6) was not the ailment which we know by that name, for the effect of the latter is to annihilate all feeling, while this slave suffered very sensible pains. By this name the ancients designated quite different illnesses, such as rheumatism, tetanus, which is so common in hot climates, etc.
[6] Probably the Ancients here alluded to are the elders of the people, and not those of the Synagogue, who are generally spoken of in S. Luke by the name of ἀρχισυνάγωγοι (Acts xiii. 15).

Jesus acceded immediately to their request.

"I will go," He replied, "and I will heal him."[1]

He followed after them, and as He was nearing the house they informed the Centurion of His approach. The Roman's surprise was great, for he had never expected to receive Him in his home, knowing that in the eyes of the Pharisees one who entered a heathen's dwelling was defiled. Desiring to spare the youthful Prophet such disgrace, he despatched some of his friends, bearing this message:—

"Lord, do not give yourself so much trouble, for I am not worthy that you should enter into my house. It was for this reason I dared not go to you; but say only one word and my servant shall be healed."

Then he himself, if we follow the text of Saint Matthew,[2] came forward to meet the divine Master, and upon the threshold of his mansion besought Him, as his only gift, to vouchsafe one single word from His mouth. Accustomed to command, he knew the power of a word.

"I, who obey another," he said, "have nevertheless soldiers under me, and I say to one, 'Go!' and he goes, and to another, 'Come!' and he comes, and to my servant, 'Do this,' and he does it."

Hearing him speak, Jesus was filled with admiration,

---

[1] "They wished to prove their gratitude for all the kindness of their fellow-citizen; and undoubtedly, to the Lord, that was a most powerful plea, that this man loved God's chosen Nation. So the Jewish Senators, who would constrain Him to restore the ebbing life of this servant who was so dear to the Centurion's heart, besought Jesus eagerly, urging that 'He deserves to be assisted by you, for he loves our people, and has built us a synagogue;' and straightway Jesus went with them and healed the serving-man" (Bossuet, *Politique tirée de l'Écriture*, livre i. article vi. proposition 2).

[2] In fact, this Evangelist puts the same words into the mouth of the Centurion which S. Luke tells us his friends uttered to the Lord. Ordinarily these two versions of the story are reconciled by asserting that S. Matthew might justly attribute to the Centurion those words which were spoken in his name. But without straining the simplicity of the sacred text so far as this, would it not be perfectly natural to suppose that the officer, meeting his Guest upon the threshold, would repeat the same words with which he had told his friends to address the divine Master? Looked at in this light, his humility seems the more impressive and touching.

and turning to the company who had followed Him, He said:—

"Of a truth I have not found any so great faith, even in Israel."

Praise like this, which exalted a Heathen above the sons of Abraham, probably gave rise to some bitter murmurings of disapproval; it may even be that the Lord had discerned some of the Sanhedrin's spies mingling with the crowd, for all at once His language grew threatening. The Jews had pictured for themselves the reign of the Messiah as it were a banqueting-board spread before them, and them alone; and they were fond of representing the confusion of the Gentiles, doomed only to gaze from afar upon their sumptuous repasts.[1]

The divine Master recalled this haughty dream in order to destroy it, and declared that Pagans coming from the East and from the West would sit down to table by the side of Abraham, Isaac, and Jacob in the heavens; while the Jews, though children of the Kingdom of Heaven, would be cast without the festal hall into the blackness of night. "There shall be weeping and grinding of teeth."[2]

Turning then to the Centurion, "Go," He said, "and may it be done unto you even as you have believed." And the servant was healed.

The Centurion of Capharnaum remains unto this day as the consummate copy set before every soul that seeks God. By praising his humility and faith the Lord has shown us that thus it behoves us to come unto Him. Of this the Church has been ever mindful; and since that

---

[1] "In mundo futuro (dixit Deus), mensam ingentem vobis sternam, quod gentiles videbunt et pudefient" (Schœttgen, *Horæ Hebraicæ*, in loco).

[2] Matt. viii. 11. That is to say, outside the circle of celestial light, in Hell: "There they shall weep and gnash their teeth, for, from afar off, they shall behold the high seats which they were to have had for their own, the crowns they were to have worn upon their heads; and all this so clearly that they shall even descry how those fair thrones are now filled by others, and those resplendent crowns upon others' brows. Then they must needs groan without avail; then will their rage force them to grind their teeth in fruitless agony of soul" (Bossuet, *Méditations sur l'Évangile*, dernière semaine, xviiie journée).

time no one draws near the Table where Jesus gives us Himself to be our Bread of Life without first rekindling in his heart the feelings of this great Captain, murmuring with reverent lips:—

"Lord, I am not worthy that Thou shouldst enter under my roof, but speak only one word and my soul shall be healed."

II. THE SON OF THE WIDOW OF NAÏM.

Luke vii. 11–17.

Jesus lingered only a little while at Capharnaum; on the next day,—so runs the record of Saint Luke,[1]—He had travelled some nine leagues thence, and had come to the town of Naïm. There was nothing unusual about this rapid journey; for, by starting in the evening, a boat could soon bring Him over to the southern shore of the lake, and leaving there about sunrise He would reach the place for which He was bound easily before nightfall.

Naïm of to-day—a poor little village—has preserved no tokens of her past, except her girdle of tombs; there is nothing now to justify her name,—"The Beautiful,"[2]—beside her site, upon the slope of a high hill, from which, in a glance, one can sweep the plain of Esdralon, and far away to Mount Tabor. But in the days of the Lord she was glowing with life, and by her faith was made worthy of receiving the Good News, and beholding His wondrous works.

At that time, the most glorious period of His Ministry, the Master walked always attended by an eager array of

---

[1] Ἐν τῇ ἑξῆς (ἡμέρᾳ). Tischendorf retains this reading, which is that of the Sinaïtic Manuscript, and the Palimpsest of Ephrem. Ἐν τῷ ἑξῆς (χρόνῳ), which is found in the Alexandrine Manuscript and in that of Sinaï (correction by a third hand), would mean that Jesus betook Himself to Naïm upon some one of the following days.

[2] Naïm, נעים, the Beautiful, the Charming City. S. Jerome (*Onomasticon*) locates this town some two miles south of Tabor and near Endor. The present village lies upon the northerly flank of Little Hermon.

faithful souls. In this manner He was making the ascent of the steep pathway which still leads up to Naim, when, from out the gates of the city, there came a funeral procession; it was advancing directly in the path of Jesus, moving toward a tomb which had been made without the walls. There is no sadder sight than a burial train in the Orient; certain of the kindred bear the body, resting on a litter and swathed in perfumes and linen bands; at their head march the flute-players, who draw shrill, plaintive notes from their pipes; the mourners send up a chorus of cries and wails, now beating their breasts, now tossing their hands to heaven, or tearing their dishevelled hair. And on this day their demonstration of woe must have been more wild and clamorous than ever, for they were seeking to give utterance to sorrow such as no tears can wash away. The Gospel with one word makes us feel how great was that grief: "he was his mother's only son, and she was a widow."[1] This weeping woman followed the body with a large company of the town's-folk.[2]

Jesus could not look upon this piteous sight without being moved.

"Do not weep," He said to her; and forthwith, coming closer, He touched the bier.

The bearers understood His gesture, and stood still. The throng waited in suspense for what was about to happen; the flute-players and the wailing women were hushed and still; through this expectant silence they heard the voice of the Saviour, —

"Young man, I say unto you, Arise!"

Instantly the dead sat up and began to speak. And Jesus restored him to his mother.

In this deed, who could help recognizing the Prince of Life, handling at His sovereign pleasure the keys of the tomb? Elias bringing back to life the son of the widow

---

[1] Luke vii. 12.
[2] From this concourse of people we cannot draw any conclusions as to the social standing of this family, nor as to the public esteem which they had won from the citizens of Naim, for it was a time-honored custom among the Jews to accompany any funeral train which they chanced to meet by the way.

of Sarepta, Eliseus restoring her child to the weeping Sunamite woman,[1] were evidently in every one's mind. But what a difference between Jesus, breaking the bonds of death by a word, and these Prophets, who must needs throw themselves upon the corpse again and again, while they revived it with their breath. Here, instead of the prolonged and laborious efforts of a restricted power, there is the simple Authority of the mighty Master! "They all were seized with fear, and glorified God, as they said, 'A great Prophet has been raised from amongst us, and God has visited His people!'"[2]

As for the child thus called back to life, and this widowed mother, assuredly it was not fear that moved them, but indeed a living faith which well-nigh overwhelmed their hearts; for it was not Jesus' custom to cure the body without renewing the soul; nor can we believe that He would have awaked the dead youth from his funeral couch, that so He might restore in him the life of the senses, without, at one and the same time, inspiring the breath of Immortality within his soul.

III. THE MESSAGE SENT BY JOHN THE BAPTIST.

Luke vii. 18–35; Matt. xi. 2–19.

For more than six months now John Baptist had been held as a captive by Herod, but from his frontier prison he still followed the course of Him for Whom he had made ready the road; and this he could do the more easily since his disciples were permitted to visit him, and could thus keep him informed of all the doings of the Christ. So, just at this juncture, he selected two from their number, and despatched them to the Saviour with this message:—

"Are you He who should come, or are we to await some other?"[3]

---

[1] 3 Kings xvii. 21; 4 Kings iv. 35. [2] Luke vii. 16.
[3] Luke vii. 19.

What is the meaning of these words? Amidst the weariness and dejection of his confinement, did John feel his courage sinking? Did he begin to lose faith in the Christ?[1] For us to harbor such a supposition would be to misjudge his character entirely. The Precursor's only design was to direct his disciples' minds by this means straight to the only Teacher Who could fully instruct them in the way of life. The Saviour, who at once fathomed John's motive, made answer by letting them witness certain deeds in which His almighty powers were manifested most strikingly. "In that same hour He healed all those who came to Him, curing them of all their diseases and wounds, and of evil spirits; and to a blind man He restored his sight."[2]

Then turning to these envoys, He said, "Go, and report to John that which you have both heard and witnessed,—the blind see, the lame walk, the lepers are cleansed, the deaf hear, the dead rise again, and to the poor the Good News is announced."

Isaias, whose words Jesus borrows here, had foretold that such marvels would mark the coming of the Messiah.[3] He indeed had not spoken of any resurrection of the dead, but the Lord could not be silent concerning that which all Naïm was now publishing abroad, and therefore He alludes also to that sovereign might wherewith He holds the powers of death at His will, adding yet another sign of which the Prophet had spoken: "the Gospel delivered unto the poor."[4]

In making this humble duty the culminating note in an enumeration of His most striking miracles, Jesus designed to set the true character of His Mission in highest relief; because He had come, not so much to do glorious deeds,

---

[1] This interpretation is given by some of the Fathers (Tertullian, *De Baptismo*, x.; *Contra Marcionem*, lib. iv. 18; *Quæstio* xxxviii. *ad Orthodoxos*, S. Justini *Op. spur.*) and it has been adopted by many Protestant scholars, but to us it seems entirely inconsistent with everything which we are told concerning "the greatest of the children of men" (Matt. xi. 11).
[2] Luke vii. 21, 22.
[3] Is. xxxv. 5, 6.
[4] Is. lxi. 1; xxix. 19.

as to teach and to comfort all such as the world despises. And yet this marvellous blending of grandeur and meekness shocked the disciples of the Baptist.

The Lord, seeing them draw away from Him, uttered that solemn warning, before their withdrawal:[1]—

"Blessed is he who is not scandalized in Me!"[2]

In their astonishment at this unceremonious departure, it would appear that the people conceived an unfavorable idea of these messengers, and were even fain to suspect the fidelity of him who had sent them, for at once Jesus spoke out in his defence.

He reminded the Jews of those reeds which they had seen waving in the wind along the banks of the streams where John was baptizing, and with these he contrasted the strong, unshaken faith of the Precursor, taking the thin and tremulous stalks as the symbol of inconstancy. Then, as His gaze fell upon certain men among them who were clothed in splendid garments,[3] He compared the lazy luxury of gay courtiers with the austerity of the Prophet, saying:[4]—

"What went you into the desert for to see? A reed shaken by the wind?

"What, then, went you out for to see? A man clothed in soft raiment?

"Nay, those who have rich robes and live in luxury do dwell in kings' houses.

---

[1] "Non Joannem, sed discipulos ejus percutit" (S. Jerome, *Epist.* cli. *ad Algasium, quæstio* i.).

[2] Luke vii. 23.

[3] These were probably some of the Scribes who were come from the court of the Tetrarch, for, since their recent reconciliation with the Sanhedrin (Mark iii. 6), the Herodians shared in the latter's espionage on the Saviour's actions. Among them it may be that Jesus recognized some members of the Sect of Manahen (father of the person of that name mentioned already, p. 205, note 4), who had yielded to the seductive charms of court life in the splendid palaces of Herod the Great, though at first he had been a rival of Hillel in the austerity of his life. His disciples had followed his example only too faithfully; throwing off the restrictions of religion, together with all zeal for the Law, they appeared in public clothed in sumptuous raiment and glittering with ornaments of gold (see *Chagiga*, fol. 16, 2; Jost, *Geschichte des Judenthums*, i. 259).

[4] Luke vii. 24-28.

"What, then, went you out for to see? A Prophet? Yea, I say to you, and more than a Prophet.

"This is He of whom it is written: Behold I send Mine Angel before Thy face,[1] to prepare Thy ways before Thee."

Was it not enough to have exalted the holiness of His Forerunner so strikingly? Yet Jesus went on to say that under the ancient Law "No one among those born of women has ever risen who is greater than John."

Still, such is the superiority of the Church over the Synagogue, that Jesus adds: "And, notwithstanding, the least of all in the Kingdom of Heaven is greater than John the Baptist;" whereby He would teach us that the lowest place by His side is to be preferred before the highest rank among the disciples of Moses.

It is this new reign of the Christ on earth "that all the Prophets had foretold, until John," and for which John himself, "the new Elias," had made ready all things with such lofty zeal. His toils and trouble had not been in vain, for at this very hour all Judea was flocking to Jesus. "Already men were taking this His Kingdom by storm, and in dense throngs were hastening to the assault."[2]

This declaration surprised the listeners, and was quite differently received. "The people and the publicans, baptized by John, acknowledged the justice and the wisdom of these divine counsels; but the Pharisees and the Doctors of the Law, who had disdained the baptism of the Precursor, now gave token of their contempt for the

---

[1] Πρὸ προσώπου σου. Here Jesus alters the wording of the Prophet Malachy (iii. 1), in which Jehovah, speaking of Himself, says, "I send My Angel before My face." By thus applying to Himself what was spoken of the Almighty, the Christ proclaims that He is co-equal with Him. This change in the Text has been studiously recorded by all three Evangelists when repeating this utterance of the Saviour (Matt. xi. 10; Mark i. 2; Luke vii. 27).

[2] Matt. xi. 12. Ἡ βασιλεία τῶν οὐρανῶν βιάζεται; "vim patitur. Vi factâ invaditur, significatur partim ardor ac studium properantium . . . partim multitudo confluentium" (Jansenius Yprentius, *Tetrateuchus*, in loco). "Vim patitur . . . vi invaditur . . . quia magna multitudine, studio, aviditate, impetu . . . ad illud rapiendum homines concurrunt" (Cornelius a Lapide, *in Matthæum*, xi. 12).

designs of God in their regard."¹ Whereupon Jesus addressed to them these reproachful words:²—

"To what shall I compare the men of this generation? To what, indeed, can they be likened?" He added.

"They are like children seated in the market-place, who cry to their companions, 'We have played for you on the flute, we have sung and you have not danced. We have chanted sorrowful hymns, and you have not wept, you have not even beat your breasts.'³

"John has come among you neither eating bread nor drinking wine, and you say, 'He is possessed by the devil;' the Son of Man comes eating and drinking, and you say, 'This is a fellow who loves good cheer and wine, a friend of publicans and sinners.'"⁴

These words of the Master must have made the Pharisees and the Scribes wince and writhe under the justice of the mortifying rebuke; for it was in the presence of all the people that He thus charged them with cherishing childish caprices, and of insisting pettishly that everything must bend to suit their humors,—at one time complaining of John because, in their hours of pleasure and happiness, his life seemed too stern and austere; and then again, displeased with Jesus, Whose condescension and charity was a scandal in their eyes.⁵

---

¹ Luke vii. 29–30. "Nota hæc verba videri potius Lucæ quam Christi. Nam paulo post sequitur: ‘Ait autem Dominus. . . .’" Ita Jansenius et alii, licet Maldonatus censeat esse verba Christi" (Cornelius a Lapide, *in loco*).

² Luke vii. 31, 32.

³ We can easily picture the scene called up by these words of the Saviour. Who has not seen children at play mimicking all that they have seen enacted by their elders? Jesus called to mind those little groups of youngsters, seated in a circle in the public squares; at such times some of them will pretend to be enjoying a concert at a grand wedding, or play at being mourners at a funeral; while there are always a certain few of their companions who will not enter into their fanciful sports, in spite of all the persistent teasing of their playmates.

⁴ Luke vii. 33, 34.

⁵ It is commonly supposed that Jesus was referring to all the Jews, as being like such fretful and peevish children. If Heaven offer them a Prophet of austere character, who urges them to do penance, and thunders forth his songs of mourning for their sins, they refuse to weep with him, but rather spurn him as a madman, overwrought by dwelling too long on

After this severe censure, the Lord proclaimed that although such was the state of this unbelieving generation, yet a time would come, and it was even now upon them, when "Wisdom would find her children, who would both defend and justify her."[1]

He might indeed have pointed out such sons of the Eternal Wisdom, as they stood there in the presence of His enemies. They were the Apostles, those lowly and humble men who surrounded Him, and who were yet to become the triumphant apologists of the New Reign.

IV. The Sinful Woman at the Banquet given by Simon.

Luke vii. 36–50.

On that same day at Naïm the divine gifts of grace were again bestowed upon mankind. While still excited by the raising of the dead youth and by the coming of John's messengers, this little city was to be the scene of one of the most touching incidents in the whole Gospel.

A Pharisee, named Simon,[2] invited the Saviour to a

---

such gloomy thoughts. Then if it send them a tender and merciful Messiah, whose words are gentle as music, a Saviour who lives their daily life, eating and drinking with them, they scorn Him as a fellow of vulgar manners! However natural this interpretation may appear, it is, nevertheless, at variance with the sacred text; it is enough to read the sequel, noting the words used by the Lord, to be convinced that it was the Pharisees whom He is comparing to children, sometimes playing the flute, sometimes intoning their lugubrious chants, but always insisting that every one else must yield to their capricious humors.

[1] The text of S. Matthew, in the Manuscript of Sinaï, and in some versions, has ἔργων, instead of τέκνων : "Wisdom is justified by her works."

[2] The Pharisee Simon must not be confounded with Simon the leper, of Bethany, who only a few days before the Passion gave a great dinner in honor of Jesus. It is true that in both instances the hosts are of the same name, and each time a woman comes to bestow her meed of perfumes upon the Master; but despite the resemblance in both these points, it seems to us absolutely necessary to separate the two events. At Naïm a sinful creature casts herself at the feet of Jesus, and bathes them with her tears ; nothing of the sort happens in Bethany. At Naïm the woman hardly ventures to anoint the feet of the Lord ; while at Bethany she pours out her

banquet. Curiosity, and the pleasure of entertaining an extraordinary personage, — perhaps, too, a secret sense of the majestic character of this Prophet, — had induced him to tender this courtesy to Jesus. However, from pride, or from fear of his Sect, he affected an air of contemptuous coldness. The usual polite ceremonials were omitted: there was no one to bathe the feet of the Stranger,[1] nor did any one kiss this Guest upon the cheek,[2] nor offer Him perfumes for His hair.[3]

Jesus made no complaint at meeting with so cold a greeting in the house of one who had bidden Him to a formal feast. He entered the banquet-hall and took His place at table. In the primitive times the Hebrews used to partake of their repasts, after the manner common among the Orientals of to-day, seated upon mats with their legs crossed;[4] but ever since the Captivity, they had dropped this custom in order to follow the prevalent fashion among the Greeks and Romans, — slipping off their sandals at the threshold, they reclined upon couches, which were ranged about the board, and helped themselves to the dainties, while leaning on the left arm, the body lying with the feet extended to the outer circle.[5]

When the great banquet-hall was thrown open to all comers (as was now the case) it was customary for a crowd of onlookers to surround the feasters with perfect freedom. In this interested circle of spectators there stood a woman

---

precious oils upon His head. In the latter occurrence the Christ sees a foretokening of His burial, and is thereby led to speak of His approaching death; at the former repast we hear no mention of any sad forebodings, nor any talk of a kindred nature. There was no ceremony of more frequent occurrence in Judea than that of scattering costly perfumes over the guests, and it would not be strange if Jesus received this token of respect and love oftener than the two instances here noted (Ec. ix. 8; Cant. iv. 10; Amos vi. 6, etc.). As to the name Simon, we know how common it was among the Jews. In his Commentary upon S. John, Hengstenberg has tried to prove that the two accounts refer to the one same banquet; but his long and scholarly argument does not strike us as successfully establishing his point.

[1] Gen. xviii. 4; Jud. xix. 21.
[2] Gen. xxxiii. 4; Exod. xviii. 7.
[3] Psalm xxii. 5, cxl. v; Matt. vi. 17.
[4] Gen. xxvii. 19; 1 Kings xvi. 11, xx. 5, 18.
[5] Esther i. 6, vii. 8.

known throughout the whole town for her disorderly life.¹ Upon hearing a rumor that the Christ was coming to this quarter of the city, she had hurried thither, clad in her usual rich garments, and clasping a vase of perfumes in her hand. She had pressed forward until she reached the Lord, and there she remained listening to Him in silence.

Very soon, indeed, the words of the Son of Mary found their way to her sin-stained soul; she threw herself weeping at the feet of the Master, humbly kissing them, drying them with her hair, and then, breaking the alabaster vase, she covered them with the fragrant incense.²

Simon looked across the table with haughty disgust at this woman who had prostrated herself before Jesus. Neither the woful shame nor the great wretchedness of a heart torn by repentance could move him to pity; he could see in this sinful woman nothing but a disgraced and odious creature, whose least touch would leave an ugly stain.³ His only surprise was that Jesus did not repulse her, as he or any other Pharisee would have done, in scorn and horror.

"If this man were really a Prophet," he mused, "he would know what sort of a woman this is who is touching him; he would know that she is a sinner." These words were not uttered aloud; but the Pharisee, if only by his silence and his contemptuous manner, let his disdain be plainly seen by all.

Jesus answered his thoughts.

"Simon," he said, "I have somewhat to say to you."

"Well, Master, say on!" replied the host.

"A creditor had two debtors; one owed him five hundred denarii, and the other fifty. As they had not wherewithal to pay him, he remitted each one's debt. Which of the two now loves him most?"

---

[1] Trench, *Notes on the Parables*, 299.

[2] The alabaster caskets destined to hold such perfumes were very fragile affairs; all that was needed to break them in pieces was a slight pressure upon the long and slender neck of the vase (Pliny, *Historia naturalis*, xxxvi. 8).

[3] "Quanto spacio a meretrice recedendum est ? R. Chasda respondet: Ad quatuor cubitos" (Schœttgen, *Horæ Hebraicæ*, i. p. 348).

Simon replied, without seeing what the Lord desired to prove from this, " Undoubtedly it would be he to whom he remitted the greater amount."

"You have judged rightly," answered Jesus; and then He turned His eyes full upon the sinner before Him. Huddled at His feet, she was shedding bitter, burning tears, —tears which Saint Augustine has called the heart's blood. But because she was humble, and was therefore more enlightened than Simon, at the very mention of debt she knew that He was alluding to Her. The Master pointed to this penitent figure, continuing still to address the astonished Pharisee.

"Simon, do you see this woman?

"I entered your dwelling; you gave Me no water for My feet, while she indeed has washed My feet with her tears, and has wiped them with her hair.

"You gave Me no kiss; while she indeed, ever since I entered here,[1] has not ceased to kiss My feet.

"You have not anointed My head with oil, while she indeed has bathed My feet with ointments.

"And so, for this reason, I say to you, many sins shall be remitted unto her, because she has loved much. But he to whom less is remitted loves the less."[2]

The Heart of the divine Master overflowed in this forgiveness which he now granted to one who was looked upon as the vilest object in all humanity, the very symbol of lost and depraved womankind. Not like Paganism, which would have devoted her to a life of shame beyond the slightest hope of escape, Jesus cast upon her a look of such deep and pure tenderness that the Pharisees themselves dared not wrong Him by an evil thought. He raised her from the earth, and though He did not lay upon her

---

[1] The Vulgate has εἰσῆλθεν, "intravit;" but nearly all the Greek manuscripts give the reading εἰσῆλθον, which implies that the penitent sinner entered the hall at the same time with Jesus.

[2] "Dictum est hoc propter pharisæum illum, qui vel nulla vel pauca se putabat habere peccata ; non enim Dominum invitaret, nisi aliquantulum diligeret. . . . O Pharisæe, ideo parum diligis, quia parum tibi dimitti suspicaris ; non quia parum dimittitur sed quia parum putas esse quod dimittitur" (S. Augustine, Sermo xcix. 6).

brow that flower of innocence which once blighted never blooms again, He crowned her with a glory far more austere, — the halo of repentance, and the great love of a pardoned soul.

And this divine fire blazed so brightly and so strong within this poor sinner's heart that it was purified at once of every ugly stain; "so much of sinfulness was forgiven her, because she had loved so much." And therefore Jesus had only to make manifest the miracle which grace had worked within her[1] by saying to the sobbing woman, —

"Your sins are remitted unto you."

Language like this, which had once roused the members of the Sanhedrin to a fury of indignation, here, among the Pharisees of Naïm, only excited mingled emotions of fear and awe.

"Who is this man," they said among themselves, "who even remits sins?"

But as for Jesus, all intent upon comforting the penitent, His only thought was to complete her conversion by making her know His infinite compassion, and so reviving her courage.

"Your faith has saved you," He said; and then He added, "Go in peace!"

Forthwith, in the peace of the Lord, the pardoned sinner went away, never again to seek happiness in carnal pleasures, destined rather to amaze the world by the unflinching rigor of her expiation.

This woman, whose name Saint Luke does not mention, is no other than Mary Magdalene. Although there is nothing in Scripture distinctly to settle this fact,[2] there

---

[1] "Negari non potest quin prius etiam tempore quam Christus illa verba proferret, Magdalena perfecte et super omnia amaret, quia Christus per illa verba non contulit amorem ad remissionem peccatorum sufficientem, sed illum supposuit, et illi testimonium perhibuit, illumque affectum declaravit" (Suarez, *De Gratiâ*, lib. vii. cap. x). The whole chapter is an admirable commentary upon these words of Jesus.

[2] In none of the passages in which the Evangelists speak of this repentant sinner, of Mary Magdalene, and of Mary of Bethany, do they say whether or not these three names belonged to the one person. The critics who have contended for this interpretation, as well as those who combat it,

are very venerable traditions of the Church which assert it; and Jewish writers add their testimony in confirmation. According to all these authorities the pardoned sinner of Naïm, Mary of Magdala, and Mary the sister of Lazarus and Martha, are one and the same person.

Of her sinful past we have no knowledge beyond a few legends in the Talmud, which speak of the beauty of Mary, the fame of her lovely hair, her wealth, and her intrigues.[1] Her husband was a doctor of the Law, Pappus, son of Juda, whose jealousy was so great that he was wont to keep her closely imprisoned whenever he left their home. The high-spirited Jewess soon broke away from this hateful restraint, joined fortunes with a gay officer of Magdala, and accompanied him to that town, where she led a life of such brilliant but unbridled indulgence that she has always kept the name of "The Magdalene."

And doubtless it was there that Jesus saw her, and so awakened in her stained and blighted heart the first seeds of a passionate regret for her lost soul. The few words at the banquet-hall in Naïm were all that was needed to bring her weeping to the Saviour's feet; and ever after that day the Fathers (whose opinion we are following now) delight in discovering tokens of her presence, as she follows the footsteps of the Master. She is among the Galilean

have supported their theories from the different narratives, and often arrive at an equal degree of historical likelihood (see Maldonatus, *in Mat.* xxvi. 7, xxvii. 56; Dublin Review (July, 1872), *S. Mary Magdalene in the Gospels;* Hengstenberg, *in Joan.* xi. 1; Smith, *Dictionary of the Bible:* MARY MAGDALENE, etc.). In a controversy where the probabilities are so nicely balanced, it would seem as though Tradition must be the only reliable resort for further light; and certainly no one denies that the most numerous and the most imposing array of witnesses have testified that under all three names the Gospel is speaking of one single woman. This has been the general feeling in the Latin Church (Tertullian, *De Pudicitiâ,* xi.; S. Cyprian, *De Duplici Martyrio;* S. Jerome, *in Osee Prologus;* S. Augustine, *De Consensu Evangel.* ii. 79; S. Gregory the Great, *in Mat.* xxv. and xxxiii.; Clement of Alexandria, *Pædagogus,* ii. 8; S. Cyril of Alexandria, *in Joan.* xi. 1). True enough, some of the Greek Fathers have combated this opinion; but even in the East Origen observes that in his time many Christians shared this sentiment (*Commentaria in Matthæum,* Migne, *Patrologie grecque,* t. xiii. p. 1721).

[1] Lightfoot, *Horæ Hebraïcæ,* in Matt. xxvii. 56.

ladies who went with Him, and waited upon their Lord. At Bethany she is seated at His feet, in deep, speechless contemplation; then too, close by the tomb of Lazarus, and afterwards at the feast given by Simon the leper, finally upon Calvary, and at the Holy Sepulchre, — everywhere whither she could tread in the pathway of Him Who had saved her.

These are the broad lines in the Magdalene's portrait, as she is depicted by Tradition, which has thus filled out the shadowy sketch left us by the Gospel. Modern critics remark very truly that there is nothing in the sacred text [1] to necessitate such a construction of the events; but surely they make a two-fold mistake when they disregard Tradition, which supplies facts omitted by Scripture, while without any sufficient proofs of their own, they contend that these three women were of different dispositions, whose like could never be combined in one person. Such writers feel sure that the noble ladies of Galilee, among whom Saint Luke mentions the Magdalene, would never have associated with an infamous character; and that Mary, the Contemplative of Bethany, has nothing allied to that impetuous ardor which Saint John attributes to the Magdalene upon Mount Calvary. These difficulties will not be stumbling-blocks to those who know what changes repentance can work in the soul. Conversion does, in truth, bestow a title of nobility which no companions of Jesus ever fail to recognize; it turns the thirst for pleasures into such passionate longing for heavenly delight that the most illustrious penitents have buried themselves in a life of contemplation. And therefore we feel no more surprise at finding the brilliant courtesan sitting silent and

---

[1] Bossuet has written a curious opuscule on this subject, and he concludes by saying "that it is more congenial with the spirit of the Gospel to recognize these women as three different saints" (*Sur les trois Madeleines*, t. xxvi. édition Vivès). In the eighteenth century this idea had acquired so much weight that very many Galilean Breviaries revised the legend in the Roman Breviary where it only speaks of the one Magdalene. The time-honored conviction of the Church has, notwithstanding, always had, and has still, many illustrious champions, — Baronius, the Bollandists, Maldonatus, Lightfoot; and in our own times Sepp, Schegg, Pusey, Farrar, Père Lacordaire, M. Faillon, etc.

subdued at the Master's feet, than when we see her still clinging to her dying Lord, or disputing with the tomb for the body of the Incarnate God. And so we are still constant to ancient beliefs, when we prefer to think of the three Marys of the Gospel as the one Magdalene, ever venerated throughout the Church.

CHAPTER V.

THE PARABLES.

Luke viii. 1-21; Mark iii. 20-35, iv. 1-34; Matt. xii. 22-37, 46-50, xiii. 1-52.

THE Public Life of Jesus might be divided into two periods: one would be that in which the Jews did not directly interfere with His Ministry; while during the latter epoch they actively attacked Him. Up to this time the Master's glory had known no diminution of its growing splendor in the eyes of the people; although Judea rejected Him at the command of the Sanhedrin, He found a warm welcome awaiting Him in Galilee, and each succeeding day saw the throngs about Him increase in number and enthusiasm. For a long time the efforts of the Sanhedrin's emissaries, who strove to stir up the populace against Him, were altogether fruitless; we have noticed at the banquet given by Simon how the power and popularity of Jesus then overawed the Pharisees themselves. But now the hour had come for a complete change in the aspect of events; and hereafter the authority of the Lord begins to wane slowly and surely, until at last His enemies are again masters of the situation.

This reversal of affairs became most apparent during a second mission which the Saviour began in Galilee. It is Saint Luke[1] who tells us of these new journeyings, when Jesus travelled again through towns and hamlets spreading the good tidings of Salvation; but he does not relate any particular occurrences. He simply notes the fact that

[1] Luke viii. 1.

the twelve Apostles were with Him, and also certain Galilean women, of whom the greater number, if not all, "had been delivered by Him either from evil spirits or from other maladies. These were Mary, called the Magdalene, Joanna,[1] the wife of Chuza, Herod's Steward, Suzanna, and many others who aided Him with such goods as they had."

These saintly companions of the Christ were evidently of distinguished character, both on account of their rank and their riches. Of Suzanna[2] we know nothing more than her name, — the gracefulest name of any borne by the daughters of Israel, since it recalls the white cup of the lily-flower. As for Joanna, her husband's title would lead us to believe that she had been at the court of the Tetrarch before she set out to follow Jesus; yet having once devoted herself to the Lord, she never was unfaithful to her vows. We shall find her again at the Sepulchre, still by the side of Mary Magdalene,[3] with whom Saint Luke associates her here.

Among all the followers of the Christ, this last-named figure is known and loved the best. We have seen how Tradition regards her as the penitent sinner, who came to the feast given by Simon. This opinion would seem to be confirmed by Saint Luke himself, for he speaks of seven devils being driven out of the Magdalene; and seven may very reasonably be considered as a symbolic number, chosen to denote the depth of degradation from which the Saviour rescued this sin-soiled creature.[4]

The Holy Virgin is not named among the women who accompanied her Son; and hence we must presume that she was now living in retirement at Capharnaum. During His sojourns at different times in that city, it would appear that Jesus did not always take up His abode with her; for after this second mission-journey, we find Him in

---

[1] Luke viii. 2, 3. Joanna · Ἰωάννα, or, according to many manuscripts, Ἰωαννᾶς.

[2] Σουσάννα, שׁוֹשַׁן, "a lily."

[3] Luke xxiv. 10.

[4] Such at least is the opinion of S. Gregory the Great, Theophylactus, Bede, and very many commentators.

a dwelling which certainly was not shared by any of His family.[1]

As always happened about this time, the multitude would besiege Him in such numbers that Jesus and His disciples could "not even find time to take food."[2] His kindred, hearing of this, entirely lost all self-control. "He is growing mad," they said, angrily, and thereupon took sides with the party who were abusing Him. Though indeed there were two of their number chosen by the Christ to be among the Twelve, who were now bearing their share in His toils and His glory, yet the other children of Alpheus — whether from jealousy, or from dread of being involved in some trouble with the vindictive Sanhedrin — shut their eyes to the light, and not satisfied with simply treating Jesus as a madman, they resolved to lay hold upon Him, and keep Him confined in their own house.

"So they started out from their home, and came thither to seize Him;" but they could not force their way into His presence, so densely packed were the masses of town's-folk about him! Just at this moment, too, there was additional cause for excitement; for some one had brought Him a possessed fellow, who was blind and dumb as well,[3] and Jesus cured him, so that the man spoke and saw.[4] And all the people were amazed and said, —

---

[1] S. Mark says that they left their own home ('Εξῆλθον) in order to go to find and seize Jesus in the dwelling whither He had retired (Mark iii. 20, 21).

[2] Mark iii. 21.

[3] After having spoken of a mission which Jesus fulfilled in Galilee, and after giving the names of the holy women who accompanied Him, S. Luke passes at once to the Parable of the Sower; however, it is quite plain that before taking up this one of the Master's lessons we ought to notice the interference of the kinsfolk of Jesus (for here we are following the more detailed order of time set down by S. Mark), and besides this, two other incidents which are reported by S. Matthew. In fact, the latter Evangelist remarks in precise terms that the healing of the demoniac, the interview which the Saviour had with some of His kindred, and the Parable of the Sower, took place upon the same day: "Ετι αὐτοῦ λαλοῦντος τοῖς ὄχλοις, ἰδοὺ ἡ μήτηρ . . . κτλ (Matt. xii. 46). Ἐν τῇ ἡμέρᾳ ἐκείνῃ ἐξελθὼν ὁ Ἰησοῦς . . . κτλ (Matt. xiii. 1).

[4] Matt. xii. 22, 23. The demoniac just now delivered by Him is not the one whose cure S. Luke narrates among the events which happened during the following year in Perea, and not in Galilee (Luke xi. 14).

"Is not this the Son of David?"

But there were some Scribes from Jerusalem present. Though for an instant they were disconcerted by the cries of delight and wonderment, almost immediately they proceeded to whisper sly hints as usual, and began to disparage the miracle.

Why need any one be surprised, said they, that this man should cast out the devils? "He is himself possessed by Beelzebub;[1] he therefore commands them in the name of their Prince."[2]

Well knowing all their underhand dealings, Jesus summoned them to come nearer, and then said:[3]—

"Every kingdom divided against itself shall be made desolate; every city, every family, so divided shall not endure. If Satan cast out Satan, he is divided against himself; how then shall he endure?"

By this the Lord does not deny that the kingdom of Satan is a state of Anarchy, but He rather insists upon

---

Many do not discriminate between these miracles, allowing themselves to be misled by the resemblance in the Lord's words on both occasions. However striking this similarity may seem to us, it does not necessarily follow that they alluded to the same deed, for Jesus healed similar maladies more than once; more than once too did He repeat the same lessons in the face of the Pharisees, who persisted so stubbornly in their evil thinking. Yet more, we should note that the two cures were performed under very different circumstances, and that the demoniac of whom S. Matthew speaks (xii. 22, 23) is dumb and blind, while the one in S. Luke is dumb only. We may believe that the latter is the same as that possessed man who was dumb as well, whose healing S. Matthew relates in his ninth chapter, verse 32.

[1] Beelzebub is the name the Jews gave the prince of devils; it signifies "Lord of the Dungheap," בַּעַל זְבוּל; "Prince of Abomination." We find this word זְבוּל in frequent use among the Talmudists when referring to idols, which in their eyes were veritable devils. According to some scholars, זְבוּל should be taken in the sense of "house;" and in that case Beelzebub would mean "the Master of the Household," that is, of this world, which is his dwelling-place. The Septuagint (4 Kings, 1, 2) and Josephus, (Antiquitates, ix. 2, 1) translates this word by Βάαλ μυῖαν, "Lord of the Flies," and Hug has ingeniously conjectured that this is the demon which was worshipped by the Philistines at Ekron, under the likeness of one of those beetles which live in heaps of muck, — the Scarabæus Pillularius, for example.

[2] Mark iii. 22.
[3] Matt. xii. 25, 26; Mark iii. 23.

the truth that it is from this single point of agreement — their hatred of God — that the divisions of Hell draw the principle of their existence; were this their one Note of unity to be lost (which is impossible), there would be at once an end of the Realm of Darkness. By the fact of His rescuing the poor victim from the infernal powers Jesus showed that He was no minister of Satan; for "No one can enter a strong man's dwelling and bear away his goods without first having bound the man of might; only then can he pillage his house." [1]

Again the Master retorts upon His enemies that their own disciples exorcised spirits in the name of Jehovah, just as He did, and hence their sons [2] would be their judges, since they could testify that Hell yields obedience to other orders beside those of Beelzebub; wherefore if He, the Christ of the Lord, in His own Name and by the Spirit of God, put the fiends to flight, this indeed is proof that the Kingdom of God has really come." [3]

Then, in conclusion, Jesus called His faithful followers about Him. "Whoever is not with Me," said the Lord, "is against Me, and whoever gathereth not with Me scattereth." [4]

The Scribes had also accused Jesus of having "an unclean spirit." [5] What did they mean by this term? Was it in allusion to His contempt for Pharisaic Ablutions or to His tenderness toward sinners? It is quite impossible to say; but we know that this calumny aroused His wrath,

---

[1] Mark iii. 26, 27.

[2] Matt. xii. 27. The sons of the Pharisees, or in other words, their disciples, practised certain exorcisms according to a Ritual (or so says Josephus) which was prescribed by Solomon (*Antiquitates*, viii. 2, 5); see p. 213. S. Irenæus gives it as an undoubted fact that, even in his time, the Jews exorcised spirits in the name of Abraham, Isaac, and Jacob: "Judæi usque nunc hac ipsâ advocatione dæmonas effugant" (*Contra Hæreses*, ii. 6, 2). S. Chrysostom, S. Jerome, and S. Hilary understand that by "your sons" is meant the Apostles, to whom the Lord apportioned His empire over the powers of Hell; indeed His adversaries could not deny that the Twelve were all descendants of Israel, their sons and their brothers according to the flesh.

[3] Matt. xii. 28.

[4] Matt. xii. 30.

[5] Mark iii. 30.

since it called from him that dreadful warning of eternal death,[1] —

"I say unto you, every sin, every blasphemy, shall be forgiven men; but blasphemy against the Holy Spirit shall not be forgiven.[2] And whoever shall have spoken against the Son of Man it shall be forgiven him; but the man who has spoken against the Holy Ghost shall not be forgiven, either in this world or in the other."[3]

In Saint Matthew's account the reply of the Lord is reported more at length.[4] He told His slanderers that they ought at least to be consistent with themselves, and should judge the tree by its fruits. If He did actually drive out devils, why did they not acknowledge the fact? The tree

---

[1] Matt. xii. 31, 32; Mark iii. 28–30.

[2] Jesus could see into the wicked minds of His enemies clearly enough: it was not from any ignorance of the Truth that they strove against Him; but they were now boldly blaspheming, recognizing the Presence of God and of His Christ, and face to face with His wondrous works so manifestly divine, and consequently seeing the enormity of their blasphemy, yet persisting in it notwithstanding. This, then, was that dreadful sin against the Holy Ghost which cannot obtain pardon, because of itself it dries up life at the fountain-head, and withstands every movement of the Spirit of Grace which strives to quicken it again to a right feeling. In order to save the heart so bent upon evil, it would be necessary to force man's freedom of will; but God always stops at the threshold of that inviolable sanctuary of the soul.

[3] The expression αἰὼν οὗτος, and others like it, ὁ νῦν αἰών (Tit. ii. 12), αἰὼν τοῦ κόσμου τούτου (Ephes. ii. 2), etc., as well as the other, αἰὼν μέλλων, were frequently employed by the Jews to designate the times which were to precede and those which should follow the Messiah. But in the New Testament they signify (as all critics agree) the present life and the future life; so then, according to the doctrine of the Master, there are sins which are only remitted in the other world, and consequently there is a place of purgation where this remission takes place.

[4] The commencement of the discourse as it reads in S. Matthew is reported by S. Mark under the same circumstances (Matt. xii. 24–32; Mark iii. 22–30). The ending, which is not now found in the second Gospel, is in every particular similar to the reply which S. Luke puts in the mouth of the Lord after the healing of another demoniac (Matt. xii. 38–42; Luke xi. 17–32). It appears very likely to us that S. Matthew, following his usual method, is here collecting different speeches of the Master which bear upon the same subject. The matter given here, which is peculiar to himself (Matt. xii. 33–37) with that which he gives in common with S. Mark, was apparently pronounced at the time which we are now describing. As to the close of the discourse, which is also found in S. Luke, there is every reason to believe that it ought to be transferred to the epoch marked for it by the latter Evangelist.

is good which bears good fruit. And yet, after all, no one need be amazed at their blasphemies, for the mouth speaks from the fulness of the heart; and assuredly these creatures, this brood of vipers, could not fail to poison their speech with the venom of malice.[1]

Jesus was still speaking when a man pushed his way up to Him.

"Your Mother and your brethren are without," he said; "they are seeking for you."[2]

The Lord's kindred, hopeless of making any headway against the crowds, had probably turned to Mary for aid; and the Virgin, startled by their wild tales, had left her retreat to go with them. Used to seeing Him yield to the lightest wish of Mary, they thought He could not resist an appeal coming from her. But the Christ could no longer be subject to His Mother. Hereafter He belonged to God and to the souls whom He had come to save.

"Who is My Mother and who are My brethren?" was His reply to the one who had informed Him of their arrival. And as the man was silent, Jesus' glance fell upon the disciples seated in a circle about Him;[3] He stretched out His hands toward them, —

"Behold My Mother and My brethren!" He said; "for every one who does the will of My Father Who is in Heaven is My brother, My sister, and My mother." Then rising, the Master left the house, and took the road leading to the lake, where He seated Himself by the beach.[4]

The insulting charges which we have just noticed, the efforts made by Jesus to enlighten the people, the uneasiness shown by His kinsfolk, — all indicate what great changes had taken place in Capharnaum during this second mission into Galilee. The creatures of the Sanhedrin had profited by the absence of the Saviour to disquiet public opinion; and though most of the citizens were still loyal to their Benefactor, the number of His enemies had so far

---

[1] Matt. xii. 33, 34.
[2] Matt. xii. 46.
[3] Καὶ περιβλεψάμενος τοὺς περὶ αὐτὸν κύκλῳ καθημένους (Mark iii. 34).
[4] Matt. xiii. 1.

increased that Jesus thought best to forego any further teaching in the simple and direct style which He had hitherto used. However much He may have differed with the Scribes, He would, notwithstanding, submit to the limitations of their forms, and hence He determined to present His doctrine hereafter in Parables, as was their custom.[1] But while these masters of Israel only employed allegory in order to hide from the public the treasures of wisdom which they wished to confine to their disciples, the design of Jesus in using these veiled figures of speech was to gain the time which was necessary for the completion of His divine instructions; for He had yet to disclose the chiefest portion of His work, — the establishing of His Church, her Constitution, her Hierarchy, — an everlasting object of undying distrust and hatred to the great ones of earth.

Such a sudden change in His manner must naturally have caused some surprise; we shall see, however, that it was not at all displeasing to their tone of mind, nor did it repel them. For, in fact, the Oriental genius, which is so different from ours, loves the mysterious, and takes no less delight in piecing together stray hints of meaning than we in firmly grasping the thought in its fulness. Hence it is that we have so many allegories and proverbs in the Old Testament; such too are the enigmas in the stories of Samson, of Solomon and the Queen of Sheba.[2] Even to-day, if an Arab chance to hear some fable or apologue, he will spend whole hours in turning it over in his mind, — like a child, or for that matter like every creature in whom the imagination rules the other faculties, he finds most pleasure in fanciful reveries, whose dreamy and indefinite forms he much prefers to the cold precision of our ideas. This fondness for mystic and figurative language, common to the Eastern mind, was an invaluable advantage for Jesus, because during the last year of His Ministry it allowed of His giving the Jews just such glimpses of His meaning as

---

[1] Vitringa *De Synagogâ*, p. 678; Schœttgen, *Horæ Hebraïcæ:* CHRISTUS RABBINORUM SUMMUS.
[2] Jud. xiv. 14; 3 Kings x. 1.

were desirable for them, while it also permitted him to display His thought even more clearly before the eyes of His Apostles and intimate disciples. These were the circumstances which prompted the Master to take up with this new form of preaching.

Jesus was not left long alone on the lakeside. Out of Capharnaum there came a great throng who crowded all the open space around Him, and stood about the beach in little knots, waiting such time as He might choose to speak.[1] There was a boat drawn up on the sand, and in this the Saviour found a seat from which He could be seen and heard. Over the heads of the people who covered all the strand His eyes could rest upon smooth fields sloping to the water's edge, beaten paths winding through rich meadows, while here and there a huge rock or clump of cactus-like thistles would give a sterner aspect to the pleasant harvest lands.

"Listen!" said Jesus,[2] stretching out His hands toward those familiar shores of Genesareth.[3] "The Sower went out to sow, and while he was sowing some grains fell into the roadway, and the birds of the sky lighted and consumed them; other some fell upon stony ground, where there was not much earth, and it sprung up immediately, because it had no depth of soil; but when the sun was up it was scorched, and as it had no roots it withered away; still others fell among thistles, and the thistles grew up and choked them; others, finally, fell in good earth and bore fruit, some a hundred, others sixty, and others thirty fold. He who has ears to hear let him hear!"

There He stopped, leaving His listeners to fathom the meaning hidden beneath the Parable. There was nothing to help them to an understanding of it; it remained a riddle not only to the Jews who were strangers to His doctrine, but even to the Twelve as well. The latter pressed

---

[1] Matt. xiii. 2.
[2] Matt. xiii. 3–9.
[3] The landscape described in the Parable of the Sower is precisely that of the hill-country whose fertile slopes border the lake from Aïn et-Tin as far as Tell Houm; therefore, when He left Capharnaum the Master must have taken the road that runs along the coast toward Bethsaïda.

about Him, and upon their asking why He spoke in this way, Jesus at once explained His conduct. If He concealed the mysteries of the Kingdom of God under the form of an allegory, it was only that His enemies might "behold without perceiving, might hear without understanding," and thus, aided by this obscurity, He might (as we have said before) gain the necessary time for the development of His doctrine, which was to make out of these lowly disciples a Holy Church, the Household of the most High God. The same truths were delivered to every hearer of His Parables, but they were not fully revealed to any hearts which were not docile enough to beg more light of the Master Himself.[1] As for the mass of the Jews, the Oracle uttered long since by Isaias [2] was now fulfilled in them, — "You shall hear with your ears, and you shall not understand; you shall behold with your eyes, and you shall not see. For the heart of this people is waxed gross; they have grown dull of hearing, they have shut their eyes, in such wise [3] that they may no longer either see or hear or understand in their hearts; neither can they be converted nor be healed."

"But as for you," continued Jesus,[4] "blessed are your eyes because they see, and your ears because they hear. In very truth, I tell you, many Prophets and just men have desired to see what you are seeing and have not seen it, and to hearken to what you are hearing and have not heard it. Therefore listen to the Parable of the Sower." But the minds of the Apostles were not yet sufficiently clear-sighted to grasp the meaning of this allegory; and for the moment Jesus was amazed at their blindness.

"Do you not understand this Parable? How, then, will you be able to understand all the rest?"[5] However, He

---

[1] Matt. xiii. 10–15.
[2] Is. vi. 9.
[3] Μήποτε, with the future of the indicative, indicates that one is apprehensive of something, and at the same time regards it as very liable to occur (Winer, *Grammatik*, par. 56, 2).
[4] Matt. xiii. 16–18.
[5] Mark iv. 13.

took pity upon their weakness, and expounded His own words.

The Church is a vast Field,[1] through which Jesus walks scattering the grain from an unstinting hand; for the gifts of God are without measure. The seed falls everywhere in an equally generous shower, — upon hearts as cold and hardened as those worn, beaten pathways, which offer it no resting-place or nourishment; upon light and superficial souls, wherein the strength of the seed, spending itself in a sudden show of growth, sends down no deep roots, and so withers beneath the first wind of temptation; upon the creatures of worldliness, who no sooner receive the gift of grace than they proceed to stifle it " beneath a weight of earthly cares and the deceitfulness of riches." But those true followers of Him are " the good ground, — they who hearken to the Word, who receive it, and bring forth fruit bearing thirty, sixty, and an hundred fold." Such was the first rough draft of the Church drawn by the hand of the Master Architect, — a Field wherein the heavenly seed is sown with exceeding plentifulness, and yet it will bear no fruit if so be that man's evil passions place an obstacle in its way.

Jesus dwelt more strongly still upon this last point by showing what perfect freedom of action He would bestow upon His earthly Heritage, the Church. He likened it to a land which, being once oversown, "produces its fruit of itself, — first the blade, then the ear, then the grain enclosed in the ear. And when it has borne its full crop, immediately they put sickle to it, because it is now the time of harvest."[2] What matters it whether the workman sleeps or watches, will not the harvest still come round? The grain takes root of itself, and grows up while he is dreaming; when once the soil is planted, there is no need of him until the time of reaping is come. In like manner the Saviour has dealt with the Kingdom of Heaven in our hearts. He came to sow, but He need never more return unto the end of Time, — until the Harvesting is come.

---

[1] Matt. xiii. 18-23; Mark iv. 13-20; Luke viii. 11-15.
[2] Mark iv. 26-29.

Strong, sharp, and clear though these first outlines were, they did not sufficiently prefigure the future development of the Church. And so Jesus cast about for new similitudes.

"Unto what shall We compare the Kingdom of Heaven," He said, "and under what imagery may We describe it?"

In order to depict the persecutions which were in store for it He gave the Parable of the Cockle,[1] — "The Kingdom of Heaven is likened to a man who has sowed good grain in his field. Now while his people were sleeping his enemy comes and sows cockle through the midst of the wheat, and goes his way.[2] The blade having sprouted and borne its fruit, the cockle also began to appear.

"And the servants of the father of the family came to him, saying, 'My lord, did you not sow good grain in your field? How comes it that there is cockle also?'

"'It is mine enemy who has done this,' he said to them.

"'Will you have us go and weed it out?' the servants replied.

"'No,' he answered, 'for fear lest in gathering up the cockle you might uproot the wheat at the same time. Let them grow up together until the harvest, and in the time of harvesting I will say to the reapers, First tear up the cockle and bind it in bundles to cast into the fire; but gather the wheat into my barns.'"

Over against this picture of the Church's sufferings Jesus set forth the scene of its Day of Triumph in even more striking contrast. He showed how humble its beginnings, how slow its growth, but at the same time how mighty is the seed of life within it; and so He called it a

---

[1] Matt. xiii. 24-30. Cockle (*lolium temulentum*), darnel, or tare, is a species of grass, which comes up with the wheat and much resembles it, so long as the ear is unformed; it owes its name (l'ivraie, drunken ryegrass, drank grass) to the intoxicating properties of its grain, which are also extremely poisonous.

[2] The savage feuds, by which tribes and families are split up in the Orient, are strikingly depicted in this Parable. The foe, the avenger, is here implacable; yet, because he is too weak to resort to violence, he lurks in the darkness and wreaks his vengeance, without exposing himself to the consequences.

Mustard Seed,[1] — the tiniest of all seeds, which becomes a tree[2] in which the birds of heaven find a resting-place; or it is the Leaven which a woman mixes in three measures[3] of meal, and which ferments the whole lump.

"All these things," adds Saint Matthew,[4] "He told to the people in Parables, and He no longer spoke to them save in parables. Thus was fulfilled what had been said by the Prophet,[5] — 'I will open My mouth in Parables; I will lay bare things hidden from the foundation of the world.'"

Nevertheless the divine Master was careful, amid all this "great number of similitudes," to say nothing "which could not be comprehended" by docile hearts, and "in private He explained everything to His disciples."[6]

To them, indeed, was committed the great trust of treasuring up the truths which were denied to incredulous Jews; not that they were always to hoard this wealth in secrecy, but that they might bring them forth at a fitting

---

[1] Matt. xiii. 31, 32. The Mustard of the Parable is the same plant which we designate by this name, whose very minute seeds produce the large, black mustard-plant. In the warmer latitudes it attains a height unknown in northern countries. When riding over the rich plain of Akkar, Thomson saw the black-mustard growing wild, and the shrubs were higher than the horseman's head (*The Land and the Book*, p. 414; along with this compare *Travels*, Irby and Mangles, March 12). Hooker testifies to the fact that on the banks of the Jordan, its bole often measures ten feet in height. And hence, comparing it with any other plants of the garden (λάχανον, "olus," Matt. xiii. 32), the Mustard may well be called a "great tree," and it is entirely unnecessary for us to suppose (as Dr. Royle has suggested), that Jesus is not speaking of the Mustard-seed here (*Sinapis Nigra*), but of the *Salvadora Persica*. (See *Journal of the Royal Asiatic Society*, March, 1844, and along with this consult Lightfoot, *Horæ Hebraicæ*, in Matt. xiii.) "Caulis erat sinapis in Sichem, e quo enati sunt rami tres, e quibus unus decerptus cooperuit tentoriolum figuli. . . . Caulis sinapis erat mihi in agro meo, in quam ego scandere solitus sum, ita ut scandere solet in ficum" (Talmud of Jerusalem, *Peah*, fol. 20, 2.)

[2] Matt. xiii. 33.

[3] Σάτον (סְאָה, in Aramean: סָאתָא) is the third part of an Ephah (a little more than 18 litres). Three of these measures made up the quantity of wheat which they were accustomed to mix for a baking of bread (Gen. xviii. 6; 1 Kings i. 24).

[4] Matt. xiii. 34, 35.

[5] Ps. lxxvii. 2.

[6] Mark iv. 33, 34.

hour to be the Light of the Church,—to be as a torch, which is not put beneath a couch, but is set within its holder that it may light all those who enter the house; "for there is nothing hidden" in the Master's doctrine "which must not be revealed, nothing done in the shadow which shall not be brought to the light."[1] This is why Jesus so earnestly beseeches His Apostles to listen to His words.

"Pay heed to what you are hearing. Whoever has ears to hear let him hear!"

And again this is the reason of His solemn warning that this great gift of wisdom is not bestowed upon them alone, but that it is to be for all; hence He threatened to take it back from such as failed to guard it faithfully,—"for it shall be given to him who hath," to him who preserves the words of the Master, "but from him who hath not, even that which he hath shall be taken away."[2]

Toward evening Jesus dismissed the throngs, and returned to His dwelling. Thither the disciples accompanied Him, and begged Him to enlighten them as to the Parable of the Cockle. Thereupon interpreting the allegory word by word, He showed plainly how the Devil is the Enemy who sows the cockle; yet at the end of the world the Angels shall gather together all the scandals, together with the evil-doers, from out the Church, casting them into the furnace of fire; while the just shall shine like the sun in the Kingdom of their Father.

To these parables Saint Matthew adds three similes which the Saviour uttered about the same time;[4] and with

---

[1] Mark iv. 21, 22.   [2] Mark iv. 23–25.   [3] Matt. xiii. 36–43.
[4] To us, it seems scarcely probable that the seven parables, as collected together here by S. Matthew, were pronounced in presence of but one audience, and all on the same day. Jesus had too intimate an acquaintance with the sordid and grovelling dispositions with which he had to deal, to overwhelm and fatigue their minds in this manner without giving them leisure to meditate upon the truths concealed beneath those mystical words. Furthermore, S. Matthew informs us that the Master uttered a great number of parables at this time (Matt. xiii. 34); so the seven now connected in this chapter are probably those which struck the writer as being more forcible than the rest,—those which would give us the clearest notion of "the Kingdom of God."

these He completed the figurative description of what His Church was to become. For some 't is a Treasure buried in a field which the toiling laborer turns up with the ploughshare; "having found it, the fellow hides it, and in his joy goes out and sells all he has that he may buy the field." For others it is the Pearl of great price which falls into the hands of a merchant who is seeking rare gems. For all of us it is a Net which drags the very depths of the sea, letting nothing escape its meshes, bearing mankind from out the fierce waves of the world up to the peaceful shores of eternity. "As fishers seated on the strand collect together the good fish and cast away the bad, even so shall it be at the end of the world. The Angels shall come and shall separate the wicked from among the righteous, and shall cast them into the furnace. There shall be weeping and gnashing of teeth."[1]

"Have you understood all these things?" added the divine Master.

"Yes, Lord," the Apostles replied; for now indeed their dazzled eyes were beginning to have glimpses of the truth, despite the surpassing splendor of His speech. Little by little they were still to descry new and lovelier verities, as the divine Light grew in glory, until the time should come for all to be made partakers in the heavenly day. This was to be their Commission; for, unlike those Doctors of the Law who communicated their doctrine only to a handful of disciples, the Apostles of the Glad Tidings were to spread the good news over all the earth. Just as a bountiful father will plunge his hand deep down in his coffers, bringing to light the hoardings of long ago as well as of to-day that he may lavish them upon the children of his household, even so the true Scribe, who has knowledge of the Kingdom of Heaven, must needs find in the Old Testament as well as in the New treasures of wisdom which shall become in his hands the noble Heritage of all mankind.[2]

[1] Matt. xiii. 44-51.   [2] Matt. xiii. 52.

CHAPTER VI.

THE MIRACLES DONE IN GERGESA AND CAPHARNAUM.

I. The Possessed Creatures of Gergesa.

Luke viii. 22-39; Mark iv. 35-41; v. 1-20; Matt. viii. 18, 23-34.

The crowds which Jesus had dismissed after the discourse by the lakeside had now gathered about His abode once more. The Saviour, seeing that any needful repose was not to be hoped for inside the city walls, resolved that same evening to seek the lonely highlands of Perea. "Let us pass over to the other side," He said to His disciples.[1] And they, after sending away the citizens, went aboard a boat; with them was the Lord, who made no preparation whatever for the voyage; for Saint Mark says "they took Him into the bark just as He was." Several other craft sailed along in company with them, each one, amid the rustling night-winds and under the starlit sky, making quiet headway toward the opposite bank.

Jesus, seating Himself in the stern, rested His head upon the pilot's pillow; very soon He was sleeping, wearied with the toils of the day. But hardly had His eyes closed in slumber when the whole outlook overhead and round about them changed. It is with surprising suddenness that the storms burst over the sea of Galilee; from the icy peaks of Hermon the tempests precipitate themselves upon the lake, and in an instant whip its waters into wild and seething waves.[2] Caught in one of these furious cloud-

---
[1] Mark iv. 35-38.
[2] Thomson, *The Land and the Book*, p. 374.

bursts, the little vessels were scattered far and wide, while that of the Master was left alone, with the waters beating into it on every side.

And now the fierce floods threatened to engulf them at every moment; yet all the time Jesus slumbered on, while the Apostles dared not waken Him. But when they felt the boat beginning to settle beneath their feet fear dispelled every other thought; they threw themselves about Him, calling upon Him with desperate eagerness,—

"Master! Master! save us! We perish!"

The wakening of Jesus was as tranquil to all seeming as His repose had been; and His first care was to calm their hearts rather than the angry waters.

"Why do you fear?" He said, "O men of little faith!" Only after this did He arise and rebuke the winds;[1] then speaking to the sea as if it had been a furious beast,

"Be quiet," He said to it; "curb thy rage."[2]

And immediately the winds ceased, and there came a great calm.

At sight of the unclouded plains of heaven, and the lake once again silent and placid, it was borne in upon the Apostles' minds how Jesus might well complain of their little faith. No matter what extreme of peril they might encounter, it were too trifling to notice in His Presence; while He is with us we have nothing to fear. Their wondering awe was shared by the sailors who were with Him.[3]

"What manner of Man is this?" they said one to another. "He commands the winds and the waves, and they obey Him."

The cry of these men of Galilee has been repeated many times since then; for the miracle performed upon the waters of Genesareth is but a type of those marvellous mercies which God has never ceased to operate by means of His Church. She likewise is sailing over blustering seas; often in the awful vortex of the whirlwind it will seem as

---

[1] Matt. viii. 26.   [2] Σιώπα, πεφίμωσο (Mark iv. 39).
[3] Οἱ ἄνθρωποι (Matt. viii. 27).

though the Master were sleeping in forgetfulness of His own; but from age to age, at the very moment when all seems lost, the Christ awakes and with one word saves the Bark. Tossed and battered though she be, so long as Jesus rests upon the Pilot's bench she is upholden by a promise which cannot fail of fulfilment, — His promise to bring us all together to the further shores of Eternity.

Jesus did not find the quiet and repose which He had come to seek in the country of Perea. He had scarcely set foot upon the land of Gergesa [1] when His glance encountered a mournful object. From one of the hills which rise above the lake a possessed creature had descried the landing of the little ship, and, emerging from the caves hollowed out of the cliff, he rushed down toward where the Lord stood.[2]

In ancient times there was no place of refuge where poor human beings could be kept when subject to such horrid afflictions as this; driven out of the towns and away from all houses, they must seek shelter in some ruined hovel or in the caverns which were used as graves. The horror overshadowing such an abode, in which no Jew could enter without being contaminated, would naturally but increase the fury of the demoniacs.

This possessed man of Gergesa was so terrible of aspect

---

[1] The name of the country where their bark came to land has been the subject of numerous alterations, in the different Versions of the Gospel. Was it called Gadara, Gerasa, or Gergesa? Tischendorf, relying mainly upon the authority of his Manuscript of Sinaï, thinks we should read in S. Mark Γερασηνῶν, in S. Luke Γεργεσηνῶν, and in S. Matthew Γαδαρηνῶν. But Gerasa, which lies upon the borders of Arabia, is too far distant to be the place referred to here; so too with Gadara, whose ruins have been discovered on the outskirts of Hieromax, a three hours' walk from the lake (Um Kreis). Hence we prefer the tradition, recorded by Origen, that a town named Gergesa stood somewhere near the shores of the lake, opposite to Capharnaum. Both Eusebius and S. Jerome make mention of it, adding that in their day a mountain near the water-side was pointed out to them as the scene of the Miracle. To-day, too, in the same region (in the Ouadi Semakh), there are some ruins which the Bedouins call by the name of Kerza or Gerza, while numerous tomb-caves are still to be seen hollowed out of the mountain-side: thus everything seems to confirm the testimony of Origen (See Thomson, *The Land and the Book*, pp. 375-378).

[2] Mark v. 2-5.

that no one dared so much as to cross his path. It was now a long time since he had torn to pieces what few shreds of clothing still hung about him. And so he roamed night and day among the lonely rock-tombs, stark and naked, uttering wild shrieks and tearing his flesh with sharp stones.[1] They had tried in vain to fetter his limbs; he would rend his shackles with their iron chains; and after this no number of men could get the mastery over him. This was the frenzied spectre which confronted the Lord almost as soon as His foot touched the land.

According to Saint Matthew's report of the scene,[2] this possessed being was not alone; another such wretched mortal came running up to Jesus with him. Frantic and violent though they were, yet (as all the others before them had been), these two were quelled by some divine charm in Him, and cowering in the dust before the Christ, they shrieked wildly [3]: —

"What is there between Thee and us, Jesus, Son of the Most-High? Art Thou come hither to torment us before the time?"

For Jesus had said to one of the demoniacs, "Foul Spirit, depart from out this man!" And as Satan was loath to obey, the Saviour added, "What is thy name?"

The fiend answered by the mouth of the possessed man, "I am called Legion,[4] because we are many."

Then shuddering and writhing before the Lord, this host of demons besought Him not to dismiss them forever from the country-side, but to allow them some place of refuge.

Now there was a great herd of swine feeding far away [5]

---

[1] One of the apocryphal writings gives it that the demoniacs gnawed at their own flesh: σαρκοφαγοῦντας τῶν ἰδίων μελῶν (Thilo, *Codex Apocryphus*, i. p. 308).

[2] Matt. viii. 28.

[3] Mark v. 6–9.

[4] The presence of the Roman armies in Palestine had made the word "Legion" familiar to the Jews; by this expression the possessed man sought to give some idea of the multitude of evil spirits whose movements he felt warring within him; in point of fact a Legion was made up of five or six thousand men. (See Lightfoot, *Horæ Hebraicæ*, in Marc. v. 9.)

[5] Matt. viii. 30. Μακράν, which is inexactly translated in the Vulgate by "non longe," "near here," indicates, on the contrary, that the herd

upon the mountain-side; and the devils begged and cried, saying, —

"If Thou wilt drive us hence, let us enter into yonder herd of swine."

"Go!" He said to them.

And the unclean spirits, rushing forth, seized upon the swine, who were carried headlong into the lake, and were stifled with the sea-waters to the number of nearly two thousand.

At sight of their herds borne in unmanageable fury to destruction, the men having charge of them at once conceived that those mad outcasts were the cause of this new misfortune; so, fearing any encounter with such ghoulish wretches, they took to flight, and spread the news as they passed along by quiet farm-houses and through the busy streets of the little city. The town's-folk sallied out at once to see what had occurred; and what must have been their surprise, on hurrying up to where Jesus stood, to perceive at His feet the much-dreaded demoniac, now quietly seated, clothed, sane of mind, and whole, — without a scream and without a single mark of recent struggle!

"And when those who had seen the thing related to them all that had happened to the possessed and to the herds,"[1] so sudden a transformation overwhelmed them with alarm; they never thought either of denying or explaining the fact; they were simply seized with such terror that they began to beseech Jesus to leave their shores.

How can we account for this overpowering fear, the like of which was never produced by any of the Saviour's miracles in Judea, — unless perhaps for the reason that this eastern shore of the lake was a very different territory, with a population far more Pagan than Jewish in thought and feeling? The ten cities which gave the name of the Decapolis to these parts were Greek, both by their origin and

---

of pigs were browsing in some place rather remote from the spot on which the possessed creature was delivered; "upon the mountain," "in the gorges," say the other two Evangelists: Πρὸς τῷ ὄρει (Mark v. 11); ἐν τῷ ὄρει (Luke vii. 32).

[1] Mark v. 15–17.

in their manners. Gadara (which was the native place of the demoniac, according to very many manuscripts) could boast of some famous poets, among them Meleager,[1] — a singer of light love songs, — and the Epicurean Philodemus, whose renown had reached Rome itself.[2]

Keen in its enjoyment of earthly pleasures, this land had no desire to hear of the Kingdom of Heaven. And so, bowing to the wishes of the agitated citizens, Jesus reembarked at once; but He did not quit their country without taking care that the Good News should be published among them.

As the man who had been healed presently supplicated to be taken along with them, the Saviour, not consenting to this step, bade him however, —

"Return to your home, to your brethren, and tell them what great things the Lord has done for you, and how He has had pity on you."[3]

The man obeyed, and thus became the first apostle of the Decapolis. "He announced everywhere the works of the Christ, and all men wondered."

II. THE BANQUET GIVEN BY LEVI. — THE WOMAN WITH THE ISSUE OF BLOOD. — THE DAUGHTER OF JAÏRUS.

Matt. ix. 10-26; Luke v. 29-39, viii. 40-56; Mark ii. 15-22, v. 21-43.

It was in the morning that Jesus delivered the two demoniacs of Gergesa, and by pushing out to sea without

---

[1] Gadara was in the neighborhood of Gergesa. Meleager, author of the *Anthology*, was born there, fifty years before Jesus Christ. We have a graceful elegy of his, wherein he celebrates the charms of his home country, the joyous spring-time in Phœnicia, the distant meadow-lands veiled over with the fine blue mists of the East, and swaying beneath their fragrant freight of purple blossoms: —

"L'alcyon sur les mers, près des toits l'hirondelle,
Le cygne au bord du lac, sous les bois Philomèle;"
(ANDRÉ CHENIÉR.)

translated from these lines in Meleager's "Spring-time:" —

Ἀλκυόνες περὶ κῦμα, χελιδόνες ἀμφὶ μέλαθρα,
Κύκνος ἐπ' ὄχθαισιν ποταμοῦ, καὶ ὑπ' ἄλσος ἀηδών.

[2] Cicero, *In Pisonem*, 29. [3] Mark v. 20.

delay He could reach the fertile land of Genesareth again that same day. A long time before they hove to and dropped anchor in the little bay eager crowds had spied the vessel which had borne Him away, and hastening down along the banks, they waited to greet Him.[1]

But none welcomed Him more gladly than Levi. Evidently this Apostle had remained behind in Capharnaum, and having in the interval called together a number of His friends, — publicans and sinners, like himself,[2] — he begged the Lord to partake of a great feast, which he immediately prepared for this assemblage.[3] Jesus showed no hesitation about accepting the invitation, and in good time sat down to the banquet, surrounded by His disciples.

That the Lord was present at this feast soon began to be noised throughout the town. The Scribes and Pharisees were the first to make their way into the great hall, thrown open wide to all comers. There they saw, enacted under their very eyes, this sad scandal, the rumor of which had so shocked them.

Verily! ay, true enough! there sat a Master of Israel, at the same table with publicans, and familiarly talking with such low company!

They were too wary now to grumble and mutter in the Saviour's hearing: but feeling that they might act more

---

[1] Luke viii. 40.
[2] Luke v. 29.
[3] After telling us the story of his vocation, S. Matthew proceeds to describe the great banquet to which he invited the Lord, the cure of a woman with an issue of blood, and the resurrection of Jaïrus's daughter (Matt. ix. 10, 26). SS. Mark and Luke put the first two events at the beginning of the first year of His Ministry (Mark ii. 15-22; Luke v. 29-39), and the latter two they place after the deliverance of the demoniacs of Gergesa (Mark v. 21-13; Luke viii. 40-56). We shall make only one deviation from the order indicated by the two latter Evangelists: considering the calling of Levi to have occurred at the same time set for it by them, we shall connect his banquet with the miracles which are to follow; for S. Matthew, on this point, speaks as an eye-witness, and he distinctly states that the three last-named events happened one after another, on the same day, and of course we cannot disregard this precise evidence. Elsewhere (p. 227) we have shown that it is impossible to suppose that the calling of Levi took place after the selection of the Twelve.

freely with the Apostles, they gave vent to their distrust and horror in their ear.

"How comes it," they said, "that you and that master of yours eat and drink with publicans and sinners?"

Censure such as this, coming from men they were accustomed to look up to with reverence, could not fail to disturb these simple minds, little versed in controversy.

Jesus, knowing every movement of their souls, discerned their trouble, and Himself replied to the formalists, "that He was not come to call the just, but sinners. For men in good health have no need of a physician, but only the sick."[1] Then, borrowing an expression common among their Rabbis, He added, —

"Go, ye, and learn[2] the meaning of those words: 'I will have mercy, and not sacrifice!'"[3] — that is, Charity rather than mere stickling for observances.

Such precepts as this uttered by the Prophet Osee conferred upon the Law its only true dignity, by permeating it with the real Spirit of Christianity before the time. But the Pharisees of Capharnaum had not so construed it; and now they refused to comprehend more than that Jesus undertook to defend His friends, and so for their part, they would refrain hereafter from all disputes with Him!

Some of John's disciples,[4] attracted thither by the hurrying throngs, had also entered the great hall. At sight of Jesus seated there, taking His part in the good things of the feast, mindful too of how the Baptist "would neither eat nor drink,"[5] and even now was languishing in the dungeons of Macheronte, — these sad memories quite broke down all their hopes. So then, the Christ had already forgotten His Precursor! Far from spending His time in fasting and tears, like these mourners over the downfall of their great Prophet, He was actually enjoying

---

[1] Luke v. 31, 32.

[2] Matt. ix. 13. Πορευθέντες μάθετε is equivalent to the expression which we find so frequently in the Talmud: צֵא וּלְמַד.

[3] Osee v. 6. The Prophet is quoted according to the Hebrew text, which the Septuagint translated thus: "I love mercy better than sacrifice."

[4] Matt. ix. 14.

[5] Luke vii. 33.

rich banquets, and diverting himself in the company of sinners!

Such a spectacle embittered their minds the more against Him, and made their disappointment over their own master's fate all the harder to bear. Finding that the Pharisees were ready to make common cause against Him, they joined them in reproaching the Lord anew.

"Why," they began, "should we and the Pharisees multiply our fasts,[1] while you and yours eat and drink?"

Jesus forgave their presumption, because their zeal made it excusable; but He recalled to the minds of John's disciples how their master had compared Him to the Bridegroom amid the marriage festivities, and continuing the figure, He said, "Would you have the sons of the Spouse[2] fasting and weeping while the Spouse is with them?" It is befitting for us to fast in seasons of mourning only; now John had foretold that the coming of the Kingdom of God would be like a wedding festival, wherein the Christ should celebrate His espousals with Humanity; and therefore, on this day of gladness, to demand that the Apostles, the friends of the Bridegroom, should abandon themselves to grief, would be to discredit the testimony of John himself.

"But a time will come," He added, "when the Spouse shall be taken from them, and they shall fast in those days."

[1] The Mosaic Law only commanded the people to fast upon the Day of Solemn Expiation, which occurred four days before the Feast of the Tabernacles, about the fifteenth of September (Lev. xvi. 29; Num. xxix. 7). After the return from Captivity, the Scribes had inaugurated four fasting-days in the year, occurring in the fourth, the fifth, the seventh, and the tenth months (Zachar. viii. 19). The Pharisees, with their usual ostentation of piety went still further, fasting twice every week, — on Thursday, in memory of the day on which Moses, according to Tradition, ascended Mount Sinai; and on Monday, to commemorate his return thence (Luke xviii. 12; *Baba Kamma*, f. 82 a). However, the Prophets do not appear to have approved of these novelties (Zachar. vii. 1-12; viii. 9).

[2] These Sons, or Friends of the Bridegroom, are the companions of the Paranymph, "the gentlemen of honor," the Best Man with the Groomsmen. This term Son is ordinarily employed in sacred literature to denote any ties which are considered as being as intimate as those of kinship: "The Sons of the Kingdom" (Matt. viii. 12); "of Hell" (Matt. xxiii. 15); "of Peace" (Luke x. 6), etc.

For the first time ¹ Jesus allowed the multitude to have some inkling of the violent death which awaited Him; but He did not dwell at any length upon this dark foreboding; indeed, He rather made haste to restore happiness and peace among Levi's guests, who had been disturbed by these ill-timed questionings.

Hereupon changing the tone of their talk, and looking round Him upon the gay furnishings which decked the board, the joyous company in their bright-colored festal robes, the tankards from which flowed sparkling wines, He began to speak in a Parable, which had now come to be His usual manner of teaching.

Under this figure He propounded a truth which would be most apt to shock the Jewish mind; for He wished to have them know that in His Kingdom the ceremonies of the Mosaic worship were to be abolished, — the bloody sacrifices, the symbolical ceremonies, circumcision, and everything else which in the Law was but a shadow of future things, would now fade away under the clear light of the Gospel. The Lord knew, were He to announce abruptly that the Ancient Covenant had already passed away, He would arouse all Judea against Him; hence He must needs prepare men's minds, as usual, with gentle condescension.

"No one," He began,² "puts a piece of unworn cloth into an old garment; otherwise the new," when damp and shrunken, "gathers up the old, and the rent is made the worse. And no more does any one put new wine into old bottles; otherwise the bottles break, the wine flows away, and the bottles themselves are lost. Rather you put new wine into new bottles, and both are preserved."

Mysterious and little understood though they were, these words could not fail to excite some surprise in the minds of His audience; perhaps they even caused renewed murmurs of disapproval. Jesus fully realized how strong the

---

¹ Heretofore He had alluded to it but once, — in the conversation with Nicodemus (John iii. 14). "Bene non dicit: Abibit ab eis sponsus, quod significasset amoris in sponso imperfectionem, sed: Auferetur ab eis sive per mortem a vobis inferendam, sive per ascensionem, a Patre" (Jansenius of Ghent, *Concordia Evangelica*, xxxiii.).

² Matt. ix. 16, 17.

attachment to time-honored observances can be, and so He added, —

"He who is wont to drink old wines does not at first relish the new, but finds the old better."[1]

As He was speaking in this way, one of the great men of Capharnaum entered the happy circle.[2] It was Jaïrus, Chief of the Synagogue, — one of those notable men of the city who had very lately sought out Jesus to implore His aid in behalf of the Roman Centurion; but this time he was come to entreat help for himself. He fell down before the feet of the Saviour, pouring forth his prayer; and in every word of it one can note how uncontrollable and distracting was his grief.[3]

"Lord, my little child, my only daughter is dying, — she is dead, — but, O come! lay your hands upon her and she shall live."

Jesus rose up at once, and followed Jaïrus.[4] The Apostles accompanied Him; behind them surged an excited throng of publicans, Pharisees, those disciples of John, and the people of the town, all eager to see what was about to happen.[5]

Now, amid this motley mass of humanity, there was a sick woman who had been subject to a loss of blood for some twelve years. Such a malady was a dreadful humiliation for any daughter of Israel; because it was looked upon as a scourge that was only laid on women of wicked character, and hence those afflicted with it were avoided and despised. The poor sufferer had paid out all her means in fees to the physicians,[6] but still in vain. She had undergone, without any benefit, all that peculiar treatment as to

---

[1] Luke v. 39. [2] Matt ix. 18.
[3] S. Matthew (ix. 18) puts these words in the father's mouth: "My daughter is even now dead," while S. Mark (v. 23) makes him say, "My little daughter is at the point of death." There is no inconsistency here, since both these expressions might have come to the lips of the distraught father, who had but just now left his child in her last agony, and so knew not whether she were yet alive or dead (S. Augustine, *De Consensu Evangelistarum*, ii. 66).
[4] Matt. ix. 19.
[5] Mark v. 24.
[6] Mark v. 25, 26.

which the Talmud gives us some curious details,[1] yet the disease grew greater every day.

She had now given up all other hope save in Jesus; but she was still held back by her timidity and shame, both because she had nothing at all to offer Him, and because her sickness was thought to be such a terrible disgrace; at last she resolved to get the gifts of grace by stealth, like a thief.

"If I can just touch His robe," she said to herself, "I shall be healed."

Urged on by this intense and lively faith, she glided through the multitude, pushed her way right up to the Master, and furtively seized the tassel hanging from His mantle[2] in her thin and wasted fingers.

Scarcely had she touched it, when the issue of blood was stopped; her trust had been rewarded. With beating heart and half choked with fear, she fell back amid the crowd.

But though no one had noticed her act, Jesus knew it of Himself.[3] Feeling at once that power had gone out from Him, He halted and turned toward the people.

"Who has touched My garment?" He said.

As each one began to plead innocence, Peter and those round Him replied, —

"Master, the people crowd about and harass you, and can you ask, 'Who has touched me?'"

"I have felt that power has gone out from Me," Jesus answered; "some one has touched Me.[4]"

And as His eyes fell upon the throng He fixed one of

---

[1] Lightfoot, *Horæ Hebraicæ*, in Marcum, v. 26.

[2] This sort of ornamental pendant was a sacred object in the Jews' eyes; they were commanded by the Law to affix tassels to the four corners of their mantle, attaching them to the seam of the garment by a blue cord. Moses intended to remind them, by means of this ornament always set before their eyes, that they were a Chosen People, and therefore consecrated to the Eternal. Two of these pendants were attached to the front, and another of them hung down below the waist, when a fold of the broad wrap was thrown back over one shoulder; probably this was the fringe which the poor woman managed to grasp.

[3] Mark v. 30.

[4] Luke viii. 45.

those grave and piercing glances which fathom the depths of the heart upon her whom He had healed. The woman, seeing herself discovered, began trembling, then tottered to Him and fell at His feet, declaring before all the people for what cause she had touched Him, and how on the instant she had been cured. The Lord had merely looked for this simple acknowledgment.

"My child, be of good courage," He said to her; "go in peace, your faith has saved you.[1]

"While He was still speaking comforting words to her, some members of the household of Jaïrus came hurrying toward them.

"Do not trouble the Master any longer," they said; "your daughter is dead."[2]

The unfortunate father had uttered no complaint at seeing Jesus make so long a wait by the road-side. Great and importunate as was his grief, it could not make him grudge this sufferer the happiness of being healed; for the nobleman's charity equalled his faith. The Master now turned back to him, and seeing him bowed in speechless sorrow, He spoke to him very gently.

"Do not fear, only believe; she shall be saved." And still followed by the throngs, He proceeded once more on the way.

At the house Jesus found the mourners already gathering, upon the first tidings of the child's death.[3] The delicate body, ready to be wrapped in its winding-sheet and

---

[1] The "Gospel of Nicodemus" gives Veronica as the name of the sick woman, and tradition says that after her cure she returned to Cæsarea Philippi, her native land, where she set up a monument of bronze, which represented her as she lay prostrate at the feet of the Saviour. There is a graceful legend to the effect that a flowering shrub grew up close by the statue, and that it was immediately endowed with the power of healing all sicknesses, from the moment that its stem once touched the hem of the Statue's mantle. During four centuries the Church venerated this touching memento of the loving-kindness of Jesus. Eusebius saw it still standing, and it was not harmed until the time of Julian the Apostate, who destroyed it, with so much beside (Eusebius, *Historia ecclesiastica*, vii. 18; Sozomenus, *Historia ecclesiastica*, v. 11).

[2] Luke viii. 49.

[3] Luke viii. 52. It is customary in the East to commence the funeral wail immediately after a person's decease.

linen bands, was lying on the cold ground; round about it the women were moaning and wailing, while the shrill keening of the flutes made their cries the more dismal.

"Weep not!" Jesus said to them; "the child is not dead, she sleeps."[1]

The mourners, hearing this speech, thought that He was mocking them, and would have continued their wail, but Jesus forbade them. He made them pass without the darkened chamber, and allowed only the mother and the father of the child, together with His three most intimate Apostles, Peter, James, and John,[2] to remain in the room.

In their presence He took the hand of the young girl, and called to her, —

"Talitha, Koumi!"[3] "My child, arise!"

At once the little maid rose and started to run, in high glee, for she was only twelve years old. The parents were beside themselves with joy, and the Lord had to remind them of such things as were necessary for the child, telling them to give her something to eat.

In working this new marvel of resurrection Jesus had yielded to his boundless love; but may He not have feared that so wonderful a sign of His Christhood would arouse all the enthusiasm of the people, and reawaken Herod's jealousy? He had not confined Himself, therefore, to merely commanding them to keep silence concerning the matter,[4] but had taken every precaution to conceal the deed beforehand. His first words had been, "The child is not dead, she sleeps;" and although these words were meant to signify that for Him it was as easy to recall her soul to life as it would be to awaken her from slumber, yet this sense of the words would be sure to escape the minds of the common people. The wondrous deed being accomplished, He probably remained in the house until the

---

[1] Mark v. 38; Matt. ix. 23.   [2] Luke viii. 51.

[3] Mark v. 41. טְלִיתָא קוּמִי. S. Peter, who was one of the eye-witnesses of this miracle, treasured up the memory of those two words, and many years after transmitted them to Mark, his Evangelist.

[4] Mark v. 43.

people outside, ignorant of what was going on within doors, gradually dropped away.

Thus Jesus avoided the first outburst of excitement; but the secret could not be kept for long. The sight of the little girl, brought back from death to life, the great gratitude of her parents, the wonder and awe of the Apostles, — all these soon betrayed the fact, "and the fame of the miracle was noised abroad through the whole country-side." [1]

[1] Matt. ix. 26.

CHAPTER VII.

THE MISSION OF THE APOSTLES.—DEATH OF THE PRECURSOR.

I. THE MISSION OF THE APOSTLES.

Matt. xiii. 54-58, ix. 35-38, x. 5-42; Mark vi. 1-11; Luke ix. 1-6.

WHEN Jesus left the mansion of Jaïrus it was in order to undertake a new mission through Galilee. It was the third (and it was to be the last) of those journeyings of His during which He preached in every little hamlet of that land. First of all, this time, He wended His way up to His old home in Nazareth,[1] and on the Sabbath began to preach in the synagogue; but He met with as cold a reception as on a former occasion a year ago; the Nazarenes were as hard and dull to the words of their fellow-Townsman as they were before.

"How does he come by his wisdom and his power?" they kept on saying. "Is not this the carpenter? Is not his mother called Mary, his brothers James and Joseph, Simon and Jude? And are not his sisters all here amongst us?" And they were scandalized at Him,—were shocked at His presumption!

---

[1] In this way we would mark a distinction between the two visits which Jesus made to Nazareth,—one being the one of which S. Luke speaks in his fourth chapter; this took place at the outset of His public life. The other, reported by S. Mark (vi. 1-6), is this instance, when he tells us that Jesus bade farewell to the household of Jaïrus, at Capharnaum, and started out for Nazareth: Καὶ ἐξῆλθεν ἐκεῖθεν, καὶ ἔρχεται εἰς τὴν πατρίδα.

Their phlegmatic bigotry and coarseness were well understood by Jesus; nevertheless on this particular day it would seem to have even surpassed His expectations; for Saint Mark tells us [1] He "was astonished thereat," as though He would indicate how entire and hopeless their incredulity was by the use of this striking expression, which sounds strangely enough when used in reference to God. The Lord grieved over their blindness, and, comparing the contemptuousness of the Nazarenes with the docility of their brethren in Galilee, He repeated what He had said of them once before, —

"A Prophet is not without honor save in his own country, and in his own home, and in his own family."

This was perforce the divine Wayfarer's farewell to that ungrateful city, where his boyhood and early manhood had been passed; now all He could do here was to heal some few of their sick folk by laying His hands upon them; then He departed from the mountain valley, never more to return.

"He went through the towns and villages,[2] teaching in their synagogues, preaching the Gospel of the Kingdom, and curing every sickness and all infirmities." The dwellers in these lands touched His heart with a great pity, — they lived so far from Jerusalem and in the very midst of Pagans, "lying uncared for and spent with fatigue," panting for breath "like a flock of sheep attacked" by wolves, "who have no shepherd to lead them."[3] However, they were all ready to receive the Good News; for Jesus, speaking of them to the Apostles, called them a rich and plentiful harvest, which only waits the coming of the reapers.

"The harvest is great," He said; "but there are few workmen. Therefore beseech the Master to send workmen into His harvest."

---

[1] Mark vi. 6.   [2] Matt. ix. 35-38.
[3] Matt. ix. 36. Ἐσκυλμένοι, literally, fleeced and flayed by the Scribes and Pharisees. Ἐριμμένοι, not merely abandoned, but spent with fatigue (jacentes, Vulgate). Perhaps the appearance of the wayworn multitude, resting on the ground all around Him, may have suggested to Jesus the idea of a stray flock, poor wanderers, homeless and exhausted.

The Twelve Apostles were to be the first to enter these fields, which had been made ripe for the coming of their Lord. Some time before Jesus had finished His own wanderings through the length and breadth of Galilee He called them about Him, "gave them strength and dominion over all devils, with the power of healing diseases, and sent them out, two by two, to preach the Kingdom of God and to restore health to the weak."[1] Before entrusting them with so lofty and august a commission He laid down the simple and severe duties of their Ministry.

For the present He wished to send them, "not to the Samaritans, nor to the Gentiles, but rather to the lost sheep of Israel."[2] All the burden of their message was to be this "announcement that the Kingdom of Heaven is close at hand," confirming the glad tidings by miracles performed in the name of the Christ.

"Heal the sick, raise the dead to life, cleanse the lepers, drive out devils; freely you have received, freely give."

A holy indifference to earthly cares was to be the peculiar feature of their ministry;[3] they might not make any preparations, but must be ready at all times to set out, in whatever circumstances they might chance to be, taking neither gold nor silver in their belt, nor victuals in their wallet, having neither a change of raiment nor travelling-shoes in the place of the sandals they ordinarily wore;[4] it would even be useless for them to get themselves a staff for the journey.[5] Having arrived in a town, their first care must be to seek out some hospitable household, which they were to accost with that

---

[1] Luke ix. 1, 2; Mark vi. 7.
[2] Matt. x. 5-8.
[3] Matt. x. 9, 10.
[4] They must start out shod with sandals only (Mark vi. 9), without buying or carrying with them the leathern buskins with which travellers ordinarily protected their feet; these S. Matthew designates by the word ὑποδήματα.
[5] "Do not purchase a staff," says S. Matthew (x. 9, 10). "Let that which you have in your hand suffice you," is S. Mark's wording (vi. 8). Μηδὲν αἴρωσιν . . . εἰ μὴ ῥάβδον μόνον. The evidence of these two, so far from being contradictory, is simply explanatory of each other.

ancient greeting, "Peace be to this house!"[1] This peace of theirs should precede them and abide upon the inmates, if they proved worthy of it; if otherwise, the heavenly gift would rather return and rest upon the Heralds of the Good News. Should they be rejected and repulsed, they were merely to shake the dust from off their shoes[2] without the dwelling, thereby proclaiming that they were not chargeable with the judgment, more terrible than that of Sodom and Gomorrah, which should one day befall its misguided occupants.

Up to this point the Lord had been speaking to the Twelve concerning their present mission only; but now, as though He would explain the duties of the Apostolic Ministry more generally, He began by marking out its two principal characteristics.

"Be prudent as serpents, simple as doves. Mark how I am sending you forth like sheep in the midst of wolves."[3]

Just at this moment (according to a tradition of the first century)[4] Peter interrupted His Master.

"But if it happen," said he, "that the wolves devour the sheep?"

"When the lamb is dead," replied the Lord, "it no longer fears the wolf. Even so fear not those who can only kill the body and have no power over the soul. But

---

[1] Matt. x. 11-15. This invocation of peace is the invariable greeting in Oriental lands: שָׁלוֹם לָךְ: in the Arab's tongue, "Shalam aleik." In these countries the guest is always welcomed with courtesy and respect; if an Apostle, he is bidden to a seat at the family board and by the hearth's side, where, from such familiar intercourse as this, he finds his opportunity to convert those who are about him.

[2] Because the Jews considered any Pagan territory as contaminated, they were accustomed, on returning to their own lands, to brush the dust from off their feet, as though it were an impurity: "All dust from a Gentile country must be to our eyes like the dry rot of the tomb" (Bartenora, *in Mischna Taharoth*, 4. 5. See Sepp, *Leben Jesu*, B. iv. k. xcii.).

[3] Matt. x. 16.

[4] The testimony of S. Clement, by whom this saying was preserved, is so decisive and important that we cannot cast any doubt upon the authenticity of these words of Jesus (*Epistola II. ad Corinthios*, v. Funk, *Opera Patrum apostolicorum*, vol. i. p. 150).

rather fear that which can send both soul and body down to Gehenna." [1]

Then the Master forewarned them that they would be dragged before the judgment-seats, flogged in the synagogues; while still in the face of the magistrates of Judea, as in the presence of the praetors of Rome, they were to bear testimony, even to the shedding of their blood for His sake; but that during all their tortures the Holy Spirit would be with them and would make answer for them.[2] Yet the Lord did not command them to go out to seek such impending perils; rather, on the contrary, He exhorted them "to fly from one town to the other," and to persevere in the faith; for in very truth "they should not complete their tale of wanderings through all the cities of Israel ere yet the Son of Man would manifest Himself on His return." [3]

The future, then, had only gloomy things in store for the Apostles; therefore, in order to strengthen and inflame their courage, Jesus reminded them of the obstacles which opposed His own Mission.[4]

Like Him, they must be calm and fearless; the heavenly Father "Who numbereth even the hairs of their head, Who lets not the littlest sparrow [5] fall from the skies upon the earth without having care thereof,"— their Almighty Father would be with them, "would acknowledge those as His own children whom His Son claimed as His disciples, and would reject all such as He disowned." [6]

Then He added that He had come to cast a drawn

[1] Matt. x. 28. For the expression Gehenna see p. 264, note 4.
[2] Matt. x. 17-23.
[3] This He manifested in innumerable ways, not only by the Apparitions which succeeded the Resurrection, but by the fall of Jerusalem, and the triumph of the Church. Nevertheless, it is not until the end of the world that this Prophecy will have its perfect fulfilment; the latter-day Apostles shall not have completed the conversion of that last remnant of the true Israel, when already the Son of Man will show Himself in His glory.
[4] Matt. x. 24, 25.
[5] One of those tiny birds which cold, hunger, and tempests have struck to the earth; such creatures are tied together and sold for a paltry price in the cities of Palestine.
[6] Matt. x. 29-39.

sword upon the earth; that very soon they should see their fathers and their children in league with the world, and eager to deliver them up to death. In the midst of raging war and of unbridled passions He bade them remain steadfast, "publishing upon the housetops that which the Master had spoken in their ear,"[1] preferring Jesus above all whatsoever they held most dear and glorious, "losing their life to find it again"[2] in Heaven, — in a word, they were "to take up their cross[3] and follow Him."

After this mystic allusion, by which He foretold His Crucifixion, the Lord uttered only words of loving consolation and splendid promise. He told His Apostles that they should stand in His stead in the eyes of the world;[4] "that to receive them as Ambassadors of God[5] would be to receive the Christ, — would indeed be to entertain God Himself and to merit the rewards laid up for the just and the Prophets."

Then, with one hand pointing to the poor folk and little children, who crowded about Him now as always, He concluded with those touching words: —

"Whosoever shall give but a cup of cold water to one of these little ones to drink, as unto one of My disciples, I say to you that indeed he shall not lose his reward."

Such were the instructions with which Jesus prepared this College of the Twelve. It may be that all were not delivered on this particular occasion, and that, following his usual custom, Saint Matthew has here collected counsels which were actually uttered at various times.[6] But whether

---

[1] Matt. x. 26, 27.   [2] Matt. x. 37–39.

[3] To our thinking there is no need to consider this saying of Jesus as founded upon a proverbial allusion to the old custom of making condemned criminals carry their own crosses to the place of execution. Crucifixion had only lately been introduced in Judea, during the era of the Roman domination; hence it is hardly probable that the popular speech would have adopted it among its colloquial figures so soon.

[4] Matt. x. 40, 41.

[5] Εἰς ὄνομα, is a Hebraism, which signifies "in the name of some one," "because he is such and such a person." To receive a Prophet because he is a prophet; a righteous man because he is righteous, as a token of respect for his justice and holiness.

[6] According to S. Luke, one part of these instructions was addressed to the Apostles, and the other to the seventy-two disciples. It may be

Jesus spoke the whole discourse before this one audience, or whether the Evangelist, divinely inspired, has connected maxims scattered through many lessons of the Master, none the less Saint Matthew's work stands as a finished and complete model for every Apostle of the evangelical Ministry; and indeed, though every priest of the Lord Christ be not bounden by the letter of these instructions, it does behove all to be quickened by their spirit. Truly every one is not bidden to press forward to the prize of the martyr's crown, yet all must follow the Master in the paths of sacrifice; the Lord God does not demand of each one of us a complete renunciation of all things, for He Himself has declared that "every workman is worthy of his meat;"[1] and yet, in proportion as zeal in the hearts of His Apostles burns higher, and the holy flame waxes purer and whiter, by so much the more joyously do they strip themselves of everything in the race unto their high calling which is in Christ Jesus our Lord. Saint Paul converted the nations of the earth while he himself toiled at tent-making for his day's bread;[2] Saint Francis Xavier took with him nothing but a cross of wood wherewith he went forth to conquer the eastern world.

Obedient to the commands they then received, the Apostles departed, going two by two.[3] Without doubt the intimate friends and the brothers would bear each other company in this sacred comradeship.[4] Peter of course would associate himself with Andrew; those two whom He had called "Sons of the Thunderbolt" would forthwith start out together, with all their characteristic impetuosity; Philip would join Bartholomew, whose two lives had been heretofore so closely linked together; then would come Thomas and Matthew; while the two cousins of Jesus, James and Jude, would naturally be companions; and

that the Lord repeated to the latter what He had already said to the Twelve; but to us it seems much more probable that S. Matthew, who does not mention the seventy-two disciples, has here simply collected these counsels of the Lord, in the same manner as he had already done with the Miracles and the Parables.

[1] Matt. x. 10.   [2] Acts xviii. 3.   [3] Mark vi. 7.
[4] Matt. x. 2–4.

finally, it was probably Simon's sad and unenviable fortune to have for his fellow-laborer in the harvest Judas.

II. Death of John the Baptist.

Mark. vi. 14-32 ; Matt. xiv. 1-13; Luke ix. 7-10.

Jesus, left alone in His own field, continued to preach in all the cities of the lake country, when the news suddenly reached them that John the Baptist was dead; his head had been struck off in the dungeons of Macheronte.[1]

After being for twelve months imprisoned in that "dark fortress,"[2] John still displayed the same spirit which had made him so terrible to sinners upon the Jordan's bank; neither caresses nor threats had moved his stalwart courage one whit, and though they did not heed him, his stern voice fell upon the ears of the tyrant in no less unsparing denunciations. Herod trembled as he listened, torn in the strife between remorse and passion. Too weak to rid himself of his fearless accuser by a crime, yet too deeply corrupt at heart to subject his will to duty, he made shift to compromise with his conscience by simply shielding the Baptist from the insatiable hatred of Herodias. The struggle between these two was prolonged and stubborn; for the rancor and venom in the heart of the adulterous woman embittered her the more against her victim the longer she was thwarted and balked in her schemes of vengeance. This creature being determined to compass the Prophet's ruin, was ever on the watch for some opportune moment; it came soon enough.

After the fashion among the Roman princes, Herod and his sons always celebrated certain memorable epochs in their lives with the greatest pomp.[3] The anniversary of

---

[1] Josephus, *Antiquitates*, xviii. 5, 2.

[2] This is the name the Rabbis gave to Macheronte (Sepp, *Leben Jesu*, B. iv. K. lxviii.).

[3] The pomp and pageantry of this prince had become proverbial, even at Rome: —

                                At quum
           Herodis venere dies . . .
                                       Perseus, v. 180.

his birth[1] chanced to occur while Antipas, with his court, was at Macheroute; there he made high festival, gathering about him all the courtiers, rich officials, and nobles of Galilee. From what we know of the wealth of the Herods, their lordly extravagance, and their gorgeous pageants, we are warranted in fancying the grandeur of the ceremonial and the brilliancy of their sports, together with the bright hangings which adorned the rugged walls of that gloomy old castle, as being altogether beyond anything ever seen among those desolate hills. Yet, beside all this, Herodias had devised for the king a night of revelry, which was fitted to intoxicate him even more surely than the fumes of wine, and would thus be likely to place him completely at her mercy.

All wanton dances brought over from Italy were well known to her; she knew which of the movements in those horrid orgies would be most apt to hold him in besotted fascination.[2] Such shameless pastimes had for some time been of common occurrence within the palace of the Tetrarch;[3] but on this evening it was Herodias' will that her own daughter should be one of the damsels taking part in those unmaidenly carousals. This young princess, descendant of Herod the Great, sprung from the seed of the Machabees, and later on destined to be the wife and the mother of kings on this night appeared in all her brilliant state, the central figure in a circle of dissolute companions. By her dancing, she so transported the prince with delight that, as the wild applause of the revellers died away, he swore that he would give her whatever she might desire of him, were it even the half of his kingdom.

---

[1] Mark vi. 21. The word γενέσια in the New Testament and in Hellenistic Greek, had come to mean the anniversary of one's birth. In Classic Greek, on the contrary, it is to be translated as the anniversary of a death (Pauly, *Real Encyclopædie:* FUNUS).

[2]
Motus doceri gaudet Ionicos
Matura virgo, et fingitur artubus,
Jam nunc et incestos amores
De tenero meditatur ungui.
      HORACE, III. *Od.* vi. 21.

[3] Josephus, *Antiquitates*, xv. 8, 1; xix. 7, 5.

Salome[1] sped quickly to her mother.

"What shall I demand of him?" she said.

The royal harlot had a ready response for this her moment of triumph:—

"The head of John Baptist."

Not even a shudder stirred the drapery of the young dancer; tripping back to the king, she repeated her mother's words, without a touch of pity or a thrill of shame.

"I will that you give me at once and on this very trencher,[2] the head of John Baptist." And as she spoke she caught up one of the great dishes with which the table was loaded.

On this request Herod was struck sad at heart; he was just wakening from the madness of passion, only to see the snare into which he had been led by his blind, brutish nature. But the vanity of the Tetrarch was proportionable to his weakness; he saw the looks his high-born guests were fixing upon him, and he had neither the courage to excite their satirical remarks, nor did he dare to brave the anger of those two unscrupulous women, who now claimed their promised prey; seeking to shield himself from any responsibility by pleading the sacredness of his oath, he gave the fatal order. The headsman[3] (according to the usage of Oriental courts) was standing behind the person of royalty, ready for the deed; a few moments later John Baptist was no more.

That very obscurity in which the Prophet had desired to be eclipsed[4] has in fact completely overshadowed his mar-

---

[1] Josephus informs us that the daughter of Herodias bore the name of Salome; that she first married her uncle Philip, Tetrarch of Iturea, and afterwards Aristobulus, King of Chalcis, by whom she had three sons (Josephus, *Antiquitates*, xviii. 5, 4).

[2] Ὧδε, just here, on this very trencher (Matt. xiv. 8).

[3] Σπεκουλάτωρ is the Latin word "speculator," and refers to one of the body-guard which surrounded the person of a prince, and often exercised the office of headsman. See Forcellini: *Speculator* et *Spiculator*. Under the latter name this officer is alluded to in that valuable passage from Julius Firmicus, viii. 26: "Spiculatores . . . qui nudato gladio hominum amputant cervices."

[4] John iii. 30.

tyrdom. No witness has ever related how he received the iniquitous decree, or with what tokens of inward peace he faced death. The executioner returned very shortly, bearing upon that charger the reverend head of the Nazarite; he handed it to the royal dancer, who carried the bleeding trophy to her mother. If we may credit certain traditions,[1] Herodias pierced with needles the tongue which she had been powerless to check in life, and then commanded that his torn and disfigured body be thrown into the chasms around Macheronte, so to become food for the dogs and foul birds of prey. But the disciples of John were keeping watch at every point; gathering together the remains of their master, they piously buried them, and then sought out Jesus to tell the sad tale to Him.[2]

God's vengeance fell upon the slayer of His Prophet without delay; from the moment when the head of the Baptist was shown to the conscience-stricken Tetrarch, there was never another hour of quiet repose for the tyrant. Always thereafter he would see now and again the tables spotted with blood, and the Prophet's cold brow, seeming more severe than in life, so drawn and white in death, while the thin lips appeared as if just about to open and rebuke the guilty adulterer.

Now, instead of his former habitual indolence, he lapsed at once into a wretched humor, fluctuating restlessly between horrid fright and vague suspicions. The fame and power of Jesus had moved him scarcely at all heretofore; but now he grew suddenly wroth at the tales which his couriers brought him.

Only a few days later, a rumor reached Macheronte that the Saviour was drawing still greater concourses of people, and that every day He performed new and more wonderful prodigies. At this Herod shuddered in great terror.

"'T is he!" he cried out. "It is John Baptist who has risen again!"[3]

---

[1] S. Jerome, *Contra Rufinum*, iii. 42; Nicephorus, i. 19.
[2] Mark vi. 29; Matt. xiv. 12.
[3] Luke ix. 7.

It was useless for the prince's familiars[1] to endeavor to quiet his alarm,—some assuring him that Jesus must rather be Elias, once again returned to earth from his flaming chariot; others asserting that He was merely one of the Prophets; while the more sceptical among them would have it that He was but a Seer, like those who were common enough in the time of their forefathers. But for Herod, whose vision was continually haunted by the grim spectre of his victim, his trembling lips kept repeating, "It is John; it is the man who baptized! He has been raised up from the dead; that is why he can work such miracles." And eager to ascertain the truth of his forebodings, he cast about for some means to see Jesus for himself.[2]

The Lord would have incurred the greatest danger from any such encounter with the furious and terrified Tetrarch; unquestionably He would have been constrained to suspend His ministry at once, at least in Galilee, while He would have been forced to forego His Paschal pilgrimage for that year, and the time for the caravans to start was already drawing near. The return of the Apostles finally decided Him to pass over into the realm of Philip without delay. Whether their mission had been finished just at this time, or whether that also was interrupted by the death of the

---

[1] Τοῖς παισὶν αὐτοῦ (Matt. xiv. 2; Mark vi. 15; Luke ix. 8).

[2] Luke ix. 9. As for Herodias, her presence beside the throne of Antipas only resulted in the destruction of that prince. Some years later, her jealousy aroused by seeing Caligula favor her brother Agrippa I., she forced her husband to visit Rome with her, in the hope of obtaining the title of king for him. Antipas, though too feeble to resist her schemes, foresaw the dangers to which he was exposing himself by yielding to her whims. The event proved that he was right. On his very arrival he was assailed with accusations by Agrippa, and as he could not clear himself, was banished to the frontiers of Spain, to Lyons (probably Lugdunum Convenarum, S. Bertrand of Cominges). (Josephus, *Antiquitates*, xviii. 7, 2; *Bellum Judaicum*, ii. 9. 6.) In misfortune Herodias showed something of the noble spirit of a daughter of the Machabees; she demanded to be allowed to share the exile of Herod, and both together ended their days in obscurity. According to the story left us by Nicephorus, the fate of Salome was even more terrible. As she was crossing a frozen stream the ice opened under her feet, and she was held fast up to her neck in water, her shoulders pinioned in the crevice. Very soon the cold paralyzed her limbs, and a mass of ice striking her head, severed it from the body (Nicephorus, i. 20).

Forerunner, at any rate the Twelve had now returned to their Master, and at one and the same time. To Him they rendered their report "of what they had done and taught;" "how they had cast out devils, anointed very many sick folks with oil,[1] and cured their illnesses."[2] Tired and spent with their long journeyings, and saddened by the fate of John, they came to seek rest and comfort by the side of Jesus; but the Lord could offer them no quiet relief, because of the crowds "which came and went, and left Him not even time to eat."

And therefore He said to His way-worn little band:—

"Let us go apart by ourselves[3] into some desert place, and there you may rest yourselves for a little time."

The sea of Tiberias was not far off from where they stood; at the Master's bidding they sought out a boat for the passage, and speedily shook out sail, heading for the north.

---

[1] This oil did not possess the supernatural virtue of Extreme Unction; it was but a figure of the Sacrament instituted by Jesus later on, for the help and comfort of the sick; "Sacramentum a Christo apud Marcum quidem insinuatum, per Jacobum autem apostolum . . . promulgatum" (Concilium Tridentinum, Sessio xiv. *De Extrema Unctione*, cap. i.).

[2] Mark vi. 13, 30.

[3] Ὑμεῖς αὐτοί: yourselves; you alone and no one else (Mark vi. 31).

CHAPTER VIII.

THE BREAD OF LIFE.

I. THE MULTIPLICATION OF THE LOAVES.

Luke ix. 10-17; Mark vi. 30-56; Matt. xiv. 13-36; John vi. 1-21.

IN the northwestern region of the lake, and near the spot where the Jordan empties its waters into the little sea, there stood a flourishing town. Its name of Bethsaïda,[1] which it bore in common with that other village in the neighborhood of Capharnaum, would indicate that at no very remote time it had been but a fishermen's station; but in the time of Jesus, Philip, Tetrarch of Iturea, had transformed this little settlement into a city, and had called it Julias,[2] in honor of the daughter of Augustus. Round about this young and vigorous town stretched great tracts of moorland, bordered on the east by hills, which were as bleak and lonely then as to-day they are; it was toward this wilderness that the Lord fixed the course of their little ship.[3] Here His disciples counted upon finding that repose of which they stood greatly in need; but their hopes were destined to be disappointed.

[1] Bethsaïda : בֵּית צַיְדָה, The Fishery House. All the geographers since the discoveries of Reland agree as to the fact that there were two Bethsaïdas on the lakeside, — one on the western shore, which always remained a village of fishermen; the other, at the northwestern end of the lake, became a celebrated town and was given the name of Julias.

[2] Josephus, *Antiquitates*, xviii. 2, 1; *Bellum Judaicum*, iii. 10, 7; Pliny, *Historia naturalis*, v. 15. "In lacum se fundit quem plures Genesaram vocant . . . ; amœnis circumseptum oppidis, ab oriente, Juliade," etc.

[3] Luke ix. 10; John vi. 1.

THE MULTIPLICATION OF THE LOAVES.

Despite the privacy and quiet with which Jesus had screened their sudden departure, some witnesses had marked the sail being hoisted and the boat drawing away from land.[1] But as they met with only contrary winds, little progress could be made; hence their arrival was anticipated, and Jesus, coming to land close to the river-mouth, found there a multitude as great in number as that which they had tried to escape. Besides the inhabitants of the neighboring villages, there were many pilgrims among them, who had come from distant lands; for it was now close upon the Paschal Season,[2] and caravans were being collected all along the seaboard.

Yet the Saviour would not swerve from His first design; setting out inland, He led the way to a lonely and retired hill, and there seated Himself with the weary little circle of Apostles.[3] But hardly had He done so, when on raising His eyes, He saw the multitude coming toward Him, — a fatigued and huddled throng, "like sheep without a shepherd."[4] Something in their forlorn and uncared-for condition so touched the Heart of Jesus that at once He forgot His own weariness and gave all His thought to them. "He spoke to them of the Kingdom of God, and healed all their sick."[5]

The sun was sinking over the distant hills of Zabulon,[6] yet still the Saviour continued His blessed office of charity; then in a few moments (for twilight lingers for such a little while in the East) night was come upon them, surprising this foot-sore and fainting flock far away out here in the wilderness. At last the disciples began to show signs of uneasiness, and gathering about the Master, finally spoke out their fears.

"This place is a desert," they said, "and the hour is late; send away the people, so that they may go into

---

[1] Mark vi. 34; Matt. xiv. 13; Luke ix. 11.   [2] John vi. 4.
[3] John vi. 3.   [4] Mark vi. 34.
[5] Luke ix. 11.
[6] Luke ix. 12, 13. Ὀψία (Matt. xiv. 15) denotes the time when the sun is sinking to the horizon, from three to six o'clock; the Greeks called it ὀψία δείλη. In verse 23, ὀψία means the later evening, commencing at six o'clock, and lasting until sunset.

the nearest farm-houses and villages, where they can find lodging and victuals."

"They have no need to go," replied the Lord; "do you yourselves give them to eat."

And as the Apostles stood staring and speechless at such an astounding proposition, Jesus turned to Philip[1] and said,—

"Where shall We buy bread to feed all this multitude?" (He spoke in this way to try him, for He Himself knew what He would do.)

"Two hundred denarii,"[2] Philip answered, "would not buy enough bread for each one to have even a small portion."

"How many loaves of bread have you?" was all Jesus said;[3] "go and see."

Andrew, Simon Peter's brother, returned immediately saying, "there is a young lad here who has five loaves of barley-bread[4] and two fishes;[5] but what is that among such a crowd as this!"

Jesus bade them bring the loaves and the fishes.

"Make the men sit down," He said to the Apostles.

They obeyed His behest; and the people sat down upon the long grass, in companies of hundreds, and fifties. It was still spring-time. The fierce heats of the sun had not yet robbed the Galilean hills of their soft garment of green; and thus the groups of friends and companions, ranged about in order, made a happy and charming scene, which, together with the glowing tints of their oriental robes, left such a vivid picture upon the memory of Peter that in

---

[1] John vi. 5, 6. Here S. John is more precise in his details than are the other Evangelists: he attributes to Philip and Andrew certain words which the Synoptic writers ascribe to all the Apostles, without discrimination.

[2] About thirty-six dollars of our money.

[3] Mark vi. 38.

[4] Barley-bread was much coarser than wheaten bread, and was the staple food of the lower classes (Smith, *Dictionary of the Bible*. BARLEY).

[5] In place of ἰχθύας, S. John employs the word ὀψάρια, which signifies "any food which we eat along with bread." In a country like Greece, where the sea is accessible from every part, fish was the food most commonly eaten with bread; this is how, in later times, ὀψάρια came to be used as a synonym of fish.

after years he described it to Mark the Evangelist as being like gorgeous beds of flowers [1] extending along the rich green-sward.

And Jesus took the five loaves and the two fishes into His holy and venerable hands, and with His eyes lifted up toward Heaven, He gave thanks to God, blessing the bread, brake, gave to His disciples, and the disciples to the people; with the fishes He did likewise. Whereupon, in the hands of the Lord, the broken bread and the portions of fish multiplied without ceasing; [2] and so He continued to give unto these His ministers until all were satisfied. Then, to mark more clearly still how plentiful are the gifts of Heaven, yet at the same time to guard against any squandering of His bounties, He said to his disciples:—

"Gather up what fragments are left, for fear they should be lost."

Each one of the Apostles, taking up his wicker pack,[3] threaded his way through the orderly bands; on their return, the twelve baskets were filled with the leavings.

In the eyes of the Evangelists this Miracle assumed the greatest importance; for each one gives us an account of it, and Saint John, by proceeding at once (as though it were the only natural sequel) to record His promise of "the Bread of Life," shows us what a lofty meaning Jesus

---

[1] Ἀνέπεσαν πρασιαί πρασιαί (Mark vi. 40), "they had spread themselves about like a flower-bed." The original expression of S. Mark cannot be translated except by developing his thought; this meaning, however, is neither uncertain nor fanciful. According to the definition of Theophylactus (in loco), πρασιαί signifies, "the ribbon-like plots in which garden-plants are set out." The repetition πρασιαί πρασιαί is a Hebraism, and gives the expression a distributive sense: in clusters; areolatim. It is the same with the words συμπόσια συμπόσια, in the preceding verse: in groups of companions, catervatim.

[2] Mark vi. 41. The aorist κατέκλασεν indicates that the act of breaking the bread lasted only an instant; the imperfect, ἐδίδου, shows that the distribution consumed a much longer time.

[3] Judæis, quorum cophinus, fœnumque supellex.
JUVENAL, Satiræ, iii. 14.

The Jews, because they regarded everything which a Pagan had touched as tainted, on their journeys carried with them osier baskets, which contained eatables, with enough straw to serve for a couch. In Galilee of the Gentiles these precautions were almost as necessary as in a foreign land.

attached to this prodigy of love. The sight of the pilgrims wending their way up to Jerusalem, the nearness of the holy festival, at which He might no longer take part without great danger to Himself, the thought of the Last Supper, whereat, just one year hence, He was to substitute for the paschal lamb an Immortal Food,— all thoughts like these impelled Jesus to declare at once and forever the great Mystery of His love.

The primitive Church was so assured of the truth of this interpretation that during five centuries, when she would figure forth the Eucharist, she represented, not the Last Supper,[1] but the Multiplication of the Loaves; and this scene she set over against the very Table of the Lord, together with the Fish, which is the symbol of the Christ,[2] and the baskets[3] overflowing with fragments gathered up by the Apostles.

And thus we know that by working this prodigy Jesus sought to prepare their minds for the reception of higher truths; but far from responding to the lofty designs of the Lord, the emotion now stirring the excited throngs had sprung from the belief that their dreams of earthly happiness were at last to be realized.

"This is He!" they exclaimed to each other.

"This is surely the Prophet who is to come into the world!"[4]

And so without doubt they had understood the promise,

---

[1] See Martigny, *Dictionnaire des Antiquités chrétiennes:* EUCHARISTIE. Representations of the Last Supper, which are so common since the Renascence, are rarely ever found in the Catacombs.

[2] "If from the five Greek words, Ἰησοῦς, Χριστὸς, Θεοῦ, Υἱὸς, Σωτήρ, you take the initial letters, by uniting them you will have ΙΧΘΥΣ, a Fish, under which name the Christ is signified in a mystical manner" (S. Augustine, *De Civitate Dei,* xviii. 23). There was no symbol more frequently employed by the primitive Church to designate the Saviour (see Martigny, *Dictionnaire des Antiquités chrétiennes:* POISSON).

[3] The baskets are always seven in number: therefore it was to the second multiplication, where the Apostles collected not twelve but seven baskets of bread, to which the Christian artists had reference. In this second prodigy, which, like the first, was a foreshadowing of the Eucharist, instead of barley-bread Jesus multiplied the wheaten bread, which is the proper matter of the Sacrament; this is one reason for their choice between the two events.

[4] John vi. 14.

thinking that Jesus would stretch forth that sceptre which Balaam had foreseen,[1] whereupon at once their oppressors would crouch before Him. He would be like to Elias descending from His chariot of fire; another Jeremy, who should restore the Mosaic Worship in all its olden splendor; and unto the Temple He would be the Ark, which, since the days of Babylon and the Captivity, had been hidden from the eyes of the faithful.[2]

The Saviour knew these passionate aspirations, as He knew well that they were already planning to bear Him along with them, and by force of arms proclaim Him King.[3] He saw, too, that the hearts of His disciples were beginning to burn high as they listened to these visions of glory, while they were gradually being filled with these ardent hopes of their fellow-countrymen. It was indeed time to forestall an uprising which would have drawn down upon Him and upon His Mission the wrathful vengeance of Herod, the Sanhedrin, and Rome.

Immediately he called the Apostles, bidding them follow Him to the beach. There He commanded them to embark forthwith, and to head for Bethsaïda in the vicinity of Capharnaum; then as they were loath to obey, the Master obliged them to set sail at once, leaving Him there upon the shore.[4]

When they had disappeared over the darkening waters, Jesus dismissed the crowds attending Him, and, profiting by the shades of night, He sought the lonely heights of the mountain,[5] unseen by any man. He went thither to fortify His Soul against the onslaught of other and sadder trials, for on the morrow Capharnaum would reject Him, even as Nazareth had done; nor was it to be long before all Galilee would follow their example; and so on, during all that last year of His Ministry, until His eyes could discern before Him only one unbroken succession of base desertions and thankless perils.

In the meantime, with the midnight, a tempest had descended upon the valley of the Jordan; beaten upon by

---

[1] Num. xxiv. 17. [2] 2 Machab. ii. 5, 8. [3] John vi. 15.
[4] Mark vi. 45, 46. [5] John vi. 15.

wild winds, the waters rose in their might and broke over the little ship of the Apostles.[1] The whole night long they struggled against the storm, rowing with all their strength, in the hope of making the port of Capharnaum; but the gale, wrenching the bark from its track, kept them tossed and buffeted amid the great seas.

At the fourth watch of the night,[2] they had gone barely half-way [3] on their course, and were still fighting against the wrack of the storm, when of a sudden they saw some one afar off, walking over the waves; it seemed to them as though He were making toward them, yet so as to cross before their bows. Believing that this which they saw was a phantom, they were filled with dismay, and in utter terror cried out aloud. But at once the calm voice which they knew so well came over the raging elements, quieting all their alarms, —

"It is I, fear not!"

And, indeed, it was Jesus, who had taken pity upon their troublous toils. They felt sure of His divine help, and eagerly made ready to welcome Him; but Peter impetuous and fiery of soul as ever, cried out, —

"Lord, if it be Thou, bid me to come to Thee upon the waters!"

"Come," replied the Lord.

Straightway the Apostle sprung from the vessel's side, hastening to meet the Master. And at first he trod the waves with unfaltering footsteps; but when he felt the fury of the whirlwind about him, terror clutched at his heart-strings, and he began to sink.

"Lord!" he cried, "save me!"

Jesus, reaching out His hand, upheld and sustained him.

"Ah, man of little faith!" He said to him, "why hast thou doubted?"

---

[1] Matt. xiv. 24; John vi. 18.

[2] John vi. 19. Like the Romans, the Jews at this time divided the night into four watches, from six in the evening to six in the morning; the fourth watch extended from three to six o'clock.

[3] "They had rowed about twenty-five or thirty furlongs," says S. John (vi. 19).

Meanwhile the others besought the Saviour with all manner of prayers[1] to come to them, certain that the Divine Pilot would bring them safely into the haven. Nor was their faith disappointed. Scarcely had Jesus entered with Peter into their ship when the winds fell; and presently they found that their vessel had reached the harbor toward which they had been so long fighting their way.

The effect which this sudden stilling of the tempest had upon the disciples' minds was altogether different from the enthusiasm caused by the multiplying of the loaves. "They had not understood the latter miracle at all," says Saint Mark, mournfully,[2] "because their heart was blinded." Too dull and too sordid of soul to conceive of any spiritual Kingdom as yet, their fancy filled with flattering dreams of high fortune awaiting them, they had met the brave hopes and resolutions of the excited people with daring encouragements; for they hoped that the Master would be moved by such zealous courage, and with a word establish His throne upon earth. Accordingly, when they saw that He meant to refuse the sceptre now offered Him, they were so sore at heart and so dissatisfied that they quite forgot the almighty attributes of their Lord, and dared to resist His commands. It required a night of anguish and terror, like this through which they had passed, to bring them to a knowledge of their fault. But this trial tore the veil from their eyes; as they beheld Jesus bidding the roaring floods be still, and holding the powers of nature beneath His feet, they recognized "Him Who spreadeth out the heavens and walketh upon the waves of the sea."[3] Throwing themselves on their

---

[1] "Ἤθελον οὖν λαβεῖν (John vi. 21): they wished to take Him into their boat, and actually did so. Indeed, θελεῖν is often used in the New Testament with the sense of wishing to do a thing and doing it. So S. Matthew says that a king "wished to look over his accounts with his servants" (Matt. xviii. 23), and we see that he did so do. Again, S. John says, "Jesus wished to depart for Galilee" (John i. 43), and so in fact He did. "The Scribes desire to walk abroad in long robes" (Mark xii. 38),—meaning that this is what they actually do.

[2] Mark vi. 52.
[3] Job ix. 8.

faces before Him, they worshipped and adored Him, saying : —

"Truly, ay, truly Thou art the Son of God!"[1]

No sooner had Jesus descended from the vessel than He was known and greeted; and instantly the rumor flew from lip to lip, until the land of Genesareth was made aware that he had returned. The multitude which was just dispersing now collected together once more, and brought with them other ill and maimed folks, beseeching Him to let them only touch the hem of His robe.[2] This prayer recalled the faith of the poor creature with the issue of blood, and Jesus healed all who approached the Divine Presence with such simple hearts of faith; afterwards He reëntered Capharnaum, welcomed on every hand with cries of delight and gratitude, — the last which it was given to Him to hear in this "His city" by adoption.

II. THE PROMISE OF THE EUCHARIST.

John vi. 22-71.

The crowds they had left behind them on the other side of the lake, in the neighborhood of Bethsaïda, had watched the ship of the Apostles making off from the shore, and knew that Jesus had not embarked with them. Somehow in the night they had lost all trace of the Master, but at dawn seeing that no other ship had quitted its moorings they made sure of finding Him speedily. So all the morning they searched over fields and plain, but of course in vain; then they concluded that He had proceeded by land, intending to rejoin His companions by some unfrequented road. In the meantime several other craft hailing from Tiberias, but now flying before the storm, had put into this harbor; and many of the Jews availed themselves of this opportunity to reach Capharnaum.

On their arrival they found the Lord seated in the synagogue, instructing the people.

[1] Matt. xiv. 33. [2] Matt. xiv. 34-36.

"Master!" they exclaimed, "when did you come here?"

Jesus looking deep down into those hearts that yearned so after earthly goods, now plainly told them the nature of their longings.

"Of a truth, yea, of a truth," He said to them,[1] "you are seeking Me because of the loaves with which you were fed. Do not toil for the food which perishes, but for that which endures in the life of Eternity. This the Son of Man will give you, for on Him the heavenly Father hath set His seal."

By these last words Jesus quickened and ennobled the hopes of the Jews, by lifting them from thoughts of earthly refreshment, setting before them that immaterial nourishment which is of the spirit. Hence He declared that it was not His design to establish a temporal kingdom, but rather to reign in the souls of men; it was to this end that God had imprinted a divine character upon His Holy One, the Christ, confirming His Mission by miracles without number. And therefore this food of which He spoke was a certain spiritual food, which He alone would impart. This the Jews comprehended, though they were too stubborn and settled in their own notions of their Law to believe that God Himself could confer upon it any more perfect dignity.

"What shall we do," they said in their amazement, "in order to labor for the works of God?"[2]

"This is the work of God," replied Jesus, "to believe in Him Whom He hath sent."

Nor does this faith, to which the Master here reduces all His precepts, imply merely a belief on our part in the word of the Christ; it means that we must likewise give ourselves to Him without a shadow of reserve. It is Faith, quickened by Charity, fastening mightily upon the Object of its love and diffusing through all human-kind the gracious gifts of God.

It is evident that the Saviour repeated this explanation more than once, and that in even clearer and simpler

---

[1] John vi. 26, 27.   [2] John vi. 28-31.

terms than would appear from this short summary of Saint John; for we know that His listeners understood well enough that He demanded of them a devotion and self-sacrifice which was unlimited and well-nigh unparalleled; He would have them follow Him as blindly as of old Israel followed Moses, leaving Egypt and its pleasures behind them.

"Our fathers," they began to say, "ate Manna in the lesert, as it is written: (He hath given them bread from Heaven to eat.) But what Miracle will you work, so that we may see and believe in you? What will you do?"

Had not all the traditions asserted that the second Redeemer would renew the wondrous deeds of the first?[1] And besides, how could anybody compare those loaves of barley-bread, multiplied so simply under their very eyes, with that nourishment which long ago fell about the plains of Sinaï? If He would prove Himself in deed and in truth the Messiah, it were needful that He too — the Christ of the Lord — should bring down from the skies that Manna which David had called "the Bread of Heaven and the Food of Angels."[2]

These objections Jesus accepted very graciously; only He explained to His listeners that it was not Moses, but God Himself who had rained down Manna in the desert;[3] telling them, too, how those perishable meats were called in a figure the bread of Heaven. While yet again to-day God, by the hands of His Christ, tendered them the very Bread come down from Heaven; and so divinely did He speak of this celestial Food, and of the life which it would diffuse throughout the world that the Jews cried out in their delight, —

"Lord, give us this bread always!"

"It is I," continued Jesus; "I am the very Bread of Life. He who comes to Me shall never hunger, and he who believes in Me shall never thirst."

---

[1] "Redemptor prior descendere fecit pro eis manna: sic et Redemptor posterior descendere faciet manna" (*Midrash Coheleth*, f. 86, 4; Lightfoot, *Horæ Hebraïcæ*, in Joan., vi. 31).

[2] Ps. lxxvii. 24, 25.

[3] John vi. 32-35.

Certainly this answer was not so mystical but that the Jews might have easily grasped its inner meaning; indeed they had often read in their sacred Books [1] that "man lives not alone by bread, but by every word which proceedeth from the mouth of God;" often they had heard the voice of Wisdom calling to their souls in words like these: "Come, eat the bread which I will give you; drink the wine which I have prepared for you." [2] Thus to eat and drink the Truth, to sate one's heart with the taste and fulness of holy words, and by study to assimilate and digest the teaching of the Master, — this was a figure as familiar to their way of thinking as it is foreign to ours.

So they at once comprehended that by calling Himself the Bread of life Jesus offered them His heavenly Doctrine as the garner wherein is stored every good gift that they could desire; and this promise once more made their hearts beat high with brave hopes. But what was still to follow did not accord with their preconceived ideas. Proceeding at once to develop His thought,[3] Jesus declared that hitherto they had only beheld Him with their eyes, without understanding Who He was. Because He had descended from Heaven, He can have no other will except that of His Father, and therefore He receives only such as come to Him from God. Now the will of the Father is that all those who believe in the Divinity of His Son should partake of that Bread of Life (which is the Christ Himself), and thereby have part in the life everlasting.

At this new revelation of His Godhead the synagogue broke out into murmurs of stern disapprobation; more than all else those words, "I am the living Bread which is descended from Heaven," aroused the deepest antagonism and disgust of which they were capable.

"Is not this Jesus, the son of Joseph?" the town's-folk of Capharnaum exclaimed. "Have we not known his father and his mother? Then how does he dare to say that he has descended from Heaven?"

Jesus did not stop to answer these malcontents; as was His wont, He deemed it enough to reiterate what He had

---

[1] Deut. viii. 3.   [2] Prov. ix. 5.   [3] John vi. 36-42.

communicated to them already, only with a more luminous simplicity, leaving it for the indwelling Truth itself to quicken and enlighten their souls.[1] Again He told them that faith is a gift of grace; and He repeated that no one can come to Him who is not prompted by the heavenly Father, — "taught of God, using the language of the Prophets," — which means that they must be touched from on high, their souls drawn by a secret influence inherent in the truth of His Word.

Still more clearly did He disclose the mystery of His Incarnation, showing them that God is too High, too Holy an Object for our earth-bound senses to encompass through human wisdom; for truly "no one can see the Father save Him alone who liveth in God;" yet this Divine Seer, this Holy Thing, Son of the Father, has become Man that He might unite Himself to mankind for love of humanity, — His Divinity taking upon Itself a dwelling of mortal flesh in order to communicate Its own life unto all men.

This was the Master's exposition of the Divine economy, whereby He sought to show us the way of Faith which leads us unto salvation. And in order to engrave this lesson within the hearts of those who hearkened to Him, He condescended to put forth the same great thoughts over and over again, reproducing them under such manifold phrases that it would seem He did but hesitate in His speech, as though He were striving to utter the language of Paradise before this wondering throng of earth-bound mortals. This is why the evangelical text contains so many repetitions, and hence arises the difficulty which we experience in tracing the connection between the various ideas.

Nevertheless the Master had one more Mystery to unveil on that same day. When the Son of God was made Man the wonder was not wrought among us that He might dwell in a human body merely for the time of His earthly pilgrimage; rather it was His will to apply the fruits of His Incarnation unto all mankind, thus being made flesh for

[1] John vi. 43–51.

each one of us, by nourishing us with His Blessed Body. It is, therefore, when we feast upon His Flesh that Jesus takes possession of these bodies of ours; it is by the mystic union of all that He is in His Humanity with all His Divinity that salvation is assured unto us of the faithful. Jesus only asked these people of Capharnaum that they love Him enough to entrust themselves implicitly to His guidance, and then, through the thick clouds which must ever shroud this Divine Mystery, they should walk forward encompassed by the Presence of their Guide and Friend; and so, led onward by the Christ, they would surely find the life everlasting in Faith,—Faith which reveals the gracious fact of the Eucharist as being in a marvellous manner inherent in the Incarnation Itself.[1] "The Bread which I will give," He added, "is My flesh [2] for the life of the world."

At this surprising announcement that they should eat the flesh of the Christ there was a louder murmur of dissent arising from all parts of the synagogue; on every hand the Jews began to dispute with each other,[3] the majority arguing, "How can this man give us his flesh to

---

[1] John vi. 52. We believe that in interpreting the words of the Master we could not follow a surer guide than Bossuet. According to that great Commentator, the burden of the whole discourse is the question of real Faith in Jesus; up to verse 15 it deals with faith in Jesus as the Incarnate God, and thereafter with faith in Jesus as He gives Himself to us in the Eucharist (Bossuet, *Méditations:* LA CÈNE, 1re partie, xxxiiie journée).

[2] All that follows that word "flesh" is unquestionably intended as specific promise of the Eucharist; for although the expressions which precede, such as "I am the Bread of Life, that has come down from Heaven," "He that eateth of this Bread shall live forever," are figures of speech common enough to the Hebrew tongue, and might naturally be taken in the sense of a master offering his doctrine to disciples, who receive it and nourish their souls with its virtues; yet this explanation does not apply to the expression, "eat the flesh of any one." The scholarly investigations of Cardinal Wiseman have proved beyond a doubt that these words, in Hebrew and in all other Semitic tongues as well, have only the one metaphorical meaning,—that of calumniating, backbiting, rending a person's fair fame with foul words (Ps. xxvi. 2; Job xix. 22, etc.). But in S. John the context certainly renders this figurative sense untenable, and consequently we are obliged to take the words in their literal sense (Wiseman, *Conferences on the Real Presence*).

[3] John vi. 53-60.

eat?" Evidently they could only comprehend that they were bidden to take a human body and feast thereon, that they must shed human blood and drink thereof.

Yet, far from abating this literal interpretation by one whit, Jesus saw fit, on the contrary, to enforce it by a double oath: —

"Amen, Amen, I say to you, If you do not eat the flesh of the Son of Man, and do not drink His blood, you shall not have life in you. Whoever eats My flesh and drinks My blood has life everlasting, and I will raise him up on the last day."

He well knew what horror the Jews felt for any such idea of blood, and how strictly they were forbidden the use of any such food;[1] and notwithstanding, He did not hesitate to assail and overturn every most cherished belief of their lives, if by so doing He might more surely establish the reality of His Body, which is eaten by the faithful, and His Blood which is their drink.

"My flesh is truly meat, My blood truly drink, and he who eats My flesh and drinks My blood dwells in Me and I in Him.[2] Whosoever eateth Me shall live by Me."

---

[1] Lev. vii. 27; 1 Kings xiv. 33; Judith, xi. 11.

[2] "All this — do you say? — is only a Mystery, an Allegory; to eat and drink means to believe; to eat the flesh and drink the blood merely means that we are to consider them as they were divided for us upon the Cross, and hence we are to look for life within the wounds of our Saviour. If this be all, O my Saviour, why didst Thou not tell us so in plain and simple words, and why didst Thou allow Thy listeners, even then, to murmur thereat, to take offence and to be shocked, and finally even to desert and disown Thee, instead of giving them Thy thought in direct and open terms? When the Saviour uttered His Parables, although they were much less involved than the long Allegory which is here attributed to Him, He explained their meaning so clearly that there was afterwards no room left for any cavilling or questioning about them; and though sometimes He did not vouchsafe to explain Himself to the Jews, who, because of their pride, deserved to be given the symbol only, and not the reality, He did never yet refuse to give His Apostles a straightforward and natural explication of His words, so that no one of them thereafter could be mistaken as to His meaning (Matt. xv. 11; xvi. 6-12; John iii. 4-7; iv. 10, 11, 13-16; vii. 38; xvi. 16-20). But now, the more His disciples and friends murmur against Him, the more pained and horrified they show themselves at such strange words, all the more does He persist in repeating those words, and so much the more does He hide His thought (so to say) in the depths of obscurity. It needed but one word from His

And now, having so clearly set forth the meaning of the Eucharist, He spoke to them of its effects; for though an ardent faith could make eternal life certain for the soul of man, and for his body obtain a glorious resurrection, yet it is the Eucharist alone which unites Jesus with the Christian who receives Him; in one only Body and one only Soul commingles the lives of two under one form, and thereby in each one of us is consummated that Union of the Christ with Humanity, even as aforetime by the Incarnation "He dwelt amongst us."

The earnestness and persistency with which Jesus reaffirmed a Doctrine so shocking to the notions of His hearers resulted in open expressions of their impatience and dislike. It was not long before the citizens of Capharnaum were joined by the pilgrims and all the rest, while even the disciples themselves finally uttered strong protests.[1] "This is a hard saying," they said; "who can hear it?"

And certainly, after the fashion in which they understood it, it would be an unbearable thought; for they imagined that they were bidden to tear the body of the Master limb from limb, and make a horrid feast of its members.

Jesus strove to drive away this unholy vision from their mind by adding that, though He was to give Himself to be their Bread of Life, yet would He none the less rise with glory into Heaven, even in such wise as He had descended to our earth, clad in this His living tabernacle of flesh; He said, too, that "His flesh," broken and dispersed among us for our Food, "would avail us nothing, if we do not partake

lips: "Why are you troubled at this? To eat My flesh means to believe in Me; to drink My blood is simply to remember Me, and all that I have just said to you means merely that you are to ever meditate upon My Death." This done, their faintest doubt and all uncertainty would have been swept away, together with every shadow of trouble. And yet this was exactly what He did not do; He permitted His own disciples to succumb to the temptation and the occasion of stumbling, for lack of one single saving word from His lips. That was not Thy way of dealing with men, my Saviour; no, of a truth, that was not Thy way! Thou didst not come to disquiet the soul of man with sounding words which were meaningless, and without grave import, signifying nothing" (Bossuet, *Médit. sur l'Évangile:* LA CÈNE, 1ʳᵉ partie, xxxvᵉ journée).

[1] John vi. 61-64.

at the same time of the Spirit" and the Godhead, which quickeneth the flesh and diffuses its life through our souls. As to the manner and the mode which He would take in order to communicate this gift to us, being an Ordinance far beyond the ken of sensual man, He saw fit to await some future day for revealing it more fully. So for the present, it was enough to prepare their minds by repeating that "His words were spirit and life," whereby He would teach them that His faithful followers must find the spirit of holiness and the life divine in the surpassing Mystery of the Communion, wherein His flesh is really eaten, though in a manner more spiritual than material.

These explanations did not dispel all disquietude from the hearts of His disciples, and among those who rebelled against this truth Jesus must have marked one of the twelve, Judas Iskarioth; for "from the beginning He knew those who did not believe in Him, and He knew him who was to betray Him."[1] The sight of these obstinate mortals still muttering against Him, so easily shocked at His Word, and already prepared to declare their outspoken disbelief, was very grievous to the heart of Jesus.

"There are some among you who do not believe," He exclaimed, "and it was for this reason I said to you, 'No one can come to Me, unless it be given Him by My Father.'"

And yet this last appeal to their nobler feelings was rejected; still they would not understand this urgent warning to ask their heavenly Father for the faith which comes from Him. Humility and obedience for them were at an end. "After this many of His disciples drew away from His company, and walked no more with Him."

However, the Apostles were still left Him. Turning toward the Twelve He said,[2] —

"Will you too go away?"

Peter loved his Master too well to doubt His words, however incomprehensible they might seem; indignant at the very thought of deserting Him, he straightway replied for all: —

"Lord, to whom should we go? Thou hast the words of

---

[1] John vi. 65-67. [2] John vi. 68-72.

Eternal Life. We believe, we know, that Thou art the Holy of God."[1]

Dear and comfortable as this confession was to the Heart of Jesus, it could not quite console Him nor distract His thoughts from the traitor in their midst.

"Have I not chosen you Twelve?" He said, "and one of you is a devil."

"By this He meant Judas, son of Simon, the man from Kerioth, who was to deliver Him up, even while he was still one of the Twelve." It is evident from these words, as we have noted before, that Judas took some part in these murmurings of the citizens and Pilgrims. Long since the struggle between greedy avarice and his heavenly vocation had been going on within him, and hence every allusion to a spiritual Kingdom filled him with vexation and anger; for it all seemed to him more visionary and foolish every day. The discourse just now delivered in the synagogue of Capharnaum completed the destruction of his faith. Hereafter, though he remained in the intimate companionship of Jesus, he had already betrayed Him in his soul. By this rebuke the Saviour graciously sought to stir the soul of the thief. Finding He could only get silence in return, He wended His way sadly from out the synagogue.

---

[1] The Vulgate and the Syriac versions have "Tu es Christus, Filius Dei;" but this reading is not found in any of the more ancient manuscripts, notably that of Sinaï, the Vatican, or Beza's Codex, which all have the reading ὁ Ἅγιος τοῦ Θεοῦ.

APPENDIX.

ΙΩΑΝΝΟΥ Α.

ἐ. ά, ιγ́.

Πᾶς ὁ πιστεύων ὅτι Ἰησοῦς ἐστῖν Ὁ ΧΡΙΣΤΟΣ, ἐκ τοῦ θεοῦ γεγέννηται, καὶ πᾶς ὁ ἀγαπῶν τὸν Γεννήσαντα ἀγαπᾷ τὸν Γεγεννημένον ἐξ αὐτοῦ. . . Ταῦτα ἔγραπσα ὑμῖν, ἵνα εἰδῆτε ὅτι ζωὴν ἔχετε αἰώνιον, τοῖς πιστεύουσιν εἰς τὸ Ὄνομα ΤΟΥ ΥΙΟΥ ΤΟΥ ΘΟΕΥ.

Testimony of the First Christians.

Every one who believeth that Jesus is THE CHRIST is born of God, and every one who loveth Him Who begot loveth Him Who is begotten of Him. . . . These things I have written to you, that you may know you have Eternal Life, you who believe in the Name of THE SON OF GOD.

SAINT JOHN'S FIRST EPISTLE.
v. 1, 13.

APPENDIX.

I.

JERUSALEM AND THE TEMPLE.

WE have noticed already how the hill-ranges of Judea run along in lines parallel with the Jordan, starting from the plain of Esdralon and coming to an end at Barsaba. Near the middle of this chain are two valleys, which are separated only by a few miles at first, but after a little they trend apart, one to the east, the other to the west, and thus enclose the plateau on whose summit Jerusalem is situated. The ravine over which you see the sun rise is called Kedron, and that through which its last beams glow is Hinnom; the latter, after cutting a chasm from north to south, branches off to the east, and again joins Kedron not far from the fountain of Siloë.

Girt on every side with these deep gorges, Jerusalem rises above the surrounding region like a lofty promontory. A tract of low ground, running parallel to Kedron, divides it into two ranges of steep bluffs of unequal height; to the west rise Sion and Akra; on the east are Ophel, Moriah, and Bezetha. In this city, where the primitive soil is often hid underneath a mass of refuse and ruins eighty feet in depth,[1] this valley (called Tyropœon) is the only landmark we can easily recognize from its general contour. But the testimony of Josephus, and that of many recent discoveries, establish almost beyond question the fact that formerly there was a gully or viaduct, starting at the present Gate of Jaffa, which connected the Tyropœon with the Temple heights and separated Sion from Akra.

---

[1] In the southwestern extremity of Mount Moriah Lieutenant Warren discovered foundations of the Temple resting on the solid rock, at a depth of about 95 feet below the actual surface.

Such were the general outlines of ancient Sion, according to the opinion of our geographers.[1] It is difficult enough to trace them in the configuration of the modern city, which is only an unshapely heap of ashes and ruins; crumbling walls of ancient edifices, scattered over the hills and choking up the glens and hollows, make it imposssible even in fancy to reconstruct from out this wreck of time the Jerusalem of David and of Jesus. It is harder still to rehabilitate the fallen city, as it now stands; for the town itself, in days of old endowed " with an unblemished loveliness," [2] is to-day a dreary spectacle; and Chateaubriand himself, skilled as he was at making his landscapes glow with color, could only give us this gloomy picture of Sion: —

"Viewed from the Mount of Olives, Jerusalem seems to lie along a steep slope, whose descent is from east to west. A battlemented wall, fortified by towers and with a Gothic castle, encloses the town on every side, leaving Mount Sion however outside this boundary line, although in former times it also included that eminence.

"In the region lying to the west and in the centre of the town, toward Calvary, the houses are crowded somewhat closer together; but to the west, following along the valley of Kedron, there is nothing to be seen but empty stretches of ground; among others of this description there is the enclosure round about the Mosque which now crowns that huge pile of ruins where the Temple once stood; then there is that other almost abandoned piece of land over which the Citadel of Antonia rose of old. The houses of Jerusalem are heavy square blocks, quite low, without either chimneys or windows; they are finished off in flat terraces or are surmounted with domes, and thus they much resemble prisons or sepulchres. The whole effect upon the eye would be that of a great field of snow, were it not for the clock-towers of a few churches, the minarets of the mosques, the dark tops of the cypresses, and occasional clumps of fig-trees, which break the monotony of the prospect. After gazing long upon these stolid squares of stone immured within a land of crumbling stone and rock, a strong feeling comes over one that those buildings over yonder are only monuments and tombs long since forgotten, out here in the midst of the wilderness."[3]

Very different indeed was the Jerusalem of Herod. We possess numerous descriptions of it, and though they are incom-

---

[1] As to the topography of Jerusalem, see Tobler, *Topographie von Jerusalem;* Robinson, *Biblical Researches;* Barclay, *The City of the Great King;* Williams, *The Holy City;* Porter, *Handbook for Syria; Le Guide indicateur* du F. Liévin de Hamme.

[2] Lament. ii. 15.

[3] Chateaubriand, *Itinéraire,* 1ʳᵉ partie.

plete and confusing as regards many points, they all describe the city as shining with a veritable splendor. Its walls surrounded the entire hill of Sion; from the present Gate of Jaffa the battlements rose up along the crest of a mountain (undoubtedly Akra); then, after dipping down again into the valley which separates that eminence from the Temple, they ascended again to the Gate of Saint Stephen; then skirting along the cliffs of Kedron Valley, they encircled Mounts Moriah and Ophel.

Above all these hilltops rose the cliffs of Sion, crowned with its radiant palace; to the south was the home of the High Priests; to the north, facing the heights of Akra, was a line of ramparts flanked by strong towers, which bore the names of Hippicus, Phasaël and Mariamne. Near the Gate of Jaffa was the new palace of Herod, whose glories Josephus details at length; not far from this was the residence of the Asmoneans, which was connected with the hill of the Temple by a bridge that spanned the narrow valley of the Tyropœon.

Mount Moriah was even richer in monuments of antiquity. The porticos, the courts, and the Sanctuary of the Temple extended from Kedron to the Tyropœon, and on the northern side of the mountain the Fortress Antonia, with beetling towers, frowned down upon the sacred porches.

The dwellings of the citizens occupied all the open spaces along these heights, as well as the lower lands lying between them, and to the south of the Temple they covered Mount Ophel as well. But these bounds, in the time of Herod, came to be too narrow and straitened. So, in one direction, houses and gardens spread around the base of Calvary (which was an elevation of Mount Akra, outside the walls); while, on the other hand, to the north and in the direction of Mount Moriah there had grown up a new town, called Bezetha, which a little later Herod Agrippa encircled with bulwarks of its own. A deep moat had been dug about this suburb in order to separate it from Antonia, and thus it stood by itself, "like an isolated mountain,"[1] — so much so that Jerusalem appeared to be raised upon four hills: Sion, Akra, Bezetha, and Moriah.

Despite these repeated enlargements, Jerusalem never covered any great territory; then, as now, it took no more than an hour to walk all round its limits;[2] and its population

---

[1] Josephus, *Bellum Judaicum*, v. 4, 2.
[2] Id. *Ibid.*, v. 6, 3; Caspari, *Einleitung*, S. 225.

never exceeded seventy thousand souls. The various Capitals along the frontier, — Tyre, Damascus, Heliopolis (Baalbek), Antioch, — even certain towns in Judea, far surpassed it in the number of their inhabitants and the vast spaces encompassed by their walls. Located at a distance from the great highroads of commerce, without either harbor or water-way, difficult of access, and perched high among these barren crags in lonely splendor, Jerusalem had none of those attractions which soon increase the activity and wealth of cities. The particular feature which won for the town its unique position in the history of the world's achievements is the Temple, erected by Solomon on Mount Moriah. It had been Herod's ambition to restore it in all the beauty of the olden times, and he had so vigorously pushed this work to completion that in less than two years the Sanctuary was finished, while the outer porches were all done in eight years; only certain accessories of the Temple had still to be supplied in the time of Jesus.[1] The edifice which was constructed by this Idumean prince is too well known to require any detailed description at this writing; it will be enough to recall the general aspect of its plan.

The plateau of Mount Moriah on which this monumental edifice was built looked to the traveller like a succession of storied terraces, three in number. The Temple crowned the loftiest, and with its pinnacles of gold towered high above the whole city.

The lowermost terrace encircled two others, and formed a court called the Porches of the Gentiles, and it extended further to the south and east than on the two remaining sides; for the Temple is not in the middle, but to the northwest of these porches. The enclosure was bounded by rows of porticos; on the east was Solomon's Gate, standing over against Brook Kedron; on the south was the Royal Portico, three times as spacious as the others; all the rest were of equal magnificence, for their columns of marble were each a solid white shaft, twenty-five cubits in height. Pagans were allowed to frequent the first court, but there were inscriptions written in various languages forbidding them to venture any further, and a balustrade of carven stone besides, to prevent them from overstepping the prescribed limit.

Beyond this barrier, a second terrace, elevated some twenty

---

[1] Josephus, *Antiquitates*, xv. 11, 56.

cubits above the first, was reserved for the Jews, and was called the Israelites' Porches. From this second enclosure there was a last stairway of fifteen steps leading to the uppermost platform, which the Levites only might ascend.

Upon this third terrace the first object to meet the eye was the Altar of the Holocausts,[1] rising in the centre of the court which was called Porches of the Priests; passing through this, you came upon the Temple, built of white marble. It was quite different from the Sanctuary planned by Solomon, inasmuch as the latter rather resembled the temples of Egypt, while the monumental structure reared by Herod was of Greek architecture,[2] and of the Corinthian order.[3] From the exterior it had something of the appearance of a basilica; but the interior was divided into three parts, — the Vestibule, the Holy Place, and the Holy of Holies. The Vestibule was a large hall, its walls resplendent with gold on the side nearest to the Holy Place; a glittering vine, of this same precious metal, was festooned over the entrance-way, and, according to the testimony of Josephus, the clusters of grapes hanging from it were equal to a man's stature in length. Before the huge door of the Golden Gate, always standing open, heavy tapestry hung, with shimmering veils waving before it, all of Babylonian fabric and glowing with brilliant colors which represented the high arch of heaven.

After the Vestibule came the great hall, called the Holy Place, which contained three sacred objects, — the Altar of Perfumes, on which the sacrifice of incense was offered; to the north of this Altar, the Table of the Loaves of Proposition; and in the middle space between the two, the Seven-branched Candlestick of gold. A double veil separated the Holy Place

[1] The sacred rock of the mosque of Omar probably marks the location of this altar (Stanley, *Sinai and Palestine*, chap. iii. p. 180).

[2] "Judaic Art in Herod's epoch was much like the Græco-Roman Art of the age of Augustus, with some traces of an oriental influence and a vegetal style of ornamentation which was its peculiar individuality" (De Vogüé, *le Temple de Jérusalem*, p. 48).

[3] To speak exactly, Josephus does not state in so many words that the temple of Herod recalled those of Rome; but (1) he says that the colonnades were of the Corinthian order (*Antiquitates*, xv. 11. 5); (2) the Golden Gate, the only part of the ruins which dates from that epoch, still displays the capitals with their acanthus leaves; (3) Herod's fondness for anything which smacked of Greece and Rome gives us good reason for believing that he would have chosen no other style of architecture but theirs when erecting the most magnificent of all his monuments.

from the Holy of Holies, — that unapproachable Sanctuary where, in the old days, once rested the Ark of the Covenant. Ever since the Captivity, this portion of the Temple had been left bare and empty, with only a huge stone to mark the spot left vacant by the Ark.

The priests alone entered these sacred precincts, and only they could describe its grandeurs; but the heathen, as well as the Jews, could behold its external magnificence; for from every part of Jerusalem the eye could descry the dazzling walls of the Temple overlooking the whole town from its high-terraced throne. Its copings were all glittering with needle-points, set there to keep the birds from nesting in its eaves or sullying its purity; and the entire roof-work, being overspread with gold, burned like a furnace from the moment it caught the first beams of the morning until the last rays of the setting sun faded over the city.

This magnificent exterior was all that Jesus saw of the Sanctuary of Israel; for since He belonged to the Tribe of Juda, He could not enter either the Holy Place, or even the Porches of the Priests. At all times when He visited the Temple He remained in the Jews' Porches, and oftener still in the first court, for that was free to Pagans and Jews alike.

II.

THE "WORD" OF SAINT JOHN.

WE know the meaning of the word "Logos" in theological language. When we speak of the Word it is to signify God's inward Utterance, His substantial Thought, His Intelligence, His Wisdom, — that is to say, it is His Speech spoken unto Eternity, wherein all things were spoken eternally, which, in the infinite play of His Attributes and by an Act (so to say), by a Sentence, forever pronounced and nevermore to cease, God has encompassed and embodied the living Truth, has manifested Himself visibly and actually as the Truth Itself. No term is more frequently employed by theologians to designate the Second Person of the Trinity; and no wonder, since there is none which more clearly declares the unspeakable and limitless Being of the Son of God.

How does it happen that this expression is found only in the

Fourth Gospel? Furthermore, how did it come to be so familiar to the Christians of Ephesus that their Apostle could make use of it without any explanation or commentary? In fine, what was the origin of this doctrine of the Word? These questions are all too intimately bound up in our subject to be passed over without attempting to give them a satisfactory answer.

Ephesus, in the time of the Evangelist, was one of the principal cities of the Eastern world. All vessels coasting along the shores of the Archipelago put in at this port; from all parts of Asia Minor the great roads of travel centred at this locality. Hence John and his flock were in constant intercourse with strangers of different races and of various religious opinions. The Xystus — the Philosophers' Hall of Ephesus — was a noted meeting-place for the learned of those parts, who were the more strongly attracted to this centre of culture because of its great numbers of intelligent auditors and the perfect freedom of speech accorded them.[1] May it not be surmised that Saint John owes his doctrine of the Word to some one of these masters of philosophy? Did he not find it set down in the sacred books of the Persians, or in the writings of Plato? None of these ingenious guesses, as we shall presently see, have been able to stand the test of historical investigation; and in order to clear up the difficulty we must have recourse, not to the profane authors of the day, but to the first Fathers of the Church.

They tell us that, in writing his Gospel Saint John's object was to confute Cerinthus.[2] This Jew (who thus became the father of Gnosticism) had endeavored to establish certain general principles, which he considered were the foundation of those beliefs always held by his ancestors, as well as of the dreams of the Platonists. In this way he was merely continuing what the Alexandrians and Philo had commenced; like the latter, he borrowed the idea of the Word from the Scribes, but he altered and disfigured it so materially as to render it wellnigh unrecognizable. In order to silence this innovator, it was only necessary that the pure Doctrine, as held by Israel at all times, should be lucidly set forth, and this Saint John set himself to accomplish.

The Holy Books, from the very first, had always given man to understand that in Jehovah there existed a Second Person,

---

[1] S. Justin, *Dialogus cum Tryphone*, i. 7.
[2] S. Irenæus, *Adversus Hæreses*, iii. 11; Tertullian, *De Præscriptione*, 33.

equal to the Most-High God; the inspired writers of later ages and the interpreters of the Law had designated this mysterious Being under the name of "Wisdom," and often as "The Word;" and so the Prologue to the Fourth Gospel is, as it were, the reverberation of this ancient teaching, revealing in its awful purity and brightness the perfect meaning of this Mystery, long since vaguely announced by the Prophets and Doctors of Israel. Such, it appears to us, were the circumstances which induced Saint John to enunciate his doctrine of the Word. From this one may easily enough fancy the nature of the answer we would make to any questions like those we have quoted above; however, let us give the principal theories a just consideration.

But at the outset we may state that there is no need to question whether the Evangelist drew any of his teaching from the Persians. The Zend-Avesta, which was unfaithfully rendered by Anquetil-Duperron, has found in M. Spiegel an exact interpreter. In the latter translation any one will look in vain for a doctrine analogous to that of the Word. It is true that in a fragment of the Vendidah, of doubtful authenticity, there is mention made of a "Word" of Ormuzd; but a glance at the passage itself will be enough to convince an impartial reader that between the so-called Mazdean Word and Saint John's lucid teaching there is not even any slight connection:—

"Then Ormuzd replied: Tell the glories, O Zoroastre, of the Mazdean Law.

"Tell the glories, O Zoroastre, of the Firmament, which itself has produced; tell of limitless Time, and the high regions of air.

"Tell the glories, O Zoroastre, of the Wind,—the swift wind created by Ormuzd, Spenta Armaiti, lovely daughter of Ormuzd.

"Tell the glories, O Zoroastre, of my Ferouer (my invisible idea);[1]

"The grandest, the best, the most beautiful, the mightiest, the most wise, the most holy,

"Whose holy Word is my soul.

"Tell the glory, O Zoroastre, of this creation of Ormuzd.

"And Zoroastre replied:

"I tell the glories of Mithra, with his vast domains, Vanquisher of vanquishers.

"I tell the glories of Shraosha, the holy one, the mighty, who has armed himself 'gainst the Devas.

[1] The Ferouers, in the Mazdean doctrine, are the innumerable invisible ideas, created by Ormuzd, and scattered over the sky in order to drive away Ahriman, the Genius of Evil.

"I tell the glories of the holy Word, that shines so bright.

"I tell the glories of the Sky, self-formed of itself, the infinite ages of Time, and the nethermost Air.

"I tell of the glories of the Wind, the swift wind created by Ormuzd, and I tell of Spenta Armaïti, his fairest and loveliest daughter.

"I tell the glories of the Mazdean Law, the Law of Zoroastre against the hosts of the Devas."[1]

It is not difficult to see that the Word in question here is not said to be a Son of the Supreme Being, but is rather the soul of a creature of Ormuzd, one of those innumerable Ferouers, or invisible ideas of visible objects which were created by the Principle of Good at the beginning of time. So that there is nothing in all this which is in any way akin to what Saint John attributes to the Word made flesh. There is neither the divine nature nor the creative power which is reserved to Ormuzd; in fact it is placed on an equality with Mithra, — one of the twenty-eight chieftains of the celestial hosts which watch over the world; it is of a like dignity with Shraosha, the holy one, with the Sky, the Wind, and in fine with all creatures begotten of Ormuzd.

So the student will find it a profitless labor to search the writings of Plato for traces of the Word of Saint John. M. Michel Nicolas has displayed much learning as well as critical acumen in the consideration of this theory. "The partisans," he says, "who claim that the Jewish doctrine of the Word owes its origin to the Platonists, are accustomed to cite in their support a passage from the Epinomis (Plato, Cousin's translation, t. xiii. p. 21), and the phrase with which the sixth of the Letters attributed to Plato concludes (ibidem, t. xiii. p. 74). These two quotations have no real bearing on the argument. The passage from the Epinomis, by being detached from the context, has been given a meaning which is not in the original. As soon as it is read in connection with what precedes and what follows it, any one will see at once that the word Logos is to be taken in the ordinary acceptation which it had in the School of Plato, and that thus it simply signified Reason in the general sense. As to that passage in the Sixth Letter, how can any one appeal to it in the present discussion when, as we all know, it has been satisfactorily demonstrated that this Sixth Letter is subsequent to the Christian Era?

[1] *Fargad*, xix. v. 42-57.

And whatever analogy there may be between Plato's Logos and that of Philo, we must always bear in mind that it was a tenet held as commonly among Greek Philosophers as by the Alexandrians and the Chaldaic Paraphrasts, that there is an Intermediary Being between God and the world, but this Intermediary Being is very different from anything ever held among the Jews. It is in the Timæus that this theory finds its completest exposition. Let us note its essential peculiarities. Before the creation of contingent beings, God began by forming the world, which He animated by setting within it a Soul, which partook of a threefold essence, — one essence invisible, pertaining to the Divine; another, which was visible, proceeding from disordered matter; and a third, derived from a mingling of the two preceding. The world of life and soul constitutes the harmony of the celestial bodies, the heavenly household of the visible and contingent gods. . . . Thus was the world commanded by God its Author to busy itself in the production of perishable creatures. . . . Now it seems impossible for any one to deny that the Intermediary Being of Jewish Theology is entirely different from Plato's concept. The Soul of the world, begotten with such strenuous effort, is after all nothing more than a contingent being; it is not in itself either immortal or indissoluble. . . . The Jewish Word, on the contrary, is a Divine Power, proceeding without any limitations from God, partaking solely and simply of His Nature, and only to be distinguished from Him as thought and action can be considered as distinct from the person who thinks and acts."[1]

Though the Evangelist is in no way indebted to the religions of Persia and Greece for his doctrine, it is however evident that he found the idea of the Word set forth in the traditions of Jewry. This last point is agreed upon now-a-days by all sides; there are many, nevertheless, who hold that Saint John borrowed his teaching, not from the true sons of Israel, but from the Jewish neo-Platonists of Alexandria, and from Philo in particular. Yet it seems to us that no reasoning could be more misleading than this. Certainly no one will deny that the doctrine of the Word exists in the writings of this philosopher, or that it even occupies an important place in his teaching. An Israel-

---

[1] Michel Nicolas, *Des doctrines religieuses des Juifs*, p. 219 and the following.

ite by birth, Philo had been instructed in the pure traditions by his early masters; but in his passion for Platonism, he altered them, in order to make the Jewish dogmas bear as great a resemblance as possible to those philosophical speculations of which he was so enamoured; his Word was not that which was taught in the schools of Jerusalem. And so when Cerinthus brought to Ephesus those doctrines which had been so disfigured and defiled at Alexandria, John felt that he must first purge out the dross from these conceptions, which had been profaned by Cerinthus and his master, if he would restore any health to the pure doctrine of the Truth. The initial page of the fourth Gospel is undoubtedly only an abridgment of his teachings upon this subject.

Philo had conceived of the Word as the "Shadow of God," but not God Himself. It was "a Divinity of the second order," which did not coexist in God, but was "between Him and the creature, the mediator between these two extremes."[1] In strong contrast to this fanciful Word, John set forth in a few short sentences the Word which had its being before the beginnings of time, existing on that first day when the universe was not, and there was naught save God, and the Son, the only begotten of the Father. He tells us of this Word, consubstantial with God, dwelling in His Bosom, never to be separated from Him, nor to depart from Him, God even as is the Father, by Whom He is begotten. And behold, he concludes, this is He Who from the beginning liveth in God.

Philo made of his Word "an instrument by whose aid God worked upon Primordial matter," preparing it, forming it,[2] quickening it into life. And notwithstanding that this Word comprised all creation in itself, and ruled all the power and thought of God, it was after all only one of these same divine ideas. It was "the first-born of the Angels;"[3] it remained their brother, and though perhaps one might not say of it "that it was born like the other creatures, still it was not uncreate in the same measure as is the Supreme God."[4] Very different indeed is the Word which Saint John adores. It is the Increate Creator; all things are made by Him, and nothing has been made which has not proceeded from His hands, for it is He who bestows life,

---

[1] Philo (*Mangey edition*), i. 6; i. 106; ii. 625; i. 683; i. 501.
[2] Id. i. 106, 162, 437.
[3] *Ibidem*, 437, 427.
[4] Philo, i. 501.

which He derives from none other than Himself. In Him life is, Who is the Source of life.

In this way the Evangelist sets himself to the task of declaring the pure doctrine of the Word, and cleansing it of foreign error. To restore it to its first and legitimate sense,—the one which it has ever since retained in Christian theology,—he had only to supply certain links in the chain of Jewish traditions, which Philo had broken, and to make use of the writings of those Scribes, disciples of Esdras, who had long since comprehended under the title of the Word all that the Old Testament has revealed concerning a Second Person abiding in Jehovah, Who thus is God even as the Father is God. But in order to conceive any just idea of this Revelation, one must needs follow it faithfully from Moses to Jesus Christ.

Commencing with the first pages of Genesis, we find vague indications of a plurality of Persons in the Divine Essence. The terms which Moses employs to describe the creative acts of God have this peculiar characteristic, that the word used to denote the action is in the singular, and yet it has a plural noun for its subject: (בָּרָא אֱלֹהִים) literally translated this would be "the Gods has made," a peculiar phraseology which seems to indicate several Persons (Elohim, the Gods), not only working together, but really acting as one single Agent and Author of being.

Certain writers have thought that this use of the plural form Elohim is a custom borrowed from the language of some polytheistic people, or a manner of speaking which was intended by the writer to lend more majesty to their conception of the Almighty. But how could Moses, knowing the evil propensities of the Jews so well as he did, dreading too their proneness to idolatry, and uncompromising as he was therefore in his zealous efforts to unite them in an unqualified belief in the One and Only God,—how would he have dared to prefer this plural form, which would naturally recall all their past errors, and this too when the Hebrew language could furnish him with the singular of the same word: El, Eloah? Could the advantage to be gained by thus bestowing a more subtle dignity upon the Name of God make him forget how fraught with dangers to his restless flock any such phraseology might be? We prefer to believe that Moses, divinely inspired, designed to inculcate a great Truth by this striking combination of plural and singular,—that in fact he meant to teach a distinction of Persons in the innermost existence of God.

Furthermore, that this was the intention of the great Prophet appears even more clearly from such words as these, the language of Jehovah Himself: "Let Us fashion man after Our own image.... Behold, how Adam hath become like to One of us.... Come, let Us go down thither, let us confound their speech;"[1] and again in the Blessing, the form of which is set down in the Book of Numbers,[2] wherein God commands that for three distinct times the Name Jehovah is to be invoked upon the heads of His people. Such rites and such expressions as these, if they were not uttered as mystical foretokenings of the Trinity, can in no other way be made to harmonize with the plans of Israel's great lawgiver, or indeed with the ethical status of the people.

Uncertain and obscure though this revelation was to the contemporaries of Moses, yet in the days of Isaiah it had come to be more clearly understood. That Hymn of the Seraphim, which the Prophet heard, is an utterance of homage to the Trinity, so express and formal that the Church has ever since repeated it, as being the most perfect praise wherewith she may celebrate this great Mystery: "Holy, holy, holy, is Jehovah, the God of hosts; all the earth is full of His glory."

Though we need not conclude from these evidences, as some theologians have done, that the doctrine of the Trinity is obviously and unmistakably taught in the Old Testament, it is, however, hardly possible not to note therein the first foreshadowings of a plurality of Persons in the Divine Essence.

The actual manifestations of God to man, which are so frequent in the history of the people of God, all contributed to the propagation of the same belief. And indeed they all partake of this one peculiarity, that Jehovah appears oftenest to mortal vision, not in His own Person, but as a mysterious Being Which Scripture calls the "Angel of the Lord." This Angel is certainly distinct from Jehovah, and nevertheless it bears his incommunicable Name, exercises the divine power, receives honors due to the Supreme Being, and at all times speaks and acts as a God. Staying the arm of Abraham, as he is about to sacrifice his son, the Angel says to him: "I know that thou fearest God, and that thou wouldst not have withheld thy son, thine only son, from Me."[3] By these last words He makes Himself one with

---

[1] Gen. i. 26; iii. 22; xi. 7.   [2] Num. vi. 23, 26.   [3] Gen. xxii. 12.

VOL. I.— 24

God the Creator, to Whom Abraham was ready to offer all that he held most dear. He promises the Patriarch that in his seed all the nations of earth shall be blessed, because he has obeyed His Voice. He appears in a dream to Jacob: "I am the God of Bethel,"[1] He says to him. But this God of Bethel, Who dwells upon the cloud-hung summits of the dream-ladder, is none other than Jehovah, the God of Abraham and the God of Isaac.[2] So also Jacob, after he had striven long in that great wrestling at Phanuel, cried out, "I have seen God face to face!"[3] And at the hour of his death, when he would bless the sons of Joseph, he called not only upon the God Who had been the Strength and the Sustainer of his youth, but upon that Divine Angel also Who had been his Safeguard in all evil days of his life.[4]

And later, in the desert of Madian, this same Angel appeared to Moses in the burning bush.[5] In this Presence the Prophet sees only Jehovah, hearkens to the Voice as to that of Elohim; he covers his face, not daring to look upon this manifestation of the Godhead, while the words which came from the flaming thicket proclaimed the Speaker to be the God of Abraham, of Isaac, and of Jacob.[6] Israel accepts the commandment to obey this Divine Messenger, for they are told that "the holy Name of God is in Him."[7]

After their adoration of the Calf of Gold, God declares He will no longer walk in the midst of this stiffnecked people of His; yet nevertheless He will leave with them His Divine Angel to be their Guide.[8] And although there is some distinction in the manner of speaking of the Lord and of His Messenger, yet the latter is still a Presence, in Whom Jehovah has His habitation.[9] And this Manifestation of the Most High continues thereafter to act, not as a creature but as a Divine Being, demanding of Joshua the same homage which He had received

---

[1] Gen. xxii. 18.
[2] Ibid. xxxi. 11; xxviii. 13.
[3] Ibid. xxxii. 1, 30.
[4] Ibid. xlviii. 15.
[5] The Vulgate has translated the Hebrew text inexactly, as "Dominus" where we read "the Angel of Jehovah," מַלְאַךְ יְהוָה (Exod. iii. 2).
[6] Exod. iii. 6.
[7] Ibid. xxiii. 20, 21.
[8] Ibid. xxxiii. 2, 3.
[9] Ibid. xxxiii. 14.

from Moses. Joshua obeys Him, and adores Him as the God of Israel. Thrice He appears in the Book of the Judges, — thrice most like unto Him Whose Name is Wonderful, girt about with strength and shining with such heavenly splendor, that Manoah cried aloud, "Surely we shall die, because we have seen God."[1]

Who was this Angel? It was the Word of God, is the answer given by the first Fathers,[2] while Saint Augustine adds with more exactness that this was some Created Form,[3] under which the invisible Word was manifested even as was also God Himself; and in this manner He condescended to accustom mortals to seeing a visible Entity, His handiwork, dependent upon Him, and nevertheless made substantially One with Him. "Thus He was preparing men for the great mystery of the Incarnation; in some such fashion He did make a beginning thereof, and so it was given us to behold Him, as it were in a kind of apprenticeship, He making trial of us after this fashion. ... All these appearances of the Son of God were a certain pledge to mankind that God did not look upon humanity as altogether abhorrent to His Own Nature, since He had resolved aforetime that the Son of God, equal in all things to His Father, should be made man like unto us."[4]

With their minds made ready by lessons like these, the Jews, little by little, acquired the habit of regarding God not as an Abstract Power, isolated in barren and unprofitable majesty, but as a fruitful and omnific Nature in Whom resides, as in its Source, all light and life and love; wherein Wisdom, the sublimest of God's attributes, is quickened into life, becomes a Person, and holds intercourse with Jehovah. We can follow this progress of Revelation all through the sapiential writings. The Author of the Proverbs[5] was content with showing how Wisdom is coeternal with Jehovah, and assists Him in the work of Creation. The Son of Sirach goes a step further; he personifies Wisdom, and attributes language like this to the Heaven-born One: "I am come forth from the mouth of the Most High,

---

[1] Jos. v. 14; Jud. v. 13-15; vi. 11-22; xiii. 6-22.
[2] S. Irenæus, *Adversus Hæreses*, iv. 7, 4; Clement of Alexandria, *Pædagogus*, i. 7; Tertullian, *Adversus Praxeam*, 13, 14, 15; S. Cyprian, *Adversus Judæos*, ii. 5, 6, etc.
[3] S. Augustine, *De Trinitate*, passim.
[4] Bossuet, *Élévations sur les mystères*, élévation vi., xe semaine.
[5] Prov. viii.

begotten of Him before all creation. I it is Who have made a light to blaze in the sky which shall never be extinguished, and Who have covered the whole earth in a vapor. I have dwelt in the high places, and My throne is in a pillar of cloud. I alone have encompassed the high arch of heaven, and I have fathomed the lowermost depths of the abyss. I have walked upon the waves of the sea, and I have wandered over all the lands. I have held sway in every nation and among every people of earth. And amongst all these I sought a resting-place; and I chose for Myself a habitation amid the heritage of the Lord. Whereupon the Creator of the Universe hath made Me to know His will; He Who hath created Me hath rested within My Tabernacle, and He hath said unto Me: 'Dwell with Jacob; let Israel be Thy inheritance.'"[1]

The Book of Wisdom more clearly still declares the relations which exist between this divine Wisdom and Jehovah, and His movements upon the face of the earth. In respect to God, 't is "a Vapor of His almighty power and a most pure emanation of His glory; 't is the Brightness of eternal light, the spotless Mirror of God's majesty, and the Image of His goodness."[2] There is no one of God's wondrous dealings with the world which may not be attributed to it. This it is Which created the first man, and still draws us away from sin; Who saved the just from the Deluge, watched over the Patriarchs, made the Israelites to pass through the Red Sea, and guided them through all their devious wanderings.[3] In a word, everything that the historical books of the Old Testament had ascribed to the Angel of the Lord, the sapiential books no longer impute to a vague and mysterious Being, but to a personified Attribute of Omnipotence, — that is, to the Wisdom of Jehovah.

Now it only remained to change this term to that sublimer title, the Word of God. And this was to be the work of those Jewish doctors who, after the Captivity, gathered together the traditions of their nation, and composed from them, in the Aramean tongue, those paraphrases of the Holy Books called Targums.[4] The most ancient of these commentaries (that of

---

[1] Ecclesiast. xxiv.
[2] Wis. vii. 25, 26.
[3] Ibid. x.
[4] Targum, תַּרְגוּם from תִּרְגֵּם: "to explain, to interpret." The Targum of the Pentateuch, attributed to Onkelos, received a definite form in the third century of our era; the others are of a later date.

Onkelos) teaches fully and unmistakably the doctrine of the Word[1] of the Lord. The Word it is Which once protected Noë, Which ratified the ancient alliance with Abraham, Which accompanied Israel into the desert, was with Isaac among the Canaaneans, and with Joseph in Egypt. At Bethel Jacob made his solemn covenant that the Word of the Lord should be his God, and again at Sinaï the people fall with faces to the ground before that breath of his nostrils Which is His Word. It would be easy to continue this enumeration through all the books of the Old Testament, for the Targums everywhere speak of the Word in places where the Historical Writings tell of the Angel of the Lord, and where the Sapiential Scriptures discourse of the Wisdom of God. From this it is evident that John had only to collect these familiar traditions, and thus from the ancient Faith prove his doctrine of the Word. And undoubtedly this was the source whence he drew the Truth; he found it in the teachings of that very Synagogue which, albeit with darkened vision and enfeebled speech, was none the less the Guardian of a deposit of true Religion and pure Belief.

III.

THE GENEALOGIES OF THE GOSPEL.

A GREAT number of writers have endeavored to conciliate the genealogies of the Gospel, but there are only two explanations which seem to us of sufficient value to merit the attention of the reader.

One of these considers the genealogy in Saint Matthew as the lineage of Joseph; while Saint Luke's, they tell us, is that of Mary.[2] This solution does away with every difficulty, and might be adopted at once were it not that it has against it not only Tradition, which has always regarded the two genealogical tables as belonging to Joseph, but there is also the text of Saint

---

[1] In the Paraphrases the Word is sometimes called מֵימְרָא, sometimes דִּבּוּרָא.

[2] This explication has been adopted by D. Calmet, Vossius, Lightfoot, Michaelis, Kuinoel, Bengel, Olshausen, Wieseler, Ebrard, Kurtz, Lange, Greswell, Kitto, Robinson, etc. The contrary opinion has been held, among modern critics, by Hug, P. Patrizi, Meyer, Mill, Lord Hervey, Ellicott, etc.

Luke, which must be twisted and deprived of its natural meaning in order to make it read as if it were the descent of Mary.

The other explanation admits that the two genealogies are those of Joseph, and, as a consequence, it undertakes the task of reconciling us to accept their contradictory statements, which would appear to be considerable. After having given the same series of generations from the origin of time as far as David, the columns separate, — one list following the line of Nathan, eldest son of the Prophet-King; the other, that of Solomon; while further on they both unite, in the time of the Captivity, under the two names of Salathiel and Zorobabel; then, starting from this point, there is another divergence, until we come to Joseph, who, Saint Luke says, is born of Heli, while Saint Matthew tells us that he was the son of Jacob.

The interpretation generally adopted is that there had been two leviratical marriages between the two branches of David's family. This Jewish custom is well known: when a son of Israel dies without children, his nearest male relative must espouse his widow, and the first-born of this new union, the natural son of the second husband, is thereafter treated as the legal son of the first. Therefore the view which we are now occupied with would have it that this Law of the Levirate was twice brought in question in this instance, — first in the time of Salathiel, and later in the time of Joseph; each of them having had two fathers, one natural, the other legal. These were, respectively, Neri and Jechonias, Jacob and Heli. And although this explanation does not suffice to enlighten us as to every obscure point, it does however shed a great measure of light upon the question; and hence we shall avail ourselves of it, for it is sustained by such an imposing array of traditions that we need only call attention to their number and nature in order to give it all the weight of authority.

From the first ages of the Church the genealogies were the object of grave discussion. Origen, when answering the attack of Celsus, reproaches him for having ignored the labors of Christian writers upon this matter.[1]

One hundred years had not passed over the world since the

---

[1] Origen, *Contra Celsum*, ii. 32. Celsus wrote in the reign of Hadrian (120). Hence the words used by Origen imply that before this time the Christians had already experienced some difficulty in reconciling the genealogies.

death of its Saviour, and already His earthly origin was obscured and forgotten. But how was it that those first Christians, living almost in the same epoch with the Apostles, did not make haste to examine the authentic sources of information? We shall have no room left for any surprise on this score, if we think for a moment upon those disasters in which Jerusalem was overwhelmed only forty years after the death of Jesus. Everything was annihilated and blotted away from this City which had sacrificed its God, and with the rest all the Genealogical Tables which were there preserved[1] became involved in the universal ruin. So that only certain traditions survived, by means of which the obscurities in their family pedigrees could be cleared up; and indeed this source was held sufficient by the Jewish converts who had thus kept alive the memory of their own family archives; and so, from Tradition and their own knowledge they could explain the genealogies of the Christ. But of course this state of affairs did not exist in the Churches founded in the various provinces of the Roman Empire. By the year 70 almost all the ministers of the Word who had heard and seen the Saviour had gone to swell that first great harvest of Martyrdom; the bishops and the doctors who replaced them had no longer the aid of their vivid memories of the Divine History; and there was no intercourse between the Christians of Judea who had taken refuge in Pella and their brethren in the East, in Greece, and in Asia Minor. In many of these last-named Churches the genealogies of the Christ soon became the theme of much unsatisfactory discussion, and oftentimes they arrived at solutions of the difficulty which were more ingenious than they were veracious. In the second century an opinion began to gain ground (in spite of the vigorous stand made against it by Julius Africanus) that the genealogies were imaginary lists of names put together with the hope of setting in higher relief the great Truth that in the person of Jesus there was the most perfect union of a lineage which partook equally of Priesthood and Royalty.[2] The only way to prevent their being looked upon as fanciful inventions was to refer to the authentic traditions of the Church; this was not done until the middle of the third century.

---

[1] Josephus, *Contra Apionem*, i. 37.
[2] The theories proposed in later times were no less plentiful. Annius of Viterbus did not scruple at making use of this curious solution, — that all the ancestors of the Saviour, after David, had a double name.

Julius Africanus, the friend of Origen, was born at Nicopolis.[1] He had acquaintance with certain of the faithful there who formed the only living remnant of the family of the Lord, and for this reason were called Desposynes.[2] From them he learned that Esther, wife of Mathan, of the branch line of Solomon, at the death of her first husband wedded Melchi, of the branch line of Nathan; and from these successive unions she had two sons, Jacob and Heli. When Heli died without issue, Jacob married his widow, and was father of Saint Joseph in the course of nature, while in the eyes of the Law Heli was his father.[3] This tradition, thanks to the high esteem in which Julius Africanus was held, came to have much authority in the Church; the Fathers welcomed it gladly, and Saint Augustine, who at first had resorted to another explanation, afterwards, in his Retractions,[4] comes back to this simple clew given him by Julius Africanus, and confesses that the Letter written by that Father to Aristides was unknown to him at the time he wrote his Treatise against Faustus.

But does it follow that, if we grant this, we must accept everything in the accounts left us by the Desposynes? We do not think so, for what they tell us of Herod's having destroyed the records of the Royal Family in order to conceal his own low origin contradicts the statements of the historian Josephus, who quotes from the genealogies of the Levites which were preserved at Jerusalem in his own time.[5] Certainly there was at bottom a foundation of truth in this tradition, and that is what we must try to disentangle from such apocryphal details as have gathered about it during two centuries of oral transmission. And indeed that is just what was done by Saint Jerome and the other Fathers. In their eyes the important point in the testimony of the Desposynes is that Joseph was born of a leviratical marriage; but they are no longer unanimous in their opinion when the question is mooted whether it was Jacob or Heli who was his natural father. Julius Africanus holds that the spouse of the Virgin Mary was born

---

[1] Now-a-days called Amouas, twenty-two miles from Jerusalem, and ten from Lydda (Antonini Augusti *Itinerarium*).

[2] Δεσπόσυνοι, "belonging to, related to the Lord."

[3] Julius Africanus, *Epistola ad Aristidem* (Migne, *Patrologie grecque*, t. x. p. 51).

[4] S. Augustine, *Retractiones*, ii. 7.

[5] *Epistola ad Aristidem* (*Patrologie grecque*, t. x. p. 51). Josephus, *Contra Apionem*, i. 37.

of Jacob; Saint Ambrose, on the contrary, gives Heli as his father.[1]

In the uncertain state in which these confused traditions leave us, is it possible to get any help toward clearing up the difficulties from the genealogies themselves? This has been the animating thought of some learned critics,[2] and so, arguing from the individual point of view taken by each of the Evangelists, they infer that Saint Matthew gives the royal ancestry of Jesus,[3] Saint Luke His natural descent.

The latter, as being the companion of Saint Paul, the Apostle of the Gentiles, and a Gentile himself, naturally would be less zealous than Saint Matthew was to make it apparent that Jesus, the Son of Abraham and David, was rightful Heir to the Kings of Israel. Saint Luke had referred to the Jewish tables of birth with the sole idea of proving that Jesus is the Man, the Second Adam, in Whom God is made incarnate for the redemption of the world. So, without stopping at Abraham, he goes back to the beginnings of time, and hence he declares that the Christ is Son of Adam, "who was the son of God."

Saint Matthew, on the contrary, is entirely engrossed with the thought of establishing his claims that Jesus is sprung of the royal stock of Israel: Βίβλος γενέσεως Ἰησοῦ Χριστοῦ υἱοῦ Δαυείδ, υἱοῦ Ἀβραάμ. And as a natural consequence he looks for that lineage for Jesus which will assure Him His lofty dignity as the Christ, the Messiah, the Anointed of the Lord; undoubtedly He is the Son of Abraham, and Heir of the Promises made to the father of all true believers; but he is still more particular to announce that Jesus is the Son of David, destined to lift up anew the Throne of His fathers upon the earth. Among all the titles which combined to render the Son of Jesse so dear to Israel, the kingly dignity is that which principally attracts Saint Matthew's attentive consideration. "David

---

[1] S. Ambrose, *in Lucam*, iii.
[2] Grotius, De Marca, Lama, Mill, Lord Hervey, etc.
[3] Some scholars look upon this term ἐγέννησε, which S. Matthew employs, as a proof that he is giving the natural generation of Joseph; but this expression, like the equivalent Hebrew word יָלַד, is not to be understood as meaning a mere carnal descent, since it is also employed frequently to indicate succession by law or adoption. The Septuagint takes it with this wider acceptation, and S. Matthew follows their example in his genealogical table Ἰωράμ δὲ ἐγέννησε τὸν Ὀζίαν, where three generations separate Osias from Joram.

the King," he repeats twice,[1] and the genealogical list, which he unfolds after David is nothing else than an historical succession of the monarchs of Juda. Now Jechonias, the last of these princes, died without issue.[2] Yet Saint Matthew, despite this well-known fact, continues the line of David down to Joseph. Must we conclude from this that Neri, the father of Salathiel, according to Saint Luke, espoused the widow of Jechonias and had a son by her; or, without resorting to this hypothesis of a leviratical marriage, is it not even more reasonable to believe that Jechonias, when he was condemned to see his own branch of the royal Household become extinct with him, adopted Salathiel, grandson of David and son of Nathan, and that he transmitted his rights to the throne to his son? Then the series of otherwise unknown names which follows in Saint Matthew's record of the royal race is that of the sons of Salathiel who should have occupied the throne, had the legitimate monarchy been perpetuated, and who thus by right of descent were the lawful kings of Juda, though in fact they never any of them mounted the throne. After eight generations the branch of Abiud, eldest son of Zorobabel, in whom resided by birthright this title to the throne of David, now in turn saw his household end with Jacob; and thus it was that Heli, a descendant of Rhesa, another son of Zorobabel, contracted that leviratical marriage with the widow of Jacob, of which Tradition has preserved a record; the fruit of this union is Joseph, who is consequently the natural son of Heli and legal son of Jacob.

[1] In fact the received text gives Ἰεσσαὶ δὲ ἐγέννησεν τὸν Δαυεὶδ τὸν βασιλέα, Δαυεὶδ δὲ ὁ βασιλεῦς ἐγέννησεν, κτλ . . . This reading is to be found in very many Manuscripts (notably that of Ephrem), and in a majority of the Versions.

[2] The malediction that fell upon Jechonias, or Conias, son of Joakim, doomed him to end his life in exile, and childless (Jer. xxii. 30); hence he either could not have had any offspring, or must have lost such as he had, before his death, for the word which the Prophet uses, עֲרִירִי, has but one meaning in the Old Testament, "without children" (Gen. xv. 2, etc.; Lightfoot, *Horæ Hebraicæ*, in Matt. i. 12). The Rabbis suppose that the repentance of Jechonias had assuaged the divine wrath, and that this prince left behind him the descendants whom we find quoted in the First Paralipomenon (iii. 17), — Asir, Salathiel, Melchiram, Phadaïa, etc." But this hypothesis is not necessary in order to conciliate the two Sacred Books; it is enough to suppose that Jechonias adopted the entire family of Neri, and thus became father by adoption of the seven sons named in the Paralipomenon.

The following table will enable one to see at a glance all that we have so far considered concerning the two genealogies —

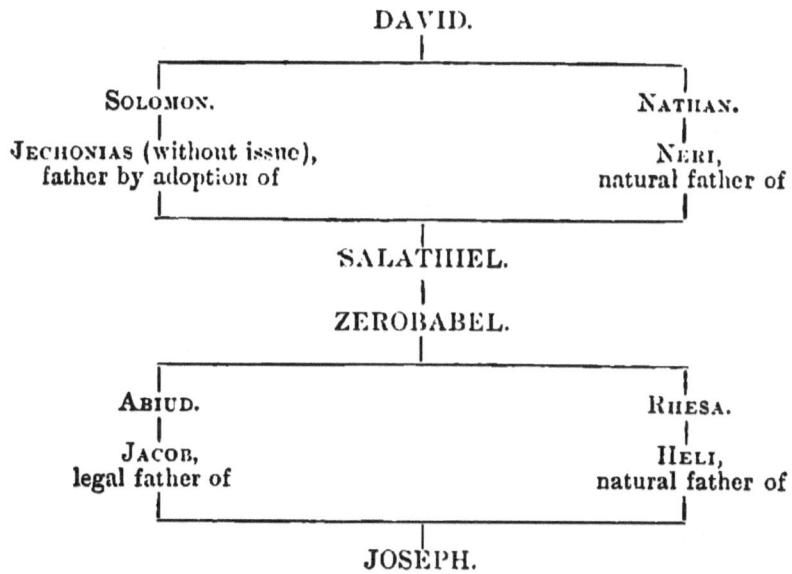

This solution, while it respects the ancient traditions, since it gives Joseph (according to the teachings of Julius Africanus) a legal father and also a father according to the Law, has the additional advantage of not multiplying the leviratical marriages unnecessarily. And finally, whether this theory be adopted or whether the generally received hypothesis be preferred, the discussion has at all events successfully proved that the contradictory statements in the genealogies are susceptible of several plausible explanations.

The only remaining difficulty concerns Saint Matthew,[1] whose genealogy is manifestly incomplete, since, in the period between David and the Captivity, he passes over three kings. — Ochosias, Joas, and Amasias. Their names are sacrificed designedly, in order to give a certain symmetry to the arrangement, and to thus divide the list into three groups of fourteen names. In

---

[1] In the second period of S. Matthew there appears to be a generation wanting, but S. Jerome long ago pointed out that we must distinguish between Joachim, son of Josias, and Joachin, who was his son, although in S. Matthew they both bear the name Jechonias. In Hebrew, Joachim is written as יְהוֹיָקִים; Joachin is יְהוֹיָכִין; from this we see that the two words are quite different.

doing this the Evangelist simply follows the general custom among the Jews, who when writing down their family pedigree were not so careful to inscribe the names of all their ancestors as they were anxious to give harmonious proportions to each genealogy. The memory retained the names better when distributed in this way; and the "mystical properties" of those numbers seven and ten, which were the usual factors in this division, conferred a higher dignity to the records of a household, which were preserved after this fashion. In the Jewish writers we find numerous examples of this arbitrary ordering of the lists. It is in this form that Philo sets apart the generations which lived between the time of Moses and the Creation of the world into two groups of ten and one of seven, in order (as he says) to display the perfect stems crowned with fruit of equal perfectness, — Noë, Abraham, Moses.[1] And therefore Saint Matthew was only consulting the popular tastes of his age when he inscribed the Genealogy of Jesus in a conventional style.

We are not now speaking of the attempts to harmonize the Gospel lists with those which we find in the Books of the Chronicles; for there are some almost insurmountable difficulties involved in the task. Among the seven sons of Zorobabel, of whom mention is made in this record, there was none called Rhesa, nor is there an Abiud; and we look in vain among their descendants for the names of Eliakim and Juda, which the Evangelists give as sons of Rhesa and Abiud. Lord Hervey has endeavored to solve this problem in his learned work entitled "The Genealogies of Our Lord." He calls our attention to the fact that Rhesa, in the Chaldean tongue, is the title of the "princes of the Captivity," who, in the first and second centuries after Jesus Christ were the Chiefs of the people (as, in fact, Zorobabel was at Babylon); from this he concludes that probably the word "Rhesa" was placed in the margin, as a comment on the text, by some Jew who had become a Christian, in order to recall the fact that Zorobabel was a prince of the House of David. From the margin this annotation passed into the text. If this be so, then Joanna, according to Saint Luke, is made the son of Zerobabel; now, Joanna is the same name as Hananiah, son of Zorobabel, if we follow the Paralipomenons (1 Par. iii. 19). In fact Hananiah, חֲנַנְיָה, is a word composed of חָנָה, "grace," and יָהּ, an abridged form of Jehovah.

---

[1] Philo, *De Posteritate Caini*, edit. Mangey, t. i. p. 259.

Joanna, יוֹחָנָן, contains the same roots, with this difference, that יוֹ, another shorter form for Jehovah, is put at the head of the compound, and חָנָן is at the end. We are therefore justified in considering these as only two forms of the same word. In the opinion of Lord Hervey Saint Matthew omits this generation. He takes Abiud, אֲבִיהוּד, whose name occurs in verse thirteen of this Gospel, to be that same Juda of Saint Luke's Gospel (in Aramean, הוּד, Jud), and also as the Hodaiah, חוֹדַוְיָהוּ, of the Books of the Chronicles (1 Par. iii. 24). The complete development of the theory regarding these names is clearly explained in Lord Hervey's Volume.

Yet, after all is said, is it necessary to recur to these very subtile hypotheses? Are not the incomplete lists which we possess, the fact of there having been so many offspring, then too the frequent unions between branches of the same family, the habit of giving the same names for generation after generation, the quite different designs animating the two Evangelists and the Author of the Paralipomenons, — are not all these sufficient to account for the fact that after two thousand years we find some difficulty in making these two genealogical tables correspond?

The same considerations are enough to deter us from any long investigation as to why Saint Luke (iii. 35, 36) places Caïnan between Sale and Arphaxad, a name which is only found in the Greek Version of Genesis (Gen. x. 24), and is not in the Hebrew text. Apparently this is an error committed by the Seventy, and so it has passed from their version into the text of Saint Luke. In fact this second Caïnan is not found either in the Samaritan text or, for the most part, in the other Versions (Vulgate, Targum, Peshito, etc.), and the Fathers have never made any mention of the name.

As to the contradiction which appears to exist between the Evangelists, who give Salathiel as the father of Zerobabel (Matt. i. 12, Luke iii. 27), and the Paralipomenons, which say he was the son of Phadaïa (1 Par. iii. 19), only a superficial difficulty is involved; for the Alexandrian Manuscript, as well as that of Cambridge, gives us Salathiel and not Phadaïa. Father Patrizi[1] prefers to admit that the Zorobabel of the Gospels is another personage from the one mentioned in the Paralipomenons.[2]

---

[1] *De Evangeliis*, lib. iii. diss. ix. 16, 2.
[2] As to the genealogies, see Lord Arthur Hervey, *On the Genealogies of Our Lord*; Mill, *Observations on the attempted application of pantheistic*

V.

THE STAR OF THE MAGI.

It was the opinion of Kepler that the Star of the Magi was only a sidereal phenomenon. Having witnessed the conjunction of Jupiter and Saturn in 1603, which included Mars in the following spring, this Astronomer observed a star of the first magnitude, and hitherto unknown, which suddenly shone out in the vicinity of these planets. The remarkable splendor of this apparition in the heavens — for it blazed with such great brilliancy that it could be seen at high noon — struck the illustrious Astronomer forcibly; and he began to question whether the Star of the Magi might not have been some such pleiad. His calculations resulted in the discovery that a conjunction of Jupiter and Saturn had in fact taken place, in the year 748 of Rome, and that the nearest point of contact for the two planets was the Sign of the Fishes. So he concludes that a star, similar to the one which he had studied, must have appeared at this period, and that this unexpected union of celestial luminaries composed the constellation seen by the Magi. As we have said, it appeared in 748, the date which Herod took so much care to ascertain, and which induced him in 750 to slaughter all the children in Bethlehem under two years of age. The thoroughly scientific methods of Kepler have established his calculations beyond any question; furthermore they have been verified and adopted by our modern astronomers.[1]

But does this phenomenon correspond with what Saint Matthew tells us of the marvellous Star? It is not sufficient to assert that the conjunction of two planets had produced in the sky a Star of more than ordinary brilliancy; but over and above this, it must be explained how, by any natural means, this Star could have conducted them from their native country to Judea, thereafter from Jerusalem to Bethlehem, and finally, in this village, indicate the dwelling-place of Jesus. After all, the

---

principles to the theory and historic criticism of the Gospels; Patrizi, *De Evangeliis,* lib. iii. diss. ix.

[1] Kepler, *De Jesu Christi anno natalitio;* Ideler, *Handbuch,* ii. 399; Pfaff, Schumacher, Schubert, Münter, Encke, etc. Mr. Pritchard has given us a résumé of the objections which modern science has raised against Kepler's hypothesis; his summing up of the matter is as powerful as it is luminous (*Memoirs of Royal Astr. Society,* vol. xxv.).

wisest plan is to admit that all the circumstances surrounding this heavenly Visitant were part of a miraculous dispensation. In ancient times Christianity never entertained any other idea on the subject. Antiquity always looked upon the Star of the Magi as a flaming meteor, upholden in the heavens as a Sign by the hand of God; and hence it must have moved in an Orbit which was not traced out for it by astronomical laws, but by the untrammelled Will of Him whose Messenger it was.

V.

THE BRETHREN OF THE LORD.

AT several different stages of the Narrative, the Gospel speaks of the Lord's brothers. Saint Matthew and Saint Mark[1] make known their names: "Is not His Mother called Mary, and His brothers James and John and Simon and Jude? And are not His sisters all here among us?" Later on three of the synoptical writers tell how they strove to push their way through the crowd.[2] In Saint John we see them coming down to Capharnaum with the Mother of Jesus, and all the time they show such disbelief in the Mission of the Christ that, six months before the Passion, they insist that He should manifest Himself to Jerusalem by some stupendous deed.[3] However, the death of the Saviour evidently opened their eyes, for we meet them once more in that upper room, where, with Mary and the Apostles, they awaited the coming of the Holy Ghost.[4]

Among these different texts there is not one which gives us to understand that these "brethren of the Lord" were actually the children of Mary and Joseph. On the other hand, we know that the Hebrew term אח, which is always translated by us as "brother," has a very much wider meaning, and denotes at times a distant relative;[5] sometimes it means they are of the same race, or from the same native city,[6] and again it is even used to indicate simple associations of friendship.[7] In order to

---

[1] Matt. xiii. 55, 56; Mark vi. 3.
[2] Matt. xii. 46-50; Mark iii. 31-35; Luke viii. 19-21.
[3] John ii. 12; vii. 3-10.
[4] Acts i. 14.
[5] Gen. xii. 5; xiii. 8; xxix. 12; Num. viii. 26.
[6] Gen. ix. 25; Num. xx. 14, etc.
[7] 2 Kings i. 26; 3 Kings ix. 13, etc.

determine what meaning the Gospel intends to convey by the expression "brethren of the Lord," we must not rest upon the received reading of the texts cited above, but must look elsewhere for whatever information the holy Books can furnish us withal concerning these kinfolk of the Lord.

One of them, the Apostle James, by word and deed, has made himself so illustrious in the Church that his name has always been considered an ample dignity of itself; and hence he is mentioned without prefix or title, whereas the other James is always called "son of Zebedee."[1] Consequently there is no question but that the Bishop of Jerusalem is the one alluded to in the various texts wherein the Gospel speaks of the father and mother of James.

The details which bear most directly upon the question in hand are to be found in the recitals of the Passion. Among the Galilean women who were present at the death of Jesus, Saint Matthew names "Mary Magdalene, *Mary mother of James and Joseph*, and the mother of the sons of Zebedee." Further on, he adds, "that those who remained at the tomb were Mary Magdalene and *the other Mary*," and that these two women, on the first day after the Sabbath, returned to look upon the sepulchre.[2] Saint Mark,[3] in relating the same events, calls "the other Mary" "*mother of James the Less*[4] *and of Joseph*"[5] in one place, "*mother of Joseph*" in another, and again "*mother of James*" in still another. Who is this woman who is thus distinguished from Mary Magdalene by the names of her sons?

---

[1] Nothing could be more natural than this preëminence, for James was the first Bishop of Jerusalem, one of the pillars of the Church, and so always associated with Peter and John (Gal. i. 19 ; ii. 9), and he was the venerated Leader of those Jews who were converted to Christianity. His authority was strikingly evidenced on many occasions. at the Council of Jerusalem, when all yielded to his advice (Acts xv. 13-22) : in his Letter addressed to those Hebrews, scattered over the world, who were converted to the Gospel (James i. 1) ; in the reverence which the Jews, even the infidels among them, displayed toward him (Eusebius *Historia ecclesiastica*, iii. 23) ; finally, in the pride which his brothers took in coupling his name with theirs, as a glorious title (Luke vi. 16 ; Acts i. 13; Jud. i).

[2] Matt. xxvii. 56, 61 ; xxviii. 1.

[3] Mark xv. 40, 47 ; xvi. 1.

[4] The title of "The Less," as applied to James, son of Alpheus, apparently indicates that this Apostle was either younger or smaller of stature than the son of Zebedee, whom Tradition alludes to as James the Greater.

[5] In S. Mark most of the manuscripts have Joses instead of Joseph, but the latter name is preserved by the Vulgate, in the second as well as in the first Gospel.

Saint John answers this:[1] "The mother of Jesus," he says, "and His Mother's *sister, Mary wife of Cleophas*, and Mary Magdalene were standing by the Cross." This passage in the Fourth Gospel clearly explains the testimony given by the Synoptical Writers, and shows that "the other Mary, Mother of James and of Joseph" and "wife of Cleophas," was a sister of the Holy Virgin, and called like her Mary.[2] It is true that in the lists of the Twelve Apostles,[3] James is named as the son of Alpheus and not of Cleophas, but it is easy to remove this last difficulty; for these two names, though apparently different, are only two modes of pronouncing the same Aramaic name, חלפא, one form being with, and the other without, the aspirate ה.[4]

We can only conclude from the texts compared thus that the father of James was Alpheus (Cleophas); that his mother was Mary, sister of the Blessed Virgin; and that his brothers were Jude, Joseph, and Simon; consequently the "brethren of the Lord" are only the cousins-german of Jesus. Such was the opinion, even in Apostolic times, according to a tradition attributed to Papias;[5] such it has remained until now, and it is the construction commonly held by modern commentators. Some of the Fathers,[6] indeed, believed that these kinsmen of the Christ were the children of Joseph by an earlier marriage; but this conjecture has no better basis than certain legends contained in the apochryphal gospels.[7] Under the more trustworthy guidance of Saint Jerome and Saint Augustine, the Latin Church has triumphantly vindicated the interpretation which, as we have seen, is amply supported by the text of Scripture.[8]

---

[1] John xix. 25.
[2] It was not an unusual thing among the Jews for brothers and sisters to bear the same name: thus among the children of Herod the Great we find two Philips, two Phasaëls, two Herods.
[3] Matt. x. 3; Mark iii. 18; Luke vi. 15; Acts i. 13.
[4] Compare the two Latin forms. "Aloysius and Ludovicus" from the same Frank word: "Ludwig," Louis.
[5] Migne, *Patrologie grecque*, vol. v. p. 1261.
[6] Origen, Eusebius of Cæsarea, S. Hilary, S. Ambrose, S. Epiphanius, Barhebrœus.
[7] Thilo, *Codex Apocryphus Novi Testamenti*, t. i. p. 228; *Constitutiones Apostolicæ*, vi. 12.
[8] See *Les Frères de N.-S. Jesus-Christ*, par le P. Corluy; Smith. *Dictionary of the Bible*: JAMES; Mill, *On Mythical Interpretation of the Gospels*, pp. 219–274.

VI.

THE SAMARITANS.

THIS little race of people, masters of the Mountains of Ephraim from the valley of Esdralon as far as Bethel,[1] formed an independent nation right in the heart of Palestine, and was composed, for the most part, of a race of strangers, with whom were mingled a few Israelites,[2] who had remained in Judea after the withdrawal of the Schismatic Tribes. The latter, when carried off into captivity by Salmanasar (721 B. C.), left Samaria so deserted and desolate that Ashar Addon was minded to send colonists thither.[3] So they came from Babylon, from Cutha, from Ava, from Emath, and from Sepharvaim. Gathered together from the remote corners of Persia and Media,[4] these Cutheans, as Josephus calls them, took the name of Samaritans from the country they had invaded; but at first they retained their old religions, and thus they defiled the holy soil of Israel with this new worship,— a monstrous union of all sorts of idolatry. The Lord, Who was wroth at their blasphemies and pollutions, sent up lions from the Jordan, that ravaged the whole land and forced the terrified Cutheans to cease from troubling the Almighty Deity of their new country; thus they became, according to a mocking phrase common among the Jews, "Lions' Proselytes." But they were to look in vain through all that lonely wilderness for some one who would instruct them in the religious rites of this ravaged land. Although a few Israelites had escaped that terrible levy of Salmanasar, still such a scanty remnant as this could not restore the ancient majestic Faith

---

[1] "Samaria," says Josephus, "commences at the village Ginea (Djennim), lying in the Great Valley, and terminates on the frontiers of the Acrabatene country" (*Bellum Judaïcum*, iii. 3. 4). This latter territory extended from Sichem to Jericho (*Antiquitates*, ii. 2, 4 ; iii. 3, 4, 5). The southern boundary of Samaria may be regarded as following a line drawn from Jaffa to Bethel, and thence to the Jordan.

[2] The Israelites were so few in number that they were almost lost in the midst of the Samaritans. This is why Antiquity always spoke of the latter as an entirely foreign race, within the confines of Israel. Consult the mass of evidence on this point collected by Suicer, *Thesaurus* · Σαμαρείτης. S. Luke calls them ἀλλογενεῖς (xvii. 18) ; Josephus, ἀλλοεθνεῖς.

[3] 4 Kings xvii. 24.

[4] Josephus, *Antiquitates*, x. 9, 7.

among these barbarians, who knew nothing of the Truth. Probably some one of the captive priests was brought on from Babylon, and thus they learned to revere Jehovah. But instead of the pure Law of the Lord, he taught them the schismatic rites which had grown to be so powerful in Israel just before the Captivity. His first care was to reëstablish the High-places upon Bethel, where Jeroboam had once raised up the Golden Calf. The Assyrian colonists now followed the idolaters' example; "each of them kept his own god, and they set them up, one and all, in the high-places which the Samaritans had built; each nation had also its own god in the city which it inhabited. The Babylonians made Sochothbenoth to be their god; the Cutheans had Nergel; the people of Emath took Asima; the Heveans chose Nebahas and Tartac; those from Sepharvaim caused their children to go through the fire, and thus burned them in honor of Adramelech and Anamelech, the gods of Sepharvaïm. . . . And though these peoples adored Jehovah, they served their own gods at the same time, according to the custom of the nations from whose midst they had been transferred into Samaria. And to this day, these peoples still follow their ancient manners. . . . They fear not Jehovah, neither do they keep His ceremonies, nor His ordinances, nor His laws, nor the precepts which He has given to the children of Jacob, whom He surnamed Israel."[1]

These were the characteristics of the Samaritans during the period of the Captivity, — a mixture of races of foreign origin, with only a faint conception of any worship of the true God. And so, when these profane adorers of Jehovah demanded of the Jews, who had returned from Babylon, that they be permitted to participate in the reconstruction of the Temple, they found that they were regarded as enemies of Juda and Benjamin,[2] and, as such, their offers were scorned and rejected. Thereafter the angry Samaritans never ceased to hate the Jews, and on all occasions sought to thwart their undertakings. Darius, son of Hystaspus reduced them for a time to a state of powerlessness (519); but after his death the old grudges and hostilities of the two peoples continued to grow in bitterness until a culminating incident brought it to a head.

During the reign of Darius Nothus (424-404) a Jewish priest, Manassah by name, and a near relative of the sovereign Pontiff,

---

[1] 4 Kings xvii. 29-41. [2] 1 Esdras, iv. 1.

married a daughter of Sanballat, the Persian governor of Samaria. Nehemiah, who was an ardent reformer of the priesthood, wished to break off this union; to this Manassah refused to consent, and hence he was forced to flee from Jerusalem, and took refuge with his father-in-law. There he made every effort to purify the Samaritan religion from the superstitions which defiled it, and he succeeded in establishing certain forms which were almost the same as the Jewish ceremonial; for, under the reign of Alexander the Great,[1] there was a sanctuary erected upon Mount Garizim which even rivalled that of Jerusalem.

This last act of the schismatics put an impassable gulf between the two peoples. Finally this temple of Garizim, the refuge of apostates from Sion, and an object of horror and detestation to Israel, was destroyed by John Hyrcanus (129); but all in vain, for the Samaritans continued none the less to worship in that place and to look upon this mountain of theirs as the holiest spot on earth. In their eyes it was everything sacred; it was the ancient site of the first earthly Paradise; it was Ararat, where the Ark once rested; and Bethel, where Jacob saw the mysterious Ladder with its shining Angels. They still showed the places where Adam, Seth, and Noë set their burnt offering before the Lord; here too (they said) was the Altar where Abraham offered his son as sacrifice, and even the thorn-tree thicket wherein the ram was caught which was to be a substitute for Isaac was likewise shown.

These traditions, which we have borrowed from the modern Samaritans of Naplouse, may have been altered in the course of so many centuries;[2] but, though we may judge them to be ever so disfigured, they none the less shed some clear and suggestive lights upon the creeds of this nation. As they had no other Sacred Books except those of Moses, their faith was always of a primitive sort, and their beliefs incomplete; they had only a vague idea of the Messiah, invoking Him (as He was revealed

---

[1] Josephus (*Antiquitates*, xi. 7, 2; viii. 4) is so precise upon this latter point that it is difficult not to accept his evidence; the historian does not, however, seem to be as exact as usual in designating the time when Manassah was driven from Jerusalem. Here he probably confounds Darius Codoman with Darius Nothus, who lived eighty years earlier. In fact, Nehemiah tells us that they banished the son of Joïada, the High priest, from Jerusalem, because he had married the daughter of Sanballat the Horonite (2 Esdras, xiii. 28). Now Nehemiah lived during the reigns of Artaxerxes the Long-handed and of Darius Nothus.

[2] See the Article SAMARIA in Herzog's *Encyclopédie*, xiii. 37.

to them in the Pentateuch) as a Converter and a Guide,[1] promised to the world, unto them who were of heathen ancestry as well as to the children of Israel. These meagre outlines seem cold and comfortless indeed, when we compare their feeble imitation with the magnificent work of Inspiration which the Prophets had filled out and made to live in the sight of the Jews; yet the latter interpreted the glowing imagery of their Seers in such a gross and material sense that in the end the confused hopes of the Samaritans came closer to the truth than the greedy cravings and gaudy dreams of the Israelites. So we have no reason to wonder why Jesus, whose Mission was to convert and guide the lost sheep of Israel's household, should still turn aside, by the wayside, to labor in these harvest-lands among strangers. For indeed He saw that they were ripe for the Kingdom of Heaven.

VII.

THE FESTIVAL IN THE FIFTH CHAPTER OF SAINT JOHN.

OUGHT we to bow to the opinion of the majority of modern commentators and agree with them that Saint John here intends us to understand the Festival of the Purim?[2] We think not, indeed; for that solemnity had nothing about it that was likely to attract the divine Master. It was celebrated one month before the Pasch, and was almost entirely devoted to profane amusements and observed as a sort of Memorial of Vengeance. The reading of the Book of Esther (the only religious act performed during the whole feast) was interrupted by shrill cries of hatred every time that the name of Haman was heard. At the same time the children clapped their hands, shook wooden rattles, and smote thin boards together on which the persecutor's name was written, as if to annihilate his memory forever. The rest of the festival was only a gay round of dancing, banqueting, and concerts, and everywhere unbounded license was condoned or encouraged; in fact it was customary,

---

[1] The Hashab, "the Converter," El Muhydi, "the Guide."
[2] Is this word of Persian origin? *Parêh*, in Hebrew פור; allied to *pars, part*. It means "a Lot," and recalls the event of Aman casting his lot on the day when the Jews were to have been massacred (Esther ix. 24–26).

if we may believe the Talmud, to reach such a state of intoxication as not to be able to distinguish the anathemas heaped upon Haman from the blessings showered upon the name of Mardokai.[1] Kepler was the first to suggest that these public rejoicings might be the festival which is mentioned so vaguely by Saint John. But, however much of weight this hypothesis may have attained [2] from its scholarly adherents, we are content with merely asking the question:— Is it reasonable to believe that Jesus would have come up to Jerusalem to countenance such saturnalian revels by His Holy Presence? Certainly He was not unaware that this institution had been censured at the outset by eighty-five Ancients of the people, of whom thirty were venerated as Prophets.[3] Furthermore, it was never a custom of the Jews to repair to the Temple on Mount Sion during this festival; it was celebrated in the synagogues, sometimes even in private residences.[4] Then how are we to explain the fact that, besides Jesus, such crowds should have been attracted to Jerusalem as Saint John describes surrounding the Pool of Bethesda?[5]

Antiquity, with clearer insight, and better informed on this subject, always regarded the Feast in Saint John's fifth chapter as one of the three great Jewish solemnities, — either the Passover, the Pentecost, or the Feast of the Tabernacles. But there can be no question as to the two last named, for they were celebrated one of them fifteen days after the Pasch, the other in the month of September, and we have seen that Jesus returned to Galilee, passing through Samaria, in the month of December, and consequently sometime after these two festivals. It appears most reasonable to suppose that by this vague expression Saint John was alluding to a second Passover in which Jesus took part. That festival was peculiarly "the Feast of the Jews;"[6] and the Christians of the first ages so understood

---

[1] *Megilla*, 7, 2.
[2] It has been defended by Lamy, Pétau, Hug, Neander, Olshausen, Tholuck, Meyer, Wieseler, Winer, Anger, Alford, Ellicott, etc.
[3] *Megilla*, 70, 4.
[4] Josephus, *Antiquitates*, xi. 6.
[5] It is proper to add that the Feast on which the paralytic was healed was a Sabbath (John v. 1, 2, 10, 13). Now the Purim was never celebrated on the Sabbath day (Reland, *Antiquitates Sacra*, iv. 9).
[6] The true reading of this first verse seems to us to be, Ἡ ἑορτὴ τῶν Ἰουδαίων. In fact, the article is left out in the manuscripts of the Vatican, Beza, and Alexandria, but the Sinaitic Codex and that of Ephrem retain it. Tischendorf has restored it in his last edition.

the term, for Saint Irenæus [1] (the most ancient of the Fathers who have treated this question) asserts that the festival mentioned is to be regarded as that greatest of all Israelite Solemnities.

It follows from this that Saint John alludes to four Paschs during the course of Jesus' Ministry. In the first the Lord drives out the hucksters from the Temple; the second is the one of which we have just been speaking; He passed the third away from Jerusalem, for it occurred about the time when He performed the miracle of the loaves; the fourth Passover was that which witnessed His death. Therefore the public life of the Saviour lasted the three years and a half which was the "Half-Week of Years" foretold by Daniel [2] after which the Christ was to be put to death; and it was the three years allotted to the Fig-tree in the Parable, wherein it was to bring forth its fruit.[3]

VIII.

THE POOL OF BETHESDA.

THE Pool of Bethesda must have been in the near neighborhood of the Temple, for it was by the Gate of the Flocks,[4] as Saint John declares, while Nehemiah, who mentions this gate,[5]

---

[1] *Adv. Hæreses*, ii. 39. His opinion is shared by Eusebius, Theodoretus, Grotius, Jansenius, Cornelius a Lapide. Friedlieb, Lampe, Hengstenberg.

[2] Daniel ix. 25–27.

[3] Luke xiii. 7.

[4] Ἐπὶ τῇ Προβατικῇ (John v. 2). Although it was not by any means usual to understand the word for "Gate" before an adjective, and though Eusebius, S. Jerome, and the *Itinerary of Jerusalem* all speak of a Pool called Probatica, or Pool of the Flocks (Προβατικὴ κολυμβήθρα, Probatica piscina, *Vulgate*), yet the text of the Book of Esdras scarcely permits a doubt as to the fact that S. John is here referring to the Gate of the Flocks, so called, without doubt, either because it was a market for live-stock, or because the cattle were driven in by this entrance. Without being able to settle the location of this gate exactly, we are told that at the restoration of the walls of Jerusalem it was built by the priests (2 Esdras, iii. 1); that it was near the Tower of Hananeël, erected in the eastern quarter of the city (Zach. xiv. 10, and the comments made by Hengstenberg in his *Christologie*). Hence it is quite probable that this Gate of the Flocks was in the immediate vicinity of the Temple.

[5] 2 Esdras, xii. 38.

speaks of it as being close to the Sanctuary. The local traditions of our day have given the name of Bethesda to two pools.[1] One, located between the site of the Temple (The Haram) and the Saint Stephen's Gate, is only a huge basin, now drained and dry; the other is not far distant, lying a little to the northwest of the Church of Saint Anne. It was discovered by M. Mauss, a French architect who had charge of the restoration of the monument of Saint Anne, and there seemed some very good reasons for supposing it to be the ancient Bethesda.[2]

These two basins were fed by springs which form a great reservoir under the Mount of the Temple. Antiquity always discoursed of them as one of the far-famed marvels of Jerusalem; and indeed they were a precious resource for the Holy City during the protracted periods of heat which it had to endure.[3] To-day, having no longer any well-built channels to regulate its flow, the waters sink beneath the soil; but if only some few feet of earth be removed streams are still to be found beneath all those masses of crumbling stone and dry refuse which now cover the ground. Quite recently the "Ladies of Sion," while laying the foundations of their Orphanage of Ecce-Homo, brought to light several ancient cisterns still plentifully supplied with water, which comes through a perfectly preserved aqueduct from the neighborhood of the Temple. Barclay, who has carefully examined the subterranean parts of the Haram, thinks that the mountain is hollow, and that (to use his expression) below the surface there is a hidden underground lake.[4] The copious outflow from these fountain-heads was a well-known fact among the Jews in all ages; for the Psalmist speaks of them as of a river the streams whereof shall make glad the City of God.[5]

---

[1] This was the case even in the time of Eusebius. According to the description which we find in the *Onomasticon*, the Pool of Bethesda was composed of two reservoirs (ἐν ταῖς λίμναις διδύμοις), one being supplied by rain water, the other with water of a reddish hue (πεφοινιγμένον). This fact is confirmed by the "*Itinerary of the Pilgrim of Bordeaux*," who visited Jerusalem in 333.

[2] See in *La Palestine*, by M. le baron Ludovic de Vaux, the note relative to the Pool of Bethesda, Appendix, v. — xxvi.

[3] "Templum in modum arcis . . . fons perennis aquæ, cavati sub terrâ montes, et piscinæ cisternæque servanis imbribus" (Tacitus, *Historiæ*, v. 12).

[4] Barclay, *City of the Great King*, p. 293; Thomson, *The Land and the Book*, pp. 656-662; Murray, *Hand-book for Syria and Palestine;* JERUSALEM, § 47.

[5] Ps. xlv. 5.

The imagery arising from these well-springs of the Temple continues to increase in strength until, as Ezechiel [1] sees them, the River becomes a great torrent, which dashes down over the sacred Rock, and from thence the risen waters flow to eastward and to westward, pouring through Kedron and through Hinnom, ever widening and deepening until it is a mighty stream which brings fruitfulness and beauty to the wilderness of the Dead Sea.

The marvel of this Pool was the coming of the Angel who was wont at intervals to move upon the waters and communicate to them a miraculous power. In our times many seek altogether to do away with the idea of any supernatural intervention; so they call in question the authenticity of the verses that speak of it;[2] while very many expounders of this passage (among them some Catholic critics[3]) would attribute its health-giving properties to certain mineral substances which it contained. To justify their view, they remind us of the abundant supply of medicinal waters in Judea,[4] and of the ruddy tinge of this one, of which both Eusebius and Saint Jerome[5] speak, which certainly indicated the presence of ferruginous particles in the waters of Bethesda Pool; hence they compare its action to that of certain gaseous waters, or hot springs, whose curative qualities are most efficacious at the moment they commence to seethe and bubble.

In the opinion of these commentators the Jews, who were but little versed in the operation of similar natural phenomena,

---

[1] Ezechiel, xlvii. 1–12.

[2] Verse 4, and the words preceding it, in verse 3, δεχομένων τὴν τοῦ ὕδατος κίνησιν, are not found in the Manuscripts of the Vatican and Sinaï, nor in the Syriac Version of the Cureton, and they have been subjected to very many different constructions in those manuscripts which do contain them. Tischendorf and Tregelles regard them as a marginal gloss, that has crept into the text. However, we believe that we should retain these words, for we find them in the Codex Alexandrinus and in many manuscripts. The Vulgate, the Peshito, and a majority of the Versions have preserved them. Furthermore, how are we to account for the press of sick folk, all thronging about the Pool at the same moment, if we reject the words which explain their presence there: "They were awaiting a movement of the waters, for the Angel of the Lord descended at a certain time upon the Pool" (see Père Corluy, *Intégrité des Évangiles*, vii. viii., ix).

[3] Jahn, Scholtz, Sepp, Maier, Schegg.

[4] To the west of Haram, we find, even to-day, "Healing Baths:" *Hummâm esh-Shefa*.

[5] Eusebius, *Onomasticon*. "Mirum in modum rubens" (S. Jerome).

attributed the wonderful powers of the Pool to the intervention of an Angel, and Saint John simply records a generally accepted belief of the people. This interpretation of the sacred text is not that of the Fathers, nor of the reverend Doctors of the Church; on the contrary, all agree in considering this fact as a supernatural prodigy.

Indeed, some among their number have apparently preferred to extend the marvellous properties of Bethesda to all streams which sprung from under the Mount of the Temple, and particularly to those of Siloë. We know that the springs which supply the latter basin, rising from the hill of Ophel, first filled the Fountain of the Virgin, and then sunk once more underground, finally reappearing at Siloë. Both these fountains are equally intermittent, and local legends attribute this fact to a dragon hidden under the Mount, who sometimes drinks up the streams at the well-head, while at other times he permits them to flow unchecked. Prudentius, who drew his knowledge from traditions which were not quite so fabulous as this, regards the movement of its waters as the visible token of a divine power which heals all evils, and thus he confounds its marvellous properties with those which the Gospel recounts of Bethesda:—

> Variis Siloë refundit
> Momentis latices, nec fluctum semper anhelat,
> Sed vice distinctâ largos lacus accipit haustus.
> Agmina languentum sitiunt spem fontis avari,
> Membrorum maculas puro abluitura natatu;
> Certatim interea roranti pumice raucas
> Expectant scatebras, et sicco margine pendent.
>
> PRUDENTIUS: *Apotheosis*, 680.

END OF VOL. I.

www.ingramcontent.com/pod-product-compliance
Lightning Source LLC
Chambersburg PA
CBHW020538300426
44111CB00008B/720